Losing an Empire, Finding a Role

Also by David Sanders

Patterns of Political Instability

Lawmaking and Co-operation in International Politics: The Idealist Case Re-examined

Losing an Empire, Finding a Role

British Foreign Policy since 1945

David Sanders

Senior Lecturer in Government
University of Essex

MACMILLAN

First published 1990
Reprinted 1991

Published by
MACMILLAN EDUCATION LTD
Houndmills, Basingstoke, Hampshire RG21 2XS
and London
Companies and representatives
throughout the world

Typeset by Latimer Trend & Company Ltd
Plymouth

Printed in Great Britain by
Billing & Sons Ltd, Worcester.

A catalogue record for this book is available
from the British Library

ISBN 0–333–44265–2 (hardcover)
ISBN 0–333–44266–0 (paperback)

FOR
GILL, JOE, BEN, ROB AND LUCY

Contents

Preface

This book grew out of a series of lectures that I first gave at the University of Essex during the academic session 1985–6. The lectures posed two main questions. What have Britain's major foreign policies been during the postwar period? And why were those policies pursued? What surprised me as I prepared the lectures was the extent to which existing studies of British foreign policy – excellent though many of them are – failed to address either question directly. While recognising the difficulty of answering either question definitively, this book does seek to answer them both. For presentational purposes, I make two assumptions: that 'foreign policy' refers to all aspects (political, military and economic) of a given country's external relations; and that the reader is intelligent but is largely uninformed of the details of Britain's postwar foreign policy.

In writing the book I benefited enormously from the advice offered by colleagues at Essex and elsewhere. I am particularly grateful to Tony King and Geoffrey Edwards for their detailed comments on the draft manuscript. Hugh Ward and Rob Stones provided invaluable advice on the treatment of economic issues. Gillian Twyman and John Sanders were immensely helpful as non-specialist readers, checking the text for ambiguity and lack of clarity. I should also express my indebtedness to two people I have not met, Bernard Porter and C. J. Bartlett, whose various works were a constant source of information and entertainment while I was writing the book. Finally, thanks to Carole Welge, Carol Snape, Geraldine Shanks and Helen Fitzgerald for their speed and accuracy in producing the final typescript. The responsibility for all errors and misinterpretations is, of course, entirely mine.

Wivenhoe
Essex

D.J.S.

Introduction

Shortly after the Second World War, Winston Churchill observed that Britain's primary overseas interests lay in three interlocking 'circles': in Europe, in the Empire and in the 'special relationship' across the Atlantic. For over two decades after 1945, successive British governments pursued a foreign policy strategy which sought to preserve their power and influence in all three of these 'circles'. It was assumed – at least until 1968 – that Britain was still a Great Power with global interests and responsibilities, and that it should accordingly seek to maintain a world role in both the military and the economic spheres.

However, Britain's continuing efforts to project this world role were confounded over the years by a series of changes in Britain's external environment. It had already been apparent in 1945 that the two emerging 'superpowers' – the United States and the Soviet Union – would henceforth be the dominant actors on the world stage. What had not been anticipated quite so clearly was the extent to which this changing alignment of forces would be supplemented by the growth of nationalism in the 'third world', a development that was destined seriously to weaken Britain's imperial grip. To make matters worse, the relative decline of the British economy, which had begun even before 1914, continued apace. In 1950 Britain's GDP per capita ranked the seventh highest in the world. By 1970 its position had slumped to eighteenth, by 1981 to twenty-first. In these changing circumstances, the British government's efforts to sustain its 'three circle' foreign policy strategy became increasingly overextended. Given the economic resources at their disposal, Britain's foreign policy makers found that they were simply trying to do too much. They were seeking to sustain a role in world affairs which reflected past rather than present capabilities. Sooner or later, Britain would have to bring both its aspirations and its commitments into line with its relatively reduced circumstances.

The resultant process of imperial withdrawal began technically with the decolonisations in India and Palestine in 1947–8. As Figure I.1 indicates, however, it was not until the late 1950s – when Macmillan's 'wind of change' brought a second and more far-reaching wave of decolonisation – that the retreat from Empire really gathered momentum. By 1968, most of Britain's colonial territories had been granted

1

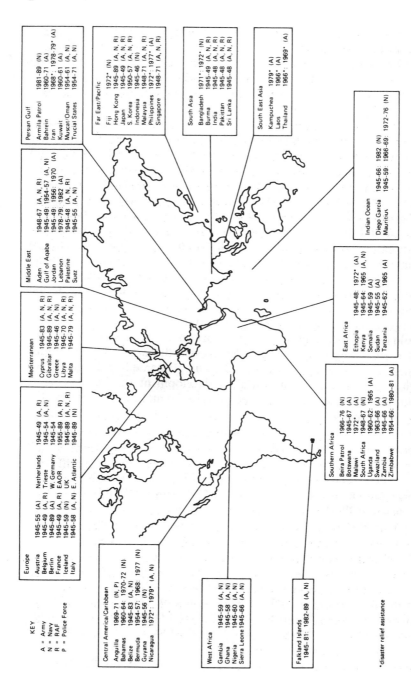

Figure I.1 Deployments of British Forces, 1945–89

SOURCES: Annual Defence White Papers, 1945–89 (for precise CMND references, see bibliography).

formal independence, and in 1971–2, as though to emphasise the fact that Britain had indeed abandoned its world role, British military forces were finally withdrawn from 'east of Suez'.

The 'retreat from Empire', however, had two important corollaries. The first was that the declining importance of the Empire was counterbalanced by a concomitant increase in Britain's involvement in western Europe. Even before the decolonisations in Africa and the Caribbean, it had been increasingly evident that the focus of Britain's external trade was already shifting away from the Empire and towards Europe. This, in turn, provided a powerful material motive for successive governments to emphasise the European dimension of their foreign policy. The second corollary of imperial retreat was that Britain's declining ability to project a world military role rendered it less able to assist American efforts to protect the general global interests of the West. Notwithstanding the continuing importance of Anglo-American collaboration inside NATO, the drastic reduction in the British government's ability after 1971 to conduct third-world operations served seriously to weaken London's ties with Washington. In short, the retreat from Empire in the 1960s was accompanied simultaneously by an upgrading of Britain's links with Europe and by a downgrading of its relations with the United States.

Yet, despite imperial withdrawal and the 'Europeanisation' of Britain's external policy, the extent and range of the British government's foreign relations remained immense. Indeed, one of the few things that could be said with certainty about Britain's foreign policy in the postwar period was that, like the weather, there was an awful lot of it about. In the late 1980s, the British government participated in a diverse array of international organisations, ranging from single-purpose associations such as the General Agreement on Tariffs and Trade (GATT) and the Universal Postal Union to highly complex 'supranational' institutions such as the European Community. London also maintained diplomatic contact with almost every other nation-state, with a plethora of embassies, consulates and High Commissions attempting to nurture innumerable sets of bilateral relations.

The sheer volume of Britain's bilateral contacts is shown in Table I.1. The table indicates the number of bilateral treaties and agreements which the British government signed with each foreign government over the period 1945–83 (for illustrative details of what these treaties involved, in a representative year, see Appendix). While such formal legal commitments clearly constitute only part of a nation's 'foreign policy', its treaty-making activities none the less do tend to reflect the differing priorities that its policy makers accord to relations with other

Table I.1 Number of bilateral treaties and agreements signed by the UK government, by country,* 1945–83

	1945–54	1955–64	1965–74	1975–83
Europe/North America				
Austria	14	13	12	5
Belgium	39	14	5	2
Canada	23	14	10	6
Denmark	34	27	10	5
Finland	13	8	6	6
France	83	27	21	35
Federal German Republic	19	47	17	9
Irish Republic	13	14	23	5
Italy	47	16	11	5
Netherlands	39	14	16	2
Norway	37	15	11	15
Portugal	26	14	9	5
Spain	14	11	3	7
Sweden	27	18	12	7
Switzerland	23	16	10	10
United States	126	93	54	30
Eastern Europe				
Czechoslovakia	17	12	5	4
Hungary	3	3	5	5
Poland	17	5	2	8
Rumania	0	1	9	11
Soviet Union	6	12	21	9
Yugoslavia	16	20	18	2
South America/Caribbean				
Argentina	12	17	14	1
Brazil	17	10	5	5
Chile	13	2	11	2
Costa Rica	0	0	5	6
Cuba	9	5	0	4
Ecuador	0	1	5	8
Jamaica	—	4	11	5
Mexico	5	3	0	3
Paraguay	3	9	13	0
Peru	4	3	9	6
Africa				
Botswana	—	—	8	9
Ethiopia	10	3	10	1

Table I.1

	1945–54	1955–64	1965–74	1975–83
Africa cont.				
Gambia	—	—	8	6
Ghana	—	5	10	7
Kenya	—	4	8	9
Malawi	—	4	9	12
Nigeria	—	4	3	3
Sierra Leone	—	3	6	7
South Africa	7	11	6	2
Zambia	—	1	12	8
Mediterranean/Middle East				
Cyprus	—	6	6	3
Egypt	26	11	12	9
Greece	22	5	6	7
Israel	6	6	8	6
Lebanon	5	4	2	7
Libya	7	1	2	0
Iraq	12	6	0	3
Jordan	3	20	23	12
Tunisia	0	3	7	3
Turkey	7	26	25	22
Asia/Pacific				
Australia	8	17	9	5
Burma	10	7	1	0
Ceylon/Sri Lanka	11	1	6	6
India	13	6	4	2
Indonesia	—	4	26	5
Japan	13	18	10	4
Laos	—	4	11	1
Malaysia	—	19	14	6
Mauritius	—	—	10	14
New Zealand	9	11	5	6
Pakistan	10	6	14	8
Philippines	4	5	0	7
Singapore	—	1	6	9
Thailand	12	8	5	8

*Countries which signed less than 10 treaties with the UK in the postwar period are excluded.

SOURCES: Clive Parry and Charity Hopkins, *An Index of British Treaties, Volume 3* (London: HMSO, 1970); *Command Papers* (CMND) (London: HMSO, various years).

countries. Thus Table I.1 illustrates (1) Britain's continuing concern with its relations with the rest of western Europe (note the high density of treaties that Britain signed with other west European countries throughout the postwar period); (2) its consistently close relationship with the United States (note, however, that the density declines somewhat from the mid-1960s onwards); and (3) the declining importance of the Empire-cum-Commonwealth, particularly after the 'second wave' decolonisations of the 1960s. The table also illustrates London's continuing interest in a variety of third-world theatres: in the Middle East (see, for example, the series of treaties signed with Egypt from 1945 onwards and with Jordan after 1955); in the Far East (note the agreements with Indonesia after 1965 and with Thailand after 1945); and in Latin America (see the continuing series of agreements signed with Argentina, Brazil and Chile). In short, Table I.1 demonstrates both the shifting priorities accorded to each of Churchill's three 'circles' during the postwar years and also the British government's determination to preserve its world-wide network of interests and contacts, even in the face of the enforced retreat from imperial power.

A genuinely comprehensive analysis of Britain's post-war foreign policy would undoubtedly need to describe and to explain the changing course of Britain's bilateral relations with each and every one of the countries identified in Table I.1 – a gargantuan enterprise given the extensive and highly variegated nature of London's postwar diplomacy. Fortunately the present study has a more limited focus. Rather than providing an all-encompassing account of Britain's postwar foreign relations, this book attempts *to outline the most important developments in British foreign policy which have occurred since 1945 and to review and assess the main explanations that have been offered for them.* Of course, such an approach immediately begs the question as to what constitutes an 'important' development. I have been guided in this matter partly by what existing academic studies consider important and partly by the priority accorded to different issues by the policy makers themselves, as evidenced by their actions, by their public pronouncements and (where available) by the official public record.[1] If this makes for a somewhat malleable notion of 'importance', so be it.

The descriptive part of the analysis presented here attempts to provide a straightforward outline of what Britain's major foreign policies have been during the postwar period. The explanatory part is conducted in terms of both the policy calculations of the key decision makers and the deeper 'structural' factors that shaped those calculations. In the context of Macmillan's 'wind of change' decolonisations, for example, this involves not only a discussion of the government's calculations about the need for a rapid withdrawal of imperial control, but also an examination of the more general 'structural' preconditions (most notably the growth of indigenous nationalism inside the colonies) that cause London to reconsider its overall imperial strategy in the first place. Without using any of the latest terminology, this book accordingly constitutes a modest attempt to examine the effects of both 'structure' and 'agency' on Britain's postwar foreign policies. Neither is assumed to be more important than the other, but both are clearly necessary if a convincing account of the major developments of the postwar era is to be provided.[2]

Chapter 1 explores the historical background to developments after 1945. In particular, it examines the way in which the failures of interwar 'Idealism' (the half-hearted attempt to substitute co-operative diplomacy for aggressive *realpolitik*) strongly reinforced 'Realism' in the minds of Britain's foreign policy makers, a Realism that was further underpinned by six years of war. The experiences of the 1930s seemed to demonstrate beyond reasonable doubt that states which opposed the international *status quo* should be firmly confronted from a position of military strength. This strongly held 'Realist' belief played a significant part in the overextended defence strategy that successive governments pursued after 1945 in their efforts to resist communist expansionism. After 1945, the conceptual model that had been devised for dealing with Hitler and Mussolini was transferred wholesale to the activities of the Soviet Union. The transfer was not in itself responsible for the subsequent Cold War but it certainly served to reinforce it, once it had begun.

Chapters 2 to 6 are organised around the major postwar developments in each of Churchill's three 'circles'. Chapter 2 examines Britain's relationship with Europe and the superpowers during the early years of the Cold War. It describes how, against the backdrop of the growing Soviet threat to European security, the Attlee government went to considerable lengths to persuade the Americans to make a long-run military commitment to western Europe's defence. The government's efforts – assisted in part by Stalin's short-sightedness – were rewarded with the creation of NATO in 1949. However, the indirect costs of American participation were to weigh heavily on the British exchequer in the years ahead. In return for Washington's assistance in Europe, Britain was expected not only to make a large contribution to NATO's continental land forces, but also to provide military support for Truman's global policy of 'containing' communist expansionism. It was this latter commitment that led to British involvement in the Korean war in the early 1950s and further exacerbated the problem of military overextension that had afflicted Britain's foreign policy strategy since 1945. As Chapter 2 also shows, however, while London was quite prepared to embroil itself in the *defence* of western Europe, it was also determined to stand aloof from French moves to create a west European *economic* community. In the early 1950s, Britain was still far too enmeshed in its 'three circle' strategy to entertain the idea that some part of its national sovereignty should be ceded to the incipiently supranational institutions of (what was to become) the European Economic Community (EEC).

Chapter 3 assesses Britain's 'Empire circle' policy between 1945 and the Suez crisis of 1956. It examines the relatively early withdrawals from India and Palestine and then describes Britain's post-1948 strategy of imperial retrenchment in the Far East, Africa and the Caribbean. It concludes that this final phase of full-blooded imperialism was carried out with remarkable skill, a series of well-timed constitutional concessions being employed to 'buy off' indigenous demands for full political participation. Suez, however, represented a symbolic watershed. The disastrous British intervention not only damaged Anglo-American relations but also provoked a thoroughgoing reappraisal of Britain's three circle strategy. After Suez, traditional European imperialism was confronted with the realisation that indigenous third-world pressures for self-determination could not be resisted forever, perhaps not even for very long. After Suez, the question of a wholesale imperial retreat came close to the top of the British government's foreign policy agenda.

Chapter 4 discusses the 'wind of change', the circumstances that produced the second wave decolonisations which by 1966 had deprived Britain of all but its smallest dependencies. It assesses the importance of the Wilson government's decision, in 1968, to withdraw British forces from east of Suez and discusses the extent to which the withdrawal succeeded in ameliorating the United Kingdom's problems of military overextension. Chapter 4 also analyses the fortuitous material shift in the pattern of Britain's overseas trade which (as noted above) was already beginning to occur before the post-Suez process of imperial retreat was fully under way.

Chapter 5 examines what was the clear counterpart to the retreat from Empire and the abandonment of Britain's world role: the British government's growing interest in Europe. Although Britain twice failed to join the thriving EEC during the 1960s, the focus of its economic activities continued to shift markedly towards Europe throughout that decade. Indeed, with its accession to the renamed 'European Community' (EC) in 1973, it seemed likely that Britain would subsequently follow a primarily European role in world politics, which would reflect its increasingly European interests and its new-found international position as a middle-ranking European power. These expectations were confirmed during the 1970s, but they were at least partially confounded in the 1980s. Margaret Thatcher's 'Gaullist' unwillingness to cede any further sovereignty to the EC's institutions severely restricted the development of a European common foreign policy and also the development of the EC itself. Indeed in the late 1980s Britain approached Europe with some ambiguity, accepting the plans for the creation of a free internal market by 1992 but distancing itself from its EC partners in terms of both financial policy and Europe's political relations with much of the outside world.

Chapter 6 reviews the main changes that have occurred in Britain's 'special relationship' with the United States in the period since Suez. It discusses the rapid repair in relations that occurred in 1957–8 following the recognition by policy makers in both London and Washington that the main beneficiary of the Anglo-American rift over Suez had probably been the Soviet Union. The chapter then examines the decay in bilateral relations which set in during the mid 1960s, as the Wilson government first refused to provide material support for the American war in Vietnam and then reduced its own geostrategic usefulness to Washington by withdrawing from east of Suez. During the 1980s, however, Britain ceased to be 'just another' European power. As an 'instinctive Atlanticist', Thatcher was as convinced as President Reagan that the West could and should use force against any government or movement, communist or otherwise, that seriously challenged the global interests of the West. The Thatcher years therefore witnessed a partial rekindling of the 'special relationship', with London seeking to add legitimacy to Washington's actions in the third world, even though the objective level of material support that Britain was able to supply was, in reality, very restricted.

Chapters 7 and 8 focus on two areas of British foreign policy – economics and defence – which, although they are analysed *en passant* in other parts of this book, raise a series of technical problems that require special attention. Chapter 7 distinguishes between the two main phases of Britain's postwar foreign economic policy: before 1968, when successive governments sought to preserve the twin financial legacies of the Empire, the reserve role of sterling and the Overseas Sterling Area; and, after 1968, when Britain experimented with a variety of approaches to currency policy at the same time as it brought its trade and investment policies increasingly into line with the requirements of the EC. Chapter 8 focuses on the two main aspects of Britain's postwar defence policy: NATO and the independent nuclear deterrent. The discussion of NATO examines the political and military underpinnings of the alliance, the changing divisions and tensions within it and the major problems that are likely to confront it in the medium-term future. The discussion of the independent deterrent analyses the deterrent's role within Britain's overall defence posture and its importance, at least in the eyes of successive governments, as a symbol of Britain's continuing Great Power status.

Chapter 9 is concerned with theoretical matters. It reviews a number of different approaches to the analysis of foreign policy and briefly assesses the extent to which each has informed the substantive analysis presented in this book. The chapter places particular emphasis on 'Realism', the theoretical model that in my view has dominated the foreign policy thinking of successive British governments for at least the last century. As argued elsewhere in this book, this commitment to 'Realist' principles has exerted a powerful influence on the development of Britain's postwar foreign policy.

Chapter 10 draws together the main substantive themes that are explored throughout the book. It assesses the extent to which, in spite of imperial withdrawal, Britain's postwar foreign policy strategy has continued to suffer from overextension and discusses the changing role that Britain has played in the international system since 1945. It is argued that, although Britain did find a role, of a sort, in the post-imperial world, its overall foreign policy strategy remained fundamentally ambivalent. During the Thatcher years in particular, the British government sought to maintain a prominent position in both the European and Atlantic circles. At a time when Britain's primary material interests were increasingly located in Europe – and when Britain was most likely to influence world events if it acted in concert with its European partners – the British government might have been better advised to commit itself more fully to the European Community.

A necessary aside: the relevance of foreign policy 'theory'

It might at first sight seem rather odd to introduce a discussion of 'foreign policy theory' into what should be a relatively straightforward historical account of Britain's postwar foreign policy. British governments, it might be observed, have pursued a particular sequence of foreign policies since 1945, and that sequence of policies has presumably been followed for a given set of reasons. All that an analysis of British foreign policy behaviour has to do is to specifiy the appropriate sequence of policies and then to identify the reasons why these policies were adopted. Where, it might reasonably be asked, does 'theory' come into it? The answer to this important question is simple, yet potentially perplexing: analysts of foreign policy invariably employ, either consciously or unconsciously, some sort of theoretical perspective when they approach their subject matter. Crucially, the perspective that is adopted not only colours the analyst's characterisation of 'that which is to be explained' (the 'appropriate sequence of policies' referred to above) but also strongly influences the specific explanations (the 'reasons') that are offered for it. In view of this profound influence of theoretical perspective upon both description and explanation, it is evident why the present 'aside' is so necessary.

The alternative approaches that are available to contemporary foreign policy analysts fall into two broad categories – those that emphasise foreign policy decision making, and those that focus on the broader 'structural' factors which shape international developments largely independently of the policy makers' decisions. At the decision-making level, the two most important perspectives are the (potentially complementary) 'Rational Actor' and 'Bureaucratic Politics' models. The Rational Actor model seeks to understand foreign policy behaviour as the goal-directed consequence of rational calculation by decision makers: rational calculations that aim in some sense to maximise 'the national interest'. The Bureaucratic Politics model, on the other hand, prefers to analyse policy in terms of the competing pressures exerted by different segments of the bureaucratic and political elites, focusing on the way in which different departmental and political factions seek to ensure that their own conception of 'the national interest' prevails.

At the structural level, three main analytic alternatives present themselves – the 'Marxist', 'World Society' and 'Structural–Realist' perspectives. The Marxist perspective stresses the way in which the exigencies of the international capitalist system constrain the decision choices of national governments and seeks to establish why (in the view of its protagonists) certain 'fractions' of the capitalist class have benefited most from Britain's postwar foreign policy strategies. In a not-dissimilar vein, the World Society perspective views foreign policy behaviour primarily as a response to transnational processes and structures, placing particular emphasis on the extent to which the increasing interdependence of the contemporary world economy has eroded national decision-making autonomy. Finally, Realism-as-structural-theory seeks to analyse changes in foreign policy strategy as the consequence of the shifting material and security interests of the state, concentrating particularly on the extent to which different states' interests tend to converge or diverge over time.

There are, then, at least five major analytic approaches to the study of foreign policy. Unfortunately, the intrusion of 'theory' into foreign policy analysis does not stop here: 'theory' also affects the policy makers themselves. Just as the analyst's theoretical position affects both his descriptions and his explanations, so the policy maker's 'world-view' – his beliefs and perceptions about the nature of international politics – influences both the way he interprets the actions of other states and the foreign policy decisions that he takes. It is, of course, virtually impossible to specify the precise 'world-views' of Britain's principal postwar foreign policy makers. None the less, it is fair to conclude that, during the twentieth century, British thinking about international affairs has been dominated by two sets of ideas: those (again) of 'Realism' and, to a lesser extent, of Idealism.

Idealism is based on the assumption that all states ultimately share a common interest in avoiding war and in maximising mutually beneficial international economic exchange. Its prescription is that, as far as possible, states should use the vehicles of co-operative diplomacy and international law in order to ensure that international disputes are peacefully resolved. Indeed, in the Idealist view, conflicts between states generally result either from injustice, mistrust or misunderstanding: a judicious combination of law and diplomacy can in principle remedy all three. Notwithstanding the British government's flirtation with Idealism in the 1920s, however, Idealist principles have never seriously informed Britain's foreign policy. On the contrary, it has been the rival tradition of Realism that (at least since the late 1930s) has constituted the foundation of the British foreign policy establishment's 'world-view'.

Although the principles of Realism are discussed in detail in Chapter 9, the frequent references to *'realpolitik* logic' that are made in Chapters 1 to 8 necessitate a brief review of Realism here. Rejecting the notion that there is, or ever can be, a global harmony of interests, Realism is founded on the assertion that, in the absence of a single 'world government', the nation–state can never be sure that it is safe from external attack. Every state permanently risks being confronted by at least one potential aggressor which, if it is given the opportunity to do so, will seek to dominate and exploit any other state weaker than itself. In these circumstances, argues the Realist, the overriding objective of a given state's foreign policy must be the achievement and maintenance of its security. This need to ensure security in turn requires both a strong defensive posture and the construction of alliances with other states which share similar security fears. (Thus, for example, in the late 1940s the countries of North America and Western Europe, fearful of the threat posed to their security interests by Soviet communism, joined together to form the NATO alliance.) Ensuring security also requires that the state does all it can both to weaken the strategic position of its opponents and to ensure that friendly governments are installed (or maintained in power) in as many other countries as possible. *Realpolitik* logic, in essence, is cynical, self-regarding calculation based on the paramount need to preserve national security.

Where does all this discussion of analysts' 'theories' and of policy makers' 'world-views' leave us? Which of the theories, if any, are relevant to the analysis conducted here and how, if at all, do they relate to the world-views of Britain's postwar foreign policy makers? In order to answer these questions, it needs to be recognised that this book adopts an essentially 'state-centric' approach to British foreign policy. In so doing, it assumes that, in spite of the growing proliferation of transnational structures and processes, nation–states remain the most important actors on the world stage; that foreign policy analysis should still concentrate primarily – though not exclusively – on a given state's dealings and relationship with other states. This is clearly not the only approach to foreign policy analysis that could be taken – indeed, Marxist scholars and World Society theorists would undoubtedly regard it as being unnecessarily limited in focus – but it probably represents the one that has been used most frequently by mainstream analysts of postwar British foreign policy.

The state-centric focus adopted here does mean, however, that more use is made of some theoretical perspectives than others. At the decision-making level both the Rational Actor and the Bureaucratic Politics models are employed: the former because it focuses on the foreign policy decisions of the nation–state; and the latter because it examines the nation–state's decision-making apparatus. At the structural level, the Realist perspective is adopted, partly because of its intrinsic explanatory power and partly because the alternative Marxist and World Society perspectives self-avowedly eschew a state-centric focus. Moreover, the use of the Realist model, at the structural level, has the additional desirable characteristic of familiarising the reader with the 'Realist' world-view shared by the vast majority of Britain's postwar foreign policy makers. Indeed a full appreciation of this world-view is essential if Britain's postwar foreign policy is to be properly understood.

Of course, any attempt to understand the decision makers' world-views immediately begs the question as to who Britain's foreign policy makers actually are (or were). The ensuing text – like many others – is replete with phrases such as 'the government decided . . .', 'London's aims were . . .', 'The British response was . . .' and 'successive governments believed that . . .'. To whom, specifically, do these synonyms refer? Who is it that actually makes British foreign policy? Any answer to these questions must begin by acknowledging that the British foreign policy making process, like its domestic counterpart, is a highly complex one, involving a variety of political and bureaucratic elites.[3] Figure I.2 identifies the main institutional actors involved in this process and describes the broad pattern of interrelationship among them. What needs to be emphasised, however, is that, although both Whitehall and Parliament can exert varying degrees of influence over particular policy issues, it is undoubtedly the Cabinet that is the key

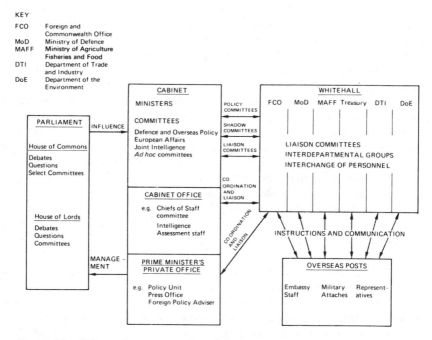

Figure I.2   Schematic representation of the contemporary British foreign policy making process

SOURCE: Michael Clarke, 'The Policy-Making Process' in Michael Smith, Steve Smith and Brian White (eds) *British Foreign Policy: Tradition, Change and Transformation* (London: Unwin Hyman, 1988) p. 86 (Figure 4.1), reproduced by kind permission of Unwin Hyman Ltd; © M. Smith, S. Smith and B. White 1988.

decision centre in all important policy matters. It is the Cabinet that defines both the general and the specific goals of Britain's external policy. It is the Cabinet that defines where Britain's primary national interests lie. And whenever there is a major policy choice to be made – whether it involves a decision to use military force or a decision to negotiate a new trade treaty – it is the Cabinet that decides upon the general course of action to be taken. This is not to say, of course, that Cabinets are invariably (or even, usually) united in arriving at their decisions, or that each Cabinet member has an equal say in determining policy choices. It is obviously the case that there is frequently dissent in Cabinet and that some ministers have more influence upon (some) foreign policy decisions than others. It would be extraordinary, for example, if the Foreign Secretary and Defence Secretary failed to contribute significantly to decisions taken in the diplomatic and security spheres; or if the Chancellor of the Exchequer was unable to exert a powerful influence over decisions relating to external financial policy. This said, patterns of ministerial influence vary from administration to administration. Through the use of the diverse political resources at their disposal, prime ministers constrain the decision-making autonomy of their individual ministers to varying degrees and in different ways. As far as the present study is concerned, this means that references to 'the British government' (or to some synonym) should be taken to refer to Cabinet – although in any given context it should also be recognised that the prime minister and one or two other ministers may well have exerted a disproportionately large influence upon Cabinet's 'collective decision'.

This book offers an unashamedly narrative account of Britain's foreign policy during the postwar era. It is a narrative, however, that is both guided and informed by theory. Following the Structural–Realist model the major shifts in Britain's postwar foreign policy strategy are analysed in terms of the changing pattern of Britain's material and security interests. Following the Rational Actor model, the policy makers' decisions are analysed primarily in terms of the calculations that were made as to how Britain's national interests could best be maximised. The analysis also reflects the extent to which the rationality of Britain's postwar foreign policy makers was consistently constrained by their Realist world-views. In essence, the foreign policy calculations of successive British governments were based on the assumption that in a threatening world the primary foreign policy goal of maintaining national security could only be achieved by the possession of an effective defence capability combined with the determination to use it. For much of the postwar period this assumption was, on balance, justified. There were also occasions, however, when the magnitude of the 'threat' was seriously overestimated and when the application of *Realpolitik* logic was accordingly misplaced. On these occasions, as will become evident, Britain's postwar foreign policy record was something less than glorious.

1
Before 1945

In the mid-seventeenth century, when the emerging European states system was in its infancy, England was a relatively unimportant regional power with primarily European interests. Over the next 250 years, with the gradual extension of its imperial acquisitions, Great Britain was transformed into a major global power with significant economic and political interests widely dispersed throughout the world.[1] How this transformation came about need not concern us here. It is none the less worth noting that both the growing strength of British sea power and the country's early industrialisation were crucial to Britain's nineteenth-century imperial pre-eminence. Indeed it is no coincidence that the 'retreat from [global] power' which characterised Britain's foreign policy after 1945 should have had its origins in the relative decline of Britain's industrial capacity and in the failure to sustain the prominent maritime position of the Royal Navy in the period after 1870.

This chapter briefly reviews the main strategic calculations which informed British foreign policy in the century before 1914. It then examines Britain's flirtation with Idealism in the 1920s and 1930s and the consequent reinforcement of Realism in the minds of the policy makers after 1936. Finally it describes the major developments of the war years which were to exert a significant influence on events after 1945.

Before 1914

The guiding principle of Britain's pre-1914 foreign policy strategy was identified in Sir Eyre Crowe's well-known 'Memorandum on the Present State of British Relations with France and Germany' in January 1907. In Crowe's view, the central objective was to ensure that

British foreign policy was 'so directed as to harmonise with the general desires and ideals common to all mankind and, more particularly, that it is closely identified with the primary and vital interests of a majority or as many as possible of the other nations'.[2] This principle, of course, had both moral and practical benefits. Not only did Britain thus conveniently demonstrate its respect for the 'vital interests' of other nations, but the overall direction of its policy – if it *could* be identified with the majority of nations – would also be consistent with the general tide of history. However, the immediate difficulty encountered in the attempt to give such a principle concrete expression was that it was not always obvious what the 'vital interests' of the 'majority of nations' actually were. Eyre Crowe's solution was to retreat into the traditional 'balance of power' principles upon which Britain had based its European foreign policy since the early eighteenth century. For Crowe, the protection of Britain's vital material and security interests lay in the continued pursuit of a general strategy which sought to prevent any other state (or group of states) from achieving the sort of *preponderance of power capabilities* which might indirectly enable that state either to weaken Britain's links with its Empire or to challenge its dominant commercial position in world trade.

In the period before 1914 Britain's efforts to sustain the 'balance of power' – to prevent the emergence of a power preponderance elsewhere – were directed in four main areas. In *Europe*, the French defeat at the hands of the Prussians in 1871 ensured that suspicions of resurgent Bonapartism were replaced by fears of German hegemonism.[3] As a result, after 1870 the need to prevent Germany from making further territorial gains at the expense of the disintegrating Austro-Hungarian Empire became the major objective of Britain's European policy.[4] The counterpart to this strategy of German containment, of course, was a more sympathetic posture towards the French – embodied in the Entente Cordiale of 1904 – since a strong and independent France would constitute a bulwark against a further German advance in the West.[5] Notwithstanding this improvement in Anglo-French relations, however, the British government continued to entertain serious suspicions about French, as well as German, intentions in the Low Countries, the independence of which Britain had jealously guarded throughout the nineteenth century in order to prevent their use as a springboard from which a sea-borne invasion of Great Britain could be launched. In the event, of course, it was Germany rather than France which in 1914 was seen as the greatest threat to the stability of the established European order; and it was the threat that German militarism posed to the integrity of the Netherlands and Belgium which was one of the important triggers to British involvement in the First World War.

In order to maintain control of the *Empire* from the mid-eighteenth century onwards, the main thrust of Britain's foreign policy was in the military sphere. This is not to say that London neglected the political need to enter into informal coalitions with local elites inside the colonies and dominions. Rather, it is simply to indicate that the fundamental means by which the Empire was maintained was (1) by the development of a relatively small but highly professional and mobile army and (2) by the commitment to maintain a navy which was larger than the size of the next two navies added together.[6] On this basis, the imperial possessions in India, in Australia and Canada, in Malaya and in Africa could be provisioned, fortified and reinforced as and when circumstances demanded. And as long as Britain could sustain the Empire, it also maintained control of the vast material resources contained therein, thus depriving any potential rival of the opportunity of strengthening its own resource-capability position.

In the *Mediterranean and the Middle East*, the primary object of British policy was to protect the military and commercial transit route to India. Thus the island bases in the Mediterranean (Gibraltar, Malta and Cyprus), the installation of a pro-British government in Egypt and the fortified bunkering facility at Aden were all required in order to allow the Royal Navy to exercise its imperial *Pax Britannica* and to prevent any other nation from interfering with British shipping *en route* to India. A second important objective in Britain's Middle East policy was the containment of Russia. In the Far East the fear of Russian expansionism had led to British involvement in the Afghan wars of 1838–49 and 1878–81. In the Middle East it led to a consistent policy throughout the nineteenth century of British support for the Ottoman Empire, the 'sick man of Europe' whose northern provinces were regarded as fertile ground for Russian annexation.[7] While London's attempts to limit *Russian* influence in Turkey before 1914 were fairly successful, Britain was not able to prevent a dramatic increase in *German* commercial involvement in Turkey between 1870 and 1914.[8] This close economic involvement with Germany, allied with Turkish suspicions that Britain and Russia, after 1914, might be in the process of concocting a deal to partition the Ottoman Empire, led the Turks to enter the First World War on the German side. However the setback to British strategy in the Middle East which the Turkish defection represented was at least partially reversed by the mandates for Iraq and

Palestine that were awarded to Britain by the League of Nations in 1920. Relations with Turkey itself were repaired after 1926.[9]

Finally, in the *Caribbean* the principal aim of British policy was not only to guarantee the security of the colonial territories themselves, but also to provide bases from which the Royal Navy could protect the shipping lanes that carried Britain's substantial and increasing trade with both North and South America. While the United States, acting under the Monroe Doctrine, exercised a dominating *political* influence in Latin America, it was Britain which – at least until 1900 – was the dominant economic power in the region.[10] None the less, so long as the United States was prepared to ensure that *all* European attempts to engineer political hegemony in Latin America would be strongly resisted, Britain was only too happy to be allowed to continue to trade there without formal political entanglement or obligation. Indeed, after 1900, London was even prepared to hand over the effective policing of the Caribbean and Latin American trade routes to the US Navy; a move that was to be extended after 1921 to include the north-western Pacific.[11]

Yet if British strategy in each of these four areas had seemed to be generally effective during the nineteenth century, it gradually became apparent after 1900 that the overall position was weakening. The most obvious and immediate signs of the incipient decline were in the very sectors from which Britain had derived its nineteenth-century pre-eminence: the efficiency of its manufacturing industry and its preponderant sea power.[12] By the early 1900s, while Britain's hold over the indigenous populations of its colonies (South Africa excepted) was as strong as ever, it no longer enjoyed the luxury of a navy which could better the combined resources of the two next-largest naval powers. Germany, Japan and the United States now each possessed sufficient naval capacity to permit an alliance of any two of them to outnumber the Royal Navy.[13] In any case, within their own regions each was already mounting a significant challenge to British dominance. The era of *Pax Britannica* was thus effectively at an end. The tacit naval understanding with the United States in the Caribbean was an implicit admission that Britain could not police the seas alone; that the very underpinning of her dominant nineteenth-century global role was beginning to weaken.

Against this background of (1) a relative decline in Britain's sea power, (2) the loss of Britain's lead in industrial production and (3) profound suspicions that the British Army was too small and too ill-equipped to participate effectively in a continental war,[14] Asquith's government found itself in August 1914 embarking on a war which was to lay waste to Europe and to squander the resources of the Empire for over four years. A large number of explanations have been offered for the outbreak of the First World War and it would be quite impossible to review them here.[15] None the less there were certainly two fundamental and immediate motives (which were also to operate in 1939) that drew Britain into the conflict: the need to defend an Empire that had been assembled, with varying degrees of commitment, over the previous century and a half; and the need to prevent Germany from controlling France and the Low Countries, the ports and resources of which could readily be used for an attack on Britain itself.[16]

Whatever causal factors 'really' operated, however, it is clear that Britain's international position in 1914 was markedly weaker than it had been a generation earlier. Yet by 1918, owing in part to the contribution of the United States after 1917, Britain had emerged as one of the victorious powers, a Great Power quite prepared to extend its global role and international commitments. With hindsight it is possible to discern that, as early as 1920, Britain was already beginning to pursue the 'overextended' foreign policy strategy which was to become so characteristic of the period after 1945. In the interwar period, however, 'overextension' was considerably less important than the tension between 'Realism' and 'Idealism', as the respective protagonists of those approaches strove for mastery in the determination of Britain's foreign policy.

The interwar years: Realism versus Idealism

If the old practices of *Realpolitik* had led to the horrors of the First World War, then the new Idealism of the League of Nations promised a fresh start in which the systematic operation of 'collective security' would replace the haphazard and unreliable workings of the 'balance of power' as the primary means of deterring war. The reality, unfortunately, was dramatically different. As will be seen in this section, (1) the Idealist experiment of the 1920s failed disastrously as a vehicle for preserving peace; (2) the public protestations of Idealist commitment – consistently made by successive British governments until the mid-1930s – were partly responsible for preventing a more 'realistic' foreign policy from emerging until it was too late to deter war; and (3) the main consequence of the failure of Idealism after 1938 was a deep commitment among British foreign policy makers to the principles of Realism. Without doubt this commitment to Realism served Britain well from the late 1930s until 1945. As will be seen in later chapters, however, thereafter it introduced a number of understandable but avoidable distortions into British foreign policy which probably operated to the country's long-term detriment.

Any event as universally traumatic as the First World War was bound to have profound long-term consequences for all of the nations involved. As far as Great Britain was concerned, the 1914–18 war had three major consequences, though each had deeper and earlier roots. The first of these concerned the promises, soon to be broken, that were made to a variety of groups in the Middle East and the Empire with the intention of securing their continued support during the war.[17] Indian nationalists were promised that their demands for greater self-government would be received sympathetically once peace with Germany had been secured. In Palestine, the Balfour Declaration of 1917 appeared to hold the promise of the coveted Jewish national homeland. And Arabs throughout the Middle East received a number of guarantees that their interests would be protected in any postwar dismemberment of the Ottoman Empire. The implications of these promises are discussed in a later chapter and so they need not detain us here.

A second major consequence of the First World War was the expansion of the Empire, a development made possible partly by the general desire to deprive Germany of its colonial possessions and partly by the defeat of Turkey which (as noted earlier) had entered the war on the German side in November 1914.[18] However, while the defeat of Germany and of Turkey released a large number of territories for distribution among the winning coalition, few of the victorious powers had a direct interest in acquiring them. The United States, at the instigation of the Senate, was in the process of withdrawing rapidly into isolation and was certainly not interested in burdening itself with quasi-colonial entanglements in either Africa or the Middle East. The new Soviet government – even if it had been consulted by the former allies of the Russian Crown – was deeply opposed as a matter of ideological principle to anything which resembled colonialism.[19] Japan was interested only in developing its power base in the Far East, and neither Germany nor Turkey had possessed territory in that region.[20] And Italy, whose participation in the war had been equivocal if not downright half-hearted, was thought not to deserve any of the spoils of war in any case, notwithstanding the promises made in the 'secret treaties' of 1915.[21]

Of the six victorious 'Great Powers', therefore, only Britain and France were in a position to acquire new 'responsibilities'. In consequence, as part of the Versailles settlement, Britain took control of the former German colonies of Tanganyika and South West Africa (now

Namibia). By 1921, under the formal auspices of the League of Nations, Turkey had been stripped of Palestine, Transjordan, Iraq and the sheikdoms of the Persian Gulf, all of which were then 'mandated' to Britain. As H. A. L. Fisher observed later, this was 'the crudity of conquest draped in the veil of morality'.[22] The crucial point, however, was that, while Britain's quasi-imperial possessions had expanded, that expansion was almost entirely the result of a peculiar set of fortuitous circumstances rather than the consequence of a genuine increase in Britain's power capability. As early as May 1920 serious doubts were being expressed as to London's ability to maintain its direct control over the newly-acquired territories as well as those which Britain already possessed. The Chief of the General Staff observed: 'Our small army is far too scattered ... in no single theatre are we strong enough.'[23] The British government's response was to adopt a tactic that decolonising governments were to emulate in the 1950s and 1960s. Under the terms of their respective mandates, 'independent' governments – with some degree of local autonomy – were established in Iraq (in 1921) and in Transjordan during the course of 1921 and 1922. Egypt, an effective British fiefdom since 1881, was accorded a similar status in 1922. And in each case, of course, great care was taken to ensure that the new government was dominated by men who could be relied upon to adopt a friendly and, if necessary, subservient posture towards Britain. As a result the British government maintained a position of considerable political and economic influence throughout the Middle East. What could have been a source of strength, however, was in fact a continuing source of vulnerability: the position of the 'thinly spread' army lamented by the Chief of the General Staff in 1920 was not substantially improved at any time during the interwar period.[24]

A third major consequence of the First World War was psychological: the determination both within the governing elite and among the public at large that this kind of general war must never occur again. The determination was hardly surprising. Not only had millions of men been killed, but millions had experienced at first hand the horror and lunacy of prolonged trench warfare. The war poetry of Wilfred Owen, Rupert Brooke and Siegfried Sassoon gave sensitive expression to the mental and physical cruelty of life on the western front; even when all was quiet. The rather more explicit details of all manner of ghastly experiences were gradually circulated among the general public by word of mouth, in direct contradiction of the government's wartime propaganda.[25] George Orwell observed that 'every [soldier and] junior officer looked on the General Staff as mental defectives' for having contemplated fighting this kind of war in the first place.[26] Arnold Toynbee later suggested that the experiences of the First World War had rendered the British people 'prematurely humanised'. It had imbued them with a determination never to fight another war. Unfortunately the tide of history had not yet provided the sort of objective international conditions in which those with such unequivocally pacifist inclinations could hope to prosper. Toynbee's description was not intended as a compliment. But it was extremely appropriate.

Yet even if it was wrong for the age, the determination that the First World War must not be repeated had powerful policy implications. Its major immediate effect was the British government's *public* commitment to the creation of a new international order which would espouse the principle of 'pacific settlement'. The new international order was to be constructed through two mechanisms, the twin pillars of interwar 'Idealism'. First, an embryonic international Leviathan was to be created through the further development of *international law*; law which had grown considerably in scope and volume since the Hague Conventions of 1899 and 1907.[27] Second, new *formal channels for co-operative diplomacy* were to be established which, along with existing bilateral arrangements and understandings, might act as a substitute for confrontation and the threat and use of force. Of central importance in this regard were to be the institutions of the newly-created League of Nations.[28]

Even from the outset, however, the commitment of the British government to the central principle of Idealism – the idea of pacific settlement through legal process and co-operative diplomacy – was severely constrained by two important factors. The first problem was the position of the United States. Despite the central role played by Woodrow Wilson in both the postwar settlement and the formulation of the principles of the League, the United States subsequently withdrew into isolation following the failure of the Senate to ratify the League Covenant in 1919.[29] As Dilks has argued, Britain would probably never have taken a leading responsibility within the League if it had been realised that the United States would not share the burden.[30] By the time of the effective American withdrawal, however, Britain was already in a position where it was unable to divest itself of its new responsibilities without destroying the League even before its official birth. Lloyd George's government was thus obliged to proceed without the assistance of its erstwhile American ally. The result was that Britain was always overstretched by its League-inspired commitments, its government lacking both the capability and the will to undertake the tasks expected of it by foreign governments and by the public at home.

A second constraint on the commitment of successive governments to the principle of pacific settlement was that the publicly-stated Idealism of the British government was never fully reflected in its private decision calculus. In private, the framers and movers of British foreign policy maintained a healthy scepticism as to the real potentialities of 'pacific settlement'. In spite of all the public posturing, the pervasive private commitment to 'Realism' – in Cabinet, in the Foreign Office, the Colonial Office and the India Office – ensured that the institutions of the new idealist international order were never even given a chance to operate effectively.[31]

A classic example of the contrast between public presentation and private calculation was Britain's dispute with Turkey in the mid-1920s over possession of the Mosul.[32] The Mosul itself was a supposedly oil-rich territory in Southern Turkey and, not surprisingly, the new Turkish nationalist government of Mustapha Kemal Attaturk wished to retain control of it. The British government, on the other hand, was determined to incorporate the Mosul into the newly-mandated territory of Iraq. Under the terms of the Treaty of Lausanne, which in July 1923 had brought an end to the four-year war of Turkish independence, Britain and Turkey had agreed to settle their dispute over the possession of the Mosul within nine months. If an agreement had still not been reached after this time, the matter was to be referred to the League of Nations Council. Thus were the principles of pacific settlement to be put into effect. When the British and Turkish governments did indeed fail to agree on a settlement, a referral to the Council was immediately effected. In December 1925, the Council, of which Britain was a leading member, awarded the territory to Iraq. Turkey, however, promptly rejected both the award and the Council's competence to make it. The Turks subsequently rejected an Advisory Opinion from the judicial arm of the League – the Permanent Court of International Justice – which had ruled that the Council's decision had been valid, and Attaturk threatened to initiate a guerrilla war in the Mosul region if a satisfactory outcome to the dispute was not forthcoming. It was at this point that London adopted the more traditional tactics of coercive diplomacy. In five months of intensive diplomatic bargaining British diplomats were able to persuade Mustapha Kemal's government that its continued rejection of the Council's pro-British decision could expect to be met with severe sanctions from the Great Powers. As a result, in June 1926, the Turks concluded a treaty with Great Britain and Iraq which recognised the Council's decision. However, while the settlement itself was to lay the foundation for the subsequent improvment in Anglo-Turkish relations, it did not represent the vindication for the process of League-sponsored pacific settlement that it was portrayed as being at the time. Rather, the Mosul settlement was a simple reflection of the balance of *realpolitik* forces: the Turks gave way not because they were converted to a belief in the sanctity of the quasi-judicial processes of the League but because the British threatened them, albeit in the most gentlemanly manner, that they would suffer 'serious consequences' if they persisted with their current 'rejectionist' strategy. For the time being, however, the public facade of pacific settlement was perpetuated: not only was Britain committed to it, but also it worked.

But if the illusion of pacific settlement could be maintained during the 1920s because the supranational decisions of the League fortuitously coincided with the interests of the powerful, that illusion could not be sustained for long. After 1930, it became increasingly apparent that *realpolitik* was once more (as perhaps it had always been) the fundamental determining force in international affairs. The disputes in Manchuria after 1931 and in Abyssinia after 1934 were settled not by the pacific mechanisms of the League – which possessed no coercive capability of its own to enforce its decisions – but by unadorned power politics: by military force. In Manchuria, the universally condemned Japanese invasion of a Chinese province went unpunished simply because none of the other Great Powers supposed that its 'vital' security or material interests were at stake. The Italian annexation of Abyssinia in 1935 attracted only token opposition (an ineffectual trade embargo) largely for the same reason.[33]

As far as the British government was concerned, however, the mismatch between public pronouncement and private calculation, which had been so evident at the time of the Mosul settlement, was all set to continue. In *private*, the Foreign Office view, typified by the position of Sir Robert Vansittart,[34] was that British interests were simply not affected by developments in Abyssinia. London also calculated that serious British opposition to Mussolini could either push him into a tighter embrace with Hitler or – if it damaged the Italian dictator's internal position – merely serve to strengthen the hand of the Italian communists.[35] Since both of these eventualities were patently unwelcome, it was better for the British government to reserve its judgement and await events: the Abyssinians would be left to their fate. In *public*, a somewhat different posture was adopted. In deference to the demands of public opinion, Britain consistently contrived to give the impression that it was seriously committed to the use of the League as an instrument for actively opposing aggression; a deliberately cultivated public image that was especially characteristic of the Baldwin government which was re-elected in November 1935. Not surprisingly, therefore, the bilateral Hoare–Laval Plan of December 1935 (which intended to recognise the ceding of large tracts of Abyssinian territory to Italy) was regarded as a clear violation of this self-avowed commitment to League-sponsored efforts at conflict resolution. A tremendous outpouring of public opposition to the plan resulted, in the wake of which Sir Samuel Hoare was obliged to resign as Foreign Secretary.[36] His replacement, Sir Anthony Eden, made rather more appropriate public noises but he could do nothing to retrieve the situation. Accordingly, the *realist* advice of the Foreign Office that British interests remained unaffected was accepted and Italy was left in *de facto* control of Abyssinia. *En passant*, 'the credibility of the League as a coercive instrument [had been] . . . completely destroyed'.[37]

But if *Realpolitik* calculation was by 1935 gaining the ascendancy in the British government's approach to the League, such calculations were less in evidence in the one context (as things turned out) that mattered most: in Britain's dealings with Hitler's Germany. As early as 1928, five years before the Nazi regime emerged, Sir Horace Rumbold, the British Ambassador to Berlin, had warned that 'the satisfaction of one German grievance . . . [serves merely to encourage] . . . new demands'.[38] This was a pattern that was to be consistently repeated once Hitler achieved power in 1933; yet it was not until 1939 that the British government grasped the nettle and decided to meet Hitler's aggressive stratagems with a suitably coercive response. In spite of Rumbold's warnings in 1933 that war with Germany could be expected within four or five years,[39] successive British Cabinets took the line that a peaceful solution to the German problem was not only desirable but also *possible*.[40] In the fashion of the 'prematurely humanised' British public, they readily seized upon any evidence that would corroborate this belief.[41] The unfortunate consequence of the continuing belief in the possibility of a peaceful, compromise solution was that the co-operative diplomatic strategy which it engendered was bound to fail for precisely the reasons that Rumbold had articulated in 1928. That failure, in turn, led to the gradual castigation of co-operative diplomacy as 'appeasement', a denigration from which it has still not fully recovered.

Hitler's first major move to revise Germany's international position came in March 1934 when he made budgetary provision for large increases in German defence spending.[42] Notes were despatched to Berlin, but nothing more was done. In March 1935 the German government formally repudiated the clauses of the Versailles Treaty which had limited German armament levels, and reintroduced conscription. The Baldwin government's response to this deliberate act of confrontation was again to back down; to continue with its policy of co-operative diplomacy: the Cabinet still hoped to negotiate with Hitler, perhaps even to the extent of restoring some of Germany's colonies if she would rejoin the League (from which Germany had left in October 1933).[43] However, the German policy of confrontation continued inexorably. In further violation of the Treaty of Versailles, Hitler remilitarised the Rhineland in March 1936. Yet, again, nothing effective was done in response. Although Foreign Secretary Eden expressed disappointment that a potentially useful bargaining counter had been lost, he still hoped for a non-aggression pact with Germany as a means of resolving the two countries' differences.[44]

In May 1937 Neville Chamberlain succeeded Baldwin as Prime Minister and the policy of appeasement continued to be the central feature of Britain's European diplomacy.[45] The period of Chamberlain's premiership provided the clearest examples of the ability of the Cabinet to seize upon any evidence that would corroborate the belief that co-operative diplomacy was the best way of dealing with Hitler. In stark contrast to the advice of the Foreign Office, Chamberlain chose to accept the judgement of Britain's Ambassador to Berlin, Sir Neville Henderson.[46] Whereas Vansittart had been calling for a determined stand against German militarism since the mid-1930s, Henderson's fundamentally benign views on the character of both Hitler and the German state held sway, bolstered by a convenient (to Chamberlain) Chief of Staff's report which concluded that Britain had no strategic interests in Eastern Europe and was therefore not threatened by any designs on the area that Germany might entertain.[47] As a direct result of the converging advice offered by Henderson and the Chiefs of Staff, Chamberlain's government simply acquiesced when Hitler's forces effectively annexed Austria in March 1938, on the pretext of being invited in by the Austrian Nazi government to restore order.

Worse was to come. In the summer of 1938 Hitler began a sustained diplomatic offensive – backed covertly by fifth-columnists on the ground – aimed at achieving the partition of Czechoslovakia and the consequent incorporation into the Reich of the German-speaking Sudetenland. In September 1938 Chamberlain travelled to Germany to discuss the Czech question with Hitler. At their final meeting in Munich – in consultation with representatives of both France and Italy, but not of Czechoslovakia – Chamberlain conceded Germany's right to annex the Sudetenland. He returned to London, waving the piece of paper which contained Hitler's assurances that he was now satisfied with the territory that had been 'retrieved' and that Germany would consult fully with Britain in the event of any future problems arising. In March 1939, in accordance with Rumbold's analysis of eleven years before, Hitler ordered his forces into what was left of Czechoslovakia. Even Chamberlain was forced to admit: 'As soon as I had time to think I saw that it was imposible to deal with Hitler after he had thrown all his assurances to the winds.'[48] The invasion of Czechoslovakia marked the end of Chamberlain's efforts to persist with a strategy of co-operative diplomacy and appeasement. Idealism, which had been comatose since 1936, was now well and truly dead. On 31 March 1939, the British and French governments announced the Polish Guarantee. With the Soviet threat to Germany effectively neutralised – for the time being – by the Molotov–Ribbentrop non-aggression pact of August 1939, Hitler's forces invaded Poland on 1 September. By 3 September Britain and Germany were at war.

With hindsight, of course, it was easy to see where first Baldwin and then Chamberlain had gone wrong. Baldwin had given his Foreign Secretary a fairly free rein to determine policy towards Germany but it was not until 1937 that Eden himself had been weaned away from appeasement. Chamberlain had relied far too heavily on the incompetent advice of Henderson, even when it was in direct opposition to almost everything else that the Foreign Office was telling him. Crucially, however, both prime ministers had failed to follow the first principle of *realpolitik*: potential aggressors will invariably remain unmoved by generous attempts to understand past injustices, by reasoned arguments about mutual interests in avoiding war, or by patient efforts aimed at securing an equitable compromise. On the contrary, what potential aggressors really understand are firm and unambiguous threats – all the more disturbing if they are politely stated – backed by military force. However, the requisite determination had been sadly lacking. The League had failed to effect a satisfactory resolution to the crises in Manchuria and Abyssinia. And co-operative diplomacy outside the framework of the League – appeasement – had failed to meet the challenge posed by German expansionism. These twin failures collectively conspired to move Realism firmly back to the centre stage of British foreign policy making. Rumbold and Vansittart had been proved correct and the general model upon which their analyses had been based would provide the broad guidelines for policy in the future: Realism would remain firmly embedded in the hearts and minds of the policy makers for over a generation.

Yet even as the central tenets of Realism were being warmly

embraced by both policy makers and scholars,[49] there were certain aspects of Chamberlain's policy – not quite in keeping with the conclusions outlined above – which were being played down. Chamberlain's commitment to co-operative diplomacy had, after all, been tinged with Realism in at least four significant respects. First, Chamberlain had been advised by the Chiefs of Staff in October 1938 that at current rates of armament acquisition Britain could not realistically fight a war with Germany before 1939 and certainly could not hope to prevail against the combined strength of Germany, Italy and Japan if the United States and the Soviet Union remained neutral.[50] In this sense, Chamberlain's strategy could have been a successful *realpolitik*-motivated attempt to play for time.[51] Second, Chamberlain did change his policy on the need for rearmament after 1937 and did make available the financial resources necessary to equip the Royal Air Force with a new generation of fighters that turned out to be crucial in the victory in the Battle of Britain in 1940. Third, Chamberlain, albeit hesitantly, took a united country into war in September 1939.[52] By that time there was a general consensus that Hitler had to be opposed by force; it can reasonably be argued, however, that any attempt to take Britain into a war before Hitler's invasion of Czechoslovakia in March 1939 would have met concerted opposition from significant segments of British public opinion.[53] Again, therefore, Chamberlain's action could be construed as being based on classical *realpolitik* security motives. A unified national effort would be essential if Britain was to survive the inevitable trial of endurance ahead; war had to be delayed, therefore, until unity had been achieved.

Now it is possible to argue, of course, that each of these three possible 'intrusions' of *Realist* thinking into Chamberlain's calculations (after 1937) were simply a prudent (delaying) response to a situation which had been created precisely because co-operative diplomacy had *already* failed. On this account it was entirely appropriate for Idealism subsequently to be so totally abandoned and for Realism to be so completely embraced: *Realist* delaying tactics had merely come to the rescue of a failed strategy of co-operative diplomacy. Such an argument cannot be sustained quite so easily, however, in relation to a fourth sense in which *Realist* calculation can be regarded as having informed Chamberlain's strategy. This particular calculation concerns British fears of Soviet Russia. Throughout the 1920s and for most of the 1930s, it was Soviet communism which was regarded as constituting the most serious threat to the interests of Britain and the Empire. In these circumstances, in the early 1930s Hitler's firm stand against communists inside Germany was viewed with favour among some sections of the ruling Conservative Party in Britain. Even as the general distaste for Hitler's internal policies grew, however, there remained a widespread belief that a strong capitalist Germany constituted a powerful bulwark against the insidious appeals of Soviet communism. With luck, Hitler might even decide to have it out with Stalin, in which case Germany and Russia might conceivably fight a mutually destructive but indecisive war, or Hitler might do the world a favour by ridding it of the communist menace for ever. While this scenario itself perhaps looked a little implausible, the overall situation none the less seemed to embody the classic balance of power dictum that 'my enemy's enemy is my friend': how better to balance the (supposedly) growing power of the Soviet Union than by allowing its capitalist near-neighbour to remilitarise and prosper? Viewed in this light, the appeasement of both Baldwin and Chamberlain could have been a *Realist* device (based, as it turned out, on faulty assumptions) aimed at coaxing Germany into the role of defender of the capitalist faith, at attempting to adjust Hitler's naturally expansionist desires so as to accord with the security interests of Great Britain. If this was an inversion of Eyre Crowe's guidelines, then so be it. This was *realpolitik*.

The problem with this interpretation of events, of course, is that it is based on somewhat equivocal evidence. There is certainly evidence that Hitler encouraged successive British politicians to believe that Germany's true mission was the obliteration of world communism.[54] There is less evidence, however, to support the notion that such a belief was pivotal in the decision calculus of any of the British governments of the 1930s: while it seems certain that the Baldwin and Chamberlain governments took account of anti-Soviet balance of power considerations, such calculations do not appear to have been crucial. According to both his 'close confidante', Sir Samuel Hoare, and his official biographer, Keith Feiling, Chamberlain seems to have been prepared to accept the incorporation of the Sudeten Germany into the Reich primarily because he believed it was *morally right*.[55] It was this belief in the moral rectitude of Czechoslovak partition, together with his gullibility in thinking that Hitler's demands for more territory would stop there, that above all else discredited Chamberlain. The tragedy was that his strategy of co-operative diplomacy was discredited along with him. In spite of the fact that there was a significant element of *Realist* calculation in appeasement (as we have seen, a remilitarised and well equipped Germany in possession of both Austria and the Sudetenland would be better able to resist Stalin), it was not Realism that was blamed for the failure to halt Hitler's programme of expansion. On the contrary, the blame was placed very firmly by the new Realist orthodoxy at the door of co-operative diplomacy, of appeasement, of Idealism as a whole. However contentious or injudicious the conclusion might have been, it was firmly in place. Henceforward, Realism would rule, OK.

The impact of the Second World War

Throughout the Second World War, as in all wars, Realism was the fundamental determining factor in all the important decisions made by the major powers. The decisions as to which powers were to be regarded as allies and which enemies, when to provide support for a friend and when to delay it, when to attack an opponent and when to await events, were all determined by calculations designed to protect and promote the security interests of the nation–state. It would not be appropriate here to analyse the details of the *realpolitik*-determined military campaigns which finally produced the Allied victory, since detailed accounts exist elsewhere.[56] It is important, however, to provide a brief synopsis of the main political developments of the war years which were subsequently to affect the context in which Britain's postwar foreign policy was obliged to operate. This task is undertaken in the first part of this section: the second part of the section offers a summary indication of the major effects that the war had on Britain's postwar international position.

Political developments during the war years

If the German invasion of Poland in September 1939 had not been bad enough, British fears for the future were further increased by the near-simultaneous seizure of large areas of eastern Poland by the Soviet Union.[57] The position worsened again in November when the Soviets invaded Finland. What on earth had Molotov and Ribbentrop agreed in August 1939? Would Britain and France have to confront the unlikely combination of both Nazi Germany and Soviet Russia? The fierceness of the Finns' resistance encouraged Chamberlain to contemplate providing direct support to the Finnish war effort, but the refusal of the Norwegian and Swedish governments to allow the free passage of supplies caused the idea to be rapidly abandoned.[58] Recognising that little could be done to resist Soviet aggressive intentions in the short term, the British government turned its attention to mobilising the public in support of the war effort at home and reinforcing the British Expeditionary Force in France. In early May 1940, shortly after

Churchill had become Prime Minister and after eight months of 'phoney war', the German offensive began, bypassing the redundant Maginot line and launching an attack on France through Belgium. By the end of May, the Expeditionary Force had been forced back to the British mainland. By June – in spite of a British offer to bolster French morale by declaring a political union between Britain and France – the French government had been obliged to sue for peace.[59] Britain's principal ally, the co-author of the Polish Guarantee, had effectively been lost and it was now even more imperative that Churchill should secure the sustained support of the United States.[60]

In August 1940, when the Battle of Britain was approaching its climax, the first intimations of American support to come were revealed in the 'destroyers-for-bases' agreement: Britain was to receive 50 destroyers from the United States in return for access to British bases in Canada and the Caribbean.[61] By January 1941 Churchill had received clear indications that the Roosevelt Administration was generally in favour of the United States joining the war on the British side, but that Congressional resistance prevented American entry for the time being.[62] Roosevelt's next best alternative was the provision of Lend–Lease, introduced in March 1941. Although the technical details of the scheme were complex – made more so by the operation of certain 'off-set' mechanisms designed to take account of any indirect contributions Britain and the Commonwealth might coincidentally make to the US economy – the practical effects of the Lend–Lease Act were fairly straightforward: Britain and the Commonwealth (and, later, the Soviet Union) would receive massive supplies of munitions, food and industrial raw materials with the repayments to be settled at a later date in a form 'which the President deems satisfactory'.[63] The monetary value of the supplies thus provided is outlined in Table 1.1; these were massive injections indeed and without them the viability of the British war effort would have been even more seriously in doubt.

In June 1941, having been thwarted in his plan to invade Britain by the RAF and the dogged response of the British public to the Luftwaffe's bombing campaign, Hitler turned eastward and launched his invasion of the Soviet Union. If his intention was to rally the support of the capitalist powers to his cause, he was sorely disappointed. Churchill's response was almost instantaneous. The real threat to British interests was from Nazi Germany; the opening of a second European front could only serve to ease the pressure in the west and in the Middle East; and now that Stalin was again Hitler's enemy (as he had been before August 1939) he could become Britain's friend. In a classic *realpolitik* manoeuvre, informal approaches were rapidly made

Table 1.1   Value of Lend-Lease, 1941-44 ($m)

	1941	1942	1943	1944
UK (excluding services)	662	2391	4579	6212
British Empire (goods and services)	1082	4757	9031	—
Soviet Union	20	1376	2436	4077

SOURCE: William Hardy McNeill, *Survey of International Affairs 1939–1946: America, Britain and Russia, their Co-operation and Conflict 1941–1946* (London: Oxford University Press, for the Royal Institute of International Affairs, 1953) p. 232.

to the Soviet government and within a month an agreement had been signed in which Britain and the Soviet Union affirmed their determination not to sign separate armistices with Hitler.[64] By October 1941, the British government had supplied Stalin with 450 aircraft and the Americans had extended Lend-Lease to include the Soviet Union.[65]

In the meantime Churchill was still trying to persuade the United States to accept a direct military role in the war against Germany. In spite of opposition from Secretary of State Sumner Welles, in August 1941 Roosevelt was persuaded into a statement of common political principles. In this 'Atlantic Charter' Britain and the United States affirmed their commitment to the principle of *self-determination*, though it was generally recognised that, while Roosevelt understood 'self-determination' to apply universally, Churchill's interpretation only extended to those areas under Nazi subjugation: for Churchill, self-determination certainly did not extend to Britain's imperial possessions.[66]

It was the Japanese attack on Pearl Harbor on 7 December 1941, however, which broke Congressional resistance and brought an immediate end to American neutrality. Japan's subsequent attacks on British territory in Malaya and Singapore (and the consequent threat to India which those attacks engendered) added yet another dimension to the convergence of security interest which the United States and Britain already enjoyed as a result of the threat of German domination in Europe. In late December 1941, Churchill met Roosevelt at the 'Arcadia' Conference in Washington. By the time the meeting ended in January 1942 the basic tacit understandings and institutional framework of the wartime 'special relationship' had been agreed. A series of 'Combined Boards' were to be established which would ensure the continuous supply of food, raw materials and munitions to Britain and the Commonwealth; a combined Chiefs of Staff Committee would meet weekly for the duration of the war to discuss joint military strategy; and in return for the supplies which the United States provided, the American armed forces would have access to military installations throughout the Commonwealth.[67] In addition to these arrangements, moreover, Churchill and Roosevelt confirmed that the first military priority would be the defeat of *Germany* (the so-called 'Germany first' strategy).[68] And along with the rest of the allies they also issued a declaration stating (1) their joint intention to engage in a unified and co-ordinated campaign against the Axis powers; and (2) their determination that any eventual armistice must be signed by all the Allied powers.[69]

In February 1942, the 'Lend–Lease Master Agreement' was signed. In deference to the demands of the State Department, this agreement named part of the price that Britain was expected to pay for the continuation of Lend–Lease through to the end of the war: the terms of repayment were to include 'provision for ... the elimination of all forms of discriminatory treatment in international commerce and ... the reduction of tariffs and other trade barriers'.[70] This, of course, was not particularly subtle coercive diplomacy on the part of the Americans. The State Department's clear (but unspecified) target was the British system of Imperial Preference established by the Ottawa Conference of 1932. Unfortunately, in the dire circumstances of early 1942, Churchill had little choice but to accept the imposition of what might prove a serious constraint on the freedom of any postwar government to determine its own foreign economic policy. It was hoped that circumstances might change in the interim, so as to render the potential constraint irrelevant, though in the event (as will be seen in Chapter 7) they did not. What mattered for the time being, however, was that the Americans were in the war and, provided that the U-boat challenge could be met in the North Atlantic, the supply of vital war materials had been ensured.

Throughout the first half of 1942, Britain's relations with the Soviet Union continued to improve and, as always, *realpolitik* calculation was at the root of change. By December 1941, the German offensive against the Soviet Union had begun to run into serious difficulties. As a result, instead of being simply a convenient and expendable diversion, Russia was becoming a genuinely useful ally capable of making an important contribution to the defeat of Germany. The Anglo-Soviet 20-year Mutual Aid Treaty of June 1942 was a symbolic acknowledgment of the two countries' improved mutual relations. However the Treaty did not lead – as Stalin had hoped – to the speedy opening of a second front in Europe and indeed the hesitancy of the British and the Americans in this regard was a continuing source of tension in their dealings with Stalin until the D-Day landings in Normandy in June 1944.

Throughout 1942 and early 1943, the attention of the Allied powers was focused on the various military campaigns that were being waged in the North Atlantic, in North Africa, in Russia and in the Far East. In November 1943, after the military tide had begun to turn in the Allies' favour, the 'Big Three' met in conference in Tehran. The intention was to try to achieve some sort of agreement on the shape of the postwar world once victory had been achieved. The attempt failed: Churchill and Stalin could not agree on either the future of Poland or their respective degrees of postwar involvement in the Balkans. Churchill and Roosevelt were deeply divided over the future role and status of France and over Britain's postwar involvement in the Middle East and in India.[71] Roosevelt, immovable in his belief that by sheer force of personality he could convince Stalin that American intentions towards the Soviet Union were genuinely benign, merely succeeded in reinforcing Stalin's conviction that American troops would be rapidly withdrawn from Europe after the war: with the British exhausted, the French demoralised and the Germans destroyed, the way would be clear for a massive extension of socialism in the postwar period.

During the course of 1944, bolstered by their joint success in the piecemeal liberation of France, the British and the Americans gradually drew closer together. They were increasingly united in their determination to prevent Stalin from installing a government purely of his own choosing in liberated Poland. And at the Dumbarton Oaks Conference in August 1944 (called to establish a constitution for the postwar United Nations) they found themselves making common cause against the Russian delegation's insistence that each member–state of the new United Nations Security Council should retain a veto over all Council's decisions.[72] From the Autumn of 1944 onwards, however, the development of the political relationships among the 'Big Three' was conditioned primarily by the course of the military campaigns in Europe. As the Red Army advanced progressively through Finland, Poland, Romania, Bulgaria, Hungary and parts of Czechoslovakia and Yugoslavia, so it became increasingly apparent that these areas were being earmarked for future incorporation into the Soviet sphere of influence. In the west a similar process, under British and American auspices, was occurring in France, Belgium, the Netherlands, Italy and Greece.

These effective 'spheres of influence' were crystallised at the Yalta Conference of the 'Big Three' in February 1945. While it still proved impossible at Yalta to reach agreement either on Poland's postwar borders or the composition of its government, Stalin was persuaded into making a general commitment that 'free elections' would be held in each of the countries liberated by the Red Army.[73] Roosevelt, however, was still insistent that American troops would be withdrawn from Europe within two years of Hitler's defeat.[74] Conscious of the fact that this would leave the Soviet Union as the preponderant power on the continent of Europe, Churchill sought to persuade Roosevelt that in these circumstances Britain would only be able to contain Soviet expansionism with the assistance of a strong, united and vigorous France. Roosevelt, however, preferred to enter into a secret arrangement with Stalin whereby the Soviet Union would join in the war against Japan after Hitler's defeat in exchange for the return to Russia of islands lost to Japan in 1904–5.[75] As a result, nothing substantial was agreed between Britain and the United States with regard to the need to strengthen the position of France; and, more significantly, nothing effective was done to limit the growing Soviet dominance in Eastern Europe.

After Yalta, the central *realpolitik* pillar of the alliance of the 'Big Three' started to crumble. With Germany on the verge of defeat, the alliance simply lost its political and military rationale: the deep-seated conflicts of material and security interest, which had been submerged in three years of war against a common enemy, rapidly began to resurface. From March 1945 onwards, the Red Army (moving west) and the allied forces under Eisenhower (moving east) engaged in an undisguised race in which each side aimed to secure as much 'liberated' territory as possible within its own sphere of military dominance. On 25 April, American and Soviet forces met at the River Elbe. On 2 May, Soviet forces entered Berlin and on 7 May the Allies accepted Germany's formal unconditional surrender.

The Potsdam Conference in July 1945 represented the final major attempt by the Big Three allied powers to achieve an amicable settlement over the future of postwar Europe. As at Yalta, however, despite their intimacy in matters of military strategy and their close collaboration in nuclear weapons development, Britain and the United States engaged in no real consultation prior to the Conference. As a result – again, as at Tehran and Yalta – Britain and the United States failed to adopt a common bargaining position towards the Soviet Union. Attlee and Bevin, newly installed as Prime Minister and Foreign Secretary, were especially concerned about the future of Poland: after all, the British had originally entered the war because of the Polish Guarantee and their military campaign in Italy had been substantially strengthened by a force of 150 000 'London Poles'. Yet at

Potsdam Poland was effectively abandoned to the Soviet Union: the agreement to recognise the incumbent Polish government was a tacit acceptance of the fact that that government would soon become (if it was not already) a tool of Soviet policy.

Crucially, what Potsdam left unresolved was the matter of Poland's eastern border with the Soviet Union and the fundamental question of the postwar form and status of Germany. Unfortunately the Council of Foreign Ministers that was specifically established in order to reconcile these unresolved differences was soon to prove totally ineffectual as a means of achieving compromise among the now clearly disunited allies. With Roosevelt's promise to effect a speedy evacuation of American forces from Europe occupying a central position in both British and Soviet calculations the tide of events seemed to be moving inexorably in the Soviets' favour. What froze the political and military situation in Europe, however, was the American atomic attack on Hiroshima and Nagasaki on 6 and 7 August. No one needed to issue an explicit threat to Stalin. He knew what this implied. It would be difficult to dislodge the Soviets from those territories which the Red Army already controlled, but for the time being – as long as the Americans remained in Europe – there was no question of the Soviet Union attempting to push further westward. The main problem for both East and West in the immediate postwar era would be how to consolidate those areas in which they already enjoyed military dominance.

The legacy of the war

The developments of the war years had a number of profound consequences for Britain's postwar international position. First, as a direct result of the war effort itself, *Britain's financial and industrial position was appalling*. By 1945, the country's gold and foreign currency reserves were virtually exhausted: almost all of the privately-owned income-earning foreign assets acquired since 1918 had been mortgaged or sold; enormous debts – for supplies received – were owed to India, Canada and Australia; and at least some reparation would soon have to be made for Lend–Lease.[76] In addition, the domestic economy was strongly geared to wartime rather than peacetime production, while exports were running at little more than a third of pre-1939 levels.[77] The general constraining effects of these problems are examined in Chapter 7, and do not require further analysis here.

We can be similarly circumspect at this stage with regard to a second major consequence of the war: *the weakening of Britain's grip on the Empire*. In what was almost a replay of what had occurred between

1914 and 1918, the exigencies of the developing situation during the Second World War produced a new set of promises to various nationalist groups throughout the Empire. In the period after 1945, however, the new promises could not be so conveniently forgotten. On the contrary, as will be seen in Chapter 3, indigenous nationalism, particularly in India and Palestine, emerged from the war more confident, more determined and better organised than ever before. The increasingly insistent demands for change could not be so easily resisted as they had been in the interwar years and, as a result, by the end of the war, Britain's hold on the Empire 'circle' was already weakening in the face of political and economic pressures which were set to grow inexorably in the ensuing years.

In relation to another of Churchill's 'circles', a third consequence of the war was clearly in evidence: *the geostrategic situation in Europe had been totally transformed.* The defeat of Germany created a political and military vacuum in central Europe which by the time of the Potsdam Conference had largely been filled by the Soviet Union. Before 1939, France and Britain together had appeared to provide some sort of counterweight to the growing German threat. Soviet Russia was only a distant worry and in any case any attempt at Russian expansionism would first have to deal with Germany itself. After 1945, with the German challenge eliminated by partition, the new threat was posed by the Soviets who appeared to possess a continental military capability far greater than any collective defensive response which the British and French might be able to muster. In these circumstances, it was only the massive American military presence in western Europe which was capable of balancing Soviet power in the east. As the leading capitalist power in the postwar world, the United States had a considerable long-term interest in insulating western Europe from the incipient communism which Soviet military hegemony already seemed to imply. Britain and France, of course, saw continuing American involvement as the only way of preserving their own immediate security: their problem in the early postwar years was to persuade the Americans of the magnitude of the Soviet threat to US interests in Europe and accordingly to encourage Truman to reverse Roosevelt's declared policy of evacuating American troops from Europe within two years of Hitler's defeat.

Of immense significance in this regard was a fourth consequence of the war: *the emergence of the Atlantic 'special relationship' between Britain and the United States.* Founded on both a traditional cultural affinity and a convergence of security interests arising out of the common wartime threat posed by Germany and Japan, the 'special relationship' had many facets. It began in the first few months of the war with a series of discussions which led to detailed technical co-operation in nuclear energy research.[78] Meanwhile the visit to London of President Roosevelt's envoy, Harry Hopkins, in January 1941, made important progress in political confidence-building.[79] The subsequent introduction of Lend–Lease in March 1941 meant that the United States was providing economic support for the British war effort on a scale unprecedented for a neutral state. And the Arcadia Conference in December 1941 not only reinforced the burgeoning economic ties (through the establishment of the Combined Boards) but also provided the institutional apparatus (the combined Chiefs of Staff Committee) for the intimate military relationship that was to follow. In short, at every level in the scientific, economic and military fields, there was a great 'mixing-up' of personnel, opinions and ideas.[80]

As the war progressed, Anglo-American collaboration increased. This was especially true with regard to atomic co-operation which not only produced the first critical breakthrough in nuclear weapons research but also led to the Quebec Agreement of August 1943 in which the British and American governments agreed that each would only use nuclear weapons against a third party if the other had first given its consent.[81] Yet even this high degree of co-operaion was surpassed in the military sphere where the complementary capabilities of the British and American armed forces were effectively integrated in a unified, global military campaign. Of course, there were inconsistencies, contradictions, reversals and occasional disasters;[82] but these would have occurred if the armed forces of a single country had been involved. As military allies the British and the Americans achieved an extraordinary degree of mutual reliance and integrated campaigning, an intimacy which was to be of considerable significance in the difficult years before the establishment of NATO in 1949.

To augment this increasing technical and military co-operation – both of which were underpinned by the growing economic ties engendered by Lend–Lease – the British and American governments also engaged in a certain amount of more explicitly political co-operation. In one sense, of course, the major decisions associated both with technical co-operation (such as the Quebec Agreement) and with military co-operation (such as the 'Germany first' strategy agreed at Arcadia) had a large 'political' component anyway. Additionally, however, there was also an informal 'high policy' agreement on the desirability of making the postwar world safe for liberal democracy; free from the ravages of fascism and communism alike.[83] By the time of Potsdam in July 1945, moreover, the views of both the Truman and Attlee governments had converged on the need to prevent further

Soviet encroachment westward and on the necessity of challenging the Soviet Union's right to exercise permanent hegemony over eastern Europe.

Yet, in spite of all these points of agreement, the 'special relationship' in 1945 was still marked by important political differences. In the *Far East* there was a significant divergence of opinion over the extent and timing of any postwar concessions that might be made to nationalism in India, Burma and Malaya; the anti-colonialist Americans favouring more and sooner, the British preferring less and later.[84] In the *Middle East*, while the Americans were intensely suspicious that London intended to restore its pre-war position of political and economic dominance, the British government for its part feared that US policy was designed principally to strengthen the position of American oil companies at the direct expense of their British counterparts; in which belief London was confirmed in February 1945 when (in the face of Senate opposition) Roosevelt was obliged to withdraw the 1944 Anglo-American Petroleum Agreement.[85] In *Western Europe* there were disagreements (in December 1944) over the composition of the new governments to be installed in liberated Belgium, Italy and Greece; with the United States rejecting British calls for the the return to power of anti-radical pro-monarchist factions which, rightly or wrongly, were regarded by the Americans as little more than Nazi collaborators.[86]

As if these 'regional' disagreements were not enough, there were also significant political differences, already noted earlier, in three other areas. First, the challenge to imperial preference represented by the 1942 Lend–Lease master agreement was viewed with considerable suspicion in Britain, where it was (rightly) regarded as part of a concerted State Department campaign to establish the United States as the pre-eminent economic power in the postwar world.[87] The abrupt termination of Lend–Lease with the defeat of Germany – when the British economy was still in desperate straits – simply added a sense of betrayal to an atmosphere already charged with gathering doubt and uncertainty.[88] Second, there was no pre-agreed united Anglo-American strategy adopted at Tehran, Yalta or Potsdam. This was in part the result of Roosevelt's desire to avoid giving Stalin the impression that the 'Anglo-Saxons' were 'ganging-up' on him, but it also reflected more general American reservations about the dangers of a resurgent postwar British imperialism. In any event, the main beneficiary of the division within the Anglo-Saxon bloc was Stalin who was able to achieve his two principal within-alliance objectives (the extension of Lend–Lease to the Soviet Union and, eventually, the opening of the second front in the west) without having to compromise any of his ambitions in eastern Europe. A third source of additional tension – after Potsdam – concerned the dispute over the best strategy for resisting the new Soviet threat in Europe. Opinion in the United States was divided but still generally in favour of the Europeans defending themselves and the Americans eventually withdrawing; the British, convinced of their own inability to resist even in combination with the French, were concerned to secure a firm American commitment to remain.[89]

By the end of the war, in short, the 'special relationship' was distinctly ambivalent. In the *military* and *technical* spheres, the degree of bilateral co-operation achieved had been remarkable. In *economic* matters the United States had rendered an invaluable service to Britain by the provision of Lend–Lease, though its sudden termination had come as a serious blow. In terms of the broader global *political* issues there were a number of significant differences which counterbalanced the common interest that Britain and the United States shared in opposing communism and in promoting capitalist liberal democracy. Not surprisingly, as we will see in later chapters, the subsequent course of the special relationship was to prove critical in the overall development of British foreign policy.

A fifth consequence of the war which merits brief attention here was *the reinforcement of the policy makers' 'Realist' world-views*. If the late 1930s had promised the future pre-eminence of *realpolitik* calculation, the experiences of the war years assured it. It had been only by the exercise of Churchillian Realism that Britain had survived and then triumphed. The callous ceding of the Burma Road to the Japanese in July 1940, for example, which had seriously damaged the war effort of allied China, was a simple reflection of the fact that Britain could not at that time afford to be at war with both Germany and Japan. Similarly, the German invasion of Russia in June 1941, by transforming 'my enemy's collaborator' into 'my enemy's enemy' provided the classic 'power politics' motive for Britain's near-spontaneous alliance with the Soviet Union; although, once the common threat had disappeared, the alliance itself disintegrated. The crucial point was that Churchill had played a hard *realpolitik* game and had won. The problem was that so had Stalin. And Stalin was *still* playing that game in a situation in which he no longer appeared to be 'on our side'. In classical Realist fashion, postwar British foreign policy makers reasoned that, if *one* party plays 'power politics' in an anarchical system, then all other parties whose interests are in consequence threatened are *also* obliged to play the same Realist game. The central concern of Britain's postwar foreign policy was thus the achievement of security in the face of the

Soviet communist threat. The direct implication was that, even though the war itself was over and the demands for demobilisation irresistible, Britain could not afford to dismantle its defences. Any British withdrawal anywhere – if the Americans could not immediately substitute their own troops for the British forces thus removed – would leave a vacuum which either the Soviets or their communist agents would be only too pleased to fill. In these circumstances, London appeared to have little choice but to attempt to maintain a military presence in all those parts of the globe that were deemed vulnerable to communist insurgence and/or expansionism. This, in effect, meant almost everywhere, and as a result Britain embarked on a global strategy which was bound to produce massive military overextension. With growing demands for more domestic consumption at home, this was the last thing that Attlee and Bevin really wanted. However, as practitioners of *realpolitik* (and after the experiences of the last decade how could they be anything else?), it was something they could not avoid. Very difficult times lay ahead.

Summary and conclusions

Before 1918, any practising British politician would probably have been surprised at the suggestion that the government's policy was conducted on the basis of anything other than *Realpolitik* calculation. To be sure, the massaging of some foreigner's ego here or the provision of a discreet financial inducement there were on occasion preferable to threats of 'serious consequences'; but where quieter methods failed it was always axiomatic that 'coercive diplomacy' (that is, threats or, if absolutely necessary, force) would be used in order to protect and promote Britain's material and security interests.

In the period after 1918 successive British governments made a series of half-hearted attempts to follow a new, more 'idealistic' style of diplomacy. If at all possible, the *legal and quasi-legal processes* of the League of Nations and its attendant institutions, with their provision for 'collective security', were to be used in order to resolve international conflicts. If this strategy failed, then the new commitment to *co-operative* diplomacy – in which the spirit of compromise reigned supreme – might still permit conflicts to be peacefully resolved. The problem, of course, was that, although most of the powers of the state system ostentatiously signed the General Treaty for the Renunciation of War in 1928, none of them had the slightest intention of actually renouncing war as 'an instrument of national policy'.[90] Although the leaders of the Great Powers paid public lip service to widespread demands for pacific settlement, their deliberations in private were strongly coloured by Realist calculation about the 'vital interests' of their respective nation states.

The irony was that, while this element of power politics calculation was sufficient to ensure the failure of both the League and the new co-operative diplomacy which it inspired, the commitment to Realism was itself so diluted by vestigial Idealist sentiment that effective strategies of coercive diplomacy were not followed either. For Britain in particular, this unfortunate cocktail of Realism and Idealism was of considerable importance. By the mid-1930s Hitler and Mussolini were pursuing policies of unashamed *realpolitik*. In contrast, the Baldwin and Chamberlain governments, perhaps the victims of 15 years of their own propaganda, retained a residual commitment to co-operative (com-promising, appeasing) diplomacy, long after the objective logic of the situation (and almost the entire Foreign Office) had suggested that a coercive response might have been more appropriate. Not surprisingly in these circumstances, the appeasement strategy of 1935–8 (notwith-standing the possibility that it provided a useful 'breathing space' during which time Britain was better able to prepare itself for war) failed to prevent war.

The failure both of the League and of Chamberlain's 'co-operative diplomacy' led after 1938 to a general rejection of Idealist principles. In their place came a return to the basic maxims of *realpolitik* (persuade and cajole if it is at all possible, but balance power and threaten serious consequences if it is not), a commitment which the war years – inevitably – served to reinforce. But the war also produced a situation in 1945 which contained something of a dilemma. On the one hand, following classic Realist precepts, the Soviet Union was beginning to emerge as a potentially serious threat to British interests both inside and outside the European theatre; and that threat, somehow, had to be met. On the other hand, the weakening ties with the Empire and the parlous state of the economy, both engendered by the war, meant that the potential threat could only be countered, in the short term at least, at the cost of sacrifices which the British public were not prepared to make. The postwar solution to this dilemma was to make use of the ambivalent – but, it was hoped, still 'special' – wartime relationship with the United States and to persuade the Americans that their own best long-term security interests lay in defending Western Europe against Soviet expansionism. As we will see, however, even though the Americans did remain in Europe, Britain's overseas commitments remained seriously overextended: the price of American support was that the British government be seen to play *its* part in the defence of the free world. As a result, Britain was obliged to maintain both a sizeable military force on the continent of Europe and a significant military presence in a variety of theatres throughout the world. The forms which this over-extension took, together with their consequences, are examined in subsequent chapters.

2

From Potsdam to Cold War: Relations with Europe and the Superpowers, 1945–55

This chapter examines the development of Britain's foreign policy in Churchill's 'Atlantic' and 'European circles' in the decade after 1945. The simultaneous examination of these two areas of policy is by no means accidental. As will be seen, developments in both circles were intimately related, not least because successive British governments were convinced that a revitalised 'special relationship' with the United States was essential if Western Europe was to be effectively defended. Britain's main problem in this context, of course, was that the 'Big Three' allies had not emerged from the war united. As the previous chapter indicated, even before Potsdam British fears of the coming Soviet threat in Europe were already taking shape and, despite the closeness of Anglo-American relations in the technical and military spheres, there were certainly significant political strains in the 'special relationship' which gave cause for concern. As things turned out, relations with the Soviet Union were to deteriorate progressively over the next ten years and as a result Britain's military links with Western Europe were to be substantially strengthened. Relations with the United States were actually set to worsen before they improved after July 1946.

This chapter begins by describing Britain's main economic and military problems in 1945. The second section examines the events in Europe which transformed American perceptions about the need to withdraw from Europe and led the United States to restore the 'special relationship' to some semblance of what it had been during the war years. At the root of this transformation, of course – in true *realpolitik* fashion – was an increasing sense that the material and security interests of Britain and the United States were again converging, with the Soviets beginning to mount a serious challenge to the global interests of western capitalism. In the third section of the chapter the main consequences of this renewed interest convergence are discussed: a renewed economic intimacy and increased military collaboration throughout the world. As will become clear, what was crucial in all these developments was the *realpolitik* view of the world taken by British and (slightly later) by American foreign policy makers. It was their mutual fear of Soviet communism that produced both the sense of interest convergence and the additional military commitments that they were subsequently to make both inside and outside Europe. These extra commitments, in turn, were to result in a significant *overextension* of Britain's military and financial capabilities by the mid-1950s.

Britain's international position in 1945

The economic problems

Partly as a consequence of nearly six years of war, by the second half of 1945 the British economy was in serious trouble. In order to support the immediate needs of the war effort, the government had forcibly sold off almost all the foreign assets held in Britain by private individuals and companies, issuing interest-bearing bonds to the former owners by way of compensation. In the short run, this had provided the government with much-needed foreign exchange with which to purchase raw materials and munitions. In the immediate postwar period, however, not only were the interest payments to bondholders a considerable drain on the Exchequer, but the economy as a whole was deprived of the invisible export income which before the war had flowed into the country in the form of repatriated profits.[1]

This problem was compounded by the size of the debts (£3567m) owed to India and the Dominions as a result of materials supplied during the course of the war. Payment for these supplies had been deferred by building up the so-called 'sterling balances' in London. The interest that Britain had to pay on these balances to the countries of the Overseas Sterling Area (OSA) was yet another drain on the British economy's slender resources. Moreover, although the 'sterling balance' debts appeared to be partially offset by gold and foreign currency reserves in July 1945 of £610m, these reserves were earmarked for the protection of the external value of sterling and accordingly could not be used for debt-reduction purposes.

A further problem deriving from the war years concernced the level of (mainly industrial) exports. In the first nine months of 1945 exports were running at some 42 per cent of the pre-war level at a time when the Treasury estimated that they needed to be at 175 per cent of the 1938 level for the balance of payments to be in equilibrium.[2] Part of the difficulty was that, under the conditions of Lend–Lease, British manufacturers had been prevented from exporting any equipment or materials of the type imported by US firms into Britain. The refusal of the Americans to relax this ruling, even for a transition period, as long as Lend–Lease continued meant that British entrepreneurs had no opportunity to attempt a *gradual* penetration of overseas markets. As a result, when Lend–Lease was abruptly ended in September 1945, British exporters were simply not equipped to produce the massive increase in export levels that was required in order to equalise the balance of payments. The only good news about the termination of Lend–Lease was that, although Britain had received over £31 *billion* worth of supplies since March 1941, the US government finally decided that only £650 *million* of it would have to be repaid.[3] However even this remarkably generous concession constituted a request for monies which Britain at that time simply did not possess.

In addition to these war-related problems, of course, Britain's postwar economy was also suffering from long-term structural weaknesses which were made to appear all the more acute precisely because of the difficulties outlined above. In 1860, Britain had been involved in 25 per cent of the total world trade in goods and services; even before the war, in 1938, its share had dropped to 14 per cent. In the 1860s, 42 per cent of Britain's exports had gone to other industrial countries; by the late 1920s industrial markets had been 'lost' to such an extent that the corresponding figure in 1927 was 25 per cent.[4] At the root of these problems, of course, were the historically low levels of domestic industrial investment that Britain had constantly achieved in comparison with its industrial competitors. While it would not be appropriate here to enter the prolonged and contentious debate abut the *origins* of this low-investment pattern,[5] it is worth noting that there has been something decidedly odd about Britain's historical tendency to export capital in vast quantities during times of peace, only to mortgage it all each time it finds itself engaged in a major war. (Whither the increased capital exports of the 1980s?)

Whatever the causes of Britain's long-term industrial decline, however, the combination of long- and short-term problems mentioned above served to produce a severe balance of payments crisis which was to last throughout the 1940s. Making the external debt problem even worse, Britain's balance of payments deficit in 1945 was £704m; in 1946 it was £386m; in 1947, £652m; in 1948, £496m and in 1949, £488m.[6] It was against this background of wartime debt and accumulating post-war deficits that the Attlee Cabinet had to confront not only irresistible demands for the extension of the Welfare State at home but also the problem of the ever-present and growing Soviet threat in Europe. If Bevin and the Foreign Office and the service ministries had not been imbued with the spirit of Realism they might have decided to ignore Stalin's machinations in Eastern Europe and to hope for the best. Who knows what might have happened if they had? As it was, however, their realist analysis told them that there clearly was cause for alarm and that remedial political and military action had to be taken. The problem was that, in the aftermath of victory, Britain was not only economically exhausted: it was also militarily overextended.

The military problems

Britain ended the war with over five million men under arms and – as in 1918 – tremendous domestic pressure for rapid demobilisation.[7] Military personnel were cut to three and a half million by December 1945 and to under one million by March 1948.[8] Before 1939, Britain in peace-time had not required a large army. It did not need to keep a military presence on the continent of Europe and the Empire could be effectively policed with a relatively small but professional mobile force. In this latter task, the British government was assisted in no small measure by a large (and loyal) locally-raised Indian army; by the fact that throughout the Empire local nationalist groups were almost invariably conveniently divided among themselves; by the Colonial Office's expertise in manipulating indigenous elites; and by the fact that the strength of the Royal Navy insulated Britain's imperial possessions from effective third party challenge or infiltration. By mid-1945, everything had changed. In Europe, Britain was already making an important contribution to the occupying forces in Germany, Austria and Italy. In the Empire, and especially in the mandated territories acquired after 1920, local nationalist groups were rapidly acquiring both a greater sense of determination and a wider popularity among indigenous populations. They were also discovering new and more effective techniques of guerrilla warfare which were to render their future suppression much more difficult.

In consequence, although the size of the armed forces was being rapidly reduced in the face of domestic demands, and although the economy was already significantly enfeebled, Britain found itself in a

Table 2.1   Countries where British forces were stationed in 1945

Austria	Burma	Aden
Belgium	Hong Kong	Cyprus
Britain	India	Egypt/Suez
France	Indonesia	Jordan
Germany	Japan	Libya
Gibraltar	Malaysia/Singapore	Muscat and Oman
Greece		Palestine
Italy		Trucial States
Netherlands		
Bermuda	British Somalia	
British Guyana	Ethiopia	
British Honduras	Gambia	
Falkland Islands	Ghana	
Jamaica	Kenya	
	Mauritius	
	Nigeria	
	N. Rhodesia	
	S. Rhodesia	
	Sierra Leone	
	South Africa	
	Tanganyika	
	Uganda	

SOURCES: CMND 6743, *Statement Relating to Defence* (Feb. 1946); CMND 7327, *Statement Relating to Defence* (Feb. 1948); CMND 7337, *Navy Estimates 1948–49* (Feb. 1948;CMND 9075, *Statement on Defence 1954* (Feb. 1954); CMND 9072, *Memo of the Secretary of State for War relating to the Army Estimates for 1954–55* (Feb. 1954).

position where its overseas military commitments were both enormous and growing. As Table 2.1 indicates, in 1945 Britain had a significant military presence in over 40 countries, for the purpose either of suppressing the local population or of deterring adventurism on the part of some potential external aggressor. In almost every theatre throughout the world, Britain was somehow involved: in the North Atlantic, the South Atlantic, the Caribbean, the Mediterranean, the Indian Ocean and the South China Sea; in Central Europe and Mediterranean Europe; in North Africa, the Middle East and the Persian Gulf; in West Africa, Southern Africa, East Africa and the Horn of Africa; in India, Burma, Hong Kong, Japan, Malaya and Singapore and Indonesia. For the government, the reason for this massively overextended commitment was clear:

The objectives of our [external] policy derive *directly from our obligations and commitments as a Great Power.* It remains the firm intention of HMG [His Majesty's Government] to maintain the forces which are needed to support its international policy, to ensure the security of the UK, to maintain its interests throughout the world, and to enable it to play its full part in the preservation of world peace. The forces which we maintain in place must be sufficient to provide an adequate nucleus for expansion in war, to meet the need for garrisons overseas ... and to furnish our contribution to the UN Armed Forces. All these duties are the inescapable responsibilities of a great Power intent on preserving peace.[9]

For a Great Power recently victorious in war, the proud possessor of a great Empire and Commonwealth which had held together through the vicissitudes of war, such commitments seemed entirely reasonable. For a medium-sized European nation–state, exhausted by six years of war, its colonial links and its economic base dangerously weakened, the commitments in many respects seemed ludicrously overextended. But Bevin *et al.* were committed to a *realpolitik* view of the world. If Britain did *not* fulfil its obligations (and the Americans did not yet seem ready, even if the Attlee government had wanted it, to step into the breach that would have been thus created) then the ever-watchful Soviets – or their proxies – would without doubt seize the opportunity and further extend their own sphere of influence. In these circumstances, Attlee and Bevin had no choice: overextend or leave the stage free for Soviet expansionism. They chose to overextend.

Differences over the 'Soviet threat'

A third aspect of Britain's international position in 1945 that merits brief attention concerns the divergence in British and American opinions about the seriousness of the Soviet threat. In Britain, Stalin's uncompromising attitude at Tehran and Yalta had certainly led Churchill to recognise Stalin as a fellow-practitioner of *realpolitik*. And the subsequent Soviet-inspired coup in Romania in March 1945 and the continuing Soviet refusal throughout the summer of 1945 to allow genuinely free elections in Poland were an unmistakable indication of things to come. The ruthlessness which Stalin had demonstrated inside Russia in the 1930s clearly continued unabated in his present foreign policy. For Churchill, and latterly for Bevin, Stalin's 'real' intentions for eastern Europe – and for anywhere else he could dominate – were all too plain: Soviet-style socialist regimes subservient to Moscow would be installed wherever possible.

Yet, in spite of this profound conviction as to Stalin's malevolent *realpolitik* intent, Bevin at Potsdam and after was for a brief period prepared to concede the *possibility* that the Council of Foreign Ministers and the UN Security Council might somehow usher in a new era of peace and co-operation. While Bevin was rapidly disabused of this optimistic belief, the Americans took somewhat longer. They had in any case always been more hopeful both about the potential of the United Nations for peaceful conflict resolution and about the Soviets' supposed desire to enter the postwar world in a spirit of partnership rather than confrontation. American analysis of the Soviet position was also coloured by lingering suspicions of Britain's intentions: in late 1945 US policy makers were still wary of the possibility either that there might be a postwar revival in British imperialism or that in contrast the new Labour government might look to Moscow rather than Washington for political leadership and ideological inspiration. Although each eventuality was unlikely, neither was to be welcomed. In any event, by early 1947 the American position had changed dramatically and, by the end of the year, the incipient 'cold war', in which Britain and the United States were very much on the same side, was fully underway. How, then, did this transformation come about? What were the major causal factors responsible for it?

Decline and recovery: the transformation in Anglo-American strategic relations, 1945–8

The sudden termination of Lend–Lease in September 1945 was followed in December by the disbanding of the wartime Combined Boards for raw materials and for production and resources. The decline of the special relationship was further hastened, however, by the McMahon Act of August 1946, in which the United States effectively ended collaboration with Britain in atomic research and development. At a time when the possession of nuclear weapons, at least in Western eyes, was intimately bound up with the whole notion of 'Great Power' status, this was a serious blow both to Britain's nuclear ambitions and to its postwar role aspirations. Yet from this lowpoint in the summer of 1946, Anglo-American relations rapidly recovered. In July 1946 the 'American loan' had already come to the rescue of the struggling British economy; in September 1946, Secretary of State Byrnes acknowledged that American forces would not be speedily evacuated from Europe; in March 1947 the 'Truman Doctrine' was proclaimed; and finally in June 1947 the Marshall Plan announced a programme of economic reconstruction that was to revitalise Western European

capitalism and thereby strengthen its resistance to communist infiltration and encroachment.

Although each of these developments has been cited as a decisive
'turning-point' in the course of postwar Great Power relations,[10] it
seems likely that the drawing together of Britain and the United States,
and the simultaneous growth of their common hostility towards the
Soviet Union, resulted from the operation of rather more gradual
processes. In particular, the improvement in Anglo-American relations, which was to prove so crucial in Britain's subsequent foreign
policy, was the consequence of two underlying factors that were much
more obviously 'gradual' in their respective effects: (1) Stalin's obstructive diplomacy in the Council of Foreign Ministers and at the Paris
Peace Conference in 1945–6; and (2) his ruthless overt and covert
'consolidation' of eastern Europe between 1945 and 1948.

Stalin's obstructiveness rapidly became apparent at the first meeting
of the Council of Foreign Ministers held in London in September 1945.
The main express purpose of the meeting was to establish a viable
framework for the peace treaties with the defeated powers, a postwar
settlement which, it was assumed, would bring the hostilities of the
Second World War to a formal close. However Molotov's insistence on
the Soviet Union's right effectively to determine the political complexion of all post-settlement governments in eastern Europe – a
position that was clearly unacceptable to both Britain and the United
States – ensured that the conference failed in all important respects.
The foreign ministers of the 'Big Three' subsequently met again in
Moscow in December 1945, but their first tentative steps towards
agreement on the peace treaties were rapidly reversed by the Persian
complaint to the UN Security Council in January 1946 that Soviet
occupation forces had still not withdrawn from the Azerbaijan Province of eastern Persia, where they were actively fomenting communist-
inspired demands for concession. By April, Molotov had in fact
relented on Azerbaijan and the Soviets agreed to evacuate their forces
by May 1946.

However this small (and uncostly) gesture of Soviet goodwill unfortunately did little to improve the atmosphere at the second meeting of the
Council of Foreign Ministers in Paris in April 1946. It had been hoped
that in Paris real progress would be made on the future of Germany.
Unfortunately, it rapidly became clear that, unless the Western Powers
retained their *de facto* military control of Germany west of the Elbe,
Moscow would use every means at its disposal to transform it into a
Soviet-dominated client state. Meanwhile the Western Powers would be
permitted no say whatever in the affairs of Soviet-occupied east

Germany. It was more than a little ironic, therefore, that at the very time that the McMahon Act was driving a wedge between Britain and the United States in the *defence* field, Britain and American negotiators were finding a new common *political* purpose in opposing Soviet diplomatic intransigence in respect of the 'postwar settlement'. The immediate result was that the Paris meeting achieved nothing except a growing realisation among American policy makers that Churchill's 'iron curtain' – evoked in his speech at Fulton, Missouri in March 1946 – was indeed 'descending across the continent of Europe' and that there was little in practice that they could actually do about it.

In July 1946, negotiators from all the Allied Powers met in Paris in order to devise draft peace treaties for Bulgaria, Hungary, Rumania, Italy and Finland. To the surprise of the Western Powers, the Soviet delegation accepted the principle that disagreements over the content and wording of the drafts could be resolved by majority voting: fairly rapid progress was accordingly made. Yet when the Council of Foreign Ministers met for the third time in New York in November 1946 in order to finalise the wording of the five draft treaties, Molotov rejected all of those parts of the drafts where a majority decision (in July) had overriden Soviet preferences. With the negotiations stalemated, the US delegation threatened to withdraw from the treaty-making process altogether. As a result the Soviets relented and in December 1946 final agreement on the five treaties was reached. Notwithstanding this agreement, however, the diplomatic damage had been done. Thereafter negotiations aimed at achieving a formal peace treaty with Germany progressed no further. Indeed, in American eyes, the Soviets had shown themselves, at least since April 1946, to be largely untrustworthy negotiators who used the treaty-making process more as an oppor- tunity for the dissemiration of vitriolic propaganda than as a vehicle for achieving peaceful compromise. This was precisely what Churchill had been telling them in no uncertain terms since Yalta; and they were now starting to believe it: the ingredients for a revitalised 'special relationship' were beginning to come together.

The crucial factor underlying the transformation in Anglo-American relations between 1945 and 1948, however, was the cynical manner in which Stalin manipulated the governments of those countries that the Red Army had liberated before the German surrender and over which the Soviet Union now exercised potential – if not actual – military dominion. The first concrete intimation of Stalin's 'defensive expansio- nism' to come was the Soviet-inspired coup in Romania in March 1945, only one month after the 'spheres of influence agreement' at Yalta.[11] This was followed in July 1945 by the installation of a Soviet-backed government in Poland. The outcome of the Hungarian election in November 1945 (in which the Communist Party vote was small) suggested that the Soviets might not invariably seek to subvert the promise made at Yalta that they would hold free elections throughout liberated Europe, but any optimism about Soviet actions in this regard was shortlived. Over the next two years, Soviet-inspired intriguing undermined the stability of a series of east European governments that dared to delay the advent of 'Peoples' Democracy'. Poland was the first to succumb in January 1947 when a new Socialist–Communist coalition government was elected in highly suspect circumstances. By the end of 1948, the Soviet-inspired communist elements within the coalition had achieved a clear ascendancy and a Peoples' Democracy subservient to the will of Moscow was accordingly declared. Similar fates befell the Romanian government in March 1947, the Hungarian government in August 1947 and the Bulgarian government in December 1947. In Czechoslovakia, where competitive elections in May 1946 produced a communist-led coalition government that showed few signs of converting itself into a one-party regime, the transition to a Peoples' Democracy was achieved in February 1948 by the simple mechanism of a *coup d'état*. The only countries in eastern Europe that escaped Stalin's efforts to consolidate the Soviet Union's strategic 'buffer' zone were Yugoslavia and Albania, which had strong and independent communist parties of their own, and Austria, where British and American forces were still in occupation.

At one level, of course, all of these Soviet machinations were understandable, if not entirely 'acceptable', to both Washington and London. After all, at Yalta it had been acknowledged that the countries involved (Czechoslovakia excepted) were outside the western sphere of influence: it had been recognised that Britain and the United States were powerless to resist determined intriguing aimed at installing regimes favourably disposed to the Soviet Union. Yet the machinations were so self-evidently the direct consequence of Stalinist *realpolitik* that they inevitably served to reinforce the reciprocal Realism that was already growing among policy makers in Britain and the United States. Even more worrying for Realists in London and Washington was the fear that Stalin's defensive expansionism would soon begin to extend beyond the confines of the existing Stettin–Trieste 'iron curtain'. In France and Italy, recent elections had returned relatively large numbers of communist deputies. In Greece, following an electoral victory for the right-wing Populist party in March 1946, civil war had broken out with communist-inspired insurgents reportedly receiving assistance from Albania, Yugoslavia and Bulgaria. And in Turkey the nationalist regime was attempting to withstand the double pressures exerted internally by communist insurgents and externally by Soviet demands for its navy to be allowed unrestricted passage through the Black Sea straits. Of course, all of this might not actually be an orchestrated campaign by Moscow, but the combination of threats to western strategic interests certainly gave cause for alarm.

The final straw was Stalin's blockade of West Berlin which began in May 1948. This was viewed in the West as a clear attempt to dislodge the Allied occupation force from Berlin where negotiation had failed: a preliminary step to extending Soviet influence in Germany more generally. The response of the Western Powers was correspondingly determined. A protracted RAF/USAF airlift ensured the survival of the British/French/American garrison in Berlin and a counter-blockade on Soviet-controlled Eastern Germany encouraged Stalin to look for a compromise solution. After various diplomatic manoeuvrings, both blockades were lifted in May 1949. Whatever Stalin's 'real' aims had been in initiating the Berlin blockade, however, its main effect – coming on top of everything else that the Soviets had done in Eastern Europe – was to bring his capitalist enemies closer together and to convince the Americans that their continued military presence in Europe was still required, even if it was now Russia rather than Germany which threatened both the liberal values and the economic stability of capitalist Western Europe. As Arnold Toynbee remarked, 'the Russians' feat of curing the Americans of isolationism staggers the imagination'.[12]

By the middle of 1948, therefore, Stalin had succeeded in reinforcing the perception among British and American policy makers that their security and material interests strongly converged. The communist encroachment in Europe provided the classic *realpolitik* raw material for a renewal of the Anglo-American 'special relationship'. The collective interests of the free, capitalist democracies were clearly threatened by a wily and mendacious aggressor playing a skilful Realist game apparently based on the 'salami' tactic of the piecemeal incorporation of adjacent territory into the Soviet 'Empire'. Inevitably, that aggressor had to be confronted by a united *realpolitik* response. A mere convergence of interest, however, was not on its own sufficient to sweep aside all of the political doubts and suspicions which had characterised Anglo-American relations in the immediate postwar years. In peacetime, when the urgency generated by fear of imminent attack is neither so pervasive nor so strong as it is in war, a convergence of vital interest has to be supplemented by a political meeting of minds in order to effect a genuine transformation in bilateral relations. The shared sense of Realism which dominated both the State Department and the Foreign Office was of course a useful start. But the crucial 'added ingredient' necessary for the full restoration of the 'special relationship' was British diplomacy.

At Potsdam Attlee and Bevin had rapidly dispelled American fears that the new Labour government, clearly 'socialist' in its domestic programmes, would look to Moscow rather than Washington for political support in resolving the postwar 'German problem'. In a number of diplomatic forums during the course of 1946 and 1947, Bevin consistently voiced his suspicions about Soviet aims and intentions and in so doing established his credentials as a worthy successor to Churchill, as a stout defender of liberal values squarely confronting the new totalitarian threat. Yet at the same time that Bevin could reasonably claim to be Churchill's heir in matters of European security, the Labour government's progressive stand on the Empire also enabled him to portray Britain as a power which fully recognised the moral importance of self-determination. And if American suspicions that this was mere public posturing still lingered, the decolonisation in India in August 1947 demonstrated that Britain was prepared to pursue colonial policies rather more in keeping with American conceptions of the way a *liberal* Great Power ought to behave. This was progress indeed. And even if this new-found spirit of British liberalism was far less important as a source of interest convergence than the threat posed by Soviet acquisitiveness in eastern Europe, it none the less made Britain a far more acceptable partner for the United States in its postwar role as primary defender of the interests of Western capitalism. This partnership, in turn, was to prove crucial in the development of British foreign policy over the next 20 years.

The consequences of Anglo-American interest convergence, 1946–55

The fundamental consequence of the renewed sense of interest convergence shared by British and American foreign policy makers in the period after 1946 was the tacit acknowledgement that, if Western capitalism was under threat worldwide from totalitarian communism, then it was better to confront that threat together rather than separately. And if the United States was now set to take over the major role in the containment of communism by virtue of its superior military and economic capability, Britain and the Empire could still perform an enormously important subsidiary role by providing the United States with both moral and material support. Obviously there would still be policy differences over Europe, the Middle East and the Empire but these could not be allowed to divert the re-emerging partnership from its primary task of opposing the communist threat.

The economic consequences of interest convergence

In the economic sphere, Britain and the United States had already begun to make joint plans for the postwar international *monetary* system at the Bretton Woods Conference in 1944. The International Monetary Fund thereby established was designed to facilitate international trade payments and thus to encourage the growth of world trade. Under the new system, the two major 'reserve' currencies were to be the dollar and sterling: joint symbols of Anglo-American dominance in the postwar capitalist world. The benefits and costs that accrued from sterling's status as a reserve currency are examined in Chapter 7 and so they need not detain us here. The important point, however, was that, as Britain and the United States grew closer together in the political–military sphere, so their established economic collaboration took on a new significance: the junior partner in the new monetary system – Britain – was now also emerging as the junior partner in the coming political–military struggle to defend the 'free world' against the ubiquitous threat of world communism.

If Britain was to play an effective 'lieutenant's' role in the defence of western capitalism, however, it had to do so from a sound economic base. And if the iron curtain was not to be extended westward in Europe, where the greatest threat in 1946–7 was perceived to be, then the west European economies also needed to be considerably strengthened. The putative solution to this problem – the American Marshall Plan announced in June 1947 – in fact offered to provide *all* of Europe, both east and west, with the financial resources necessary for rapid economic reconstruction. However, Soviet suspicions that the extension of the Plan to eastern Europe was merely a ploy to insinuate American capital (and therefore influence) into the Soviet sphere of hegemony led to the rejection of the offer throughout the Soviet bloc. As a result, when the distribution of Marshall Aid actually began in March 1948, it effectively became a vehicle for rebuilding the economies of *western* Europe.

This had two obvious benefits: not only would the provision of a solid economic base head off deprivation-induced dissent at home, but it would also provide the resources necessary for a more formidable west European defence against external attack. As far as Britain was concerned, Marshall Aid provided the economic underpinning for the new North Atlantic politico-military partnership that was already emerging. For the Americans it was, in addition, a means of strengthening western Europe's commitment to capitalism. In any event, the provision of Marshall Aid had a profound impact on the recipient economies, laying the foundation for the economic rejuvenation of Western Europe in the 1950s.

The political–military consequences of interest convergence

The main consequences of the renewed convergence of British and American interests in the late 1940s, however, were in the politico-military sphere. Inside Europe, it led to a new military alliance which, although always subject to important strains and tensions, was to provide the foundation for British defence policy for the next 40 years. Outside Europe it produced defence collaboration in a variety of theatres aimed at protecting western interests worldwide.

Anglo-American co-operation inside Europe, 1946–55. Several of the 'milestone' events which marked Britain's closer ties with the United States from mid-1946 onwards have already been mentioned. In July 1946, Congress ratified the Anglo-American Financial and Trade Agreement – the 'American Loan' of $3.75bn which provided (on very reasonable terms)[13] a desperately needed boost to the flagging British economy. The loan not only indirectly enabled Britain to maintain throughout Europe and the Mediterranean military forces which otherwise might have had to be withdrawn, but also 'seal[ed] Anglo-American political solidarity' to such an extent that 'subsequently Stalin had to face a common Anglo-American front'.[14] In September 1946, Secretary of State Byrnes tacitly acknowledged that the Truman administration had reversed its previous commitment to Roosevelt's policy of withdrawing American troops from Europe as quickly as possible. Indeed, in a speech at Stuttgart, having stressed the United States' 'permanent and inescapable involvement' in global affairs, he asserted: 'I want no misunderstanding. We will not shirk our duty. We are not withdrawing. We are staying here. As long as there is an occupation army in Germany, American forces will be part of that occupying army.'[15]

The Truman Doctrine of March 1947 proclaimed the Administration's determination to provide assistance to any 'free peoples who are resisting attempted subjugation'.[16] Although never as all-embracing in practice as it sounded in principle, the doctrine constituted an important symbolic affirmation of America's global responsibilities in the defence of the 'free world'. The main practical effect of the doctrine, however, was that the United States took over the primary responsibility for supporting the beleaguered Greek and Turkish governments in their separate domestic struggles against subversion, a responsibility which in February the British government had announced it was shortly to abandon as a result of its overextended military commitments.[17]

Finally, the Marshall Plan, announced in a speech by the new Secretary of State at Harvard in June 1947, not only provided for the economic reconstruction of Western Europe but also marked the formal abandonment of American hopes that the Great Powers might act in concert in the postwar world. As early as April 1946, the UN Security Council had degenerated into little more than a propagandising talking-shop and a similar fate had befallen the Allied Control Commission in occupied Germany. Marshall's Harvard speech was the first major public affirmation of the US commitment to 'one *free* world' rather than to the more general 'one world'.[18] The rhetorical switch was not accidental: after the Harvard speech, the *containment* of the Soviet communist threat became the main concern of Anglo-American strategic thinking.[19] The world was clearly dividing – if it had not divided already – into two antagonistic camps, each convinced of its own moral superiority and its opponent's aggressive intent. As far as the Truman and Attlee governments were concerned, for two years one co-operative diplomatic gesture after another had met with a Soviet rebuff. The time for sterile talking with Stalin was over; what was now needed was a liberal dose of *realpolitik*.

As the Marshall Aid funds began to flow in March 1948, however, its European recipients remained concerned that the main intention underlying Washington's generosity might actually be to 'get Europe on its feet and off our backs.'[20] These fears were compounded by the suspicion that the Brussels Treaty of March 1948, in which Britain, France and the Benelux countries, with American approval, had created the 'Western Union' and bound themselves together in a mutual assistance pact, would be viewed in Washington in the same detached way. Perhaps this demonstration of European determination on security matters would simply provide the Americans with the excuse they were looking for to withdraw from Europe. With Marshall Aid serving to strengthen Europe's economic base, US military assistance might no longer be considered necessary. Fortunately for London, there was an alternative (and rather more accurate) interpretation of American intentions. As Bevin correctly predicted, the Brussels Treaty was in fact seen in Washington as a clear indication that the Europeans were prepared to make an effort to help themselves.[21] Such fortitude, moreover, was deemed to deserve American support. Five days before the Brussels Treaty was signed, the Truman administration entered into preliminary negotiations with a view to establishing some sort of Atlantic Pact.[22] The Vandenberg resolution, passed overwhelmingly in the Senate in June 1948, confirmed American intentions. Although the wording of the resolution was imprecise, its import was undeniable: the United States would provide material support to any regional security organisation in the western sphere of influence which sought to bolster collective resistance to the communist threat.

The process of increasing American involvement in European security culminated in the signing of the North Atlantic Treaty in April 1949: the Brussels Pact was extended to create NATO, which from January 1950 onwards became a mutual assistance pact with a permanent military command structure. The message to the Soviets was unequivocal. The United States was now tied formally and directly to the defence of Western Europe: any Soviet incursion in western Europe would without doubt be met with the combined resistance of all the Western Powers, and in particular with the full force of the US Strategic Air Command.

Yet, in spite of this uncompromising external stance, London remained concerned throughout the early 1950s about the real extent of the American commitment to European security. The problem was that, throughout the negotiations that preceded the formation of NATO, there had been two conflicting strands of American strategic thinking – one associated with the State Department and one with the National Security Council (NSC) – about the role that the United States should play in NATO. Even after the Berlin crisis of 1948–9, the State Department view – associated particularly with George Kennan, the head of its Policy Planning Staff – was that the Soviets were already strategically overextended and that they were consequently extremely unlikely to attack Western Europe in the foreseeable future. For Kennan, the creation of a US-dominated North Atlantic alliance would inevitably provoke the remilitarisation of Europe, divided into eastern and western camps. This was undesirable for two reasons. First, it would divert resources away from the fundamental task of economic and political reconstruction which in the long term was the best defence against the real threat of Soviet-inspired subversion *inside* western Europe. And second, remilitarisation would lock both the United States and the Soviet Union into a set of European entanglements from which they might not subsequently be able to extricate themselves even if they so desired. For Kennan, therefore, the primary responsibility for the defence of Western Europe should lie with the West Europeans themselves, with Washington providing only limited assistance if absolutely necessary and for a limited time period.

The position of the National Security Council, however, was rather different (and rather more simplistic). The NSC had witnessed Stalin's ruthless consolidation of eastern Europe between 1945 and 1948, his provocative posturing over Berlin, his covert support for communist subversion in the Mediterranean and in Western Europe and his overt backing of the communists in the Chinese Civil War; from all these actions, the NSC deduced an aggressive, expansionist Soviet *intent*. According to American intelligence reports, moreover, whereas the Red Army had 175 divisions at its disposal at the beginning of 1949, Western Europe had a combined total of 12: here was a massive superiority in *capability*.[23] For the hardline realists in the NSC, intent plus capability meant only one thing. At the first sign of a weakening in the West's resolve, the Soviets would be likely to attack. Since little could be done about Stalin's intentions, in these circumstances it was absolutely essential that the capability imbalance in Europe be re-dressed; a situation that could only be remedied – in the medium term at least – by a significant and continuing *American* military presence in Western Europe.

The views of the NSC were embodied in a document (NSC-68) published in April 1950, which called for a 'massive projection of American military power abroad' in the fight against communist expansionism.[24] Yet even though NSC-68 became official administration policy on 25 April, the State Department's position was at that time still being accorded considerable weight in Washington. What swung the balance decisively in the NSC's favour was the outbreak of the Korean War in June 1950. (The war itself is discussed below.) Suspecting that the Korean episode might simply be a feint to divert the West's attention and resources away from the defence of Western Europe, the Truman administration became all the more determined to strengthen its commitment to NATO.

The difficulty for the administration, however, was that in the short term it needed to concentrate its limited resources on the war effort in Korea. The position was further complicated by the fact that Truman also needed to persuade the British to make as large a contribution as they could to the western force. This latter requirement gave Washington a powerful incentive (1) to play down the seriousness of the Soviet threat to Europe (how could Britain send troops to Korea if a Soviet attack in Europe was imminent?); and (2) to encourage the Europeans (and especially the British, who in 1950 were still producing

30 per cent of all West European industrial output) to increase their overall defence spending to more 'realistic' levels. Not surprisingly, this combination served to fuel British fears of a revival of incipient Kennanism: notwithstanding NSC-68 and Washington's formal membership of NATO it was possible that the Americans were once again contemplating trimming their European commitment.

The Attlee government's response in December 1950, as it had been in early 1948 when Bevin had instigated the Brussels Pact, was to demonstrate the seriousness of Britain's commitment to the defence of Europe and the free world. In addition to despatching the Commonwealth Brigade to Korea in July 1950 as a show of solidarity, on 19 December 1950 Bevin announced the government's plans for a massive rearmament programme.[25] If the expected cost was to be a doubling of defence spending over the next three years, the intended benefit would be a further strengthening of the American commitment to Europe.

Unfortunately, even while British and American troops were fighting side by side in Korea, the controversy about the extent of Washington's European commitment continued unabated as a result of disagreements over the *European Defence Community* (EDC). The French had produced the Pleven Plan for an EDC in October 1950 and its main attraction had been its proposal to create a West European army to which the newly-independent Federal German Republic could subscribe:[26] NATO would obtain a sizeable increase in the number of divisions at its disposal without the (then) politically unacceptable reconstitution of the Germany Army. Britain's response to the plan, as it had been to its economic counterpart, the (May 1950) Schuman Plan for a European Coal and Steel Community (ECSC), was sympathetic but non-committal. Like Truman, Attlee and Bevin were in favour of the Europeans doing more to build up both their defences and their economic strength. In contrast to American preferences, however, the British were not willing to participate directly in either the EDC or the ECSC. Britain was prepared to accept some sort of associate membership of the EDC but anything more would compromise both its sovereignty and its '*global* responsibilities'. As a result, when the EDC treaty was signed by the continental European powers in May 1952,[27] the Eisenhower administration and the new Churchill government merely signed an appended bilateral agreement stating that they would assist the signatory states if they fell victim to some future aggression, a commitment which they had already made in any case through their joint membership of NATO.

However, in the months after the signing of the EDC treaty, and before it had been ratified by the various national Parliaments,

Secretary of State Dulles became increasingly concerned that Britain should assume a more prominent role in European defence. He warned Foreign Secretary Eden publicly that the US commitment to Europe would have to undergo an 'agonising reappraisal' if the EDC plan foundered, though he largely left open the question as to whether it would be the British or the Americans who would suffer the most 'agony' if this did indeed occur.

To the consternation of the British government, in August 1954 the French National Assembly failed to ratify the EDC treaty. The alacrity with which Eden toured the capital cities of Western Europe in September 1954 was a measure of the importance that Britain accorded to Dulles's threats. However, following a series of meetings in London and Paris in September and October of 1954, a satisfactory compromise solution among all the Western allies was reached. The plans for a European Defence Community were shelved but the now clearly-rehabilitated Federal German Republic would be allowed to join NATO in 1955, the size of its military contribution to be determined by the newly-constituted Western European Union. However, the crucial development in the last months of 1954 was that the Americans, having secured the principle of German rearmament within a political framework that was acceptable to the Europeans, were now genuinely committed to making a permanent and substantial military contribution to the defence of Western Europe: henceforward over 300 000 troops would be permanently stationed in Europe. With the constant fear of the continuing Soviet threat, this was precisely what British policy in both the European and Atlantic 'circles' had been aiming for since 1946. To be sure, there had been a convergence of British and American security interests in Europe, with their common interest in opposing the westward expansion of the Soviet Empire, since the time of the American loan. But the course of true *realpolitik* interest convergence never runs smooth: it had taken almost a decade of manoeuvring on both sides of the Atlantic to achieve a mutually acceptable compromise on the practical form that the western alliance should take.

Yet, even though a lasting compromise had now been achieved, there was still a sting in the tail. Just as Bevin had been obliged to strive for European agreement on the Brussels Pact in 1948 (and to initiate a costly rearmament programme in 1950–1) in order to convince Washington of Britain's commitment to European defence, so Eden had to pay a heavy price for America's renewed commitment to NATO in 1954–5. Over 50 000 combat personnel – four divisions of the British Army of the Rhine and the 2nd Tactical Air Force – were to be assigned to the defence of continental Europe for the indefinite future. The open-ended commitment thus engendered was to contribute significantly to the military overextension that was to plague successive British governments for the next 25 years.

What has been repeatedly suggested in this section, then, is that the basis of Anglo-American collaboration in postwar Europe was the joint perception that both countries were confronted by a common Soviet threat: the long-run interests of both Britain and the United States would have been seriously damaged if Western Europe had succumbed to Soviet domination, leaving almost the entire Eurasian landmass under Stalin's control. It has also been suggested that the fundamental character of the NATO alliance was stabilised only after several years of tortuous negotiation. While the British believed an effective European defence was impossible without the participation of the United States, the Americans were not prepared to make a *permanent* commitment unless the Europeans would shoulder a larger share of the defence burden. The delay in resolving these differences was not the result of the policy makers failing to appreciate the urgency of the situation: achieving the right compromise in an extremely complicated situation simply took a long time.

Anglo-American co-operation outside Europe, 1946–55. Outside Europe, collaboration between Britain and the United States was based on the community of interest that the two countries shared in insulating pro-Western regimes throughout the third world from communist infiltration.[28] In the decade after 1946, this shared interest was of particular importance in the Middle East and in Korea.

The *Middle East* was of interest to Britain and the United States in the postwar period for three main reasons. First, as noted above, according to the 'bipolar' realist model which Western policy makers were increasingly employing in their dealings with Stalin in Europe, any territories which 'defected' from the Western sphere of influence constituted an automatic gain for the 'other side' There was therefore a continuing incentive to ensure that as few territories as possible were left 'unguarded', so as to avoid leaving a vacuum that the Soviets might fill.

A second reason underlying British and American interest in the Middle East derived from the strategic contingency plans that the Chiefs of Staff in Washington and London were obliged to make during the postwar period. Whatever assumptions were made about the likely extent of a Soviet advance in Europe – whether it was assumed that the Red Army could be held at the Elbe, the Rhine, the English

Channel or the Atlantic – [29] the network of British bases stretching across the Mediterranean and North Africa into Egypt, Sudan, Iraq and the Gulf took on considerable strategic significance. All of the bases were potential springboards for future counter-offensives in Southern Europe and those bases east of Cairo could in principle be employed as sanctuaries for long-range strategic bombers capable of launching air attacks (nuclear or otherwise) on Soviet cities. It was of course hoped that such contingency plans would never need to be put into effect, but at the same time conditions in Europe were sufficiently tense to underscore the enormous potential importance of these strategic assets.

A third reason for Anglo-American interest in the Middle East, inevitably, was oil. If it was important to prevent the Soviets from encroaching into any of the territory currently within the Western sphere of influence for fear of the additional resources which the Soviets might accordingly control, it was doubly important that a region rich in such a vital strategic resource as oil should not fall prey to Soviet machinations. Anglo-American collaboration in oil policy had in fact begun in the 1930s when Iran and Iraq had been tacitly acknowledged as the preserve of the British, and Bahrain and Saudi Arabia the preserve of the United States; Kuwait had enjoyed the privilege of being plundered by them both.[30] In the immediate postwar era there was no pressing need to alter these rather comfortable arrangements: the question of whether it was British or American companies that held the oil concessions was less important than the fact that the oil states were solidly entrenched in the Western sphere of influence.

All this said, the actual collaboration between London and Washington in terms of concrete policy was rather limited, notwithstanding Marshall's announcement in December 1947 that the two countries would henceforward be pursuing 'parallel policies' in the Middle East.[31] Although the Americans did provide some assistance in restoring the Shah of Iran to power in August 1953, which resulted in the British-owned Anglo-Iranian Oil Company receiving some compensation for the assets that had been nationalised in May 1951, this barely merited the description 'Anglo-American collaboration'. Indeed the most tangible aspect of Anglo-American co-operation that occurred in the Middle East in the decade after 1945 was the encouragement that the Americans gave to British efforts to maintain their network of bases throughout the region.[32] Defence planning in both countries from 1947 onwards was predicated on the assumption that, in the event of war with the Soviet Union, American forces would have free access to

Britain's Middle East bases as and when they needed it. As things turned out, of course, the bases were never actually required: war in Europe never materialised and by the late 1950s rocket technology and doctrines of mutal assured destruction had substantially reduced the military potential of the bases anyway. However their availability was an important ingredient in the increasing closeness of relations between London and Washington in the late 1940s: for the Americans, Britain's possession of the bases made it an ally worth having in the Middle East; for Britain, American support for at least a part of its global role was a welcome symbolic acknowledgement of Britain's continued status as a Great Power. The United States, of course, did not provide any specific financial assistance to Britain in order to support the upkeep of the bases. None the less the American loan and then Marshall Aid did provide a general subsidy to the British economy which enabled the government to continue to service its overextended global military commitments without having to make hard choices (yet) about where those commitments should be reduced. As a result, in spite of the withdrawal from Palestine in May 1948 and the downgrading of the British presence in Egypt after the Arab nationalist coup in 1952 (both of which are discussed in Chapter 3), Britain maintained a significant military capability in the Middle East throughout the Cold War.

The main arena for Anglo-American collaboration outside Europe, however, was in Korea where western involvement was predicated mainly on the *realpolitik* need to avoid 'losing' territory to the communist 'enemy'. The Korean peninsula itself had been dominated by the Japanese since its military victories over China (in 1896) and Russia (in 1904–5). The Japanese had then used the area as a base for further expansion into Manchuria and beyond in the 1930s and 1940s. After the Japanese defeat Korea had been subjected to *de facto* partition along the line of the 38th Parallel, the point where the advancing Soviet and American liberation forces had met (and briefly negotiated) in 1945. Predictably, in the years after 1945, there were significant local tensions between the communist North and the American-backed South, with each side seeking to achieve reunification on its own preferred terms. In January 1950, however, notwithstanding the State Department's avowed global strategy of containing communist expansionism, Truman and Secretary of State Acheson both made speeches indicating that South Korea, unlike Japan and the Philippines, was *not* included in what was described as the United States' 'defence perimeter'. It seems clear that it was this statement, together with assurances of support from Moscow, that provided the trigger to the North Korean invasion of the South in June 1950. The

South Korean government immediately appealed for assistance to the UN Security Council where, with the Americans having second thoughts about the 'real' extent of their 'defence perimeter', their request met with a favourable response. By accident or design the Soviet delegation was at that time boycotting the Council[33] and as a result the American forces which supported the South Koreans from July 1950 onwards did so under the auspices of the United Nations. By January 1951, in support of the American effort, Britain had despatched a 10 000-strong Commonwealth Brigade – which constituted the largest non-American contingent in the UN force – together with a sizeable naval task force that was to be stationed in Korean waters.

But why was Britain involved in this relatively obscure part of the Far East when there were so many prior and pressing commitments elsewhere? The immediate justification at the time was that the action was necessary to uphold the UN Charter, though it now seems fairly clear that this claim was no more than moralistic window-dressing. A second explanation advanced (later) by a junior foreign minister in Attlee's government was that British support for the US action had been an 'instinctive reflex': not to have provided assistance to Britain's closest ally would have been, quite simply, unthinkable.[34] While there may be an element of truth in this explanation, it seems likely that British involvement was based on a rather more calculated assessment of the risks and benefits involved. Of particular importance in this context was the belief that, if Britain wanted continued American support in Europe in the future, then it would have to provide a clear demonstration now of its moral and material commitment to the 'defence of the free world'. As the Cabinet was told in November 1950,

> If we were to withdraw our support for US strategy in the Far East, the US government would be less willing to continue their policy of supporting the defence of Western Europe: and without their full assistance in Europe, we have little chance of withstanding a Russian aggression there.[35]

There was also a significant element of hard calculation in the government's assumption that, by joining the United States in its Korean campaign, Britain would be better able to restrain the Americans from taking a course of military action that might lead to an escalation of the conflict. Bevin and Attlee did not want to see either the Chinese or the Russians drawn into the war since it might then prove extremely difficult to prevent the conflict from spreading to Hong Kong or Malaya or even to Europe.

Perhaps the most important of all the factors underlying British involvement in Korea, however, was the fundamentally 'Realist' set of assumptions adopted by the leading members of the British Cabinet in their analysis of the developing situation. Although recent historical research has tended to emphasise the local tensions between the two Koreas as the primary source of the conflict,[36] it was widely believed at the time that the Soviets were not only supplying the North Korean war effort, but had *instigated* it as well. In July 1950, Secretary of State Acheson informed Foreign Secretary Bevin in no uncertain terms that 'the aggression was *ordered* by the Kremlin and is being actively directed by key Sov[iet] personnel [emphasis added]'.[37] Whether or not the information was correct, it was in general believed.[38] Certainly Attlee and Dalton believed it, and inside the Cabinet their views carried considerable weight. The invasion of South Korea was seen as a Soviet-inspired act of aggression not dissimilar in its fundamentals to Hitler's expansionist strategies of the 1930s. It was 'America's Rhineland' and accordingly the failures of appeasement must not be repeated.[39] The least that Britain could do was to assist its ally in its attempt to resist aggression and thereby prevent further communist encroachment: if action was not taken in Korea now, then Indochina, Hong Kong and Malaya would soon be the next targets on the communists' list.[40] In these apparently threatening circumstances, and with the need to provide the Americans with a public show of support, it was perhaps not surprising that the Attlee government should find itself embroiled in a war in a far-off country with which Britain had no historical ties.

In October 1950, however, the position worsened considerably. A UN General Assembly resolution sympathetic to the reunification of Korea was used by General MacArthur, the Commander-in-Chief of the UN forces, as a pretext to invade North Korea.[41] The Chinese in turn used the incursion into North Korea as a pretext to launch their own intervention, in November 1950, against the UN force. They made rapid progress and by the end of the month were threatening to overrun South Korea itself. Amid rumours that the Americans were considering using nuclear weapons against the Chinese or the North Koreans, or both, Attlee hastened to Washington in early December with the express purpose of persuading Truman of the immense folly of such a course of action: it would not only be immoral but would also encourage an escalation of the conflict well beyond the confines of the Korean peninsula. It is possible, of course, that Truman had no intention of crossing the nuclear threshold, but in any event Attlee emerged from their discussions satisfied that the Americans would not use atomic weapons without first consulting Britain.[42]

Attlee's success in Washington did little to calm the Cabinet's fears of imminent war with the Soviet Union. Even though Bevin had been able to inform the Cabinet in September 1950 of his belief that 'the Soviet Union wishes to avoid provoking a major war', by December 1950 the Chiefs of Staff Committee was reporting to Cabinet that 'preparation for war should be based on the formula, "war probable in 1952; possible in 1951"'.[43] While these estimates, which were also typical of those being supplied to Britain by the United States,[44] were clearly a reflection of Soviet *capabilities* rather than an estimate of Soviet *intent*, they were none the less extremely alarming. They certainly served to reinforce the pervasive sense that Britain's vital interests were seriously threatened by the Soviet Union and in so doing made any chance of a thawing of the Cold War for the foreseeable future seem increasingly remote. It is not clear whether Stalin was deterred from extending the Korean conflict by the massive British and American rearmament programmes that began in 1951 or whether he had no serious intention of risking war in the first place. In any event, notwithstanding the dire warnings of the strategists, a major global war was avoided: the Soviets continued to supply the Korean war effort but never gave the slightest indication that they were prepared to become directly involved in the fighting themselves. In Korea itself, by March 1951, with MacArthur removed from his command, the military position had stabilised at the 38th Parallel, the original line of partition. Two years of military stalemate ensued and an armistice signed at Panmunjon finally brought a formal end to hostilities in July 1953.

As far as Britain was concerned, however, the legacy of Korea was to endure well after Panmunjon. The distorting effects on the domestic economy of the 1951–4 rearmament programme were considerable. And the deep suspicion of China and the Soviet Union – of communism generally – had been strongly reinforced. But perhaps the most important consequence of the Korean episode stemmed from the very obvious fact that the UN forces had successfully achieved their primary objective of containment. In the final analysis the 38th Parallel had been maintained. Whereas Britain and France had failed to act in Manchuria in 1931 and in the Rhineland in 1936, in Korea the United States and Britain had actively opposed aggression and, in the end, opposed it successfully. To be sure, the costs in terms of lives and materials had been considerable, but this did not vitiate the fact that the seductive appeal of appeasement had been successfully resisted and a cynical aggressor forced to withdraw. Indeed London and Washington were so convinced of their own joint determination to continue to resist communist aggression in the Far East that they speedily assembled SEATO (in September 1954), a defensive alliance of capitalist powers in South-East Asia, the security of which would be jointly guaranteed by Britain and the United States. The crucial point, however, was that without doubt an important lesson had been learned: aggressive expansionism *could* be profitably resisted if appeasement was avoided and a determined political and military stand taken. Unfortunately, within three years, this entirely valid principle was to be horribly misapplied in Egypt. That way lay Suez.

Summary and conclusions

Underlying all of Britain's dealings with the European and Atlantic 'circles' in the decade after 1945 was a continuing perception that Western interests were seriously threatened by an aggressive and potentially expansionist Soviet Union. As a direct response to this perceived threat Britain sought both to strengthen its political and military ties with Western Europe and to convince the United States that it should join the Europeans and underwrite their collective defence. By 1947, when the Cold War began in earnest, the Americans were fairly receptive to London's overtures. They could see that, if the Soviets were allowed to dominate Western Europe, the resources of the industrial economies therein would not only be denied to North American capitalism but would instead be at the disposal of Moscow's strategic planners. At the same time, however, the Americans also remained convinced that the Europeans themselves were sufficiently well-equipped to mount their own response to the Soviet threat. A combination of Soviet diplomatic intransigence, Stalin's strategy of 'consolidation' in Eastern Europe and Bevin's diplomacy transformed the American position. By 1949, Washington was ready to join the Atlantic Pact and to make Strategic Air Command formally available as a deterrent to Soviet aggression in Western Europe. Yet even though American involvement in European security now had an air of permanency about it, Washington's long-term commitment to NATO was still extremely tenuous. In consequence the British government not only had to make the correct noises and gestures to assuage American reservations about unnecessary European entanglements, but it also had to take appropriate *action* as and when required to persuade Washington to maintain its European presence. Britain's involvement in the Korean war, its financially crippling rearmament programme between 1951 and 1954, and its decision to station 55 000 troops permanently in Germany in 1954 were all essential demonstrations of Britain's commitment to the defence of the West. Without them, the Americans might simply have left Western Europe to fend for itself.

And, in the view of successive British governments, the Europeans, Britain included, would not have been equal to the task.

The extra commitments thus engendered, however, were additions to an already overstretched British defence capability. The problem for the government was that no compensating reductions could be made to existing commitments: the security of what was left of the Empire still had to be maintained; and the global aspects of the renewed 'special relationship' required the preservation of the bases in the Mediterranean and the Middle East. The result was that Britain's foreign policy strategy in the period after the war remained fundamentally overextended. The overextension, moreover, was likely to continue for the foreseeable future. The main reason for this was that the foreign policy makers themselves remained convinced that Britain was still a Great Power of the first rank with global responsibilities. The Soviet threat had to be met and if the United States was not yet prepared to meet it alone – and no other country in the period after the war possessed the capability even to consider it – then Britain would have to shoulder a significant share of the burden. In these circumstances existing commitments could not be cut or new commitments refused unless there was either a significant reduction in the perceived magnitude of the Soviet threat or a radical revision in Britain's perception and definition of her role in world affairs. The problem was that, while Soviet antagonism towards the West remained unabated, Britain had not yet suffered the sort of external trauma (such as a defeat in war) usually associated with a fundamental role reappraisal. Throughout the late 1940s and early 1950s, therefore, the intense fear of the Soviet Union, the belief in Britain's Great Power status and the overextended strategy were all sustained, draining ever greater resources from the fragile British economy. Perhaps fortuitously, both a softening in the Soviet attitude and the requisite external trauma – Suez – were close at hand.

However, the concern with the Soviet threat and the consequent need to re-establish the 'special relationship' in the decade after 1945 had serious consequences for Britain's relations with Western Europe. Following the framework outlined in the Schuman Plan of 1950, European economic 'reconstruction' became increasingly based on the principle of economic integration. The European Coal and Steel Community was created in 1952 and by 1957 the 'functional cooperation' that it inspired had led to the creation of the European Economic Community. In the early 1950s, the Americans encouraged Britain to consider leading West European efforts at integration. The British, however, demurred: they were not yet ready to cede sovereignty to a supranational institution such as the ECSC and they feared that participation in Europe would damage relations with the Empire and Commonwealth. With hindsight, it was relatively easy to see that, with its diminished capabilities after 1945, Britain's best long-term interests lay primarily in the European 'circle'. As Nicholas Henderson observed: 'We had every Western European Government eating out of our hand in the immediate aftermath of the war. For several years our prestige and influence were paramount ... we could have stamped Europe as we wished.'[45] What was evident to later observers, however, was not so obvious to contemporary policy makers who had to make decisions amid genuinely felt fears of the ubiquitous Soviet threat. Britain flirted with Europe economically and politically, but concentrated most of its European efforts in the *military* sphere: in the Brussels Pact and NATO, where the European and Atlantic 'circles' overlapped. This of course was the very aspect of the European circle which not only incurred the most clear-cut cost but which also produced the least tangible gain. Though the security which NATO provided was obviously crucial to *survival* (the 'gain'), the *effort* which went into sustaining it (the 'cost') did nothing to reverse Britain's fundamental long-run problem: the decline of its economic base. In any event, the opportunity to lead Western Europe economically and politically had been missed. And when Britain was finally allowed to join the European club in the 1970s it was very much on the terms laid down by the existing members. In the meantime, however, there was still the Empire.

3

The Road to Suez: British Imperialism, 1945–56

Throughout the nineteenth century, Britain's dominance as an imperial power extended well beyond those territories that were administered from the Colonial Office and the India Office. In addition to the *formal* Empire of the colonies and dominions, London also exercised considerable economic and political influence in China, Latin America and the Middle East. By 1914 Britain's position in China and Latin America had been undermined by commercial and naval competition from Germany, Japan and the United States. However the consolidation of Britain's *informal* empire in the Middle East progressed steadily as the government took effective control of Egypt in the early 1880s and then acquired possession of the 'mandates' over Iraq and Palestine in 1920.

This chapter reviews the major developments in both the formal and the informal empire between the end of the Second World War and the Suez débâcle of 1956. The story of the period, somewhat paradoxically, is simultaneously one both of 'withdrawal' and of 'retrenchment'. The first section examines the build-up of forces that led to the rapid withdrawal of British authority in India and Palestine in the late 1940s. It is argued that these withdrawals derived principally from indigenous pressures for autonomy that in the years immediately after 1945 grew irresistibly. The second section, in contrast, briefly describes Britain's strategy in Malaya, in the Caribbean and in Africa where the government's main concern after the war – partly as a result of what had happened in India – was a retrenchment aimed at preventing any further erosion of the British sphere of influence. It is argued that this retrenchment is best explained by classic *realpolitik* security calculations: the counter-insurgency operation in Malaya after 1948 was largely a response to the global Cold War tensions of the period; British policy in Africa and in the Caribbean reflected the belief of successive governments that Britain could ill afford to make further major concessions to nationalist movements which, if they proved successful, might conceivably look to Moscow rather than London or Washington for moral inspiration and material support. Finally, consideration is given to the Suez affair, in which an unsuccessful attempt at Imperial retrenchment was followed by an enforced and embarrassing withdrawal necessitated mainly by the external pressure exerted by the United States.

India and Palestine apart, Britain in the late 1940s and early 1950s still possessed sufficient military capability to resist nationalist pressure throughout the Empire and Britain was accordingly able to maintain much of the imperial *status quo*. After Suez, though not necessarily because of it, the balance between British capability and nationalist pressure was to be quickly reversed and, in consequence, as we will see in later chapters, substantial changes to the *status quo* were to be rapidly introduced.

Withdrawal: India and Palestine

India

Nationalist resistance to imperial domination had always been a force in India since the early days of British involvement. The Indian Mutiny of 1857, though triggered by religious rivalries and differences, was fundamentally a nationalist rebellion which expressed the resistance of the indigenous population to the legal and social changes that the Raj had introduced. The suppression of the Mutiny did not mean the end of Indian nationalism. Though not supported by the traditional Indian elites, anti-British nationalist sentiment continued to make gradual progress throughout the late nineteenth century inside both the Moslem and Hindu communities, punctuated by periodic civil disturbances which served to remind the British that eventually some sort of concession to nationalist demands for autonomy would have to be made. The first clear sign of compromise came with the Montagu Declaration of December 1917, in which Lloyd George's government announced its intention to introduce 'self-governing institutions with a view to the progressive realisation of responsible government in India'.[1]

The 'Montagu–Chelmsford reforms' embodied in the 1919 India Act which followed held out the promise of a future 'dyarchy' in which the British would retain responsibility for the internal and external security of India while the Indians themselves would progressively obtain control of all other areas of policy.[2] The promise failed to materialise, however, and in 1927 the Simon Commission was despatched to India to consult with the All-India Congress and other interested parties in order to assess the possibilities for future constitutional reform. The eventual result of Simon's investigations, after much heart searching and discord within the ruling Conservative party,[3] was the 1935 India Act. Under the provisions of the Act, while the Indian provincial governments were to achieve fuller self-government, the dyarchy principle at federal level was to be retained: in federal matters the Viceroy would still maintain control of the key areas of internal and external security. The 1935 Act, however, like its counterpart in 1919, failed to have any real practical effect. Indian nationalists of varying religious and ideological persuasions soon came to recognise the Act for what it was: a continuation of the British policy of side-tracking demands for independence, a device for diverting nationalist pressure and sentiment away from the issue of fundamental reform. Indeed, if anything, the Act had the opposite effect of that which had been intended: instead of acting as a kind of safety-valve by siphoning off dissent, it merely served to convince nationalist leaders that the proposed concessions were a sign of British weakness. Moreover, such displays of weakness merely invited further demands.

The progress of Indian nationalism was interrupted, albeit briefly, by the Second World War. Some nationalists, inevitably, regarded the war as just the opportunity they had been waiting for: the anti-colonial forces should strike against British rule while the imperialists' attention was focused on their own survival. Gentler counsels prevailed, however. Notwithstanding the occasional riot and Gandhi's civil disobedience campaign of 1940–1 there was relatively little serious open resistance to the Raj during the war years. This absence of outright nationalist opposition was partly a reflection of the recognition that the Japanese – poised to attack India from their bases in Burma – were even more undesirable as potential colonial masters than the awful British. It was also partly a consequence of the widespread confidence that internal pressures for change would be so great once the war was over that the British would in any case be obliged to introduce fundamental constitutional reform. Indeed nationalist leaders were so confident of major concessions to come that they rejected the Cripps plan of March 1942, which would have instituted postwar reforms that went well beyond anything envisaged in the Acts of either 1919 or 1935.

In any event, after 1945, it rapidly became clear that the rule of the Raj was drawing to a close. The British were obviously incapable of resolving either of the two major (and interrelated) problems that confronted the Indian subcontinent: the growing civil unrest which produced intercommunal violence of increasing ferocity, and the refusal of the Moslem League to accept the Hindu-dominated All-India Congress Party's plans for a united post-imperial India.[4] A significant turning-point was the Great Calcutta Killing of August 1946, in which a Moslem massacre of Hindus produced a Hindu retaliation of unprecedented proportions.[5] Amid the repeated and escalating counter-retaliations which followed, the three-million British and Indian troops of the Raj were simply unable to maintain anything approaching law and order. Aware of the danger that the resultant anarchy might provide fertile ground for ideological zealots even more unattractive than the Moslem and Hindu fanatics who were actively fomenting the present intercommunal strife, the Attlee government decided to adopt a high-risk strategy. In February 1947 – before any agreement between the rival Islamic and Hindu factions in the nationalist struggle had been reached – it was announced that June 1948 had been set as the date for Indian independence. The effect of the announcement was salutary. Having observed the scale of the slaughter on both sides of the religious divide which had occurred since August 1946, the Congress leaders realised that their attempts to pacify the secessionist demands of the Moslem League would in all probability be no more successful than those of the British. As a result, Congress elected to compromise and to accept the principle of partition. Yet it was not until June 1947, when Mountbatten announced that the date for independence would be brought forward to August 1947, that agreement was reached on the precise form that partition would take. On 15 August India and a geographically divided Pakistan became independent nation–states, their new-found independence being accompanied by mass migrations of Moslems to Pakistan and Hindus to India. Over 500 000 people were killed in the continuing intercommunal strife which the migration provoked and as a result the British were roundly condemned for adding to the slaughter by their precipitate withdrawal. However, given Britain's proven inability to maintain civil order after August 1946, it seems probable that further delay would only have made matters worse.[6] To its credit, the British government had granted independence to two states which were subsequently to achieve a degree of domestic stability. The added bonus as far as Britain was concerned was that both India and Pakistan (and Ceylon, which achieved its own independence in February 1948) decided to remain with the Commonwealth, thus maintaining many of the economic and diplomatic ties which were of potential benefit both to the former colonies and to the ex-imperial power.

Crucially, the Attlee government had firmly eschewed the interwar strategy of seeking to delay – or even to avoid – decolonisation by promising constitutional reforms which in the event failed to materialise. It had recognised that the Raj could not be preserved in the face of continued and growing nationalist-inspired civil disorder. In these circumstances it had been far better to cut and run, leaving a relatively well-disposed Congress in control, than to attempt to maintain British hegemony and to risk fuelling further dissent: this might conceivably have produced an anarchic power vacuum and thereby have provided an opening for Britain's Cold War enemies. Given how awful things could have been, Indian decolonisation had been a remarkable success.

Palestine

Throughout the Middle East, as in India, there had long been indigenous pressures for greater local autonomy. Indeed, as the dominant European power in the region since the late nineteenth century, Britain had not been averse to encouraging nationalist sentiment in certain contexts, particularly if temporary support in the prosecution of some greater struggle could be bought by vague promises of future independence. This was precisely what had happened during the First World War when London had succeeded in making mutually contradictory promises to the rival Arab and Jewish communities in Palestine. In order to encourage an Arab revolt against their then Turkish masters, the McMahon letter of June 1916 had promised that Britain would 'recognise and support the independence of the Arabs'; in order to appease Jewish opinion both at home and in Palestine, the Balfour Declaration of November 1917 had announced the British government's commitment to the principle of a national homeland for the Jewish settlers who had been arriving in Palestine since the 1880s. If Britain had had no formal responsibilities in the Middle East after the First World War, these promises could have been quietly forgotten, or someone else blamed for their non-implementation. However, the acquisition of the Palestine Mandate in 1920 meant that the British government was obliged to confront the competing demands of both Arab and Jew. In fact, throughout the interwar years, notwithstanding a series of Arab riots in 1936, Britain still possessed sufficient military capability to contain the more aggressive elements within both communities.

Britain's hold on Palestine was seriously weakened, however, by developments during the Second World War. The Nazi holocaust in Europe not only swelled the numbers of Jewish immigrants into

Palestine but also simultaneously stiffened the Zionist resolve that in future the Jewish people must be masters of their own destiny.[7] At the same time the growth in Palestinian Arab nationalist consciousness – itself partly the result of the accelerated influx of Jewish settlers after 1930 – increased Arab demands for complete autonomy from British rule. In the immediate postwar period these different demands found expression in escalating intercommunal violence and in increasingly ferocious attacks on the beleaguered British garrison forces. In these circumstances, the Attlee government was confronted with an unenviable choice. On the one hand, withdrawal was not an attractive option. Not only was Palestine important in its own right if Britain was to retain its dominant position in the Middle East, but the base facilities which Palestine provided could also be offered to Washington's strategic planners as part of the price for the continuation of an American military presence in Europe. In these circumstances, a complete British withdrawal from Palestine – since the bases would presumably then be unavailable to both London and Washington – might prejudice Bevin's entire Atlantic/European strategy. On the other hand, if withdrawal was undesirable for reasons of strategic *realpolitik*, the internal security situation had deteriorated so badly by the beginning of 1946 that there was also no point in trying to sustain the *status quo*. The 'natural' solution which presented itself in this difficult situation was to instigate some form of *partition* – if Arab and Jew could not live together in the same state, then the problem could be resolved by creating two separate states – in the hope that close relations with at least a part of the divided territory might be restored at a later date. Unfortunately, in 1945 and 1946, the fear that partition in Palestine would reinforce demands for partition in India (where London's policy was still predicated on the paramount importance of post-colonial unity) meant that even this sort of compromise solution had to be rejected.[8]

What freed the British government from its state of near-impotent immobility was the growing conviction during the course of 1947 that, with Palestine ungovernable, the British military bases there were in any case an unusable resource. Moreover, once the decision to abandon India to partition had been taken in June 1947, there was clearly no longer any need to deny the possibility of partition in Palestine merely to prevent the contagion spreading to the Raj. With a specially constituted UN Commission backing the principle of partition, Britain announced in December 1947 that it would withdraw the mandate on 15 May 1948: Palestine east of the River Jordan – the mandated territory of Transjordan – would achieve independence as the Hashemite Kingdom of Jordan; the fate of Palestine west of the river would be determined by negotiation between the rival indigenous and settler communities. The British tactic of announcing a date for withdrawal had produced a negotiated compromise (albeit a bloody one) in India: why not reproduce the experience in the Middle East?

Unfortunately what had worked – just about – for India was not appropriate for Palestine. Between December 1947 and May 1948 no serious negotiation between the Arab and Jewish communities took place. On the contrary, intercommunal violence increased as militias on both sides of the religious divide prepared for armed confrontation once British troops had departed. Outrages were undoubtedly committed by both sides but, following the Deir Yassin massacre in April 1948, there was a mass exodus of Palestinian Arabs from the territory that David Ben Gurion proclaimed as Israel when the British did indeed withdraw in mid-May. The surrounding Arab states immediately initiated the first Arab–Israeli war, seeking to destroy the infant Zionist state at birth. Their efforts proved unsuccessful, however. Israel tenaciously held on to (what were at that stage) its preferred borders and the Palestinian Arabs merely retained the so-called 'West bank' territory which was formally incorporated into Jordan in May 1948, being subsequently seized by Israel in 1967. Not surprisingly, the Arabs felt that their interests had been betrayed by Britain: through their rapid withdrawal the British had tacitly offered their approval to the emergent Zionist state at the direct expense of the indigenous Palestinian Arabs. This had certainly not been London's intention but that was the way things were viewed in Cairo, Damascus and Amman: Anglo-Arab relations were set to be discordant for several years to come.

What, then, can be deduced from the withdrawals in India and in Palestine? How can they best be explained? What implications did they have for Britain's subsequent external policy? Consider, first, the main alternative *explanations* for the withdrawals. In the context of India and Palestine, there was very little justification for arguing – as British politicians were inclined to do when discussing the 'second-wave' decolonisations in the late 1950s – that independence had been granted because the colonial peoples, after years of British tutelage, were now 'ready' for self-determination. Such a thesis was immediately disproved by the horrible massacres that were occurring on all sides in both territories. There was also no real basis for arguing that beneath the indigenous challenge to imperial rule in India and Palestine lurked the insidious machinations of some Soviet-inspired communist conspiracy. The fact that neither Moscow's diplomacy nor Marxist ideology made any significant progress in either India or Israel (where the *Kibbutzim* movement certainly had socialist aspirations) in the years after the British withdrawal suggested that such 'external subterfuge' arguments were largely irrelevant.

As has been repeatedly intimated, it seems much more likely that the root cause of the British withdrawals of the late 1940s was the increasing strength of indigenous nationalism in India and Palestine and the concomitant inability of the British-sponsored security forces to maintain internal order. Without doubt, the British government would have preferred to maintain a presence in both countries if it had been at all possible: in Palestine, because long-range aircraft based there could reach targets in the Soviet Union, and in India, because of the lingering suspicion that Lord Curzon's gloomy prediction might actually prove correct – that without India Britain would 'drop away as a third rate Power. The rest would become the tollgates and barbicans of an Empire that has vanished.'[9] In both India and Palestine, however, the meagre British forces were unable to cope with either the generalised mass rejection of British rule or the blind fratricidal hatred of rival religious groups. The combination of both proved irresistible. Even the *timing* of the withdrawals was conditioned largely by the pattern of events inside the colonial territories: in each case, to have delayed further would have been pointless. Withdrawal was a recognition of the new facts of colonial life: it simply brought the *de jure* position into line with *de facto* conditions on the ground.

The major *implications* of the two withdrawals were also relatively clear-cut. Their most immediate and unambiguous consequence was the decline in Anglo-Arab relations that resulted from the manner of the British withdrawal from Palestine. The rapidity of the evacuation and the failure to achieve a prior negotiated settlement were widely perceived in the Arab world as evidence both of London's pro-Zionist sympathies and its determination to do nothing to protect the interests of the indigenous Arab inhabitants of what had become Israel. Far more important than Arab resentment, however, was the additional impetus to *further* withdrawal which the two decolonisations had provided. Further withdrawal was in principle now more likely, for two reasons. First, Indian decolonisation had again raised the possibility that the loss of India would significantly impair the strategic coherence of the Empire. The British bases both in the Middle East and in Singapore, for example, had been acquired primarily as vehicles for protecting the routes to India and the removal of India from the system of imperial defence undoubtedly diminished their immediate strategic relevance: why not execute further withdrawals, therefore, and ease the financial crisis at home? A second reason for supposing that further withdrawal would be more likely in the future was that developments in India and Palestine had clearly increased the danger of an imitative increase in nationalist consciousness elsewhere in the Empire. Unchecked, the contamination would undoubtedly spread and could only serve to increase the pressures for greater local indigenous autonomy in the future. However, in spite of these increased pressures for futher withdrawal, successive governments – ever convinced of Britain's Great Power status – stood firm. The deepening Cold War of the late 1940s made it imperative that Britain should follow the *realpolitik* principle of ensuring that potentially useful strategic sites remain within the western sphere of influence. In consequence, the process of withdrawal was suspended and a new policy of retrenchment adopted. For the next decade or so nationalist demands of independence would in general be contained wherever possible: only when the indigenous pressure proved irresistible would real concessions to local democracy actually be made.

Retrenchment: Malaya, the Caribbean and Africa

From mid-1948 onwards the British government was determined both to prevent a repetition of the violence that had occurred in India and Palestine and especially to avoid making further major concessions to demands for self-determination. This desire to retain as much as possible of the old imperial sphere of influence was in turn a response to 'natural' *realpolitik*-motivated fears that were increasingly exacerbated after 1947 by the Soviet/Communist Cold War threat. Throughout the remainder of the Empire, the result was a policy of careful but consistent retrenchment: while local nationalists might be granted some concessions by way of greater participation in local decision making, the ultimate power of decision on major issues would still lie with either the British government or its representatives.

Malaya

The Malayan peninsula and adjacent islands had been under British domination since the early nineteenth century. Before the Japanese occupation in 1942 Malaya had been more a 'geographical expression' than a political entity: a collection of Crown colonies (Sarawak, North

Borneo and Singapore) and internally autonomous British protectorates (notably Brunei). After the Japanese surrender in September 1945, the Attlee government became increasingly concerned to consolidate the position of Malaya within the Western sphere of influence by achieving some sort of political union among the various Malay states. Unfortunately its plan for a Malay Union outlined in 1947 was rejected by most indigenous Malay groups on the grounds that it gave too much (that is, a proportionate share of) power to the large ethnic Chinese minority. The announcement in February 1948 of a modified plan for a Malay Federation – which restricted Chinese participation in the political process – merely served as the trigger to a communist-inspired insurgency among ethnic Chinese Malays that necessitated the declaration in June 1948 of a state of emergency which was to last until 1958.

Arguably Malaya was the first genuinely 'hot front' of the Cold War, if only because the insurgency posed such an obvious threat to western (and particularly British) interests in the Far East: Malaya not only provided one-third of the world's rubber and one-half of its tin, but it also provided the Overseas Sterling Area (OSA) with over a third of its dollar earnings, without which the OSA would very probably have collapsed.[10] What made the situation even more alarming was the victory of Mao's communists in the Chinese Civil War in October 1949. Thereafter the communist insurgents in Malaya had an obvious community of interest and outlook with the regime in Beijing. The need for Britain to resist the insurgency was reinforced even further by the outbreak of the Korean War in June 1950. Indeed, with the entry of the Chinese into that conflict the following November, the whole situation in the Far East looked as though it might erupt into the sort of generalised capitalist *versus* communist conflagration which – whatever its consequences for Korea itself – would almost certainly overwhelm the relatively meagre British forces in Singapore and Hong Kong and threaten the whole of Asia with a communist takeover.

Notwithstanding the covert material support which the Beijing regime provided to the Malayan revolutionaries, however, the British-backed counter-insurgency campaign eventually proved successful. The estimated number of active terrorists, which in 1951 had been over 8000, was reduced by January 1956 to 3000.[11] Indeed the security situation was so improved by the end of 1956 that Malaya was granted independence in August 1957 and in the following year anti-terrorist operations were ceased altogether. Two principal factors had underpinned Britain's success. The first was the pursuit of a patient military strategy closely tailored to the contingent needs of the situation. While the Royal Navy had made it increasingly difficult for the insurgents' backers to provision their island-based guerrillas with supplies, the Army, in conjunction with local security forces, had succeeded in isolating the revolutionaries from their potential support base by developing a system of 'protected' settlements which the guerrillas were increasingly unable to penetrate. Turning Mao's dictum on its head, the counter-insurgency campaign had effectively prevented the revolutionary fish from swimming in the sea of the people. Sound military strategy on its own would never have been sufficient to contain the insurgency, however. The second – and critical – factor was the widespread support which the majority non-Chinese Malay population gave to the British-sponsored anti-terrorist campaign. Although the majority population wished to be free of British interference, it certainly did not want either to be ruled by ethnic Chinese communists or to see Malaya fragmented into rival communist and non-communist mini-states. In these circumstances, it was hardly surprising that the British government should have received the support of the majority community and that, partly as a result of that support, the British-led military campaign should have proved successful.

The favourable outcome of the Malayan campaign nevertheless had two disturbing implications for Britain's subsequent foreign policy. First, the achievements in Malaya seemed to provide additional confirmation that the British government's overall foreign policy strategy of maintaining Britain's position of influence in all three of Churchill's 'circles' – of maintaining the 'world role' – was being successfully prosecuted. The strategy had been devised, of course, on the assumption that, while close links with Western Europe and North America were necessary for Britain's immediate defence, it was also essential to nurture the forces of anti-communism in the Empire if the long-term economic and political interests of the West were to be protected. The tactical success in Malaya served to dispel the suspicions – which had been increasingly voiced after the rearmament programme of 1951 – that the three-circle strategy itself might be damagingly overextended: in doing so, it indirectly contributed to the continued pursuit of the strategy at a time when it was becoming increasingly apparent that Britain no longer possessed the economic capability to sustain it.

A second and even more troublesome implication of the Malayan campaign was its reinforcement of the belief that the communist threat to western strategic interests in the third world could be productively resisted by military means. If Korea had shown that *external attack* could be successfully opposed by a determined strategy of Western confrontation, Malaya demonstrated that the same principle applied with regard to communist-inspired *internal subversion*. As a result, in the period before Suez, the Malayan campaign – like Korea before it – served to strengthen the commitment of Britain's key foreign policy makers to Realism. Since Western interests throughout the world were increasingly open to challenge by the agents of communism, appeasement should at all costs be avoided. A decisive and determined stand must be taken against any attempt to subvert the international *status quo*. Suez beckoned.

The Caribbean and Africa

In the immediate wake of the withdrawals from India and Palestine, indigenous demands for change in Africa and the Caribbean were neither sufficiently focused nor so intense as to oblige the British government seriously to contemplate similar acts of decolonisation elsewhere. To be sure, during the course of 1948 there were riots in both the West Indies and West Africa which, though partly the result of purely local grievances, were also a potentially ominous manifestation of the sort of imitative 'contagion' effect that the imperialists feared.[12] The disturbances were not particularly well-organised, however, and in the event were quickly and relatively easily suppressed. The longer-term task that confronted the Foreign and Colonial Offices was how to prevent the situation in the remaining parts of the Empire from degenerating into the sort of ungovernable chaos which had characterised India and Palestine in the run-up to independence.

The specific tactics that London subsequently pursued in Africa and in the Caribbean obviously varied from country to country. None the less, in a wide range of contexts, the same basic principles seem to have been followed: (1) retain British authority for as long as possible and in as many policy areas as possible; and (2) keep internal dissent to a minimum by increasing indigenous participation in the local legislature and – if absolutely necessary – in the local executive. As in the Indian case, the motivation underlying these principles could be interpreted in two rather different ways. On the one hand, Britain could be portrayed as a benign liberal power that was gradually preparing its subject populations for self-rule: colonial peoples needed a gradual introduction to the ways of responsible government and administration; independence would come only when indigenous populations were ready for it. On the other hand, Britain could also be characterised as a self-interested Realist power which in the face of growing indigenous nationalism sought to postpone independence by making constitutional concessions which would divert dissent into politically acceptable, institutionalised channels: relatively minor concessions made at the appropriate time would enable Britain to retain control of the major levers of power. Inevitably it is extremely difficult to establish which of these characterisations is correct. Indeed there is probably an element of truth in both of them. None the less, the fact that Britain did so little in real terms to prepare its black subject populations for power – apart from the self-educative benefits of imprisonment which it bestowed on most of their more prominent leaders – suggests that the *realpolitik* characteristation was perhaps the more accurate of the two.

It is clearly not possible here to provide a detailed description of the constitutional developments that occurred in each of Britain's colonial territories in the immediate postwar period. A brief summary of the main changes that were introduced is worthwhile, however, since it shows that the policy of retrenchment – pursued after the loss of India and Palestine as a means of stemming the tide of imperial decline – was already exhibiting signs of erosion well before Suez. Of course, in some of the colonies, limited constititional reforms had been instigated even before 1948. *Nigeria*, for example, had already been favoured with a modest increase in African representation in its national legislative council in 1946, and similar reforms were introduced in *Sierra Leone* in 1948, though in both cases the councils remained firmly under the domination of British-sponsored nominees. In the Caribbean, a similar adjustment had been effected in *British Guiana* in 1943 and new constitutions based on adult suffrage (yet which still left ultimate power in the hands of the Governors) had been introduced in *Jamaica* in 1944 and in *Trinidad* in 1946. In terms of real black participation in government, of course, all of these reforms had been largely cosmetic. Moreover, as noted above, after the withdrawal from Palestine successive governments had become even less well-disposed to the notion of radical colonial change. However, events on the ground were soon to force a series of breaches in this strategy of imperial retrenchment, although, by the introduction of various transitional arrangements, London doggedly sought to delay the full transfer of power for as long as possible.

Despite the best endeavours of successive governments, between 1948 and 1956 *Sudan* followed the model that had been established in India in the period after 1918. Although nominally an Anglo-Egyptian condominium, Sudan had been effectively controlled from Whitehall since 1899. In June 1948, however, Sudanese representation on the legislative and executive councils was increased, and in 1952 – partly as a result of Egyptian pressure aimed at securing Sudanese–Egyptian union – the powers of the councils were expanded and those of the

British-appointed Governor commensurately curtailed. In August 1955, an army mutiny was followed by widespread insurrection and in the midst of the chaos (in January 1956) Ismail al-Azhiri's National Unionist Party issued a *de facto* declaration of independence which Britain was both powerless to resist and (since Nasser's designs on Sudan would thus be thwarted) willing to accept. A not-dissimilar developmental path was simultaneously being followed in *Ghana* (Gold Coast). The reforms of 1946 – which had produced a black majority in the legislative council – did nothing to prevent serious rioting from occurring throughout the colony in February and March 1948. Britain's eventual response was to hold elections in 1951 and 1954 which produced clear victories for Kwame Nkrumah's nationalist Convention People's Party. In the face of further nationalist pressure the powers of the Governor were radically circumscribed during the course of 1955 as a prelude to the granting of full independence in March 1957.

In east and central Africa, partly as a result of the existence of small but influential white settler communities, nationalist progress in the decade after 1945 was slower. In *Uganda*, where African participation in the legislative council had first been permitted in 1945, appointed colonial officials continued to dominate both the legislative and executive councils well into the 1950s. In *Tanganyika*, it was not until 1948 that four African and three Indian representatives were allowed to participate in the 24-member legislative council, though the revised 1955 constitution did accord equality of representation to the (variably sized) African, Indian and European communities. In *Kenya*, where the white settler community was more firmly entrenched and more determined to sustain its racial dominance, progress was only achieved after four years (1952–6) of Mau-Mau guerrilla insurgency; constitutional reforms introduced in 1956 mirrored the changes introduced a year earlier in Tanganyika by instituting equality of representation among the three main racial groups. Throughout east Africa, however, serious reforms favouring the interests and aspirations of the indigenous majority would have to await Macmillan's 'wind of change' in the early 1960s.

A similar delay would also prove to be in evidence in central-southern Africa where the protectorates of *Northern Rhodesia* and *Nyasaland* and the self-governing colony of *Southern Rhodesia* were joined together in August 1953 under the auspices of the British sponsored Central African Federation. The Federation was widely seen as a vehicle for sustaining white rule and throughout its ten-year existence was subject to sporadic but increasingly violent opposition from black nationalist groups. The challenge to the existing order was insufficient, however, to require much in the way of a concessional response and it was not until 1964 that Northern Rhodesia (as Zambia) and Nyasaland (as Malawi) achieved independence under conditions of majority rule.[13]

What conclusions are suggested by these various developments in Africa and the Caribbean? What is clear is that, after India and Palestine, the fear of contagion led successive British governments to conclude that further demands for self-determination should be resisted. Not only was it unseemly for a Great Power to be seen rapidly to divest itself of long-cherished imperial possessions, but there was also the question of who else might benefit from British withdrawal: the exigencies of the Cold War dictated that Britain, as the second ranked western power, could not retreat from its imperial responsibilities only to allow Moscow to make easy progress in the territories thus vacated. Indeed for the next eight years or so it seemed that the historical pattern established in India and Palestine would be repeated throughout the remainder of the Empire and possibly even over the same time-frame: indigenous nationalists would demand greater autonomy but London – using whatever means were at its disposal – would delay self-determination for as long as possible. In the hope of diverting dissent and, therefore, of delaying fundamental change, concessions would be made only when the strength of indigenous pressure was irresistible. By 1956, Sudan, no longer governable from London, had actually been granted independence, and significant (though not necessarily democratic) moves towards local self-determination had been made in Ghana, in Kenya, Uganda and Tanganyika, in the Rhodesias and Nyasaland, and in the West Indies. For the time being, however, the post-1948 policy of imperial retrenchment appeared to be working. The Empire was still largely intact and the separate decisions of India, Pakistan and Ceylon (though not Burma or Palestine) to remain within the Commonwealth boded reasonably well for the maintenance of British influence in the future. However, indigenous pressures for change were already gaining in strength and momentum throughout the Empire. And they were about to be given an important psychological boost.

Retrenchment and withdrawal: Suez

Writing in the late 1950s, Martin Wight observed that, although Suez ranked with Ireland and the United States as one of Britain's greatest imperial failures, the episode itself had been 'of small historical effect'.[14]

With hindsight, Suez does seem to have been more of a 'turning-point' – if such things exist – than Wight implied. To be sure, Britain's position of relative power was in decline well before Suez, just as indigenous pressures for change in the Empire were already growing apace. However, the crucial significance of the Suez affair was that it provided an important external psychological shock – analogous, perhaps, to defeat in war – that enabled British foreign policy makers to undertake a fundamental reappraisal of Britain's role in the world and the changing nature of its imperial system.[15] Although some of the consequences of the reappraisal were not felt immediately, Suez was an important watershed in Britain's postwar history: the perhaps necessary prelude to the large-scale withdrawal from the Empire and the shift towards Europe which occurred after 1960.

Britain's close political and military involvement in Egypt itself had begun in 1881. What had started as a classic piece of gunboat diplomacy – a debt-collecting mission – ended with London in effective control of a semi-autonomous Egyptian government which, though notionally a part of the Ottoman Empire, in effect became a British strategic base from which the routes to India could be protected. After 1881, Egypt, and especially the Canal Zone, was very much a part of Britain's 'informal empire' and in 1914, when the Turks sided with Germany, Asquith declared it a protectorate. In 1922 Egypt was granted independence, though Britain retained both formal control of the Canal Zone and a considerable amount of informal influence over the Egyptian government. Under the terms of the Anglo-Egyptian Treaty of 1936, although Egyptian autonomy was strengthened, the British government maintained the right to garrison the canal. Together with the condominium status of the Sudan, this continued military presence represented a continuing affront to the Egyptian government's desire to exercise sovereignty over what it perceived to be all of its rightful territory.

In the years immediately after 1945, Egypt, under its conservative monarchy, was not particularly troublesome to Britain, in spite of its attack on Israel in 1948 in the cause of pro-Palestinian solidarity. The Neguib–Nasser coup of July 1952, however, drastically changed the character of the Egyptian regime, providing it with a new commitment both to land reform and to Pan-Arab nationalism.[16] Long suspected as the power behind Neguib's throne, Nasser assumed full control of the Egyptian state in December 1954. Although highly critical of Britain's historical role in Egypt, Nasser in fact showed a preparedness to negotiate which suggested that some new sort of Anglo-Egyptian accommodation could be reached. The Agreement on the Canal Zone of July 1954, however, seemed to involve the British government doing most of the accommodating. Indeed, according to one account, London's agreement to withdraw its troops from the zone within 20 months was enough of a concession to merit it being described as the 'equivalent of the [1947] transfer of power in India';[17] though as a supposedly independent sovereign nation Egypt had every right to expect that such a concession would be made.

It has been suggested that, if the 1954 Anglo-Egyptian agreement had remained the basis for subsequent Anglo-Egyptian relations, then the Suez fiasco might never have happened.[18] Unfortunately events proved otherwise. Throughout 1955 and early 1956, the Egyptian government entered into separate negotiations with Britain, the United States and the Soviet Union with a view to securing finance for a series of development projects. In early June 1956, the Suez garrison completed its withdrawal from the Canal Zone and a few days later Nasser was elected President of Egypt. Given the new President's penchant for socialist rhetoric and his continuation of the ousted Neguib's policies of land reform, Nasser's continued discussions with the Soviet Union increased concern in London and Washington that he might be about to move Egypt into the Soviet sphere of influence. In the hope of weakening the Egyptian leader's domestic position, on 19 July the Eisenhower administration withdrew its offer to provide finance for the Aswan Dam project. A week later Nasser nationalised the Anglo-French Suez Canal Company. Although on the Canal question the Egyptian government was acting well within its rights under international law, Prime Minister Eden was outraged. He regarded the nationalisation as a clear violation of the spirit of the 1954 Agreement and in response established the Egypt Committee – a six-man inner cabinet – which engaged in three months of intense analysis of the implications of Nasser's actions.

Anglo-Egyptian relations remained tense throughout the summer of 1956, despite several attempts at negotiation involving both the UN Security Council and an 18-Power Canal Users Conference in London in September. The real obstacle to an improvement in Anglo-Egyptian relations was that, while Nasser had adopted an immovable stance on the Canal, the Egypt Committee's main concern from the beginning was not to seek a further compromise but to conjure a set of circumstances in which Britain could take effective military action against the Egyptian government.

In spite of strenuous denials at the time, it is clear that Britain colluded with France and Israel in order to create politically acceptable conditions in which – it was hoped – the two European powers could intervene against Nasser.[19] The arrangements were finalised at a series of meetings in Sèvres between 22 and 24 October. Israel would provoke a 'border conflict' with Egypt; Britain and France would intervene on the pretext of 'separating the combatants'; the Egyptians would be obliged to withdraw from the Canal Zone; and, it was hoped, Nasser would be toppled from power and someone more amenable installed in his place. The Israeli attack began on 29 October; the next day an Anglo-French ultimatum demanding the withdrawal of Israeli and Egyptian forces from the vicinity of the Canal was rejected by both sides; on the 31 October British aircraft bombed Egyptian airfields; and on 5 November British troops were parachuted into the Canal Zone itself.

Unfortunately for the British government, world opinion was not at all taken in by Eden's stated pretext for military action. The Americans in particular were astonished both at the apparent collusion and at the crass attempt to revive 'gunboat diplomacy'. They were strongly critical both of the *means* (force instead of law) which Britain had used in its attempt to weaken Nasser and of the *timing* of the invasion which not only came in the politically sensitive run-up to the presidential election but also let the Soviets off the propaganda hook over their intervention in Hungary on 24 October.[20] Apart from using the normal channels of diplomatic persuasion, the Eisenhower administration also took concrete action to thwart Eden's plans. The Sixth Fleet, stationed in the eastern Mediterranean, was ordered to use all peaceful means to obstruct Anglo-French operations.[21] Far more significant, however, was the dramatic run on sterling which occurred during the first week of November. Reputedly orchestrated from Washington, this financial crisis was made all the more serious by the US Treasury's insistence that the International Monetary Fund (IMF) would not be permitted to bail Britain out. London's near instantaneous response on 6 November was to call a halt to its military action (the French rapidly followed suit). In the face of continuing American threats to let the pound sink even further if Britain did not withdraw altogether, British forces were completely evacuated from Suez by mid-December.[22] In a matter of days – which from a purely military viewpoint had been quite successful – Britain had experienced a symbolic political reversal which had displayed prominently to the world what even Eden had already suspected: that Britain could no longer compete with the two superpowers in the race for global influence.[23] Relations with the United States had been damaged, but they would soon be repaired. The blow to Britain's prestige, however, would prove rather more permanent in its effects.

But why had it happened? Why over Suez had Britain embarked on a strategy that seemed bound to incur both near-universal condemnation and the extreme displeasure of Britain's closest ally, the United States? Why, against the advice of almost the entire Foreign Office,[24] did the Egypt Committee choose to take military action to resolve Britain's dispute with Nasser? Given the many analyses of the Suez episode that have been offered since 1956, it is hardly surprising that a wide range of explanatory factors have been cited as having been partly responsible for the Egypt Committee's decision to intervene militarily. Three factors seem to have been especially important however. The first of these was the legacy of the Egypt policy that successive governments had pursued between 1881 and 1952. Throughout the period Britain had contrived to preserve its economic and political hegemony through a combination of threats and carefully judged elite manipulation. This in turn had enabled London to maintain a military presence in the strategically vital Canal Zone. For Britain, the 1954 Anglo-Egyptian Agreement had constituted an acceptance of the fact that British dominance over Egypt could no longer be sustained. However Nasser's nationalisation of the Canal within days of the evacuation of the British garrison looked suspiciously like an attempt to replace British dominance with British subordination; an unequivocal abuse of London's liberal gesture of 1954. For Eden, such a situation was intolerable. It demanded a retrenchment – a reversion to the pre-1952 *status quo ante* – that would remove Nasser from power and enable a more malleable government to be installed. This was what the Suez invasion was supposed to provide: a means of restoring Britain's traditional position of dominance in Egypt. The disastrous political outcome of the intervention merely meant that such hopes were irretrievably lost.

A second major factor underlying Britain's military intervention was (yet again) the fear of 'contagion'. In view of the nationalisation of the Anglo-Iranian Oil Company in 1951, the danger was that the nationalisation of the Canal might encourage the development of a pattern; in which case British-owned assets throughout the Middle East, and possibly further afield, would be increasingly at risk. In these circumstances a determined show of force was perhaps necessary *pour décourager les autres*, to warn other third-world nations that similar acts of nationalisation would meet with severe sanction. Of course, as things turned out – as will be seen below – the *failure* of the British strategy counter-productively served to reinforce the aggrandising tendencies various radical regimes were soon to display: for the next decade and more, Arab radicals were to hold up Nasser's achievements against British imperialism as a model which could be used for liberation throughout the Arab world.

The third, and by far the most important, factor underlying the Egypt Committee's decisions, however, was the influence of Realism; especially the Realist world-view of Sir Anthony Eden. As with many of his contemporaries, Eden's political beliefs had been profoundly influenced by the events of the 1930s. In Eden's case, the impact was particularly strong, if only because of his direct association with 'co-operative diplomacy' (as a junior minister at the Foreign Office) between 1935 and 1937 and his subsequent public rejection of 'appeasement' (by resignation) in February 1938. For Eden all the major international conflicts that occurred in the years after 1938 – German and Japanese expansionism, Stalin's ruthless 'consolidation' in Eastern Europe, the Communist aggression in Korea – served to reinforce his belief in the importance of *realpolitik* calculation and especially to demonstrate the need to confront aggressive dictators with force rather than mere diplomacy.

From the outset of the Suez crisis in July 1956, Eden clearly identified Nasser as being very much in the mould of the great dictators of the 1930s. This perception, given Eden's dominant position in the Cabinet, seems in turn to have coloured all the deliberations of the Egypt Committee. Britain had made important concessions to Egypt in July 1954 and now Nasser was seeking to make further political and economic gains directly at Britain's expense by the use of the *fait accompli*. For Eden the parallels with Munich were all too obvious: Chamberlain's 'paper agreement' with Hitler had done nothing to prevent German troops marching into Poland one year later; the 1954 agreement had failed to prevent Nasser nationalising the Canal. Where would it all lead? Would Sudan be next? Or Libya? As Eden commented in his memoirs,

> To take the easy way, to put off decisions, to fail even to record a protest when international undertakings are broken on which the ink is scarcely dry, can lead only one way. It is all so much more difficult to do later on . . . the insidious appeal of appeasement leads to deadly reckoning.[25]

Given Eden's determination to resist 'appeasement' the Egypt Committee's major calculation became not whether to intervene against Nasser but when. The Soviet intervention in Hungary which began on 24 October may have had some small effect on the timing of the Anglo-French-Israeli action, but far more significant were the practical logistical problems of organising the military campaign and the political problems of agreeing a joint strategy with France and Israel. In any event, when the intervention did come it met with enormous political resistance both from Britain's enemies and from its friends. Crucially, even the Americans – in spite of all the difficulties they had experienced by rejecting the temptation to adopt a strategy of appeasement in South Korea – remained unconvinced that Nasser's Canal policy constituted part of some greater plan aimed at securing Egyptian hegemony in either North Africa or the Middle East.

Eden's main failing throughout the Suez affair had been his application of the wrong historical model to Nasser's behaviour. Although he was right to see the nationalisation of the Canal as a challenge to Britain's immediate economic interests, in the period after 1956 there was in fact never any question of restrictions being introduced on the free movement of commercial shipping through the Canal. Eden's fundamental error, however, lay in assuming that the way to treat Nasser was the way (he now believed) Hitler *should* have been dealt with over German rearmament in 1935, over the remilitarisation of the Rhineland in 1936 and over the annexation of the Sudetenland in 1938: by determined resistance and, if necessary, by force.

Unfortunately, as historians have frequently noted, the comparison between the expansionism of Hitler's Germany and the nationalist aspirations of Nasser's Egypt was not well-founded. After 1936 Hitler clearly had his sights set on the territory of *other* countries, whereas, over Suez, Nasser was simply trying to regain full sovereignty over a piece of *Egyptian* territory which, under foreign control, had represented a continuing affront to Egyptian national pride. Similarly, whereas Hitler wilfully and openly violated international legal commitments in pursuit of his grand strategy, in nationalising the canal Nasser was acting well within his rights under international law. The historical comparison which Eden perhaps should have made was not between Nasser and Hitler or Mussolini but between Nasser and Kemal Attaturk, the Turkish dictator of the interwar period. Indeed the parallels between Anglo-Turkish relations during the period 1923–36 and Anglo-Egyptian relations in the early to mid-1950s – though never apparently considered – were striking.

First, both Nasser and Attaturk were dictators who none the less enjoyed mass popular support in their respective attempts to carry out a radical domestic policy programme. Second, both were nationalist leaders whose respective countries had just achieved some semblance of 'real' independence: Attaturk's Turkey after the 1920–3 War of Independence; and Nasser's Egypt after the 1952 Neguib coup and the 1954 Anglo-Egyptian agreement. Third, the countries which they led were both being vigorously courted by the Soviets: in Attaturk's case this was partly because the Soviet leadership in the 1920s saw Turkey as a fellow-victim of Western imperialism and partly because of the strategic importance to the Russians of having an ally which could in principle control the straits between the Black Sea (wherein lay the Soviet's only warm water ports) and the Mediterranean; in the Egyptian case, Nasser was viewed as an agent of 'progressive' change in the Middle East whose success could only serve to weaken the West's political and economic stranglehold over that region. Fourth, when each leader had achieved power his country had enjoyed very poor relations with Britain: in Attaturk's case this was because the 'War of Independence' had been fought primarily against what was seen as a British-sponsored attempt to dismember the Turkish national homeland; and in Nasser's case, the 1952 coup had ousted Britain's preferred candidate for the Egyptian leadership, King Farouk. Finally, with regard to the major source of contention in each set of bilateral relations, neither nationalist leader was seeking to annex any foreign territory. On the contrary, both were simply seeking to (re)gain national control of what was perceived as an important national asset: Attaturk wished to return the Straits – which had been internationalised in 1923 under the Treaty of Lausanne – to Turkish sovereign control, Nasser to take charge of a strategic asset which had for too long been a symbol of foreign domination in Egypt.

Notwithstanding this series of remarkable similarities the British government apparently paid no heed to the fact that a strategy of patient and unaggressive diplomacy towards Attaturk had been extremely successful in transforming Anglo-Turkish relations from a position of extreme antagonism in 1926 to one of firm cordiality by 1932.[26] Eden, of course, plainly believed that quite enough 'patient diplomacy' towards Nasser had already been practised between 1952 and 1954 and that the time was now right for decisive *action*. Yet Nasser was asking for no more in 1956 than Attaturk had requested, and duly received, when in 1936 under the terms of the Montreux Convention Britain had accepted Turkey's right to remilitarise the Straits. The Egypt Committee seemed unable seriously to consider the possibility that a continued strategy of non-violent co-operation towards Egypt – even in the face of the loss of ownership of the Canal – could have maximised Britain's long-term interests. Rather than regarding the nationalisation as a hammer-blow to British interests in the Middle East, London could have chosen to accept it as an inevitable concession to what after 1954 was in effect a newly-independent state striving to achieve a sense of national identity. The continued ownership of the Canal by British citizens was not sufficiently important to merit the British government's seriously damaging its relations with the entire Arab world by resorting to force. Indeed the logic of self-interest

– as well as the need for a Great Power to be seen to adhere to international legal norms – suggested the reverse: that Britain's wisest strategy was patient diplomacy aimed both at maximising the compensation payable for the forfeiture of the Canal and at preserving Britain's good relations with the Arab states; and that a policy of persuasion and accommodation was far more likely to promote Britain's long-term goals in the Middle East of securing oil supplies, retaining strategic bases and maintaining pro-western regimes wherever possible. The Foreign Office was well aware of the depth of feeling in the Arab world generally about the importance of Egyptian control of the canal; and it advised Cabinet accordingly. Eden, however, chose to ignore that advice. Within the confines of his particular version of Realism, Nasser was seen as an expropriator who must be opposed, if necessary by force, rather than appeased. The potential lessons offered by Britain's interwar Turkey policy were in consequence ignored and disaster ensued.

Summary and conclusions

Britain's 'Empire circle' policy in the years immediately after 1945 was a combination of withdrawal and retrenchment. In India and in Palestine – where as late as 1946 it had been hoped that some sort of British presence could be maintained – Britain was obliged to effect rapid withdrawals: a simple response to the fact that in each country London was no longer in *de facto* control. By way of contrast, in the Far East, in Africa and in the Caribbean, a broadly successful policy of *retrenchment*, designed to maintain British dominance, was facilitated by the relative weakness of indigenous nationalism. In Egypt, a brief attempt in 1956 to reverse a policy of withdrawal that had been grudgingly accepted two years earlier met with such determined resistance from the United States that an immediate and ignominious withdrawal was unavoidable.

The decolonisation in India in 1947 was the culmination of a long sequence of events in which Britain had periodically introduced limited constitutional reform with the intention of softening dissent and thus enabling British dominion to be maintained for as long as possible. By 1947, however, the diversionary potential of the British strategy had been exhausted. In these circumstances the British withdrawal merely represented a *realpolitik*-inspired recognition that in conditions of near anarchy a quick transition to independence – rather than further delay – would be more likely to leave behind regimes relatively well-disposed towards British interests. In Palestine, the postwar situation was not dissimilar, though obviously the time-scale of British involvement had been much shorter and the building of indigenous pressures for change more rapid.

The critical factor underlying Britain's loss of control in Palestine and her resultant withdrawal was Hitler's anti-Semitic extermination campaign in Europe. The holocaust not only swelled Jewish immigration into Palestine but also increased Zionist determination to achieve a Jewish national homeland at a time when guilt and compassion had rendered London's will to resist those Zionist pressures correspondingly weak. All things considered, however, the British withdrawals from India and from Palestine were accomplished with only minimal damage being done to British interests: India and Pakistan joined the Commonwealth; Jordan and Israel remained in the western sphere of influence. In the conditions of the time these two outcomes were probably the best anyone could have hoped for.

After 1948, Britain's imperial strategy became broadly one of retrenchment, though it was a retrenchment sufficiently flexible to permit further withdrawals when circumstances were clearly beyond London's control. In fact, in Malaya, where the desire to avoid imperial withdrawal was overlain with a determination to prevent further communist gains in the Far East, no major concessions were necessary, at least in the period before Suez. This was largely because the communist threat had been successfully resisted – thanks partly to an outstanding military campaign and partly to the ethnic composition of the Malayan population (which undermined the popular appeal of the ethnic Chinese communist insurgents). In Africa and the Caribbean the danger of communist subversion was considerably smaller than in the Far East. None the less the continuing need to protect British political and commercial interests and the corresponding need to keep the remaining colonial territories firmly within the British sphere of influence meant that the Colonial Office had to carry out the chosen strategy of imperial retrenchment with caution and sensitivity. It did so with considerable success. As in India between the wars, nationalist demands for full self-determination were, for the time being, held at bay by a variety of constitutional concessions which allowed for some (and often increasing) indigenous participation in the decision-making process, but which simultaneously ensured that the British government remained the source of final authority. This was not to say, however, that nationalist pressures could everywhere be contained. Where indigenous demands for autonomy were especially strong and/or the problems of ungovernability particularly intense, then Britain was still prepared to bow to the inevitable and withdraw: hence the agreement to evacuate Suez by 1956 and the abandonment of the Sudan at the end of 1955.

Yet it was in relation to Egypt that the whole post-1948 imperial strategy began to founder. In 1954 Britain had accepted that the new Egyptian government had the right to full sovereignty over the Canal Zone and had set out a timetable for British withdrawal. However the subsequent nationalisation of the Canal Company itself was regarded as such a provocation that Britain opted for a return to the strategy of retrenchment: of attempting to restore Britain to the position of influence which it had enjoyed in the period before 1952. Unfortunately the specific form of collusion that was adopted by the Egypt Committee displayed neither the subtlety nor the understanding of local conditions which had characterised Britain's policy of retrenchment in Malaya and Africa. Indeed the politically unacceptable nature of the intervention in Egypt led to the rapid abandonment of the attempted retrenchment; a complete and permanent withdrawal quickly followed.

What is clear from the foregoing discussion, however, is that the Realist world-views of Britain's foreign policy makers were extremely important in generating this variegated pattern of retrenchment and withdrawal. It was certainly Realism – in both the everyday and the technical senses of the term – that led Britain to evacuate India and Palestine: a simple recognition of the fact that, when the imperial power is no longer able to govern its dependencies, then its own interests are best served by achieving an accommodation – on the most favourable terms possible – with those who look as though they can. It was certainly Realism, given the apparently growing communist threat to western security interests in the Far East, which underlay Britain's determination to eradicate the Marxist insurgency in Malaya. It was certainly Realism that led to the strategy of retrenchment in Africa and the Caribbean: while there was no serious *security* threat to western interests in these areas in the late 1940s and early 1950s, the twin necessities of maintaining safe overseas markets and protecting the sterling area's dollar earnings meant that material-interest *realpolitik* calculation continued to dominate British government policy. And it was certainly Realism – forged out of the experiences of the Second World War, the Cold War and Korea – that encouraged Eden to misapply the principle that aggressors should be actively resisted rather than passively appeased, with such unfortunate consequences at Suez.

The real paradox of imperial policy in the decade after 1945 was that a string of *tactical* successes could have added up to something approaching *strategic* failure. As has been repeatedly observed, the decolonisation in India and the withdrawal from Palestine were completed with minimal damage to British interests; the guerrilla insurgencies in Malaya and Kenya were successfully resisted; nationalist pressures in Africa and the Caribbean were successfully contained. Yet Britain's military capabilities, given its Cold War commitments in Europe, the North Atlantic and Korea, were seriously over-stretched. The competing resource demands of rival spending programmes at home and the chronic balance of payments difficulties that the British economy was encountering merely made things worse. In this curious situation of faltering strategy and tactical success it was more than a little ironic that the one notable tactical failure of the 1945–56 period, Suez, should have been largely responsible for the broad strategic reappraisal which subsequently took place. Without the trauma of Suez, Britain might have attempted to sustain its overextended 'three circle' strategy well after 1956, continuing to improvise brilliantly in increasingly difficult circumstances. Without Suez, the subsequent self-conscious analysis of Britain's diminished role in the world of the superpowers might not have been so intense or the indigenous demands for change in the colonies so insistent.

The road to Suez had been tortuous and by no means inexorable. If the Conservative Party had decided to skip a generation and pass over Anthony Eden when the question of Churchill's successor arose in April 1955, it is possible that Suez might never have happened at all. In the event it was perhaps just as well that it did. Without the stimulus of humiliation, Britain might have stumbled on in its strategy of overextension, determined to hang on to its remaining imperial possessions until they were forcibly prised from its grasp. It was far better to recognise the strength of the 'wind of change' that was blowing through the Empire; to come to terms with reality quickly; and to act accordingly.

4

The Wind of Change: The Empire Circle after 1956

In the years after 1956, Britain progressively withdrew from the Empire 'circle'. Although the pace of withdrawal varied – at times accelerating and on occasion even going into temporary reverse – it none the less proceeded inexorably. At the root of this process, of course, was the relative decline in Britain's international economic position which had begun well before the First World War. However, while Britain's relative economic decline might have been a necessary condition for the downgrading of the Empire, it was never a sufficient condition for such an eventuality. Crucially, in the period after 1956, economic weakness was complemented by two other processes that encouraged withdrawal: the increased intensity of *indigenous nationalist pressures for real local autonomy* and the seemingly *autonomous shifts that were taking place in the pattern of Britain's overseas trade*. In the decade or so after Suez, the juxtaposition of these three factors produced tremendous pressures for a strategic shift in Britain's external policy. Fortunately successive governments after 1957 were sufficiently well-schooled in the principles of *realpolitik* to recognise not only that the economic significance of the Empire had diminished but also that Britain's traditional military position within it could no longer be sustained.

This chapter begins with a review of the major effects which Suez had on Britain's international position. Although the affair itself does not seem to have provoked a thorough-going formal reconsideration of Britain's world role,[1] it undoubtedly gave added impetus to deep-seated changes that were already occurring within the Empire; changes which were quite beyond the British government's ability to control. The second section of the chapter provides a brief account of the 'second wave' decolonisations that occurred throughout Africa and the Caribbean in the decade after 1956: as with India and Palestine, the critical factor in this process was the pressure of indigenous nationalism. The third section examines the withdrawal from east of Suez after 1968, a manoeuvre of enormous symbolic significance which was undertaken largely in order to reduce the size of the overseas defence budget. The final section reviews British policy towards the Empire circle in the period since 1968 and attempts to assess how far Britain – despite its formal imperial withdrawal – can still be regarded as an imperialist power.

The effects of Suez

Notwithstanding the domestic political furore which accompanied the Suez crisis in the autumn of 1956, the affair itself did not in the short term appear to have a major effect on the British government's empire circle strategy. In one sense this was odd. It might have been expected that Britain's most serious diplomatic humiliation in modern times would have occasioned a major review of Britain's international position in what was now clearly the age of the two superpowers. Yet no such review took place. Indeed in the immediate aftermath of Suez the main political fall-out was limited to the discreet removal from Cabinet of those politicians who had so consistently chosen to ignore Foreign Office advice. As a result, Britain's overextended, three circle strategy – including its commitment to an imperial world role – continued largely undiminished, at least for the time being.

The wider ramifications of Suez were considerable, however. In Britain's informal Empire in the Middle East, the government's standing plummeted. The Iraqi government suggested publicly that Britain should be expelled from the Baghdad Defence Pact; Jordan abrogated the 1953 Anglo-Jordanian defence treaty; Syria and Saudia Arabia broke off diplomatic relations with London; and at a summit meeting in Beirut, the Arab Heads of State considered the possibility of combined economic sanctions against Britain.[2] Inside the Commonwealth the response was little better. Although Australia, New Zealand and South Africa were non-committal, Canada publicly announced its regret that Britain had failed to engage in consultation with its allies; Ceylon conveyed its vigorous disapproval of British policy; and Pakistan and India expressed their outright condemnation of Britain's actions.[3]

These immediate responses were of less significance, however, than the longer-term implications of the Suez affair. While it is clearly not possible to describe all of the consequences which Suez had for

Britain's international position, three of the more important ones – which were of direct relevance to the subsequent pattern of imperial withdrawal – require brief review here. The first of these was the damage which Suez inflicted upon Britain's prestige abroad and in particular upon its ability to pose as a champion of international morality. From the mid-nineteenth century onwards British military involvement in both Europe and the third world had always been more or less plausibly justified in terms of some moral principle or other. Wherever the British government had been obliged to resort to force it had done so either to uphold international law or to defend some weak state threatened by external aggression, internal subversion or both. Even if in the mid-twentieth century the maintenance of colonial control could no longer be justified as part of 'the white man's burden', Britain could still claim that it had an obligation to discharge its responsibilities of 'trusteeship' towards its colonial dependencies in order to provide appropriate conditions in which self-government could eventually be introduced. The problem with the Suez intervention was that none of these moral justifications applied. Nasser was operating within his rights under international law; he was clearly not acting aggressively against some weak third party; and Britain could in no sense claim a 'trusteeship' over internal developments in Egypt. In these circumstances the British intervention was widely interpreted by the international community as evidence of London's general preparedness to resort to power politics if it failed to get its way by persuasion. After Suez, foreign diplomats and nationalist leaders pressing for independence were even less likely to believe that British diplomacy was instinctively more civilised and more benign than that exercised by either the United States or the Soviet Union (both of which made significant advances in the Middle East in the decade after 1956). An important reserve of goodwill had been lost and without it subsequent demands for self-determination were to prove much harder to resist.

A second long-term consequence of Suez concerned the Commonwealth. The more ardent imperialists at home had always hoped that the Commonwealth would help Britain to maintain its postwar world role by acting as a kind of surrogate Empire.[4] In the mid-1950s there had been several good reasons for supposing that the strategy might be successful: the cultural ties which bound the Commonwealth together were still strong; trade interdependence was still high, bolstered by the monetary underpinning of the sterling area; and the participation of the Commonwealth Brigade in the recent Korean War suggested that Commonwealth governments were agreed that co-operation among the liberal democracies was still important in resisting the global threat of communist expansionism.[5] However, Suez meant that, although the Commonwealth survived as a formal institution, it lost what coherence it had possessed as an economic and diplomatic bloc. Of particular importance in this context was the reaction of India. Prime Minister Nehru was so incensed at Britain's aggressive manoeuvring that he initiated a series of diplomatic moves which were to result in 1962 in the creation of the non-aligned movement. Crucially, Nehru gained the strong support of Kwame Nkrumah, Prime Minister of the newly-independent state of Ghana and the leading African nationalist of the period. While the non-aligned movement itself never achieved the diplomatic coherence that its creators had hoped for, the support which the 'new' (black) Commonwealth members accorded it in turn meant that London was unable to use the Commonwealth as a device for sustaining British influence in the rest of the third world. On the contrary, during the 1960s the Commonwealth increasingly provided little more than a forum in which ex-colonial states could express their disapproval of the British government's domestic and foreign policies and at the same time seek to secure special concessions from Britain's overseas aid budget.

A third major consequence of Suez was that Britain had demonstrated a new vulnerability in its dealings with less powerful states. Even with its superior military capability – which was in any case already diminished in comparison with that of the two superpowers – it could not prevail over a weak opponent. Here was a lesson for would-be nationalists both in the 'informal Empire' and in the remainder of Britain's colonial possessions: with the right political strategy 'perfidious Albion' could be successfully resisted. In the Middle East Nasser's example was soon to provide the inspiration for a series of attempts to subvert the western-dominated *status quo*. In the immediate aftermath of Suez, oil pipelines throughout the Gulf region were sabotaged; Bahrein and Kuwait were subject to a wave of strikes and serious rioting; and there was an upsurge of anti-government guerrilla activity in Yemen.[6] In July 1958, the pro-British Iraqi monarchy was ousted in a *coup d'état* following a radicalisation of the Syrian government which had taken place during the course of 1957. Notwithstanding the changed climate in the Middle East, however, the most profound effects of Britain's new vulnerability were felt in the increasingly insistent demands for decolonisation in Africa, the Caribbean and the Far East. To be sure, Suez itself had not *created* these demands for change, but it certainly gave them a significant boost. It is these developments which are now examined.

The 'second wave' decolonisations: Africa and the Caribbean after 1956

As noted in Chapter 3, some concessions to African nationalism had already been made well before Suez. Sudan, for example, had effectively been granted full independence in January 1956. The plans for decolonisation in Gold Coast (Ghana) had been formalised several months before Nasser nationalised the Canal. Yet, in spite of these concessions, it was still London's broad intention in mid-1956 to continue its policy of 'trusteeship' over its remaining colonial territories into the indefinite future. However, partly as a result of the new 'vulnerability' that Suez revealed, in the period after 1956 there was a fairly rapid change both in Britain's overall imperial strategy *and* in the conditions on the ground inside the colonies. In terms of the overall strategy there was an increasing recognition both in Cabinet and in the Foreign and Colonial Offices that Britain no longer possessed the military and economic capability to sustain its imperial role in the third world. Crucially, by the early 1960s it was also recognised that a fairly rapid withdrawal would be less painful for all concerned than a lengthy campaign to retain control of possessions that would eventually be lost anyway: to move quickly would permit a transition to a cordial interdependence between ex-colonisers and ex-colonised; to delay would be to risk an escalation in violence and the possible development of irreconcilable antagonisms.[7]

The immediate reason for this transformation in the collective perceptions of the British foreign policy establishment was the changing balance of grass roots political forces inside the colonies themselves. Quite simply, indigenous nationalist sentiment in the late 1950s and early 1960s was rapidly becoming more articulate, more widespread and more determined. Throughout Africa and the Caribbean, political discourse was experiencing a radicalisation. Anti-imperialist propaganda received much wider currency than even before and the membership of nationalist organisations accelerated significantly. A new generation of black intellectuals – Fanon in North Africa, CLR James in the West Indies, Nyerere in Tanganyika and Nkrumah in Ghana – found its ideas gaining increasingly wide acceptance, especially among the politically active sections of the colonial populations. A black political consciousness was emerging that was all too aware of the nature and extent of the oppression and exploitation that colonialism engendered. The new generation of nationalist leaders was much less ready to accept a slow retreat from Empire and far more prepared to countenance the use of active and, if necessary, violent resistance to imperial domination.[8]

The result of this strengthening of indigenous nationalism was a series of acts of decolonisation which by 1966 had left Britain with the merest residue of an Empire consisting of territories considered too small to be viable as independent nations. As Table 4.1 indicates, between 1957 and 1966 Britain granted formal autonomy to some 22 major colonial territories. Independence was not granted unconditionally, however. If the Realist world-views of the policy makers had forced the recognition that imperial control could no longer be sustained in the face of rising indigenous demands for independence, then Realism also required that, wherever possible, the newly sovereign regimes should be well-disposed to Western – and especially to British – interests. The British government had gone to great lengths in Malaya, resolutely suppressing a guerrilla insurgency in the decade after 1948, both to ensure the survival of a friendly government after independence and to guarantee the installation of a Westminster-style political apparatus through which subsequent political conflicts could be resolved. Following classic *realpolitik* principles, the Colonial office made great efforts to ensure that this pattern of well-disposed governments, underpinned by liberal–democratic constitutions, was continued throughout the subsequent decolonisation process in Africa and the Caribbean. If the Westminster model was in fact inappropriate to societies riven by ethnic and linguistic divisions – where the need to achieve a sense of national unity and identity was more important than the possession of a competitive party system – then this was unfortunate but unavoidable. The British government believed in the virtues of liberal democracy and the least that it could do was to bestow liberal-democratic institutions upon its newly-liberated colonial peoples. The fact that liberal democracy was so short-lived in so many of the ex-colonies (see the right-hand column of Table 4.1) is a sad testament to the failure of successive governments fully to comprehend the depth of the economic and political problems that Britain bequeathed to the colonies which it had ruled so benignly, yet exploited so thoroughly.

Explaining the rise in indigenous nationalism

But if the pressure of indigenous nationalism was the critical factor which induced decolonisation, what had been responsible for the upsurge in nationalist sentiment in the first place? Had the retreat from Empire been unavoidable? Or could something have been done either to divert or to suppress the rising tide of nationalist demands? As has been repeatedly intimated, a key factor in Britain's inability to resist the increase in nationalist pressure was Britain's long-run relative

Table 4.1 Dates of independence and abandonment of party competition in British colonies and dependencies[9]

Colony/Country	Year of independence	Year in which competitive party system abandoned	Colony/Country	Year of independence	Year in which competitive party system abandoned
Sudan	1956	1958	Zanzibar (with Tanganyika became Tanzania)	1963	1963
Ghana	1957	1966	Nyasaland (became Malawi)	1964	1966
Malaya	1957	—	Northern Rhodesia (became Zambia)	1964	1973
British Somaliland	1960	1969	Malta	1964	—
Cyprus	1960	1964	The Gambia	1965	—
Nigeria	1960	1966	Southern Rhodesia (announced UDI; became Zimbabwe 1980)	1965	1965
Sierra Leone	1961	1967	British Guiana (became Guyana)	1966	—
Cameroons	1961	—	Bechuanaland (became Botswana)	1966	—

Country			Country		
Tanganyika (with Zanzibar became Tanzania)	1961	1962	Basutoland (became Lesotho)	1966	1986
Jamaica	1962	—	Barbados	1966	—
Trinidad and Tobago	1962	—	Leeward Islands	1967	—
Uganda	1962	1969	Windward Islands	1967	1978
			Aden (became Yemen)	1967	1967
Singapore ⎫ North Borneo ⎬ joined with Malaya to become Malaysia* Sarawak ⎭	1963	—	Mauritius	1968	—
			Swaziland	1968	1973
Kenya	1963	1982	Fiji	1970	1987
			Bahamas	1973	—
			Grenada	1974	1980

*Singapore seceded in 1965.

economic decline. If Britain had retained the industrial and financial pre-eminence which it enjoyed before 1914, then it might have remained impervious to nationalist demands. Certainly a thriving economy might have provided the British government with the physical wherewithal to suppress a widespread outbreak of colonial dissent. However, while economic decline was almost undoubtedly a precondition of imperial withdrawal, it certainly does not explain the *timing* of the second wave decolonisations. Neither does it explain the upsurge in nationalist demands for self-determination which actually provoked the decision to decolonise.

At least three general explanations for this upsurge in nationalist activity can be identified. One explanation, frequently advanced in the popular press of the time, attributes the upsurge to *the machinations of the Soviet Union* and its agents at home and abroad: the Soviets were alleged to have trained nationalist leaders, supplied them with arms, assisted with the dissemination of anti-British propaganda, or some combination of the three.[10] While it seems unlikely that Soviet agents were entirely uninvolved in the various nationalist struggles around the world in the 1950s and 1960s, there is no evidence to suggest that their participation was in any sense decisive in the ground swell of indigenous support for rapid decolonisation. While the covert nature of anti-*status quo* operations obviously militates against the discovery of any direct evidence of Soviet intrigue, it is worth noting that in the years since independence none of Britain's ex-colonies has moved into the Soviet sphere of influence. Apart from Somalia – which briefly strengthened its commercial and military ties with the Soviets, between 1971 and 1977 – none has signed a Friendship Treaty with the Soviet Union and none has been induced to enter the Soviet's economic club, Comecon, as Vietnam did in 1979 after the withdrawal of US forces. Such a record of subsequent Soviet exclusion provides indirect support for the claim that Soviet involvement in the process of decolonisation itself was never significant: otherwise, it seems likely that the Soviets would have sought to realise their 'investment' as quickly as possible by supplanting Britain as the 'sponsoring' external power.

A second explanation for the increase in nationalist resistance to imperialism in the late 1950s and early 1960s concerns the mutually reinforcing *contagion effects of British and French (and to a lesser extent Belgian) decolonisations*. The argument runs along the following lines.

1. The crucial feature of the postwar world was the shift in the global locus of power away from Western Europe and towards the United States and the Soviet Union. With the loss of their hegemonic

position, it was only a matter of time before the great Western European empires collapsed. Indeed Britain initiated the process by conceding independence in India and Burma.

2. Notwithstanding *Britain*'s subsequent attempts at imperial retrenchment, the success of these 'first wave' decolonisations acted as both *a stimulus and a model* to nationalists in Indochina. Accordingly *France* was obliged to withdraw from Laos, Cambodia and Vietnam in the mid-1950s.

3. The success of south-east Asian nationalism in turn encouraged nationalist liberation movements in French North Africa, provoking the crisis in Algeria in the late 1950s.

4. Inspired by the Algerian model, Ghanaian nationalists demanded their own independence, which they were granted in 1957.

5. Once one of the major *British* West African states had achieved autonomy, the demands for independence from *French* West Africa became irresistible, and accordingly the French decolonised their West African possessions in 1960 (at the same time as the Belgians were obliged to withdraw from the Congo).

6. This 'wind of change' was clearly far too strong for a liberal power like Britain to resist. Unable either to offer any plausible public justification as to why it should retain control of its colonies or to provide the military capability which might render such a public justification unnecessary, the British government bowed to the inevitable. Following the French example, in 1961 it effectively foreclosed on the Empire by initiating a sequence of major decolonisations throughout Africa and the Caribbean which was to last until 1966.

While the 'contagion' explanation has a ring of intuitive plausibility to it, it is extraordinarily difficult either to determine what the precise transmission mechanisms of such 'contagion' effects actually were or to demonstrate that such effects did indeed operate. More importantly, the contagion explanation does not really address the fundamental question as to why the colonial populations were *susceptible* to 'contagion' in the first place. The postwar shift in the global balance of power might explain why Soviet and American imperialisms replaced West European imperialism in the period after 1945. It might explain the loosening grip of the West European powers on their respective colonial possessions. It does not explain why indigenous nationalism should almost universally have become such a potent force for change in the 1950s and 1960s.

It is in this context that a third explanation – what might be termed the 'social mobilisation' explanation – assumes relevance.[11] This explanation centres on the long-term economic and political effects which imperialism itself had on the colonial territories of the European power. It suggests that, *by developing the colonies, the imperial powers created the very conditions which encouraged the colonised peoples to challenge imperial rule.*[12] The process began with the improvements in long-range transportation which accompanied the second industrial revolution of the late nineteenth century and which accelerated the incorporation of the newly-acquired third-world colonies into the emerging global economy. This insertion of the African and Caribbean economies into the international division of labour produced important changes within those economies. People began to move away from subsistence agriculture in the rural areas to paid employment in the cities and small towns. In the early part of the twentieth century the extent and importance of this migration was limited. In the period after 1945, however, as the world economy entered a 30-year period of increasing prosperity, there was a dramatic increase both in the productive capacity of the colonial territories and, crucially, in the numbers of people moving to the urban centres. It is difficult to overestimate the profound consequences which rapid urbanisation can have for an undeveloped society and economy, especially when it is combined, as it was throughout the Empire in the postwar years, with an expansion of the available channels of political communication. Of particular importance is the fact that the entire social and political milieu of the newly-urbanised migrant is totally transformed. Old loyalties, allegiances and social networks are broken. The migrant is exposed to new ideas and to the influence of new organisations – on the streets, in the workplace, even in the home.[13]

In conditions of rapid urbanisation – of *social* mobilisation – the potential for *political* mobilisation of the frequently impoverished urban migrant under the banner of any new ideology is inevitably greater than the equivalent potential encountered under the static conditions of rural subsistence.[14] In the 1950s the rate of social mobilisation in Africa and the Caribbean was at historically unprecedented levels; and the new ideology with the most obvious mass appeal was anti-colonial nationalism. In these circumstances it was perhaps not surprising that indigenous nationalism should have experienced such an upsurge in the late 1950s and early 1960s and that it should have had such profound consequences for European imperialism.

Yet the pressures of social mobilisation and contagion did not produce decolonisations everywhere in Africa. For several years three of the major West European colonies apparently remained immune to indigenous nationalism: the white settler regimes in Mozambique, Angola and Southern Rhodesia. The critical factor in their survival was their geographical proximity to the apartheid regime in South Africa: with the firm political and economic support of Pretoria they were able to fight temporary holding operations in order to delay the transition to majority rule.[15] It was Rhodesia – the only British colony of the three – which held out the longest. Confronted with the imminent introduction of universal suffrage, Ian Smith's government had made a Unilateral Declaration of Independence in November 1965. From the outset, the illegal Smith regime posed severe difficulties for the British government. To have handed over the problem to the United Nations (as some critics advised) would have involved an abdication of British responsibility and sovereignty that was unacceptable to a country which still aspired to Great Power status. To have attempted to remove Smith from power by military force (and there was no guarantee that such a strategy could be effected successfully) would have seriously over-stretched Britain's military capability and split both Parliament and Cabinet at a time when the Labour government had a Commons majority of only four. In the event, successive governments, in collaboration with the United Nations, chose to apply economic sanctions against Rhodesia and to await developments.

Throughout the 1970s, as indigenous demands for majority rule grew progressively stronger, the Smith regime's efforts to resist the combined guerrilla onslaught of Robert Mugabe's ZANU and Joshua Nkomo's ZAPU became increasingly ineffective. By the late 1970s the security position of the settler regime had been so weakened that Smith was ready to negotiate. In January 1980, after a series of diplomatic false starts, the British-sponsored Lancaster House Conference reached agreement on a new, compromise constitution that was acceptable both to ZANU and ZAPU and to the ruling Rhodesia Front Party. Although Britain had never been in a position to exert a determining influence upon the military situation in Rhodesia itself, Lord Carrington's diplomatic efforts were undoubtedly important in persuading Smith that a rapid transition to majority rule was inevitable and that the interests of the settler community would be best served by accepting the limited constitutional concessions to the white minority that Mugabe and Nkomo were still prepared to make. Crucially, at Lancaster House, Britain had fulfilled its formal legal obligations as the decolonising power: with the independence of Zimbabwe, in April 1980, the 'second wave' phase of decolonisation was complete.

Why, then, did the 'second wave' decolonisations occur? In one sense, the answer is fairly clear. The decision of the Macmillan government to opt for a broad strategy of imperial withdrawal was based on classic *realpolitik* calculation. In the face of escalating indigenous demands for independence abroad and a relatively weakened economic base at home, decolonisation was a simple matter of trimming Britain's overseas involvement to match its declining overseas capability. Such an answer, however, immediately begs another question: what factors were responsible for producing the conditions that underlay this *realpolitik* decision? As we have seen, the 'external subterfuge' argument – in the absence of any compelling evidence to support it – cannot be seriously entertained. A similar conclusion can be drawn with regard to the frequently articulated contemporary claim that independence could now be granted because, thanks to Britain's previous 'educative' endeavours, the colonial peoples were now 'ready' for full self-rule: such a contention is strongly contradicted by the dismal record of militarism and instability which characterised much of British Africa after independence.

But if these factors were not particularly important, certain things did matter. Britain's relative economic decline and its postwar eclipse as a leading world power were undoubtedly significant as background preconditions. However the two major conditioning factors underlying the realist decision to curtail Britain's imperial responsibilities were (1) the acceleration in social mobilisation which accompanied economic development inside the colonies; and (2) the imitative contagion effects which seem to have linked different nationalist movements in various parts of the third world. The economic development of the colonies created the structural conditions in which indigenous nationalism could flourish; the achievement of independence in one colonial territory served as both an inspiration and a model for nationalists elsewhere. The process was inexorable and the imperialists had neither the will nor the capability to resist it.

The withdrawal from east of Suez

In spite of its commitment to the process of decolonisation, Britain in the mid-1960s still retained much of the global network of bases that it had assembled in order to protect the Empire. Sizeable military forces were still maintained in the Far East (in Singapore and Hong Kong), in the Middle East (in Aden and the Persian Gulf), in Southern Africa (at the Simonstown base in South Africa) and in the Mediterranean (in Malta and especially in Libya, which had become increasingly important since the 'loss' of Egypt in the 1950s). There were three major reasons why successive governments attempted to sustain this partial *Pax Britannica*. First, Britain still had unambiguous treaty obligations which required it to assist in the external defence of its allies. Under the SEATO 'Manila Pact' of 1954, Britain was obliged to defend Malaysia, the Philippines and Thailand; under the CENTO 'Baghdad Pact' of 1955, it had a responsibility towards Pakistan and Turkey;[16] and under a series of separate bilateral treaty arrangements it was also committed to defend Malta, Libya, the South Arabian Federation, Bahrain, Qatar, Muscat and Oman, the Trucial States and Kuwait.[17] Clearly, if Britain was to discharge its responsibilities in all these contexts effectively, it had to maintain military forces locally which would not only act as a deterrent to any potential aggressor but which could also be rapidly deployed should the deterrent fail.

In addition to these formal legal commitments, a second reason why Britain remained apparently wedded to its global military role was the potential military–strategic value of British bases. To be sure, the strategic rationale of those bases had been questioned both after the loss of India in the late 1940s and after the loss of Suez itself in 1956. None the less even if Britain, having now abandoned all of its major colonies, no longer needed to protect exclusively British interests in the third world, it could still provide a useful supplement to American efforts to defend the general interests of the West: interests which in an era of decolonisation the Soviet Union was doing its very best to subvert. In these circumstances, the continued deployment of British forces in areas where London had traditionally exercised an imperial influence represented a very convenient way of insulating the global *status quo* from communist-inspired challenge. Thus, in terms of strategic contingency planning, the bases in Singapore and Hong Kong could still be used for the 'forward defence' of Australia and New Zealand and for the protection of Malaysia; the British presence in the Persian Gulf was still required to ensure that the West retained a firm grip on Middle Eastern oil supplies; and Aden and Simonstown were necessary for the protection of the increasingly important oil tanker traffic which used the Indian Ocean and the Cape. A continued British presence was obviously no guarantee that Western interests in these regions would be safeguarded, but equally obviously it would reduce the chances that Soviet intrigue would prove successful in the future.

A third factor underlying British involvement east of Suez in the early 1960s was the 'bureaucratic inertia' of the foreign policy-making process itself, the general tendency of Britain's foreign policy makers to avoid hard choices and to delay making a major decision until events foreclosed on all the options. This tendency has certainly been evident in Britain's foreign policy making throughout the postwar period and, according to Wallace, was undoubtedly involved in the matter of the British military presence east of Suez in the early 1960s.[18] On this account, a major reason why Britain retained its far-flung network of bases in the face of both decolonisation and the loss of Suez itself was simply that British forces had been stationed east of Suez for over a century. While a conscious strategic decision was necessary to end this involvement, the highly bureaucratised nature of the decision-making process itself militated against such a radical policy departure unless circumstances made it unavoidable,[19] which until 1966 they did not.

The decision to withdraw

When Harold Wilson's Labour government achieved office in October 1964, it did so committed to retaining a British military presence east of Suez. Indeed, in the face of PLP criticism, Wilson was still defending the need to maintain Britain's global role as late as June 1966.[20] There were several good reasons for doing so. In the Middle East, following the shock administered to the American defence establishment by the Cuban Missile crisis of 1962, Britain's naval presence in the Gulf now had the blessing of the United States.[21] In the Far East, Britain's support for Malaysia in its border dispute with Indonesia after September 1963 had been invaluable in preserving Malaysian territorial integrity: without it, there was no telling how the situation might have escalated. In addition, in the face of the rapidly growing communist threat to Indochina, the Americans were now prepared to accept the need for an indefinite continuation of Britain's military role in the Far East. It appeared that Britain, having lost an Empire, might conceivably have confounded Dean Acheson and found a role acting as the United States' second lieutenant, defending Western strategic interests where the Americans – for whatever historical or contingent reasons – feared to tread.

But if this was the way things appeared in 1965, the situation was not to last beyond the publication of Denis Healey's Defence Review in February 1966.[22] Although the Review stated that the Labour government intended to retain its naval presence in Singapore and Malaysia, it also placed great emphasis on the 'overstretch' of Britain's defence capabilities. By insisting that this 'overstretch' was to be eliminated at the same time as the Defence budget was to be cut from 7 per cent to 6 per cent of Britain's Gross Domestic Product, the Defence Review effectively anticipated the end of Britain's presence east of Suez. Against a background of overall defence cuts, it was only possible both to maintain Britain's commitment to NATO (now clearly designated as the first priority) and to avoid 'overstretch' by reducing Britain's global commitments. The Review also asserted the government's clear intention to withdraw from Aden in November 1967, when South Arabia was scheduled for independence. In February 1967, the process of withdrawal was further bolstered when the annual Defence White Paper asserted that British forces would withdraw from Simonstown in a matter of months and that only Britain's 'core responsibilities' would be maintained in the Gulf. Finally, in July 1967, it was announced that Britain would withdraw all of its forces from east of Suez by the early 1970s. This was confirmed formally in the 1968 Defence Review which expressed the government's intention to evacuate British forces from Singapore, Malaysia and the Gulf by the end of 1971.[23] In anticipation of the fact that these withdrawals would effectively prevent Britain from discharging its existing treaty responsibilities, Britain would also cease to 'declare' ground forces to SEATO from March 1969 onwards, convene a special five-power conference to arrange for the future defence of Malaysia and Singapore by delegating greater responsibility to Canberra, and make bilateral arrangements with each of the Gulf States in order to ensure their continued security.[24] The new – and much diminished – world role that Britain might play in the future was neatly symbolised by the tiny contingent of unarmed British 'bobbies' that was despatched to the Caribbean dependency of Anguilla in the summer of 1967: in combination with some skilful diplomacy, the contingent's benign presence brought a potentially dangerous constitutional crisis to a swift and peaceful end.

Explaining the withdrawal from east of Suez

But why had it all been necessary? Why had the British government found it expedient to bring to an end a traditional commitment that was intimately bound up with the perception – both at home and abroad – of Britain as a world power? Why had London wilfully turned its back on the 'second lieutenant' support role, apparently well-suited to Britain's post-colonial status, which dovetailed so neatly with the American view that the Western powers could operate a mutually beneficial division of labour in the defence of Western interests in the third world?

Several factors seem to have been important. At the decision-making level, by far the most important consideration in all the deliberations over east of Suez policy was cost. By 1965, although Britain still had an abundance of post-imperial responsibilities, it no longer possessed the financial capability to discharge them. In terms of GDP per capita Britain had declined from seventh position in the world 'league table' in 1950 to twelfth position in 1965, having been 'overtaken' by France, West Germany and Denmark (see Table 4.2). With the exception of the United States, it was spending a higher proportion of its GDP on defence than any of its major industrial competitors.[25] And given the Wilson government's determination to increase state spending on both industrial investment and social welfare provision, the Treasury not surprisingly insisted on commensurate cuts in defence expenditure.[26] In 1965 Britain had over 55 000 military personnel stationed east of Suez, at a cost of £317m per year or 15 per cent of the total defence budget of £2120m.[27] Notwithstanding the support which the British military presence east of Suez provided for a number of friendly regimes, it was not easy to see how this considerable drain on defence funds actually contributed to British security. The two major bases east of Suez – Aden and Singapore – had originally been acquired in order to defend, respectively, the western and eastern approaches to India. With the 'loss' of India – and it was certainly lost after 1956, if not in 1947 – both bases had lost their principal strategic *raison d'être*. It might well have been worth paying 15 per cent of the annual defence budget in order to defend the Jewel in the Crown; it was certainly not worth paying simply to maintain isolated pockets of British influence in the third world – or to curry favour with the Americans – when serious financial crises threatened at home.

These cost concerns were exacerbated, moreover, by the suspicion that the same wind of change that had produced the 'second wave' decolonisations was also responsible for increasing the extent to which Britain's commitments east of Suez were being activated. The pacification of the old empire had always been a relatively easy task: rarely, except during the years of the two world wars, had it been necessary to wage campaigns in more than one territory at any given time. However, the early 1960s had witnessed a violent confrontation between Malaysia and Indonesia, serious internal subversion in Bahrain and in Kuwait, and a prolonged armed insurrection in the South Arabian Federation; all of which required a determined and sustained military response from the British government. If this pattern was representative of things to come, reducing Britain's overseas commitments might well be preferable to increasing the resources available for fighting the necessary military campaigns effectively. In these circumstances, given that it was the Atlantic Alliance which was at the core of British security concerns, the commitment to maintain forces east of Suez was

Table 4.2 Britain's place in the world GDP/capita rankings, 1950–81 ($US per capita per year)

1950

1	United States	1593
2	Canada	914
3	New Zealand	900
4	Switzerland	894
5	Australia	761
6	Sweden	740
7	UK	644

1960

1	United States	2804
2	Canada	2229
3	Sweden	1865
4	Luxembourg	1629
5	Australia	1586
6	New Zealand	1576
7	Switzerland	1560
8	Iceland	1385
9	UK	1358

1965

1	Kuwait	4877
2	United States	3142
3	Sweden	2342
4	Canada	2270
5	Switerland	2002
6	Australia	1825
7	Iceland	1746
8	France	1743
9	Luxembourg	1733
10	West Germany	1697
11	Denmark	1678
12	UK	1584

1970

1	United States	4789
2	Sweden	4109
3	Kuwait	3639
4	Canada	3884
5	Switzerland	3349
6	Denmark	3159
7	Luxembourg	3136
8	West Germany	3092
9	Australia	2948
10	Norway	2880
11	France	2775
12	Belgium	2652
13	Qatar	2531
14	Netherlands	2429
15	Iceland	2422
16	Finland	2251
17	New Zealand	2237
18	UK	2194

1975

1	Kuwait	11726
2	Switzerland	8463
3	Sweden	8459
4	US	7087
5	Norway	7058
6	Denmark	7006
7	Canada	6995
8	FRG	6871
9	Qatar	6500
10	Australia	6364
11	France	6360
12	Belgium	6352
13	Luxembourg	6102
14	Netherlands	5949
15	Iceland	5665
16	Finland	5645
17	Austria	4996
18	New Zealand	4417
19	Japan	4133
20	UK	4089

1981

1	United Arab Emirates	32 555
2	Qatar	32 317
3	Kuwait	17 657
4	Saudi Arabia	16 990
5	Switzerland	14 979
6	Norway	13 966
7	Sweden	13 529
8	US	12 763
9	Canada	11 824
10	Australia	11 597
11	Denmark	11 348
12	FRG	11 097
13	France	10 602
14	Luxembourg	10 587
15	Finland	10 277
16	Iceland	10 260
17	Austria	10 185
18	Netherlands	9936
19	Belgium	9701
20	Japan	9670
21	UK	8982

SOURCES: *United Nations Statistical Yearbook, 1982* (New York: United Nations, various years). *United Nations Statistical Pocketbook/Second Edition: World Statistics in Brief* (New York: United Nations, 1977).

an obvious target for defence cuts: as with decolonisation, it was a matter of trimming involvement to match capability.

But if cost was the major reason underlying the *policy decision* to withdraw from east of Suez, there was another important *structural* factor which also operated to encourage the retreat from empire. This concerned the changing pattern of Britain's international trade, and in particular the changing pattern of its export markets. The essence of the change was that while the second wave decolonisations were actually taking place – and immediately prior to the withdrawal from east of Suez – Britain's vitally important export trade was experiencing a dramatic shift away from the Empire 'circle' and towards western Europe and the United States. To be sure, as Table 4.3 shows, exports to the Overseas Sterling Area (OSA) countries of the Empire and Commonwealth increased between 1955 and 1965. However, while exports to the OSA increased by £403m, total exports to Western Europe and North America – from a lower base – increased by the much larger figure of £1390m. As Table 4.4 indicates, between 1955 and 1965 the share positions of the two groupings were almost exactly reversed: the OSA share of total exports *fell* from half to a third while the Europe/United States share *rose* from a third to half over the same period. (As Table 4.4 also indicates, this trend was to continue right through to the mid-1980s.)

Now, of course, it is extremely difficult to establish that these shifting trade patterns were in any sense a 'cause' of imperial withdrawal. It is entirely possible, for example, that the relaxation of imperial control associated with the second-wave decolonisations had the effect of 'losing' British export markets to foreign competition. However, even if the relative decline in imperial trade can be thus explained away as a consequence of decolonisation, it is less clear why imperial withdrawal should have so radically stimulated Britain's export trade with Europe

Table 4.3 **British exports to selected areas, 1955–65 (£m)**

	1955	1965	Change 1955–65	
African and Caribbean	57	235	+ 178	total change
Old Commonwealth	731	866	+ 135	in OSA
India/Pakistan/Ceylon	188	183	− 5	exports
Malaysia/Singapore/Hong Kong	99	159	+ 60	+ 403
Gulf States	0	35	+ 35	
Western Europe + USA	993	2383	+ 1390	

SOURCE: *Annual Abstract of Statistics* (HMSO, various years).

Table 4.4   Percentage of British exports destined for selected areas, 1955–84

	1955	1965	1975	1984
Exports to W. Europe ⏐ USA as % total exports	34.2	50.5	56.3	70.5
Exports to OSA as % total exports	49.2	34.8	22.3	13.2

SOURCE: *Annual Abstract·of Statistics* (HMSO, various years).

and North America. It was not the decision to decolonise which accelerated Britain's export trade with Europe and the United States. Rather, it was the changing consumption patterns in those advanced economies which autonomously increased the demand for British goods and services. The reason for this was simple. The economies with the fastest growing market potential in the 1950s and 1960s were those of the rich industrialised world. As a result, British exporters increasingly found it easier to sell their goods and services in Europe and the United States rather than in the generally poorer economies of the Empire and Commonwealth. Crucially, the focus of Britain's *economic* activity was shifting away from the Empire and towards Europe: as a result of the aggregate effect of innumerable individual business decisions in Europe and the United States, trade with the empire circle was becoming progressively less important to the British economy. In these circumstances, it was only a matter of time before the British government's *political* commitments followed the same path: if Britain's material–economic interests were shifting autonomously towards Europe, then in classic *realpolitik* fashion its military–strategic commitment was sure to follow. Viewed in this light, the political downgrading of the Empire 'circle' associated with both the second wave decolonisations and the withdrawal from east of Suez was simply the policy response to deep-seated economic forces which were already operating inside the rich western economies and which were drawing the locus of Britain's trading activity away from its imperial roots.

In addition to Britain's long-term economic decline, then, the two major factors that led to the withdrawal from east of Suez were also primarily economic: (1) the need to cut the size of the overseas defence budget; and (2) the changing pattern of Britain's export trade. But if these underlying preconditions made an eventual withdrawal from east of Suez inevitable, the *timing* of the decision to withdraw was also shaped by a number of shorter-term – mainly *political* – factors. First, while Britain was supporting Malaysia in its border dispute with Indonesia between 1963 and 1966, a strategic withdrawal from east of Suez was unthinkable; however, once the local participants had settled their differences, as they did in August 1966, the constraint was clearly removed. A second short-term factor was the endemic sterling crisis which plagued the Wilson government between 1966 and 1968 and which created enormous pressure for cuts in public spending. Given Britain's declining international economic position and the recent discarding of its imperial possessions, defence expenditure was an obvious target for cuts. Decolonisation had enormously diminished Britain's world role: why not now take the process to its logical conclusion by terminating a military commitment which had originally arisen primarily as a means of protecting an Empire that had now disappeared? The final short-term factor was the fact that a Labour government was now in power. Although the Conservatives had presided over much of the process of decolonisation, a Conservative government would also have been sorely tempted to retain a presence east of Suez both to preserve the appearance of a continued British 'world role' and to appease the influential Tory right wing. A Labour government was far less likely to experience internal party dissent as a result of a decision to end a military commitment which had outlived its political and economic usefulness. It was consequently far better placed to carry through a policy that squarely faced up to economic realities by offering a symbolic affirmation of the fact that Britain no longer had pretensions to an imperial role. The question that remained, of course, was how far Britain – in the wake of decolonisation and the withdrawal from east of Suez – would continue to act as an 'imperialist' power. Had the retreat from Empire really meant an end to Britain's 'world role'? Or would imperial domination and exploitation simply be continued with a mixture of other means. It is these questions which are addressed in the next section.

After 1968: imperialism without colonies?

In the late 1960s, it became fashionable among writers of the 'new left' to argue that, in spite of the widespread decolonisations which had taken place over the previous 20 years, imperialism – even without colonies – was still rampant.[28] The main target of this critical onslaught was the United States which, as the leading capitalist state of the postwar era, was portrayed as having taken over from the western European powers as the exploiter-, manipulator-, and dominator-in-chief of the underdeveloped third world. The United States was not only alleged to extract an immense economic surplus from the countries that it dominated. It was also considered to maintain that domination by preserving those countries' economic underdevelopment and by the ruthless, if often subtle, manipulation of their governments. These criticisms were not focused exclusively upon the United States, ho vever. In principle, most of the arguments that were adduced about United States dealings with the periphery could also be applied to any rich country which had extensive political and economic ties with the third world. In these circumstances it is appropriate to ask whether there was anything that Britain did – or failed to do – in the period after 1968 that could reasonably be construed as the actions of a neo-imperialist power. The ensuing discussion attempts to answer this question in two ways: first, by examining Britain's major *political* entanglements in the old Empire 'circle'; and second by assessing Britain's *economic* record towards the third world in general. The overall verdict is that in political terms Britain's performance since 1968 has been relatively benign, continuing the process of imperial retreat which began in 1947; in economic terms its sins – like those of the rest of the prosperous North – have been largely ones of omission rather than commission.

Political entanglements in the Empire circle after 1968

Not long after the decision to withdraw from east of Suez had been publicly confirmed, a serious blow was dealt to British interests in the Mediterranean. The Libyan monarchy, which since 1956 had increasingly been regarded as Britain's major ally in the Near East,[29] was ousted in a *coup* which brought to power Colonel Muhamoor Qadafi, champion of Arab nationalism and ardent anti-imperialist. British interests were almost certain to be damaged by the change in regime, as indeed they were in January 1972 when Libya dissolved its alliance with Britain, and again, in September 1973, when all foreign-owned companies were nationalised.[30] However, the Heath government responded with commendable circumspection. There was no question of a repetition of the sort of crass intervention which had produced such calamitous results at Suez. With some justification, Britain was unwilling to confront the international opprobrium which would undoubtedly have greeted any attempt to intervene in the internal affairs of a sovereign nation-state: as a result, the opportunity to engage in yet another piece of modern-day gunboat diplomacy was firmly rejected.

A similarly responsible reaction greeted Idi Amin's *coup* against

Milton Obote's government in Uganda in January 1971. Although it was rumoured at the time that Amin's actions had the blessing of the Foreign and Commonwealth Office (FCO)[31] because of Obote's recent shift to more radical domestic and foreign policies, there is no evidence whatsoever that the British government had any part in either the planning or the execution of the *coup*. On the contrary, Britain certainly did not benefit from it. It seems far more likely that London's policy from the outset was designed to avoid any British involvement in the internal conflicts of an ex-colony. This was certainly the position that had been adopted with regard to the *coups* in Nigeria and Ghana in 1966 and with regard to the Nigerian Civil War of 1967–70. It was a policy which was also to be adhered to as further *coups* afflicted West Africa after 1970.[32] As with Libya, in all these cases the British government's awareness of its own physical inability to impose a military solution – as well as the strongly antipathetic international reaction which intervention would have invoked – counselled a policy of caution. It was better to do nothing and risk a gradual loss of influence and investments than to embark on a vainglorious campaign to restore pro-British regimes which could only survive with continued – and substantial – military support. This was classic *realpolitik* calculation on the part of the British government, but in the straightened economic circumstances of the time it implied post-imperial *non*-involvement rather than further efforts at colonial subjugation.

Throughout 1971, as the date for the final withdrawal from east of Suez approached (and as promised in the 1968 Defence Review), the Heath government negotiated a series of defensive and quasi-defensive treaties with the countries from which British forces were to be removed. Between August and December 1971, a series of Friendship Treaties were signed with the Gulf States which variously provided for the future stationing of British forces in the Gulf in certain circumstances.[33] However the newly unobtrusive nature of Britain's post-imperial involvement in the third world was best expressed in the agreements which Britain signed separately with Singapore and Malaysia in December 1971. Intended as a direct substitute for Britain's hitherto intimate involvement in the defence of the region, the texts of these agreements revealed clearly that it was the governments of Malaysia and Singapore which would dictate the terms and conditions of any future British involvement in their defence. The United Kingdom–Malaysia Exchange of Notes, for example, asserted that the *Malaysian government '. . . may* after mutual consultation *permit a UK force to be stationed or present in Malaysia* upon agreed terms [emphasis added].[34] It was also made clear that all future rights and facilities accorded to British forces would have to be agreed with the Malaysian government.[35] As far as the British government was concerned, these residual commitments were in no sense a surreptitious vehicle for the maintenance of indirect imperial domination. On the contrary, they were simply assurances that London felt obliged to make in order to avoid leaving friendly governments cruelly exposed should their security be threatened by some nearby regional conflict (such as the war in Indochina, which was then raging).

But if a relatively benign view can be taken of the arrangements that Britain made for the protection of its allies after its withdrawal from east of Suez, rather more cynicism is in order with regard to the Diego Garcia Agreement which Britain reached with the United States in October 1972. The British evacuation of both Singapore and Aden had not only signalled Britain's unpreparedness to provide strong material support for the United States in its global efforts to defend the strategic interests of the West. It had also left the Indian Ocean exposed to Soviet infiltration. With the radicalisation of the People's Republic of South Yemen after 1968, Soviet warships had begun, by the early 1970s, to use the port facilities which the British had vacated in Aden. In addition, Siad Barré's *coup* in Somalia in 1969 had led to a Soviet–Somali Friendship Treaty which in turn had given the Soviet navy access to the deep-water facilities at Mogadishu. The combined effect of these changes was a significant increase in Soviet naval activity in the Indian Ocean, a development which was construed, rightly or wrongly, by strategic planners in London and Washington as a threat to Western shipping. The British response was swift. Having already granted limited port facilities to the United States Navy on the strategically placed Indian Ocean island of Diego Garcia in 1966,[36] London decided that, if the Royal Navy was no longer able to police the Indian Ocean, Britain should at least provide the Americans with the means to do the job properly. As a result of the 1972 Agreement (which was reinforced by a subsequent Exchange of Notes in February 1976)[37] the United States was given a virtual *carte blanche* to fortify and enhance the facilities of the Diego Garcia base as it wished. This may not have been overt neo-imperialism on the part of the British government, but it was certainly yet another example of *realpolitik* calculation intended to maximise the strategic interests of the West rather than the interests of a subject population over which Britain still exercised sovereignty.

Meanwhile, in Southern Africa, the Rhodesian crisis slowly rumbled on throughout the 1970s. As the decolonising power that had so far failed to decolonise properly, Britain had residual responsibilities towards Rhodesia which it exercised after 1965 by supporting the diplomatic isolation of the Smith government and by orchestrating an international campaign of economic sanctions against the rebel regime. Given the fairly sophisticated sanctions-breaking operation which, with South African assistance, was subsequently put into effect, it is unclear how far British policy was actually responsible for the downfall of the Smith regime. None the less, as noted earlier, as the armed struggle of the black nationalist movement reached its climax in the late 1970s, London returned much more directly to the fray by organising the Lancaster House Conference which, in January 1980, established a framework for a peaceful transition to formal independence and majority rule. In strictly legal terms, Britain's actions in 1980 were those of an imperial power. Realistically, however, the government possessed no practical capability to influence events on the ground: Lord Carrington's skilful diplomacy merely provided a suitable environment in which black and white Zimbabwean leaders could agree to resolve some of their more significant differences. This was certainly not imperialism in any malign sense: it was simply Britain undertaking a minor role on the world stage which, in virtue of its imperial past, it was uniquely qualified to perform.

With Zimbabwe independent, it seemed as though virtually all of Britain's overt imperial responsibilities had been discharged. In future – with luck – Britain's imperial role would be limited either to the sort of occasional minor policing operation that had been undertaken so successfully in Anguilla or to providing training assistance for the armed forces of ex-colonies which specifically requested British advice.[38] However such calculations reckoned without the Falklands affair of 1982. Britain had occupied the Falkland Islands since 1828. Throughout the ensuing period, successive Argentine governments had claimed sovereignty over the islands but had taken no overt military action to reclaim them, a result principally of Britain's obvious determination to retain control over what had always been regarded as an important strategic base. The 1981 Defence White Paper, however, had announced significant cuts in the size of Britain's surface fleet.[39] One consequence of these cuts was the withdrawal in November 1981 of the only remaining Royal Navy frigate to have been permanently stationed in Port Stanley. This action was clearly viewed in Buenos Aires as an indication of Britain's weakening commitment to maintaining a presence in the South Atlantic. With negotiations over the possession of the islands deadlocked, General Galtieri's government decided to wrest control of them by a *fait accompli*.

The Argentine invasion of March–April 1982 had not, however, anticipated the reaction of the Thatcher Cabinet which immediately began preparations for the repossession of the islands. Three factors were crucial to Thatcher's position. First, after 150 years of continuous occupation, Britain had a strong claim to ownership of the islands under international law. Second, as an attack on a British colony, the invasion was a direct challenge to British sovereignty which could not go unpunished. And third, the vast majority of the islands' 1800 inhabitants fervently wished to remain under the British Crown.[40] As a result of an outstanding military campaign, by October 1982 British forces had regained control of the islands and British sovereignty had been restored. At the considerable expense of the British taxpayer, a substantial garrison and naval contingent were permanently stationed in and around the islands thereafter.[41] This continuing military presence not only acted as a deterrent to further Argentine aggression but also represented an unequivocal public affirmation of Britain's intention to carry out its remaining imperial responsibilities to the full even if the scope of its Empire had been radically compressed since decolonisation.

Yet, in spite of the scale and the determination of the British response to the Argentine intervention, the Falklands episode was nothing more than a temporary reversal of the long process of imperial retreat. While, after 1982, the chances of a British withdrawal from the Falkland Islands were now remote, it was equally unlikely that the British government would seriously consider embarking on a similar venture of (post)-imperial self-assertion elsewhere in the world. Quite apart from the fact that there were now so few colonial dependencies left, there were two main reasons why this should have been so. First, given that by the mid-1980s the British government was already spending some £250m per annum in defence of the Falklands, an *additional* commitment of a similar magnitude would have seriously prejudiced the quality of Britain's top-priority military commitment: the defence of Western Europe. Second, the decision to send the task force to repossess the Falklands was based on a Realist assessment of international circumstances that were themselves unlikely to be repeated in the foreseeable future. Although much of the third world was opposed to the British government's policy, the United States (after four weeks of attempted mediation between London and Buenos Aires) and the European Community countries provided firm backing for Thatcher's stance. The Soviet Union, for its part, though it was prepared to express its verbal condemnation of the British military action and to conspire in the mobilisation of diplomatic support for Argentina, could not be seen to provide material assistance to one of the most odious right-wing military governments in Latin America.

Thus, deprived of potential support from powerful allies, Argentina was from the outset a relatively weak opponent whose military campaign could be effectively stifled through the intelligent use of the Royal Navy's superior sea-power. Crucially, given that such a fortuitous combination of strategic and diplomatic circumstances was unlikely to recur, the resurgent imperialism which characterised Britain's Falklands War was clearly an ephemeral historical aberration. Rather than presaging a renewed attempt to restore Britain to its world role, the Falklands campaign merely represented the last gasp of imperialism in retreat.

That the heyday of perfidious Albion was long gone was confirmed in Britain's negotiations with the People's Republic of China over the future of Hong Kong between 1983 and 1985. Although the size of the Hong Kong garrison had been reduced at the time of the withdrawal from east of Suez, a continued presence had been maintained there after 1971. This was partly to accord with the wishes of the indigenous population and partly because to have withdrawn in the immediate aftermath of the Cultural Revolution might have been construed in Beijing as an invitation to intervene. With the gradual softening of China's position towards the West during the 1970s, the prospects for a negotiated settlement over the future of the colony increased. Yet in the early 1980s there was still reason to suppose that such a settlement would prove elusive. Britain had consistently been unprepared to concede sovereignty to Argentina over the Falklands question: why should it behave any differently towards China over Hong Kong? The two situations, after all, were in many respects similar. In both cases, the territory had been acquired by military force over 100 years before; the adjacent power had a longstanding – though contentious – legal claim to possession of the territory; and the indigenous population, apparently, wished to remain under the Crown in order to avoid being dominated by a much larger neighbour. Yet where Britain had refused as a matter of principle to make concessions to Argentina, by December 1984 it had formally agreed to a complete withdrawal from Hong Kong by 1997, after which date – with certain safeguards – the territory would revert to the People's Republic.[42]

The reason for these very different approaches to two similar problems was in fact very simple: *realpolitik*. Whereas Britain could have reasonably expected to resist any Argentine threat to the Falklands, it would have been powerless to resist had Communist China chosen to take Hong Kong by force. In the wake of the Falklands War, the agreement on Hong Kong represented a rapid reversion to the long-term pattern of gradual imperial withdrawal that had first found expression in the decolonisation of India. As always, even if diplomacy had been important in determining the timing and the conditions of withdrawal, at the root of the withdrawal itself were the ubiquitous forces of Realist calculation: with Britain's military capability in progressive relative decline, a major diplomatic concession on Hong Kong had always been inevitable.

To summarise, then, Britain's political actions in the Empire 'circle' after 1968 – with the notable exception of the Falklands War – were those of an imperial power in continuous retreat. To be sure, as the process of withdrawal proceeded, prudence demanded that help be given to old friends. But it was help generally given on terms determined by the recipients; and when British assistance was firmly rejected, as in Libya after 1969, the rejection was accepted in London with good grace. As in the Macmillan years, frantic efforts to subvert the forces that were pressing for further imperial withdrawals were studiously avoided. But if responsibility, admittedly inspired by Realism, reigned almost supreme in the political sphere, what of Britain's *economic* activities in the Empire 'circle'?

Post-imperialism: the economic record after 1968

It has become almost an axiom of modern Marxist political economy that formal decolonisation made no difference to the economic exploitation of the third world. In spite of the relaxation of formal political control that occurred in the 1960s, the forces of international capital, using the rich 'Northern' capitalist states as their instrument, continued to extract a large 'economic surplus' from the impoverished 'South'.[43] According to this view, in the economic sphere the British government did not need to take any specific action after 1968 in order to continue to be 'imperialistic'. Simply by participating in the existing international division of labour – by maintaining the exploitation of the 'South' – the British government laid itself open to the charge of 'imperialism without colonies'.

What evidence is there – if any – to support this characterisation? Consider, first, Britain's reaction to international attempts after 1970 to change the global economic order. In this context, Britain's record has not been distinguished, but it has certainly been no worse than that of the other major 'Northern' powers. First, Britain participated in the United Nations Conference on Trade and Development (UNCTAD) meetings of the 1970s which sought to secure a New International Economic Order (NIEO) that would herald a 'fairer' deal for the underdeveloped economies of the South.[44] Along with the rest of the

Organisation for Economic Co-operation and Development (OECD) governments, however, Britain refused to make any real concessions to southern demands. Second, in the late 1970s Britain combined with other rich industrialised nations to establish a series of *commodity funds* that were intended to stabilise the export earnings of third-world countries which were dependent on the production of a limited number of primary commodities.[45] However, given that it was higher – as opposed to stable – export earnings which were required, these schemes did little to ameliorate the problems of their supposed beneficiaries. And third, in partnership with the other members of the European Community, Britain was also a party to the Lomé Conventions of 1975, 1979 and 1985. These conventions sought to provide the African, Caribbean and Pacific (ACP) group of countries[46] with easier access to European markets for most of their exports, a greater degree of export price stability than they had hitherto enjoyed and additional aid. Unfortunately the evidence is mixed as to whether the concessions made under successive Lomé conventions did anything substantial to ease the chronic economic problems of many of the ACP.[47] Crucially, like UNCTAD and the commodity funds before it, the Lomé process did little to alter the global distribution of economic power which remained heavily weighted in favour of the North. The countries of the South, frequently burdened in the 1980s by debt repayments almost as large as their export revenues, were still consigned to a position of dependence and impoverishment which laid them wide open to continued Northern exploitation: to economic imperialism. Through their concerted inaction, Northern governments passively maintained an international economic system which systematically operated to the detriment of the South.[48]

But if the North committed sins of omission by its failure to change the international economic order, what specific evidence is there that *Britain* continued to extract an 'economic surplus' either from the third world in general or, more particularly, from the territories that were formerly under its direct colonial control? Given the large volume of writing on the relationship between Northern affluence and Southern poverty, it is somewhat surprising to discover that there is in fact little hard evidence to show that Britain – or for that matter any other rich country – does indeed 'exploit' the third world. While British companies certainly extract profits from their operations in the South, for example, it is also the case that they can only do so once they have brought desperately needed investment funds to the 'host' economy. Moreover, contrary to what is often claimed by critics of Western neo-imperialism, the notion that the level of repatriated profit exceeds the extra income which is generated by the investment activities of foreign corporations still awaits firm empirical corroboration.[49] The fact that most third-world governments, notwithstanding their awareness of the potentially exploitative behaviour of multinational corporations, continue to welcome foreign capital suggests that they at least must believe that the domestic benefits of foreign investment outweigh the costs incurred as a result of profit repatriation.[50]

A similar problem of lack of evidence is encountered in relation to *trade*. Critical observers of North–South relations feel instinctively that the North benefits disproportionately from its trade with the South; that the terms of trade favour the former at the expense of the latter. However, while it is possible to show that the third world's overall terms of trade did become less favourable during the 1980s,[51] it is extremely difficult to demonstrate that the North extracts a measurable economic surplus simply by trading with the South. The core of the problem is that, if Southern countries derived no benefit from exporting their products to the North, they would presumably cease trading altogether: the fact that they do not implies that trade must be to some degree mutually beneficial. The question as to whether the North benefits 'more' than the South – to an 'exploitative' degree – in these circumstances essentially involves a normative judgement that is not susceptible to empirical corroboration.

This failure to demonstrate that trade of itself involves the extraction of an economic surplus does not mean, however, that those trade statistics which are available are entirely irrelevant to the question of Britain's possible post-colonial 'imperialism'. On the contrary, even if it is assumed that any North–South trade does involve the extraction of an economic surplus from the South, the available evidence suggests that since decolonisation Britain has, in relative terms, extracted substantially less of an economic surplus than it did previously. As Table 4.5 shows, in the mid-1950s all of the countries in the Empire 'circle' sent a significant proportion of their exports (average: 28.5 per cent) *to* Britain and received a significant proportion of their imports *from* Britain (average: 35.2 per cent). By the mid-1980s the position had altered considerably with corresponding figures of 6.9 per cent and 9.4 per cent respectively. This diminution in British economic dominance was clearly not an *intended* consequence of the government's post-colonial foreign policy. (Successive governments would obviously have preferred British companies to have retained those markets which, after decolonisation, were increasingly opened to foreign competition.) None the less, the failure to maintain market share has meant that protagonists of the benevolence of Britain's post-imperial role can

Table 4.5 Britain's declining importance in the trade of ex-Empire countries: imports from and exports to Britain (ex-colonial 3rd world states) 1955–84

	1955		1984*	
	Imports from UK as % of all imports	Exports to UK as % of all exports	Imports from UK as % of all imports	Exports to UK as % of all exports
Barbados	40.0	41.5	7.4	6.9
Kenya	43.6	27.4	14.1	18.3
British Guiana (Guyana)	47.3	35.5	15.9	25.8
British Honduras (Belize)	35.2	n.a.	15.8	21.9 (1980)
British Somalia (Somalia)	25.7	1.8	29.0	0 (1981)
Burma	25.4	8.3	0	0
Ceylon (Sri Lanka)	21.0	26.7	4.9	5.9
Cyprus	50.0	26.8	11.3	17.0
Gambia	54.5	53.7		
Ghana	47.1	34.8	16.1	11.1 (1981)
Hong Kong	11.8	9.9	3.9	5.2
India	25.4	27.8	5.7	4.7
Jamaica	40.0	50.0	5.7	12.7
Jordan	15.7	0	6.9	0
Malaya (Malaysia)	18.0	18.3	3.5	2.7 (1983)
Singapore			2.6	2.7
Nigeria	46.3	69.7	18.5	1.2
Pakistan	28.1	15.2	6.5	6.2
Bangladesh	—	—	3.7	5.8
Zambia (N. Rhodesia + Nyasaland)	42.7	n.a.	12.9	6.6 (1982)
Sierra Leone	59.6	70.7	11.4	11.7
Sudan	30.1	27.9	11.6	0 (1983)
Trinidad	38.0	39.2	11.5	3.5 (1983)
South Africa	34.5	30.8	11.1	4.3
Zimbabwe (S. Rhodesia)	42.7	n.a.	11.5	11.4 (1983)
Uganda	43.6	27.4	n.a.	n.a.
Tanzania (Tanganyika)	43.6	27.4	n.a.	n.a.
Egypt	13.1	5.7	4.4	0 (1982)
Iraq	27.8	14.1	0	0
Libya	25.1	19.1	8.0	0
Average	35.7	28.5	9.4	6.9

*Except where stated.   n.a. = not available.
SOURCE: *United Nations Yearbook of International Trade Statistics* (New York: United Nations, various years).

reasonably claim that decolonisation was followed by a reduction in British economic domination within the Empire 'circle'. Even if trade with the third world necessarily implies the extraction of an economic surplus from it (and there are good reasons, identified above, for doubting whether it does) Britain was a much less serious offender in the 1980s than it had been in the 1950s. Ironically, Britain's relative decline as a world trading power – the result of its own inefficiency – meant that charges of a continuing neo-imperial role after decolonisation were increasingly ill-founded.

Where does this leave us? Was Britain's more benign political approach to the Empire 'circle' after 1968 matched by a concomitant reduction in the extent of its economic imperialism? Unless the orthodox Leninist line is taken – that all advanced capitalist states are *by definition* imperialist – the answer must be equivocal. In terms of its failure to press for a 'fairer' deal for the South – for a NIEO – Britain could be adjudged to be passively imperialist: its inactivity helped to maintain an international economic system which appears to sustain the economic underdevelopment of the South. Yet in terms of the crucial indicator of neo-imperialism – the extraction of an economic surplus from the 'periphery' – the evidence is both sparse and indecisive. On the one hand, there is no systematic evidence whatsoever that the economic surplus which accrues to Britain as a result of repatriated profit exceeds the economic surplus which accrues to the third world as a result of British investment. On the other hand, the available information on trade flows suggests that since decolonisation Britain's economic dominion over the Empire 'circle' has significantly diminished. This weakening dominion is likely to continue in the future; the plausibility of claims that Britain remains a neo-imperialist power is likely to decline with it.

Summary and conclusions

The story of the Empire 'circle' after 1956 was fundamentally one of withdrawal. As the Empire simultaneously became both less manageable and less crucial to the preservation of Britain's vital interests, so London relaxed its imperial grip and progressively abandoned the 'world role' which Britain had played for almost two centuries. The major step in the process of imperial retreat was obviously the 'second wave' decolonisations which took place between 1956 and 1966. The withdrawal from east of Suez in 1971 represented the British government's symbolic affirmation that the retreat was to be both comprehensive and irreversible.

Yet in spite of the seemingly inexorable nature of the forces which provoked this 'retreat from power', successive governments from the late 1950s onwards had good reason to hesitate. Their main fear was that British withdrawal, in addition to bruising innumerable egos in both Cabinet and Whitehall, would leave a power vacuum in the third world which the Soviet Union, either directly or indirectly, would be only too happy to fill. In the colonial territories themselves the dilemma was resolved (if only temporarily, given later developments) by installing friendly governments and liberal democratic constitutions before independence and by making *ad hoc* defence arrangements with the newly-independent nations on request. In the strategically important Indian Ocean – vacated by the Royal Navy after the withdrawal from east of Suez – the solution was to provide the United States with facilities at Diego Garcia that would enable it to replace Britain as the guardian of Western strategic interests in the region. Despite the occasional set-back, the strategy was in general fairly successful: Soviet influence in Britain's ex-colonies remained limited and the American naval presence in the Indian Ocean effectively counterbalanced any threat which the Soviet navy might pose to western shipping.

But why had the withdrawal itself been necessary? The *decisions* over both decolonisation and the withdrawal from Suez were undoubtedly based on classic *realpolitik* cost–benefit calculation. On the one hand, Britain increasingly lacked the military capability to contain the growing demands for independence inside the colonies. On the other, the focus of Britain's material economic interests was shifting away from the Empire and towards Europe. If the potential communist threat resulting from a British military and political withdrawal could be effectively neutralised – which, as we have seen, was possible in principle – then the obvious solution was to reduce Britain's overseas commitment to a level commensurate with its remaining capabilities: better to do less effectively than to attempt more and fail ignominiously.

However, to assert that the decision to opt for a strategy of imperial withdrawal was based on Realist criteria does not explain why the particular circumstances arose that made such a decision necessary. It has been argued in this chapter that, in addition to Britain's long-term relative economic decline, two principal 'structural' forces were responsible for the 'emptying out' of the Empire circle.[52] The first of these was the increase in indigenous nationalism which arose from the economic development of the colonies. The acceleration in world economic growth that occurred in the postwar years created economic and social conditions throughout the colonial world in which nationalism could thrive. Rapid urbanisation and the move away from subsistence agriculture combined to produce a major social upheaval which rendered almost all of Britain's colonial peoples much more susceptible to the appeal of anti-imperialist ideologies. As a result, nationalist movements throughout the Empire – with their views clearly articulated by a new postwar generation of third-world intellectuals – found increasing support. It was this indigenous nationalist pressure which constituted Macmillan's 'wind of change': a force for imperial retreat that could not be sensibly resisted.

The second major 'structural' factor underlying the withdrawal from the Empire circle was the apparently autonomous change in the pattern of Britain's external trade which occurred from the mid-1950s onwards. Between 1955 and 1965 – *before* the end of the Sterling Area and *before* Britain's entry into Europe – the Empire circle declined significantly as a destination for British exports. This was almost certainly not a result of any policy decisions taken by the British government. It was simply a reflection of the fact that European and North American consumers expanded their demand for the sort of goods and services that British business was increasingly willing and able to supply. The main consequence of this secular change was that Britain's economic ties with the Empire circle became progressively less important for the health of the domestic economy: here was a powerful economic force which could only serve to reinforce the existing political pressures for an imperial withdrawal.

After the withdrawal from east of Suez in 1971, the retreat from Empire continued. In the political sphere, this principally involved the granting of independence to most of the remaining smaller colonies and resisting the residual temptation to intervene in those parts of the third world where indigenous regime changes threatened to damage British commercial or strategic interests. It also meant playing a diplomatic role in the formal decolonisation of Zimbabwe in 1980 and in the 1984 agreement to return Hong Kong to the People's Republic of China by the end of the century. The only major departure from this long-term trend was the Falklands crisis of 1982 which led to a powerful reassertion of Britain's commitment to the defence of the islands. However, in spite of the fact that this particular commitment seemed destined to continue for the foreseeable future, the Falklands episode was likely to remain an isolated exception to the general rule: that Britain had indeed retreated from its world role and that it no longer possessed the capability to sustain it.

Even in the economic sphere, British imperialism continued to retreat. From the mid-1950s onwards, largely as a result of increased competition from other industrialised countries, Britain found its share of Empire circle markets in serious decline. Indeed, by the mid-1980s, Britain's economic dominance in the third world had declined to such an extent that accusations of a specifically British neo-imperialism seemed misdirected. The only sense in which Britain might have been deemed to participate in the continuing imperialistic exploitation of the third world was as one of the large group of rich Northern powers which exercised a generalised dominion over the world economy; but even in these circumstances there was no compelling evidence to demonstrate that Britain actually extracted a disproportionate economic surplus from its dealings with the South. By the mid-1980s, British imperialism – both political and economic – was very largely a thing of the past: most of the action was concentrated in Europe.

5

The Search for a New Role: The European Circle after 1956

As noted in earlier chapters, throughout the postwar period successive British governments found it increasingly difficult, in the face of Britain's long-term relative economic decline, to sustain the strategy of maintaining British influence in all three of Churchill's 'circles'. In Chapter 4 it was suggested that, from the mid-1950s onwards, partly as a result of indigenous nationalism and partly because of the diminishing importance of Britain's imperial trade, Britain's involvement in the Empire circle was gradually reduced. As will be seen in Chapter 6, by the 1960s, with the process of decolonisation well under way, Britain was also becoming less important to the United States as a strategic ally in the global struggle against 'communist expansionism'. The obvious corollary to this reduction of influence in both the 'Empire' and 'Atlantic' circles was for the focus of Britain's foreign policy to shift towards Europe. It was increasingly recognised in the years after Suez that it was here that Britain's primary economic and political interests were located; that if Britain wished to retain a significant voice in world affairs, then it would have to do so in concert with its allies in Western Europe. The strategic shift towards Europe was not accomplished without difficulty, however. Significant problems were encountered in the 1960s as Britain attempted to institutionalise its European connections. And even after Britain finally 'joined Europe' in 1973, its residual commitments and responsibilities in both the Empire and Atlantic circles frequently served to reinforce the widely-held impression that the British were fundamentally 'reluctant Europeans', only partially committed to the ideals of European co-operation that the original six members of the EEC had so strongly – and productively – embraced.

This chapter begins with a review of Britain's increasing involvement in the European circle in the period up to 1972. It briefly examines Britain's failure to participate in the early efforts at European economic co-operation in the 1950s and then describes both its abortive attempts to join the EEC in the 1960s and its successful accession to the Community in 1973. The first section also assesses Britain's developing relations with *Eastern* Europe, which from 1956 were an important complement to its closer economic and political ties with Western Europe. The second section seeks to identify the principal causal factors that lay behind the strategic shift towards Europe. At the decision-making level, the crucial factor was the apparent benefit which it was believed EEC membership would bestow upon the British economy; at the structural level, the major causal influence was the autonomous shift in the pattern of Britain's external trade – away from the Empire and towards Europe – that was observed in Chapter 4. Finally Britain's evolving relations with Europe in the period after 1973 are examined. As will be seen, notwithstanding the continued recalcitrance of British policy in European budgetary matters, by the late 1980s Britain had shed at least a part of its 'reluctant European' image and – with reservations – joined with other Community members in their efforts to achieve some degree of foreign policy co-ordination in certain limited policy areas. There was very little evidence, however, to suggest that a common European foreign policy was anything but an extremely remote possibility.

Increasing involvement in the European circle, 1956–72

As observed in Chapter 2, in 1945 Britain's position as the dominant power in Western Europe provided it with the capability to play a determining role in the political and economic evolution of the entire region. Yet, in spite of American efforts to persuade London to take a leading role in establishing a new European co-operative political order, the Attlee government demurred. Although Bevin was actively involved in the formation of the Council of Europe in May 1948,[1] the Council itself never became anything more than a 'talking shop' in which European foreign ministers (in the 'Committee of Ministers') and Parliamentarians (in the Council's 'Assembly') could exchange views on matters of current concern. Jealously guarding the principle of national sovereignty, the British and Scandinavian delegations insisted from the outset that the Committee of Ministers should play the primary role in the Council's activities. This in turn prevented the

Assembly from developing any sort of authority, thereby dashing the hopes of contemporary European 'federalists' who had hoped that the Council as a whole – but especially the Assembly – might provide the basis for an embryonic European federation analogous to the model developed in the late eighteenth century in the United States.[2]

The response of European internationalists to the limitations of the Council of Europe was to develop the idea of *functionalist integration.* Federalist internationalism had foundered because of the refusal of national governments to cede any part of their sovereignty to the would-be federal body. The central principle of functionalism was that the process of economic and political integration in Western Europe could be started without the need for an open-ended commitment on the part of national governments to transfer decision-making power to some supranational institution. On the contrary, the integrative process could be started by achieving functional co-operation in a limited number of narrowly-defined areas of economic activity. Once the benefits of such functional co-operation became evident, there would be pressure to extend it elsewhere: functional collaboration in one sector would 'spillover' into others.[3] In short, greater political and economic integration – which was impossible to achieve in the short run because of the continuing commitment of national governments to the preservation of their own sovereignty – would be achieved by 'stealth' over a period of time.

The French-sponsored Schuman Plan of 1950 was very much a reflection of this new functionalist logic and in January 1952 it resulted in the creation of the European Coal and Steel Community (ECSC). Under the terms of the enabling legislation, the constituent members of the Community[4] delegated a large measure of decision-making power to the 'High Authority'. This meant that the High Authority was from the outset a genuinely supranational body which did not require the unanimous consent of member governments for its actions: it was thus able to develop a common policy for the coal and steel industries of the member countries on the basis of *majority* decisions. However, the British coal and steel industries remained outside the High Authority's purview. Fearful of the damage that membership of the ECSC might inflict on Britain's Empire circle trade, London was still unprepared to accept any diminution of its sovereignty even in so specific a policy area: British involvement was accordingly limited to an agreement in December 1954 which regularised Anglo-ECSC relations.[5]

Even without British participation, however, the ECSC flourished. Indeed it was such a success that at a summit meeting in Messina in June 1955 the member governments decided to act upon the 'spill-over' principle and extend their collaboration by forming the European Economic Community (EEC) and the European Atomic Community (EURATOM). The Treaty of Rome of March 1957 duly established that these two additional 'functionalist' institutions would be created in January 1958. The three main aims of the EEC were (1) the elimination of intra-community trade barriers; (2) free mobility for capital and for labour; and (3) a common external tariff. As with the ECSC, however, the British government expressed no desire to join the new venture. There were two principal – and related – reasons for this lack of interest. First, in the mid-1950s Britain had yet to experience the autonomous shift in the balance of its external trade – away from the Empire circle and towards Europe – which was to become so evident over the next decade.[6] Second, while the British government would probably have been happy to accept both the abolition of internal tariffs and the free mobility of capital and labour, it was widely feared that a common external tariff would seriously damage what was left of 'imperial preference', the special trade relations with the Empire and Commonwealth which had been established at the Ottawa Conference in 1932.[7] The result of London's prevarication was clear, however: Britain again 'missed out' in Europe, as it had in 1952, at a time when the EEC was still young enough for the British government to have decisively influenced its rules and structure. Although, by way of a partial substitute, Britain turned instead to the creation of the European Free Trade Association (EFTA) (established in January 1960 in collaboration with the three Scandinavian countries, Austria, Portugal and Switzerland), this was merely a diversion which London was content to pursue temporarily until the time was ripe for a closer British relationship with the EEC Six.

The abortive attempts to join the EEC 1961–2 and 1967–8

While the Macmillan government was busying itself with the establishment of EFTA, certain other changes were taking place – both in Britain's bilateral relations with the major European powers and inside the European communities – which were to lead to two British attempts to join the EEC. Throughout the late 1950s and early 1960s, British collaboration with Western Europe increased in a wide range of policy areas. In July 1956, for example, Britain signed an agreement with the Federal Republic of Germany (FRG) in which the two powers undertook to co-operate in the field of non-military nuclear energy.[8] A similar undertaking was reached with Italy in December 1957.[9] In June 1957 the FRG, in the first of several 'offset' arrangements, agreed to pay part of the foreign exchange costs of the British Army of the Rhine.[10] And throughout 1960 and 1961 various measures were taken to facilitate private travel between Britain and continental Europe.[11]

However these largely cosmetic changes, while indicative of a growing closeness between Britain and Europe, were not as significant as the return to power of General de Gaulle in France in December 1958. Hailed as the only man who could resolve France's long-running Algerian crisis, de Gaulle was as committed to the principle of national sovereignty as the British leaders of the early 1950s who had preferred to remain aloof from the integrative experiments of the ECSC and EEC. Accordingly, de Gaulle deliberately tried to put a brake on the integrative, supranational momentum of the EEC, attempting instead to transform it more into an association of independent sovereign states which would collaborate pragmatically for the sole purpose of their mutual economic benefit.[12] This view of the Community squared very well with the British government's long-held view of European co-operation and as a result, in October 1961, Prime Minister Macmillan entered into a series of negotiations aimed at securing Britain's entry into the new 'Gaullist' EEC. De Gaulle for his part welcomed Britain's approaches, hopeful of building a genuinely European *security* community – independent of the United States – as well as an economic one more suited to his liking. Negotiations, inevitably protracted given the complexity of the undertaking, continued for over a year, with apparent success. However, in December 1962, the 'special relationship' interposed itself. For largely technical reasons, the Americans cancelled the Skybolt nuclear-tipped missile system which Britain had contracted to buy in order to strengthen its deterrent capability in Europe. De Gaulle apparently regarded the cancellation as a great opportunity both to develop Anglo-French military – and especially nuclear – collaboration and for Britain to reduce its military links with the United States.[13]

But if Macmillan was ready to draw closer to Europe in economic terms, he remained unconvinced that such involvement should in any way prejudice London's close military and political relationship with Washington. Within a week of the Skybolt cancellation, Macmillan met President Kennedy at Nassau, where, by way of replacement, he negotiated the purchase (on extremely favourable terms) of the submarine-launched Polaris missile system.[14] It is possible that the Polaris Agreement may have been the excuse that de Gaulle was looking for in order to prevent Britain's entry into Europe. Alternatively the agreement may have represented a symbolic decision on the British government's part that caused the French leader genuinely to change his view of the desirability of Britain's membership of the Community. In any event, on 14 January 1963 the French government announced its intention to veto the British application. By convincing de Gaulle that the United Kingdom still retained strong political and military ambitions inside the Atlantic 'circle' – that Britain was still in effect a near-dependency of the United States – the special relationship, as manifested at Nassau, had succeeded in preventing Britain moving more fully into the European 'circle'.

In October 1964, the incoming Labour government was not in favour of British membership of the EEC. The Labour left had always regarded the Community as a 'capitalists' club' which should be studiously avoided if socialism was to make any progress either in Western Europe in general or in Britain in particular. In July 1966, however, George Brown, the party's deputy leader and an ardent Europeanist, became Foreign Secretary. Under his influence, first the Prime Minister and subsequently the Cabinet and the Parliamentary Labour Party were gradually persuaded of the merits of UK membership.[15] As a result, in May 1967, Britain initiated its *second* attempt to enter the newly-designated 'European Communities'. Negotiations over the terms of UK entry proceeded for almost a year before being halted in February 1968 by the 'Soames Affair'. In a private dinner conversation with the British Ambassador to Paris (Sir Christopher Soames), General de Gaulle had indicated that the French would favour British entry provided that it meant (1) less European reliance on the United States, (2) a change in the character of the EEC, making it principally a free trade area with special provisions for agricultural prices, and (3) a more powerful decision-making role for the largest member countries.[16] If this information had remained confidential, Britain's application (at that stage, informal) might well have proceeded smoothly. However the details of the conversation were leaked to the Federal German leadership, which subsequently informed the other EC governments. In the ensuing diplomatic furore, Anglo-French relations plummeted to their lowest point since January 1963, while the remaining Community members – fearful that British entry might prove to be a Trojan horse intended to destroy the Community from within – began to treat British requests for a sympathetic hearing with extreme suspicion, if not open hostility. The simple result was that the second British attempt to join the Community failed by default: with the Council of Ministers deadlocked on the question of British entry, the Wilson government avoided pressing its application any further.

Entry, 1972–3

The turning-point in Britain's relations with the Community was de Gaulle's resignation from the French presidency in April 1969. The fact that his successor, Georges Pompidou, inclined far more towards a supranationalist view of the Community itself did much to allay the fears of other member states that British entry would create an Anglo-French axis opposed to the partially supranational basis of the Community's existing decision-making procedures. At a summit meeting at The Hague in December 1969, the heads of government of the Six declared themselves to be in favour of British membership. The election victory of Edward Heath – a long-standing advocate of British entry into the Community – in June 1970 provided the final trigger. Formal diplomatic negotiations began in May 1971 and in January 1972 a series of treaties were signed confirming Britain's accession to the Communities as from 1 January 1973.[17] For good or ill, the long journey into the European circle had been given formal, institutional expression. It remained to be seen how far Britain's new status as a 'European partner' would affect its dealings with the Empire-cum-Commonwealth and with North America.

The East European dimension

In spite of Britain's closer relations with the countries of EFTA and the EEC in the years after 1956, it would be wrong to give the impression that the increasingly European focus of British foreign policy was confined solely to the western, democratic part of the continent. Important changes were also occurring in British policy towards the communist countries of Eastern Europe. To be sure, underlying these changes was the continuing conviction that the Soviet Union and its Warsaw Pact allies[18] constituted the major threat to the security of the West. And, as a key member of NATO, Britain was obviously obliged to maintain its strong deterrent military posture towards the Soviet bloc. None the less, the continuing perception of the Soviets as 'the enemy' did not prevent successive British governments from engaging in 'partial co-operation' with the Warsaw Pact countries in relatively non-contentious policy areas well removed from security matters.[19] The NATO deterrent would inhibit Soviet aggression for the time being: in the long run, partial co-operation might effect a gradual warming in Anglo-Soviet relations, replacing the sense of mutual hostility so prevalent since the late 1940s with something more akin to guarded cordiality. This was not only the sort of 'dual-track' strategy towards opponents that Churchill had counselled in 1953:[20] it was also in accordance with the classic *realpolitik* maxim that statesmen should 'speak softly and carry a big stick'.[21]

The first tentative steps towards 'partial co-operation' had in fact been taken by Eden in April 1956 with Khruschev's visit to London; though the Soviets' subsequent support for Nasser during the Suez crisis prevented the co-operative process from being advanced any further. In May 1959, however, a five-year Anglo-Soviet trade agreement was signed, followed in December by a two-year scientific, technical and cultural agreement; both of these were regularly renewed throughout the 1960s.[22] In the early 1970s the Heath government extended the principle of partial co-operation to embrace the rest of the Warsaw Pact. In April 1971 a long-run trade agreement was reached with Poland;[23] and similar accords were achieved with Hungary, Czechoslovakia and Romania during the course of 1972.[24] Scientific and technical agreements were signed with Poland and the German Democratic Republic in 1973.[25]

While it would clearly be wrong to regard any or all of these agreements as constituting a major breakthrough in Britain's relations with Eastern Europe, they were none the less indicative both of the more Eurocentric focus of UK foreign policy after 1956 and the determination of the British government – like its West German counterpart – to build diplomatic bridges wherever possible, even with states which were collectively regarded as a serious military threat. In spite of the added East–West tensions which were generated as a direct result of the Soviet invasion of Czechoslovakia in August 1968, both Britain and the FRG (the latter operating under the banner of Willy Brandt's *Ostpolitik*) continued to combine a posture of firm military confrontation with a preparedness to negotiate and compromise in non-military areas. The ultimate objective was clearly the achievement of a gradual thaw in the relations between the two halves of Europe. The comparatively cordial record of those relations after 1970 suggested that the strategy did indeed meet with some small degree of success.

By the early 1970s, then, Britain had established very close relations with Western Europe and was even beginning to co-operate – admittedly on a limited scale – with the communist states of the East. Why had this major change in the content of Britain's external policy taken place? It is this fundamental question which is addressed in the next section.

Explaining the shift towards Europe

Any major foreign policy development is obviously the consequence of a large number of causal factors. There were nevertheless four critical factors – some already mentioned in other contexts – which were of overriding significance in Britain's strategic shift towards Europe after 1956. At the decision-making level the three most important considerations were (1) the apparent economic benefits of Community membership, (2) American approval of closer British ties with Europe, and (3) the declining political significance of the Empire-cum-Commonwealth. At the structural level, the principal influence was the shift in the focus of Britain's overseas trade.

The economic benefits of closer ties with Europe

The economic benefits of ECSC membership were already becoming evident by the time the Six signed the Treaty of Rome in 1957. All of Europe – Britain included – was benefiting from the worldwide postwar economic boom which Marshall Aid and the expansion of the US economy had done so much to create. Unfortunately Britain's economic performance lagged significantly behind that of its European competitors. As Table 5.1 shows, even by 1956 it was clear that, in comparison with other major West European economies, Britain's record on industrial growth was unimpressive. Obviously there was a variety of possible reasons why this should have been so. For one thing, the continental European countries, with their economies shattered by the war, had begun their industrial expansion from a lower production base, which in turn meant that they could achieve relatively large *percentage* increases in production rather more easily. In addition, it was widely suspected that an overvalued pound, inefficient British manufacturers protected from foreign competition, and unnecessarily powerful trade unions were also, in their separate ways, contributing to Britain's poor economic performance. The problem, of course, was that there was no way of establishing definitively which – if any – of these possible explanations was correct. A final possibility, moreover, was that the ECSC, with its supranational orientation, its factor mobility and its common external tariff, was genuinely achieving better collective results for its members than any of them could have secured individually. Indeed, as noted earlier, it certainly appeared after Messina in 1955 that the Six themselves were sufficiently convinced of the benefits of functional co-operation for them to elect to expand the functional domain of the entire community.

Table 5.1   Percentage growth in industrial production in selected countries, 1950–6

Federal Republic of Germany	100
Italy	63
France	49
Belgium	36
Britain	21

SOURCE: Mancur Olson, *The Rise and Decline of Nations: Economic Growth, Stagflation and Social Rigidities* (Cambridge Mass.: Harvard University Press, 1982) p. 17.

As the debate about the relative merits of Britain's fuller participation in Europe gathered momentum in the early 1960s, the available evidence on different national growth rates certainly suggested that Europe was performing rather more effectively than Britain. As the first column of Table 5.2 indicates, throughout the 1950s the average annual growth rate within the ECSC/EEC countries was 4 per cent compared with a figure of 2.3 per cent for Britain. There was, of course, some reason to suppose that functional co-operation among the Six was *not* the critical factor in the genesis of these differential growth rates: Belgium, for example, was inside the Community and yet had a lower growth rate than the United Kingdom; Austria was outside and yet had a growth rate almost as high as the FRG. The main comparison that *was* made, however, was between Britain and the three other countries which since the late nineteenth century had been regarded as the most important powers in continental Western Europe: France, Italy and (West) Germany. Here the contrast was clear-cut: an average annual growth rate of 2.3 per cent for Britain, compared with 5 per cent for the other 'Big Three'. The inference that was drawn accordingly was that, if Britain had been a member of the ECSC/EEC from the outset, its economic growth might have been considerably greater. Compounded over the years – and, more importantly, projected into the future – these differences in growth performance were alarming. Certainly by the early 1960s the Macmillan government was convinced that, if the British economy was not to be further disadvantaged in the future, Britain would have to become a full member of the Community. This perception even extended to 'public opinion': in December 1962, immediately prior to the French veto, two-thirds of the respondents to a Gallup survey who expressed a preference declared themselves to be in favour of British entry.[26]

Table 5.2 Average annual growth of GDP in selected countries, 1950–80

	1950–60	1960–70	1970–80
Belgium	2.0	4.1	3.2
France	3.5	4.6	3.0
FRG	6.6	3.5	2.4
Italy	4.9	4.6	2.1
Netherlands	3.3	4.1	2.3
(Av. ECSC/EEC)	(4.08)	(4.2)	(2.6)
Denmark	2.5	3.9	2.2
Ireland	1.8	3.8	2.3
Britain	2.3	2.3	2.0
Austria	5.7	3.9	3.8

*Excluding Luxembourg.
SOURCE: Mancur Olson, *The Rise and Decline of Nations: Economic Growth, Stagflation and Social Rigidities* (Cambridge Mass.: Harvard University Press, 1982) p. 6.

After the failure to secure British membership in 1961–3, Britain's overall economic performance continued to stagnate throughout the 1960s. As column 2 of Table 5.2 shows, between 1960 and 1970 even the lowly Belgian economy outperformed its British counterpart. Indeed, while British growth remained stuck at 2.3 per cent per annum, the average EC rate rose to 4.2 per cent. In these circumstances the tempting prospect of easier access to an expanding market of over 250 million consumers was quite enough to persuade both Conservative and Labour leaders that somehow or other Britain must join the European Club. It was also hoped that, as a partner in Europe, Britain would be in a much stronger bargaining position in international negotiations over tariff reductions, a perception which was strongly reinforced following the difficulties encountered by Harold Wilson during his dealings with the United States in the 1968 'Kennedy Round' of tariff negotiations.[27] The tragedy was that, shortly after Britain finally did accede to the Community in 1973, Community growth rates – for a variety of exogenous reasons discussed below – fell sharply (see column 3, Table 5.2). The result of this fall was that for the 1970s as a whole there was a levelling-down of Community growth rates rather than the levelling-*up* of British rates which had been anticipated. With hindsight, it seems sensible to conclude that it was *not* Britain's exclusion from the ECSC and EEC which led to its comparative low postwar growth rates: the causes of Britain's economic failure lay much deeper than its non-membership of a successful economic club.[28] However this is not to suggest that the *promise* of economic improvement was anything other than a crucially important element in the decision calculus of successive governments in their respective attempts to join the EEC.

The importance of American support

A second continuing factor underlying Britain's greater involvement with Western Europe was the consistent support lent to the idea by successive American administrations. As observed in Chapter 2, immediately after the Second World War Truman and his Secretary of State Dean Acheson encouraged Ernest Bevin to take a leading role in stimulating political and economic co-operation in Western Europe: a strong united Europe, which was inconceivable in 1945 without British participation, would be a solid bulwark against Soviet expansionism. As also noted in Chapter 2, however, what the Americans failed to appreciate in 1945 was that Britain could not simultaneously lead the process of (west) European unification *and* maintain its strong imperial links. None the less, the fact that through to the late 1950s successive governments chose to emphasise London's ties with the Empire circle rather than with Europe did not prevent US leaders, ever suspicious of a resurgence in British imperialism, expressing their continued desire to see Britain pursuing a primarily European role in world affairs. Increasingly after 1949, Britain's economic integration with the rest of western Europe was, for the Americans, the natural corollary to Britain's military role in the European wing of NATO.

But why should the British government have been concerned to receive United States approval for any of its actions? Although the answer to this question is explored more fully in Chapter 6, the fundamental reason lay in the *military* relationship between London and Washington. There were two senses in which this relationship engendered an acute British sensitivity to the policy preferences of the United States. First, Britain's national security relied heavily on a strong American commitment to NATO and in particular to the continued presence of a large United States conventional force in Western Europe. No British government after 1949 would have been prepared to entertain a projected foreign policy strategy which might weaken that commitment. A second sense in which the United Kingdom was concerned to appease American sensibilities was in the context of the British independent nuclear deterrent. The continuing belief within Cabinet that Britain's status as a Great Power required the maintenance of an effective and up-to-date nuclear capability was confronted from the late 1950s onwards with the unpleasant fact that Britain could no longer afford to build one itself. This in turn meant that London was increasingly obliged to rely on the Americans for the necessary technology. Yet, if the Nassau agreement of December 1962 was a symbol of this dependence, the fact that no other nation received such preferential treatment was an affirmation of the special place which Britain still occupied in United States global strategy. The problem that confronted the British government in the mid-1960s – and after – was that this 'special place' looked increasingly precarious. Not only had Britain failed to support the American war effort in Vietnam but it was also contemplating leaving the United States with an increased military burden in the Far East, an eventuality which would inevitably follow if London pressed ahead with its plans to withdraw from east of Suez. To have deliberately flouted Washington's long-standing preference for a closer British association with Western Europe in these circumstances would undoubtedly have been to undermine Britain's privileged position as the sole overseas recipient of American nuclear technology.

It was a happy coincidence, therefore, that after 1966 British policy towards Europe accorded well with the publicly-stated preferences of the United States. Britain could thus take an active part in the newly-created 'Eurogroup' of NATO and press forward with its attempts to join the EEC, secure in the knowledge that it did so with the blessing of Uncle Sam. To be sure, French (and, after Soames, German) resistance ensured that Britain's formal passage into Europe was both hesitant and protracted, but if Britain had attempted to join Europe in the face of *American* resistance, its passage would have been even more difficult. It would also have put at risk both the unity of NATO and the survival of the independent deterrent, neither of which Britain was prepared to countenance. Britain certainly did not join the EEC just to please the Americans. None the less, Washington's approval of London's repeated applications was a welcome facilitating condition, essential to the success of British efforts to give formal institutional expression to the United Kingdom's increasing involvement in the European circle.

The declining significance of the Commonwealth

A third major factor underlying Britain's shift towards Europe after 1956 was the further decline of the Commonwealth as an instrument for maintaining British influence inside the old Empire circle. As noted in Chapter 4, after the decisions by India, Pakistan and Ceylon to become members, it had been hoped that the Commonwealth would act as a sort of surrogate Empire, fostering the preservation and spread of Anglo-Saxon democratic principles across the black–white racial divide. With luck, it might even provide the nucleus of a global network of alliances among democratic states capable of resisting any challenge which the communist states might collectively pose. As also noted in Chapter 4, however, such hopes were soon dashed. The Suez affair seriously tarnished Britain's image in the eyes of both the recently liberated and the soon to be liberated colonies. Combined with the new third-world consciousness of oppression that was already developing in the mid-1950s, the general disillusion with western neo-imperialism that had been exacerbated by Suez led to the emergence of a new international political bloc which sought to establish a 'middle way' between the rival imperialisms of East and West. Moreover the fact that two of the Commonwealth's most prominent third-world leaders – Nkrumah and Nehru – were among the prime movers of this Non-Aligned Movement was a clear signal to London that the new Commonwealth nations felt very little diplomatic allegiance to the old 'mother country'; a conclusion which was soon to be reinforced by the tendency of those nations to fail to support the Western Powers in critical votes in the UN General Assembly.[29]

The internal coherence of the Commonwealth was further weakened by a series of crises during the 1960s. South Africa's continued membership of the Commonwealth had been a source of considerable contention since its introduction of the *apartheid* system in 1948. With an increasing number of newly-independent black states acceding to the Commonwealth after 1957, demands that 'something be done about South Africa' grew inexorably. Over a decade of 'gentle persuasion' directed from London had failed to soften the hardline racism of the South African government. As far as the new states of Asia and Africa were concerned, the continued presence of such a regime in a commonwealth of nations that formally espoused non-racial principles was wholly unacceptable. Indeed their deeply-felt opposition produced a concerted diplomatic campaign during 1960 and 1961 which resulted in London's preferences being overridden and South Africa withdrawing from the Commonwealth in May 1961. The enforced withdrawal not only constituted a defeat for Britain's 'quiet diplomacy' – the Macmillan government had argued that South Africa would be more amenable to persuasion if it remained inside the Commonwealth – but also symbolised the racial tensions which permeated what was supposed to be an essentially multiracial club.

These tensions resurfaced sporadically during the 1960s. In the process they gradually weakened not only the unity of the Commonwealth itself but also Britain's already limited ability to exercise political influence over the association's new members. Harold Wilson's half-hearted response (economic sanctions) to Ian Smith's Unilateral Declaration of Independence (UDI) in Rhodesia in the period after 1965, though entirely justifiable, given Britain's physical inability to do more, was not well-received by black Commonwealth leaders who naturally felt that Britain should have acted far more decisively in order to effect a speedy transition to majority rule. The British government's relations with the black Commonwealth were further damaged by the two UK Immigration Acts of 1965 and 1968 which placed heavy restrictions on the ability of (especially new) Commonwealth citizens to become resident in Britain. Both of these Acts were widely viewed abroad as being racist in their implications, if not in their intentions; both increased Commonwealth suspicions that London's public commitment to a *multiracial* association of nations was largely disingenuous. Finally, Britain's persistent refusal (which was to endure through to the late 1980s) either to withdraw its investments from South Africa or to boycott South African products continually aroused the resentment of the black Commonwealth states.

The continual eruption of all of these racial differences during the 1960s made it extremely difficult for Britain to exercise any sort of political influence over the Commonwealth nations. Indeed it was doubly unfortunate from Britain's point of view that this further erosion of its *political* influence should have coincided with the decline of the Overseas Sterling Area (OSA), an international monetary arrangement which since the 1940s had operated to the mutual advantage of Britain and the majority of the 'Empire circle' countries. (The OSA itself is discussed in detail in Chapter 7.) With the final abandonment of the OSA in 1968, Britain lost not only a valuable source of international liquidity but also a potential *economic* lever that could have been used to exert pressure on individual Commonwealth nations had the need arisen. In a situation where Britain found it increasingly difficult to exert either political or economic pressure on individual Commonwealth members, the Commonwealth itself rapidly began to look less like the surrogate Empire of the postwar imperialists' imaginings and more like the loose association of (somewhat like-minded) sovereign states which the founding Statute of Westminster had formally envisaged in 1931. By the mid-1960s the British government's calculations, based, as ever, on sound *realpolitik* principles, suggested a very simple conclusion. If Britain's ties with the Commonwealth – with the residue of Empire – were no longer benefiting the United Kingdom either politically or economically, then there was absolutely no point in allowing those ties to hamper Britain's relations with Europe, as they had done since the early 1950s when London had first rejected the Schuman Plan. In these circumstances, Britain might just as well accept that its principal material interests now lay in the European rather than the Empire 'circle': the urgent institutionalisation of its increasingly close links with Europe must now be a top priority.

The increasingly European focus of Britain's trade

The fourth – and probably the most important – factor which underpinned Britain's strategic shift towards the European circle after 1956 was the changing pattern of Britain's overseas trade. Notwithstanding some contemporary claims to the contrary,[30] from the late 1950s onwards – as discussed in Chapter 4 – the focus of Britain's trade shifted dramatically away from the Empire circle and towards Europe. The fact that the change was already occurring well before Britain's entry into the EEC in 1973 is shown very clearly in Table 5.3, which reports the percentages of British exports to and imports from the EEC countries for selected (but representative) years between 1935 and 1983. In the prewar period, about 20 per cent of Britain's trade was with the eight countries that were destined later to become members of the EEC. As a result of the industrial devastation engendered by the war this figure fell slightly after 1945. However, by 1954 the prewar share had been restored, a position which remained more or less stable until 1960.

Table 5.3   **Percentage of British exports to and imports from the EEC**

(All figures include The Six + Ireland + Denmark)

	British exports to EEC as % of all British exports	British imports from EEC as % of all British imports
1935–8	21.7	18.6
1948	16.7	13.1
1954	21.5	18.4
1960	20.9	20.2
1971	29.3	29.9
1979	41.8	43.1
1983	43.8	45.6

SOURCE: *Annual Abstract of Statistics* (HMSO, various years).

Yet by 1971, *before* Britain's membership application had been successful, the EEC share in Britain's trade had risen to almost 30 per cent.
This trend continued after 1971, so that by 1979 the EEC share had
risen to well over 40 per cent.

This 'Europeanisation' of Britain's external trade was not confined
solely to the *EEC* countries, however. As Table 5.4 indicates, Britain's
trade with the *whole* of Western Europe increased considerably after
1955: Sweden, Switzerland, Austria, Greece, Portugal and Spain also
became much more significant as United Kingdom trading partners in
the period after 1955. This can be seen very readily by an examination
of the figures displayed in column 5 of Table 5.4. This column indicates
the magnitude of the increase in British exports to each country
between 1955 and 1984. As the first row of column 5 shows, total
British exports to all countries were 24 times greater in 1984 than they
were in 1955. By comparing the country-by-country 'magnitude of
increase' figures with this baseline figure of 24 we obtain a very clear
picture of the changing pattern of Britain's trade. What is immediately
apparent is that, whereas the vast majority of Empire circle countries
exhibit 'magnitude of increase' figures considerably below the baseline
figure of 24 × (empire average: 9.6 ×), *almost all the West European
nations exhibit 'magnitude of increase' figures well in excess of the 24 ×
baseline* (West European average: 45.1 ×).[31] Column 6 of Table 5.4 –
which effectively controls for both inflation and the overall increase in
trade which occurred between 1955 and 1984 – is even more revealing.
It shows, for example, that France and Germany were four times more
important as destinations for British exports in the mid-1980s than they
had been in the mid-1950s; Western Europe as a whole became twice as
important as a destination over the same period.

What all of these figures demonstrate beyond reasonable doubt is
that from 1955 onwards – as was suggested in Chapter 4 – Britain's
major trading interests were becoming ever more concentrated in
Western Europe. Here was a powerful material reason why, during the
1960s and 1970s, the leaders of all three major political parties should
have begun to stress Britain's role as a primarily European power: this
was, increasingly, where Britain's main material interests lay.

Of course, to some radical observers the link between the changing
pattern of trade and the changing political posture of Britain's political
parties during the 1960s was not just a matter of the latter recognising
'where Britain's main material interests lay'. In the Marxist view, the
unseen hand of financial capital was a major influence upon the policy
of successive governments.[32] Increasingly after 1955, it was not the
interests of Britain, but the interests of financial capital – the interests

Table 5.4 UK Exports to major trading partners 1955–84 (£m)

Exports to:	1955	1965	1975	1984	Magnitude of increase	Corrected** magnitude of increase index
All countries	2905	4723	19 929	70 511	24x	0.30
Ghana	(10)***	41	51	82	8x	0.54
Nigeria	57	73	512	768	13x	0.25
Zambia	(10)	15	80	66	6x	0.70
Kenya	(10)	35	86	176	17x	0.25
Tanzania	(10)	11	42	60	6x	0.25
Trinidad & Tobago	(10)	25	52	113	11x	0.45
Jamaica	(10)	24	61	48	5x	0.21
Australia	284	280	631	1 186	4x	0.16
New Zealand	139	125	254	367	3x	0.12
Canada	141	200	538	1 183	8x	0.30
South Africa	167	261	685	1 205	7x	0.29
India	130	114	164	781	6x	0.25
Pakistan	36	50	77	282	8x	0.30
Ceylon (Sri Lanka)	22	19	0	0	—	—
Malaya (Malaysia)	(48)	94	157	556	22x	0.91
	73					
Singapore	(25)					
Hong Kong	26	65	159	897	34x	1.42
Egypt	29	20	108	427	15x	0.62
Iraq	(10)	22	137	343	34x	1.42
Libya	(10)	18	107	246	24x	1.00
Cyprus	(10)	16	27	146	14x	0.58

Bahrain	(10)		61	138	13x	0.54
Qatar	(10)		56	133	13x	0.54
Abu Dhabi	(10)	35	91	215	21x	0.87
Dubai	(10)		105	298	29x	1.21
Oman	(10)		98	390	39x	1.62
Iran	(10)	38	495	703	70x	2.92
Algeria	(10)	65	78	272	27x	1.12
Lebanon	(10)	—	69	76	7x	0.29
Irish Republic	108	176	907	3 393	31x	1.29
Finland	42	72	264	684	16x	0.67
Sweden	95	219	826	2 888	30x	1.25
Norway	74	86	391	968	13x	0.54
Denmark	74	125	443	1 197	16x	0.67
West Germany	77	255	1 304	7 458	97x	4.00
Netherlands	106	193	1 115	6 128	58x	2.42
Belgium	63	170	922	3 051	48x	2.00
France	72	177	1 164	7 082	98x	4.08
Italy	58	109	563	2 902	50x	2.08
Switzerland	27	89	805	1 549	57x	2.37
Austria	(10)	35	165	320	32x	1.33
Greece	(10)	31	117	354	35x	1.46
Turkey	14	18	143	331	24x	1.00
Portugal	(10)	40	158	385	38x	1.58
Spain	(10)	95	295	1 234	123x	5.12
Soviet Union	23	45	211	735	32x	1.33
Yugoslavia	(10)	20	94	163	16x	0.67
Czechoslovakia	(10)	—	51	71	7x	0.29
Romania	(10)	—	39	71	7x	0.29
Poland	(10)	24	183	170	17x	0.71

Table 5.4 UK Exports to major trading partners 1955–84 (£m)

	1955	1965	1975	1984	Magnitude of increase	Corrected** magnitude of increase index
United States	183	493	1 789	10 149	55x	2.29
Japan	(10)	53	309	925	92x	3.83
Thailand	(10)	18	56	149	14x	0.58
South Korea	(10)	—	57	219	21x	0.87
Philippines	(10)	14	55	91	9x	0.37
Argentina	23	27	68	5	—	—
Brazil	7	20	161	238	34x	1.42
Venezuela	(10)	25	92	102	10x	0.42
Chile	(10)	10	36	75	7x	0.29
Mexico	(10)	19	112	150	15x	0.62
Ecuador	(10)	—	19	34	3x	0.12
Total exports	2905	4723	19 929	70 511	24x	
Total Sterling Area exports	1431	1645	4 454*	9 324*		
Sterling Area as % of total	49.2	34.8	22.3	13.2		

*Estimates derived from summing UK export revenues from pre-1968 Overseas Sterling Area countries.
**Magnitude of increase index obtained by dividing column 5 by 24. An index figure of 1 indicates that a country is exactly as important a destination for UK imports in 1984 as it was in 1955.
***UK Export volumes less than £10 m were not recorded in 1955. For countries thus affected, a figure of £10 m is none the less recorded here to prevent the 'magnitude of increase' numbers from approaching infinity.
SOURCE: *Annual Abstract of Statistics* (HMSO, various years).

of the banks and financial institutions of the City – that were shifting towards Western Europe. The promise of free capital mobility, envisaged by the Treaty of Rome, was a particularly attractive incentive in this context in the sense that it would allow capital to be moved around Europe to where wages were lowest and profits highest. What British financial capital now needed, apart from a share in Europe's newly mobile capital market, was more *political* influence inside the EEC itself: British membership of the Community was one of the more obvious means by which this could be achieved.

Like so many contemporary Marxist arguments, this account sounds fairly plausible. Unfortunately there is very little conclusive empirical evidence to suggest that it is actually correct. Britain's membership of the EEC might well have been 'in the interests of financial capital', but it is entirely possible that it was *also* 'in the interests' both of industrial capital and of labour. After all, in the 1960s, industrial capital – as evidenced by the growth in exports summarised in Table 5.4 – was already achieving greater market penetration in Europe; the ever easier access to these markets which would follow from Britain's entry into the Community would presumably raise the possibility of yet higher sales and higher profits. By the same token, labour could reasonably expect that it too would benefit from the added production possibilities engendered by Britain's membership of an enlarged and expanding market. Moreover, if British entry meant that there would be fiercer foreign competition inside domestic British markets, then those new competitive pressures would be felt by labour, industrial capital and financial capital alike. There was certainly no ineluctable reason for supposing that financial capital would be either the only or even a disproportionate beneficiary from Britain's closer involvement with the Community.

In essence, financial capital was no more important than any other economic interest or grouping in provoking Britain's strategic shift towards Europe. The Europeanisation of UK trade which took place after 1955 was a phenomenon that affected the interests of the British economy as a whole, not just selected parts of it. The fundamental cause of the trade shift, as noted in Chapter 4, was the fact that changing patterns of production and consumption in the European economies autonomously increased the demand for the goods and services which British industry and commerce could supply. To be sure, these structural changes were reinforced by the general liberalisation of the international trade regime which occurred in the decade or so after 1958. None the less, the changes themselves were so deep-seated in character that they profoundly altered the basic focus of the British economy. As has been repeatedly observed, in the period after 1955, Britain's material economic interests shifted towards Europe: the three attempts to join the EEC in 1961–2, 1967–8 and 1971–2, whatever the express calculations of the decision makers themselves, were merely the response of a political system trying to catch up with economic realities.

Britain's relations with Europe after 1972

Once Britain, along with Denmark and the Irish Republic, had actually joined the European Communities (EC) in January 1973, the main foreign policy question that arose was how far membership would affect the government's general European circle strategy. The broad answer was 'not very much': although changes did occur in certain policy areas, they were invariably both slow and incremental. British policy towards Eastern Europe, for example, exhibited remarkable continuity: the strategy of partial co-operation – of gradually building bridges in non-contentious policy areas – continued steadily with yet more trade and scientific co-operation agreements being negotiated with the countries of the Warsaw Pact. However, the main focus of London's European circle activities after 1972 was in the West. Here, too, Britain's overall foreign policy posture was largely unaffected by its membership of the EC. As the first part of this section indicates, Britain's relations with the other Community members – though always good in comparison with *non*-member states – were consistently marred by the continued British preference for a Community in which sovereignty, especially in foreign affairs, ultimately remained with the *national* governments. As the second part shows, this continued preference was a major reason why the EC failed to develop a coherent common European foreign policy during the 1970s and 1980s.

Britain's foreign policy towards other Community members

The fictitious Whitehall mandarin of the early 1980s, Sir Humphrey Appleby, frequently referred to Britain's new European partners as 'our European enemies'.[33] The sentiment underlying the description – though not the characterisation itself – was probably an accurate portrayal of the continuing belief in both Cabinet and Whitehall that the fundamental task of government in the field of foreign relations was the protection of Britain's national interests. Wide-ranging and pro-tracted international co-operation of the sort engendered by the EC was all very well, and always welcome, but it could never be permitted to interfere with the vital national interests of the United Kingdom. It could also be safely assumed, moreover, that several other EC member governments viewed the Community in a similar light.

Notwithstanding this important reservation, however, Britain's relations with other EC members were from the outset remarkably good. There were obviously periodic diplomatic disagreements, but these were never so important as to impair the fundamental convergence of material interest which had motivated the British government to apply for EC membership in the first place, and which continued to inform relations with the Community thereafter. After all, the United Kingdom's new European partners, though still 'enemies' in the sense that they were by definition not actually British, were far closer to Britain economically and politically than any other sovereign country or group of countries. They shared with Britain not only geographical proximity but also a common commitment to competitive party democracy, common membership of NATO and an increasingly interdependent trade network.[34] All of these shared interests had made for comparatively good relations before Britain's entry and, not surprisingly, they continued to do so afterwards.

In formal-legal terms, from the time of its accession to the EC, Britain's behaviour towards the Community's institutions was exemplary. As anticipated at the time of entry, during the 1970s London accepted without question a new form of international legal obligation – the regulations and directives of the European Communities – which circumscribed the behaviour of member-states in a variety of different contexts.[35] Similarly, the decisions of the supranational Commission, in areas where, by prior agreement, it was competent to make them, were generally accepted without challenge, as were the decisions of the European Court of Justice.

Yet, in spite of this formal obeisance to the supranational practices and institutions of the Community, the British still contrived to give the impression that they remained somewhat 'reluctant Europeans'. This reluctance was reflected in the two major issues which arose between Britain and its European partners in the years after 1972: the 'terms of Britain's entry' into the EC and the continuing problem of the Community budget.

Each of Britain's three attempts to join the Community in the 1960s and 1970s had encountered difficulties with regard both to the size of Britain's contribution to the EC annual budget and the implications which Community membership – and especially participation in the Common Agricultural Policy (CAP) – would have for British farmers and existing overseas foodstuff suppliers. As a subject for international bargaining, the size of the budget contribution was a fairly simple matter to resolve. Britain obviously wanted to contribute as little as possible to central Community coffers, but at the same time it would have to make a contribution that was acceptable to the existing members. This was clearly a position which was always capable of being resolved by simple haggling.

The agricultural problem was rather more intractable, however. In the early 1960s, Britain had still wanted its Commonwealth suppliers to retain their privileged access to British markets. At the same time, British farmers were extremely unhappy about the change in the system of farming subsidies which would be necessary if Britain were to accept the principles of the CAP. In the event, of course, the United Kingdom government's failure to secure membership before 1972 meant that difficult choices could be delayed. By the time Britain's successful negotiations were under way in 1971–2, however, London had already downgraded the Empire circle in its overall foreign policy strategy. In consequence, notwithstanding the special arrangements made for Commonwealth sugar and for New Zealand butter and lamb, the interests of Britain's Commonwealth suppliers could be largely disregarded. Meanwhile Britain's farmers were not sufficiently important as a domestic lobby for the United Kingdom to risk prejudicing its entire application solely on their account. The result was that, as part of the 1973 terms of entry, the Heath government not only accepted the imposition of a discriminatory tariff against *all* non-EEC imports to Britain, but also acquiesced in the indefinite preservation of the CAP.

However, having achieved membership of the Community on terms apparently agreeable to all sides, London soon began to recant. In 1975, in order to appease the left wing of the Labour party, the recently elected Wilson government was obliged to hold a referendum on whether or not Britain should remain inside the Community. Lord knows what would have happened if the popular verdict had been in favour of withdrawal. Fortunately the referendum produced a strong statement of approval for Britain's continued membership.[36] The die had been cast, however. For Britain's partners in Europe the fact that London could even consider subjecting Britain's continued membership of the Community to such a grave risk was clear evidence of its lack of commitment to European ideals. The error was compounded by the attendant efforts of both the Wilson and Callaghan governments to 'renegotiate the terms of entry' in 1974–5 and again in 1978–9. The results of their endeavours in terms of a 'better deal for Britain' were at best marginal, the disillusion with the recalcitrant British which their efforts occasioned considerable.

With Mrs Thatcher in power after June 1979, European suspicions of Britain's lack of commitment to the Community intensified. Even if it was now impossible to renegotiate the 'terms of entry' yet again, Britain was still unprepared to accept that the contribution which Britain was obliged to make to the EC budget was 'fair'. Accordingly, from 1980 onwards, the Thatcher government engaged in a form of 'megaphone haggling' which invariably resulted in an annual budget settlement that London at least clearly regarded as unsatisfactory. A breakthrough of sorts was eventually reached at Fontainebleau in June 1984, however, where the Community heads of government, meeting as the European Council, finally agreed on an algorithm for budgetary contributions which took account of the fact that income per capita in the United Kingdom was among the lowest in Western Europe.[37] Yet even after this achievement Britain did not retreat substantially from its 'reluctant European' image. Through to the late 1980s the Thatcher government made strenuous efforts to effect a major revision in the CAP: the policy not only resulted in excessive over-production but also constituted both an enormous drain on the Community Budget and a serious violation of the free-market principles in which the Thatcher Cabinet so firmly believed. Indeed London was so determined to force the pace of reform that, in June 1987, Thatcher effectively vetoed the entire Community budget for the coming financial year – to the considerable consternation of the other EC heads of government.

British recalcitrance towards the Community, then, transcended the party-political divide. From their different ideological standpoints, Labour and Tory governments in the period after 1972 were equally obstructive in their general approach towards Europe. But *why* should successive governments, notwithstanding the significant convergence of material interests that Britain shared with other EC members-states, so consistently have advertised their own latent anti-Europeanism in their policy towards the Community? At least three possible explanatory factors can be identified. The first of these can be dismissed fairly rapidly. It might be expected that the obstructionism of successive British governments could have resulted from *the ideological opposition of other member governments*: the 1974–9 Labour government, so the argument runs, suffered from a predominantly right-wing European political environment, the Conservatives after 1979 from a predominantly socialist one. Unfortunately, this appealing hypothesis is simply not borne out by the facts: the European political balance in the 1970s if anything inclined towards the left; in the 1980s it certainly shifted to the right.[38]

A second factor that encouraged Britain's diffident posture towards the Community after 1972 was the fact that her relatively late entry meant that she joined a Community in which *the economic interests of the original Six were already well entrenched and in which French and German political influence predominated.*[39] In this sense, the continual wrangling over the 'terms of entry' and Britain's budget contribution simply reflected the government's attempts to effect changes in the EC's internal economic and political arrangements that would enable Britain to play a role in intra-Community affairs rather more commensurate with its status as a Great Power. By the mid-1980s, this particular objective had in fact to some extent been achieved, and as a result Britain was beginning to behave – and was being seen to behave – as a more 'normal' member of the Community. And although the UK government still clearly had important reservations about the current and projected supranational character of the Community, it was no longer quite the 'late-comer in search of self-aggrandisement' which it had appeared to be before the Fontainebleau settlement in 1984.[40]

A third factor underlying Britain's continued recalcitrance towards the EC concerned *the decision-making arrangements of the Community itself.* As detailed descriptions of these processes exist elsewhere, it is unnecessary to review them here.[41] It is sufficient to note that all major policy decisions of the Community required the assent both of the supposedly supranational Commission and of the nationally-nominated Council of Ministers. The critical feature of this dual arrangement was that in all important matters the Council required unanimous agreement: this in turn meant that each member-government possessed an effective power of veto over any new Community initiative with which it disagreed. Britain had entered the EC in the full knowledge that it could use its ministerial veto in order to prevent the Community as a whole from introducing changes in either institutions or practices which appeared contrary to British interests. (Indeed, if such a protective provision had not already been available, Britain would never have joined the Community in the first place.) Once Britain had secured membership, however, the United Kingdom was all too ready to use the threat of the veto not just as a means of preventing progressive supranational change within the EC, but also as a bargaining counter with which it might extract concessions from other member-states in its attempts to produce a Community more to its liking. The decision-making apparatus of the Community, by making provision for legitimate nationalist reservations, simultaneously armed Britain – a state which felt increasingly during the 1970s that EC rules and regulations worked systematically to its disadvantage – with the diplomatic weaponry necessary to prosecute its own narrow, nationalist case. Many

Europeans had feared that a British government steeped in centuries of *realpolitik*-based diplomatic practice would find the temptation to use such weapons irresistible, even among friends. London's behaviour after 1972 merely served to confirm their suspicions.

The French, of course, were not entirely disappointed with this turn of events. As noted earlier, under de Gaulle they had always preferred to see the EC develop as a highly co-operative association of sovereign states rather than as a genuinely integrative supranational community. Under Giscard in the late 1970s and Mitterrand in the 1980s they were quite content to witness the rapid dissipation of the supranational momentum of the Community under the weight of British membership. Like the British, they were also anxious to admit yet more members to the EC. When Spain, Portugal and Greece joined the Community in the mid-1980s, the prospects of diluting the Community's supranationalism were enhanced even further. The Gaullist vision of the Community which had proved so embarrassing at the time of the Soames Affair in 1968 was now surreptitiously becoming a welcome reality. The remaining founder members of the Community were not quite so amused.

In 1973, then, Britain had joined a Community which had already achieved quite a high level of economic integration (in terms of a common external tariff and the free internal mobility of goods, capital and labour) and which was advancing along the road to supranational decision making. Even before Britain's entry, however, both the process of economic integration and the moves towards supranationalism had already begun to peter out. Although this stagnation was certainly exacerbated by British intransigence, London was by no means primarily responsible for it. Indeed, the response of the Community's main protagonists was not to apportion blame but to search for new policy areas where Community-wide co-operation would yield such obvious benefits that the impetus towards supranationalism would be restored. What seemed to offer the most promise in this regard was the development of a common European foreign policy. One of the original attractions of the Community had been the idea that its members might at some stage wield a collective influence in world affairs which was greater than the sum of their individual contributions: if this could indeed be achieved now, then the supranational momentum of the EC as a whole might be revived.

A common West European foreign policy?

Although a common European foreign policy had always been on the political agenda of the European federalists, the integrative activities of the Six during the 1950s and 1960s were almost entirely restricted to the economic and social spheres. The first real sign that a common European foreign policy might indeed be emerging was the introduction of the so-called 'Davignon Procedure' in 1970.[42] The resultant system of European Political Co-operation (EPC) aimed to extend the principle of harmonisation – previously confined to the economic and social policies of the Six – to include foreign policy as well. EPC provided a set of procedures whereby European Foreign Ministers (including those of the Six and of the EC's four intending members: Britain, Denmark, Norway and the Irish Republic) could engage in detailed consultation and negotiation prior to a major policy decision being taken. This was a considerable departure from the previous diplomatic practice, which even at its most co-operative had been restricted to the exchange of 'information' and 'assessments'.[43]

Within months of Britain's accession to the Community in 1973, European Political Co-operation appeared to bear its first (small) fruit. With the outbreak of the fourth Arab–Israeli war in October 1973 and the subsequent Arab threat to western oil supplies, Europe found itself more or less united in its opposition to American policy in the Middle East. While the United States firmly maintained its position of 'Israel right or wrong', the Europeans – fearful that their oil supplies might dry up altogether if they antagonised the oil sheikhs still further – were rather more sympathetic (in public at least) towards the plight of the Palestinians. (The rift with the United States, although serious, was rapidly repaired at the NATO Heads of Government Conference in Ottawa in June 1974.)[44] What seemed especially promising from the European point of view was that the European nations, in the face of stern American opposition, had established something approaching a common position on what was undoubtedly a highly complex and difficult issue. However, in case anyone should get carried away with enthusiasm, it was also recognised that the achievement of this common position had probably been due less to the procedures established under EPC and more to a clear convergence of material interest in an urgent and threatening situation. The protagonists of EPC nevertheless remained undaunted. In the years after 1973 the Foreign Ministers of the Nine continued to attempt to carve out a distinctively European position on the whole Middle East question. Their efforts culminated in the June 1980 Venice Declaration which recognised that negotiations aimed at achieving a Middle East peace settlement must include the Palestine Liberation Organisation (PLO). The declaration also initiated a long-running dialogue between Western Europe and the more moderate Arab states that was intended as Europe's contribution to the

Middle East peace process. Unfortunately European efforts in this regard, though commendably 'harmonised', had '[very little] influence on the affairs of the region' itself.[45]

There were two other policy areas in which, after 1972, some progress was made towards a common European foreign policy. In the defence sphere – predictably, given the overlapping memberships of NATO and the EC – there was considerable agreement not only over military strategy, but also over arms procurement[46] and the need to engage in confidence-building measures with the countries of the Warsaw Pact.[47] Perhaps the main achievement, however, was in the *EC's economic relations with the third world.* In 1975, the EC member states negotiated a major trade and aid package with the Afro-Caribbean-Pacific (ACP) group of third-world countries. This first Lomé Convention, which was followed by others in 1979 and 1985, made provision both for privileged ACP access to protected EC markets and for special development-aid grants to the poorest third-world economies. Although – as discussed briefly in Chapter 4 – the Lomé process was ultimately of limited benefit to most ACP countries, the fact that the EC member-states had acted as a single bloc in so complex a set of negotiations implied that a common European approach to a wider range of policy issues might indeed be possible in the future.

In retrospect, however, it is clear that such optimism was misplaced. In many respects the Venice Declaration, Lomé and the agreements on defence were merely 'islands of agreement amid a sea of matters'.[48] They were exceptions to a general pattern of *non*-agreement in matters external to the Community: isolated examples of the successful co-ordination of national foreign policies rather than the embryonic embodiment of an emergent Community foreign policy. The main reason for this dearth of genuinely European foreign policy was simple. It is extraordinarily difficult for any group of nation-states, no matter how ingenious the procedural arrangements which it has established, to achieve agreement on complex matters of external policy when individual members of that group continue jealously to guard their own national sovereignty and national interests. Notwithstanding the sentiments underlying both the Treaty of Rome and EPC, this was precisely the position inside the European Community throughout the 1970s and 1980s. Ceding sovereignty to NATO in the military sphere had been unavoidable; ceding sovereignty to the Commission in the internal economic sphere had been positively beneficial; but political relations with states outside the Community remained the prerogative of the national governments: it would only be possible to achieve a common foreign policy on those rare occasions when, for whatever external reasons, the different national governments found themselves in agreement.

The British government, moreover, was one of the prime offenders in this regard. During the *Lomé negotiations* in the late 1970s, the British delegation frequently seemed to imply that, as a result of Britain's long experience with the Empire and Commonwealth, it was better placed than its European counterparts to understand the needs and aspirations of the impoverished peoples of the South – a posture which inevitably made it much more difficult for the EC negotiators as a whole to reach agreement with the ACP group. Similar problems arose in the mid-1980s with regard to the *Middle East* 'island of agreement'. Having accepted in 1980 the terms of the Venice Declaration, which recognised that the PLO had a crucial role to play in any attempted peace settlement, Mrs Thatcher's government unilaterally abandoned this position in October 1985 when it prevented a joint Jordanian–Palestinian negotiating team (which it had previously invited) from entering Britain. The express reason offered for the cancellation of the invitation was that, as PLO members who subscribed to the Palestine National Covenant, the Palestinian delegates did not accept Israel's right to exist within secure borders. This was a clear defection on Britain's part from the agreed European position which had insisted that, despite the hardline stance adopted in the Covenant, no progress on a negotiated settlement could be achieved without the participation of the PLO. Here was an 'island of agreement' that was rapidly sinking back into the sea, and at the British government's behest.

The fact that British diffidence had tarnished the EC's would-be common foreign policy even in those few areas where it had achieved limited success was not lost on Britain's European partners. They were equally irritated by the United Kingdom's posturings in areas where *no* common European position had been reached. In the context of *Latin America*, for example, where several of the continental European countries had extensive investments as well as a significant share of lucrative markets, London's actions during the Falklands crisis were a distinct embarrassment. On the one hand, the need to protect Europe's economic interests in Latin America pointed to a quiet neutrality; on the other, Britain *was* a partner in Europe and there *was* intense diplomatic pressure from both London and Washington aimed at persuading all of the Community countries to express their public support for British policy. In the event, Britain's European partners came out solidly in favour of the United Kingdom's robust stance against Argentina.[49] The consequence, however, was the loss of a considerable amount of Latin American goodwill; a loss which was immediately translated into a commensurate European irritation with Britain. The British refusal even to negotiate with the civilian Alfonsin regime after 1984 merely served to reinforce that irritation.

A similar divergence of opinion between Britain and its fellow Community members also arose over the question of *South Africa*. While the British government championed the maintenance of trade and investment connections with the apartheid regime in order that Pretoria might be gently persuaded to mend its ways, Britain's partners inclined more to the view that South Africa would only introduce real internal reform in the face of vigorous coercive diplomacy from other advanced industrial states. In these circumstances there was no prospect of a distinctive European approach: once again, the recalcitrant British appeared to be a major obstacle to the development of a common European foreign policy.

By the late 1980s, then, Britain appeared to be adopting a rather different position from the rest of Europe on a series of policy issues (economic relations with the third world, the Middle East, Argentina and South Africa) which might otherwise have provided the nucleus for an emerging Community foreign policy. Indeed, in the late 1980s, there was no common European foreign policy. At best the consultative procedures of EPC ensured that the foreign policies of the Twelve were *co-ordinated*.[50] And the British government's determination to pursue a very public 'independent' line ensured that even this co-ordination was severely limited. What was especially disappointing for serious supporters of further European integration was the declaration by the Community in 1985 that henceforward members would (1) 'inform and consult' one another on foreign policy matters and (2) 'develop and define ... common principles and objectives'.[51] This was past failure masquerading as good intent: (1) had been official policy since the inception of EPC in 1970; and (2) was merely an example of the classic bureaucratic formula which recommends that the insoluble problems of today should be left for resolution (preferably by someone else) tomorrow. Unfortunately the problems of 'developing and defining common principles and objectives' were always likely to prove as intractable in the future as they had done in the past. This was a clear indication that in the late 1980s European Political Co-operation was at a standstill.

Summary and conclusions

Britain's shift towards Europe after 1956 was the natural complement to its decreasing involvement in the Empire-cum-Commonwealth. What has been suggested in both this chapter and the last is that the major causes of this 'emptying out' of the Empire circle and the attendant 'infilling' of the European one were essentially *structural*: the emptying out and the infilling would have occurred anyway, whatever policy choices had been made by successive British governments. The shift in the focus of Britain's trading activity away from the Empire and towards Europe – which occurred over a decade before the United Kingdom's accession to the EC – represented a fundamental change in Britain's material economic interests that no government, no matter how determined, could have resisted. This is not to suggest, however, that policy calculations and policy decisions were unimportant in determining events in Europe after 1956. On the contrary, the precise institutional form which Britain's greater involvement would take, as well as the timing of that greater involvement, was very much a matter for governmental decision. It was not really the British government's fault that, having decided that the United Kingdom's destiny lay inside the EEC, its formal entry into 'Europe' should have been delayed for so long by an intransigent French president with a personality problem.

In any event, all three of Britain's attempts to join the EEC between 1961 and 1972 were based on entirely rational assessments both of the strategic shifts in Britain's international position which were taking place and of the likely costs and benefits of British membership. These calculations ran broadly as follows.

1. While Britain in the early 1960s was still strong enough to be deemed a Great Power, its pre-war world role had clearly been eclipsed by the rise of the two superpowers. Decolonisation, the withdrawal from east of Suez and the end of the Overseas Sterling Area – all, for different reasons, unavoidable – were clear indications that Britain's ability to undertake a world role was in serious decline. The best course of action, therefore, would be to recognise realities and seek to identify a new role that Britain would be capable of playing.

2. The Commonwealth was becoming increasingly redundant as a vehicle for projecting either British interests or British views abroad. In these circumstances, any attempt to build a new post-imperial role on the remains of the old Empire circle was doomed to failure.

3. Closer economic co-operation with the EEC promised to bring faster economic growth in Britain, thereby bringing about a reversal of the long-term economic decline which had been at least partly responsible for Britain's failing grip on its imperial possessions.

4. The Americans, upon whom Britain was so dependent both for the continued defence of Europe and for the supply of the hardware for the British independent deterrent, strongly supported Britain's incorporation into the West European economic club.

5. Given that even the British government was capable of interpreting trade statistics, it became increasingly clear in the 1960s that Britain's primary material economic interests now lay in its close trading contacts with western Europe. The fact that the Europeans had already started their own co-operative enterprise several years earlier could not be helped.

6. The obvious international role for Britain in the future was as a leading member of a dynamic European community which could itself expect to wield considerable political and economic influence on the world stage in the years ahead. The logic was impeccable; the conclusion inescapable: Britain applied to join Europe.

Yet once the application had finally been accepted, the vision of Britain as an active and thrusting 'European partner' seemed to fade. The United Kingdom government never appeared to be totally committed to its new 'European' role, consistently giving the impression abroad that the British were 'reluctant Europeans'. This failure to develop a genuinely European role in the 1970s and 1980s was the result of two major factors. The first was London's continuing 'Gaullist' view of the EC primarily as an association of sovereign states rather than as a fundamentally supranational community in which national interests would eventually be submerged. This position immediately set Britain at odds with most of the other Community members and in these circumstances it was clearly extremely difficult for Britain to play a leading role in EC affairs. The second factor was Britain's continued intriguing in pursuit of its residual pretensions and responsibilities in the old Empire circle. The belief that Britain's long imperial experience provided its government with a superior understanding of the problems of the third world not only produced significant policy divergences between Britain and its European counterparts but also made the task of developing a common European foreign policy much more difficult. Again, in circumstances such as these, Britain's behaviour seemed to justify accusations that it was not fully committed to the new European role which it had apparently so fervently wished to adopt between 1961, when it first applied for Community membership, and 1973 when it finally achieved it. Indeed, as the 1980s progressed, it became less and less clear what sort of role in world affairs the Thatcher government actually wished to play. Britain's frequent refusals to compromise its position in order to satisfy the sensibilities of its European partners suggested that it no longer saw Britain's role as a primarily European one. Yet London no longer possessed the capability to exercise anything other than minimal influence in the Empire circle. And although relations with Washington were good, the Cabinet was well aware that Britain was far less important to the United States as a strategic ally than it had been in the 1950s. By failing to commit itself more fully to the supranational principles and objectives of the EC, Britain had effectively disqualified itself from playing a leading role in Europe. Unfortunately it no longer had a distinctive role to play anywhere else. Where would it all end? Chapter 10 considers the problem.

6

The Changing 'Special Relationship', 1956–88

As was seen in Chapter 2, the 'special relationship' between Britain and the United States was forged during the vicissitudes of the Second World War. Yet as Chapter 2 also showed, in the late 1940s that relationship received a severe buffeting. The abrupt termination of Lend–Lease in September 1945 seriously weakened an already over-stretched British economy. The passage of the McMahon Act in August 1946 unilaterally ended five years of intimate Anglo-American nuclear collaboration and obliged the Attlee government to initiate its own independent programme of nuclear research. American diplomatic pressure was an added factor in provoking the British withdrawal from Palestine in May 1947.[1] And the US government's insistence on sterling's free convertibility in July 1947 produced a catastrophic run on the pound.[2]

Notwithstanding the considerable Anglo-American collaboration that took place both inside NATO after 1949 and under the auspices of the UN peace-keeping force in Korea after 1950, the 'special relationship' continued to experience traumas throughout the early 1950s. The exclusion of Britain from the ANZUS defence pact between the United States, Australia and New Zealand in September 1951 was interpreted in London as clear evidence of Washington's long-term intention to increase its influence in the Pacific at Britain's expense. Similarly, the US failure to join the Baghdad Pact in February 1955 was seen as an indication of America's refusal to underwrite an alliance which might enable Britain to preserve its political influence with existing client states in the third world. Suez was the final straw. Who *did* the Americans think they were? How on earth could Britain continue to enjoy a 'special relationship' with an 'ally' which had so malevolently ambushed British diplomacy in its hour of need?

The remarkable feature of Anglo-American relations in the years after 1956 was how quickly the 'special relationship' was restored. The first part of this chapter describes the rapid improvement in relations that occurred immediately after Suez, the decline that set in during the mid-1960s, and the partial revival that was effected during the Reagan–Thatcher period after 1980. The second part examines the major causal factors which underpinned these changes and suggests that the course of Anglo-American relations always depended primarily on *realpolitik* calculation. It also seeks to assess how far the 'special relationship' still existed in the late 1980s.

Developments in Anglo-American relations, 1956–88

There were three main phases in Britain's post-Suez relations with the United States.[3] For almost a decade after Suez, strenuous efforts were made on both sides of the Atlantic to repair the damage that Eden's Egyptian adventure had wrought. The efforts were largely successful. By the early 1960s, with Britain's decolonisation programme well under way (a development vigorously applauded in Washington), London looked set to adopt a significant support role behind the United States in the latter's attempts to protect the global strategic interests of the West. However this position did not survive the death of John F. Kennedy in November 1962 and the political demise of Harold Macmillan in October 1963. By 1965 it was clear that Britain no longer possessed the physical capability to sustain an extensive global military presence: as London became increasingly unwilling to commit resources to out-of-(NATO)-area operations, Britain quite simply became less *useful* to the United States. As a result, the 'specialness' of the 'special relationship' gradually faded, with Britain increasingly taking on the character of 'just another' European ally. During the period after 1980, however, relations experienced something of a revival. The common commitment of Margaret Thatcher and Ronald Reagan to market economies at home and strong anti-communism abroad led to a resurgence in Anglo-American collaboration in a variety of diplomatic, economic and military contexts. To return to the heady days of the wartime special relationship was of course impossible. None the less, under Thatcher the government loudly proclaimed its determination to preserve and strengthen Britain's ties with the 'Atlantic Circle'.

Phase 1: Repair, 1957–63

The political breach between London and Washington over Suez had undoubtedly been serious. The British in particular had been deeply wounded by the diplomatic humiliation which they had suffered at the hands of the Eisenhower administration. Yet the Soviet threat in Europe – underlined by the Soviet invasion of Hungary only a week before the Suez fiasco itself – and the continuing global threat of communist encroachment remained serious enough to merit a rapid restoration of bilateral relations. After all, the United States was still the world's leading capitalist power. And Britain, although its step was now clearly faltering, still possessed the ambition and the capabilities of a Great Power. As ever, classic *realpolitik* principle dictated that the common interests of both powers (above all else, preventing the spread of communism) would be better served by friendship and collaboration than by further discord and mutual recrimination.

The initial repair was effected by renewed co-operation in the military sphere. Throughout the 1950s – at a time when Britain's strategic air deterrent still relied totally on the RAF's increasingly outdated fleet of bomber aircraft – American (and Soviet) scientists had been making significant advances in the military application of ballistic missile technology. The Macmillan–Einsenhower meeting in Bermuda in March 1957 effectively gave Britain access to the fruits of the American research: some 60 Thor missiles were to be stationed in East Anglia under the joint ('dual-key') control of both British and American operational commanders. The US decision to share the new technology was an important symbolic concession: it not only indicated Washington's intention to heal the diplomatic rift over Suez but also reaffirmed the fact that the Anglo-American partnership remained at the heart of the defence of Europe.

The need to repair bilateral relations was made even more urgent by the Soviet launch of *Sputnik* in October 1957. There was no telling what this (temporary, it was hoped) Soviet victory in the 'space race' might imply for the delivery of nuclear warheads. In any event, prudence suggested that the two great capitalist allies should pool their scientific knowledge in order to meet the new challenge. The outcome, in July 1958, was the repeal of the 1946 McMahon Act (which had abruptly terminted the intimate Anglo-American nuclear collaboration of the war years) and the signing of the Agreement for Co-operation on the Uses of Atomic Energy for Mutual Defence Purposes (which effectively restored the nuclear-sharing *status quo ante* of the pre-McMahon years).[4] To be sure, the treaty would probably not have been signed if

Britain had not had something useful to offer as a result of having maintained its own independent nuclear research programme through-out the 1950s. Yet it was certainly of greater political import than its prosaic title might have suggested. Nuclear sharing would have been inconceivable without the high levels of mutual trust enjoyed by the political and military establishments of both countries: the smooth operation of the treaty's provisions in the years after 1958 served to reinforce that sense of trust and to maintain an 'island' of intimacy long after the 'special relationship' itself had ceased to have any real geostrategic significance.

The new post-Suez spirit of collaboration was not confined solely to nuclear weapons technology however. In the immediate wake of Nasser's diplomatic victory over Britain and France, Eisenhower had offered to provide anti-communist regimes in the Middle East with any economic and military assistance which they might require in order to strengthen their resistance to either external or internal threat.[5] In July 1958, in response to separate requests from King Hussein of Jordan and President Chamoun of the Lebanon, combined Anglo-American forces were urgently despatched to the Middle East. The civil distur-bances in Jordan and the Lebanon were both quickly suppressed and the authority of their respective governments accordingly restored. This was joint global policing *par excellence*, the two great Western allies acting in tandem to ensure that the Western sphere of influence in the Middle East would not be eroded by Soviet subterfuge and stealth: Suez was merely an unhappy memory now largely erased by the need to meet the undiminished and still ubiquitous challenge of Soviet expansionism.

The new convergence of interest and policy in the Middle East did not mean, however, that Anglo-American relations were entirely free of discord. The 'Colonel Zinc' affair in 1959 and the dispute over the RB47 engine in 1960 demonstrated that in certain policy areas old antagonisms could still disturb the increasingly smooth surface of Atlantic affairs.[6] At heart, however, relations remained excellent. In June 1960, following three months of intensive negotiation, Washington agreed to supply the newly-developed Skybolt missile system – capable of delivering nuclear warheads to Soviet bloc targets – to Britain's armed forces.[7] As far as London was concerned this was an even more important accord than the introduction of American Thor missiles in 1958: whereas Thor had been deployed under a dual-key arrangement, Skybolt (once it had been supplied) was to be solely at the disposal of Britain. If it were still needed, here was clear evidence that the 'special relationship' had indeed been restored. No other ally of the

United States had even come close to achieving the kind of deal which Macmillan had secured over Skybolt. And with the reinvigoration of the Cold War, provoked by the erection of the Berlin wall in August 1961, close Anglo-American relations would perhaps become even more necessary.

Unfortunately, in November 1962, it was announced that Skybolt, the new symbol of Anglo-American nuclear co-operation, simply didn't work. In London, suspicions that had previously been suppressed began to surface. Perhaps the Americans had not really wanted to assist Britain's nuclear weapons programme in the first place and the whole Skybolt deal had been a charade. Or perhaps Washington had had second thoughts about the British government's reliability and no longer wished to facilitate Britain's continued membership of the 'nuclear club'. Although the doubts seemed well-founded, they were firmly swept away by the agreement reached between Kennedy and Macmillan at Nassau in December 1962. Under remarkably generous terms,[8] the United States agreed to supply the United Kingdom with the Polaris submarine-launched missile system. And, although the missiles were officially designated for NATO purposes, it was clear that in supplying Polaris the Americans were effectively enabling Britain to maintain its independent nuclear deterrent without having to incur the enormous (and possibly prohibitive) costs of a full research and development programme.

The Nassau agreement, moreover, had come in the wake of the Cuban missile crisis of October 1962, when the world had waited with bated breath to see if Khrushchev would accede to Kennedy's demand that Soviet missile installations be removed from Cuban soil.[9] There is some disagreement as to what the crisis implied about the character of Anglo-American relations. According to some accounts, the crisis revealed the effective demise of the 'special relationship' itself: Washington's persistent disregard of London's views demonstrated the irrelevance of Britain's 'world role' posturings in the post-Suez era of the two superpowers.[10] In contrast, however, more recent evidence seems to suggest that throughout the crisis Kennedy in fact solicited advice from Macmillan on a frequent and regular basis.[11] Viewed in this light, in the last quarter of 1962, the 'special relationship' was apparently in better shape than at any time since early 1946. The Americans were prepared not only to supply Britain with the latest nuclear weapons technology but also to consult closely with London in what had undoubtedly been the most threatening international crisis since 1945. Almost inevitably, however, this position was not to endure for long. Although during the course of 1963 British and American negotiators continued to collaborate intimately in their discussions with the Soviets over the Partial Test Ban Treaty,[12] from the end of 1963 onwards relations between London and Washington, though they remained friendly, undoubtedly entered a period of gradual but inexorable decline. It is the character of this decline which is now examined.

Phase 2: Decay, 1964–79

Very few of the major changes which occur in international politics are without (deep) historical roots. The decay in the special relationship after 1963 was no exception. Even though the Nassau agreement could reasonably be presented as an indication of the closeness of relations, the agreement had in fact been reached in the face of strong opposition from the 'Europeanist' lobby inside the US State Department.[13] This lobby – centred upon Secretary of State George Ball – was strongly opposed to the continued British possession of an independent nuclear deterrent for two main reasons: first, it would encourage nuclear proliferation and thereby threaten the stability of Soviet–US mutual deterrence; and second, it might serve to weaken the resolve of Western Europe to provide sufficient conventional forces for the effective operation of NATO's flexible response strategy which was strongly favoured by the United States. The response of the 'Europeanist' lobby in December 1963 was to persuade newly-installed President Johnson to support their proposals for a multilateral force (MLF) which would incorporate Britain's nuclear deterrent into a combined West European force. The British reaction to MLF, not surprisingly, was extremely cool. After all, the retention of the independent deterrent was still considered necessary for the maintenance of Britain's Great Power status. In the run-up to the October 1964 General Election, however, the MLF issue receded from prominence. None the less, in November 1964, the new Labour government issued a series of counter-proposals for an 'Atlantic Nuclear Force' (ANF) which would combine the entire nuclear forces of Britain and France with the submarine capabilities of the United States.[14] By this time, however, the Johnson administration had become less convinced of either the efficacy or the desirability of a unified European nuclear deterrent and it accordingly abandoned its plans for MLF. Having suggested ANF principally as a bargaining counter to prevent MLF, the Wilson government was in turn only too ready quickly to shelve its proposals.

If the diplomatic impasse over MLF and ANF had done little more than ripple the surface of Atlantic relations, much deeper – and far more disruptive – currents were soon to make themselves felt over

Vietnam. Although the United States had been providing military assistance to the Diem regime in South Vietnam since 1961, during the course of 1964 American involvement, in a progressively deteriorating security situation, had increased considerably. Indeed at the beginning of 1965 the United States looked set to make further major deployments in order to resist the communist insurgency which was clearly being orchestrated from Hanoi. In an apparent attempt to emulate Attlee's visit to Washington in December 1950 (when the British premier had sought – unnecessarily – to dissuade Truman from using nuclear weapons in Korea) Wilson requested an urgent audience with Lyndon Johnson in order to counsel against deeper American involvement in South-East Asia. His approaches to the American President met with a rebuff, however, and he was sharply informed: 'I won't tell you how to run Malaysia and you don't tell us how to run Vietnam.'[15]

The real problem, of course, was that the differences between London and Washington over Vietnam ran much deeper than the contents of one irate telephone call between Harold Wilson and Lyndon B. Johnson. The Americans were desperate to receive international backing for their South-East Asian campaign: even a token British force would have constituted an important propaganda *coup* for the US administration. Unfortunately, the deep anti-American strain inside the Labour left, combined with Wilson's slender majority in the Commons, made it quite impossible for the Labour government seriously to consider sending a British contingent, no matter how small, to Vietnam in support of the American action. The Americans were understandably furious. Here was Washington's closest ally – which only two years earlier had been given the latest nuclear weapons technology at a knock-down price – refusing to lend even token assistance in a military campaign which the US administration deemed essential if the whole of South-East Asia was to be saved from communism. Secretary of State Dean Rusk was moved to observe that "All we needed was one regiment ... don't expect us to save you again.'[16] By mid-1965 the 'special relationship' was certainly looking a lot less special than it had at Nassau.

An even more serious blow to the special relationship, however, came with the Wilson government's 1967 decision – clearly presaged in the 1966 Defence Review – to withdraw from east of Suez. The decision to reduce Britain's world role and to concentrate its defence efforts primarily within Western Europe inevitably meant that in future Britain would be far less able either to play the sort of anti-communist trouble-shooting role that it had performed in Malaya between 1948 and 1956 or to furnish the sort of continuous anti-Soviet 'deterrent' presence which the Royal Navy had provided in the Indian Ocean throughout the postwar period. In a world still fraught (in American eyes) with communist danger, the British withdrawal from east of Suez was a serious abdication of responsibility. If the British were no longer available to patrol the South China Sea, the Indian Ocean and the Persian Gulf – and there was certainly no other Western nation ready to act as a satisfactory replacement – then the Americans would be obliged to undertake the task themselves. And although Wilson attempted to sweeten the pill by providing the United States with extensive naval facilities at Diego Garcia,[17] such a concession to the needs of global *realpolitik* did little to compensate Washington for the considerable extra expense that it would incur as a result of having to extend its own global naval commitments. Moreover, as far as the Americans were concerned, the timing of the British withdrawal – between 1968 and 1972 – could not have been worse, coming as it did when the Americans' morale-draining involvement in Vietnam was at its peak. For twenty years the British presence east of Suez had lightened Washington's burden in its efforts to make the world safe for capitalism and liberal democracy: with the British gone, the burden was inevitably increased and the Americans became commensurately more resentful. By reducing the potential for Anglo-American collaboration in out-of-(NATO) area operations, the British withdrawal from east of Suez had further weakened the 'special relationship'.

Yet if the withdrawal from east of Suez had reduced Britain's global strategic value in the eyes of the United States, it was also associated with a change in the *self*-perceptions of the British foreign policy establishment. Crucially, the withdrawal 'got rid of the psychological constraint of [the British government] thinking [of] itself as the United States' universal and indispensable number two'.[18] In essence, therefore, the withdrawal from east of Suez weakened Britain's ties with the residue of Empire *and* with the United States. And in so doing, of course, withdrawal paved the way for Britain's greater subsequent participation in the European circle, which itself served further to diminish – for policy makers in Washington – any 'specialness' that Britain might once have possessed.

If anyone in Washington had thought that the increasingly unhelpful British posture of the 1960s was simply the result of having a Labour government in office – and that it might be reversed by the swing of the political pendulum – they were rapidly disabused of such a belief by Edward Heath's actions after June 1970. In the first place the new Conservative government failed to make more than cosmetic adjustments to the deep defence cuts which had originally necessitated the withdrawal from east of Suez. In its desire to establish Britain's credentials as a 'good European', the Heath government then chose to ignore Henry Kissinger's somewhat extravagant plans to make 1973 the 'Year of Europe'. Worse still, in October 1973, Heath proceeded to make common cause with Britain's European partners in refusing base facilities to the American aircraft which were supplying Israel in its 'Yom Kippur' war with the Arab states.[19] All of these developments, inevitably, did little to endear London to Washington. Britain was merely behaving like any other self-regarding West European state: incessantly complaining about the cost of deterring the Russians; relying on the Americans to do the job for it; and refusing to provide material assistance to the United States when it was really needed for fear of what the Arabs might do in retaliation. It simply was not good enough. Wilson had been right when he had observed in December 1964 that Anglo-American relations were by then merely 'close' as opposed to 'special'.[20] With the German Federal Republic now supplying the biggest European troop contingent to NATO[21] and with the NATO *Eurogroup* well established,[22] Britain's relative importance to the United States in the security field was declining both inside *and* outside the NATO area of operations. By 1973, Anglo-American relations were indeed becoming distinctly ordinary.

The decline continued – without drama – throughout the 1970s. Within the context of NATO, of course, there was still clear agreement on the need to continue to deter Soviet aggression. Outside Europe, however, with Labour again in power from February 1974, London and Washington seemed to take increasingly divergent views of developments in world politics. Events that were viewed with alarm in Washington – such as the overthrow of the right-wing Salazar dictatorship in Portugal and the resultant revolutions in Angola and Mozambique in 1974–5 – were received with relative equanimity in London. In the Middle East, President Carter's diplomacy between 1976 and 1979 was focused primarily on achieving a peace accord between Egypt and Israel;[23] in contrast, the Callaghan government, along with its European partners, attached rather more importance to the fact that the Carter-sponsored peace process did almost nothing to alleviate the plight of the displaced Palestinians. In Latin America, whereas the Americans were happy to provide financial and military assistance to the right-wing dictatorships in Chile under Pinochet after 1973 and in Nicaragua under Somoza until 1979, London expressed rather more sympathy, respectively, for the assassinated Chilean President, Salvador Allende – a Marxist – and for the avowedly socialist Sandinista resistance. Notwithstanding the diplomatic support that the United

States had given to Britain in the latter's attempts to resolve the Civil War in Zimbabwe–Rhodesia in 1977 and 1978,[24] by May 1979 Anglo-American relations were at their lowest ebb for over a generation. And although continued Anglo-American collaboration inside NATO seemed assured, with the left clearly on the ascendant within the Labour party, the prospects for anything resembling even the 'close' relationship of the Wilson years seemed dim indeed. Yet much was about to change: in May 1979, Margaret Thatcher was elected Prime Minister with a sizeable majority in the House of Commons.

Phase 3: Revival, 1980–88

It might have been expected that, as in 1970, the election of a Conservative government would make very little difference to Anglo-American relations. Just as Edward Heath had failed to restore Britain's pre-1965 role as the United States' 'indispensable number two' (largely because of the secular decline in Britain's relative economic strength), so, it might have been supposed, Margaret Thatcher would also prove unable to halt the increasing tendency during the 1970s for London and Washington to adopt divergent positions on major international issues. British and American interests were slowly diverging; an increasing policy divergence would naturally follow. Such expectations, if they were ever seriously entertained, were soon confounded. Where Heath had been a self-avowed and highly committed 'European', the newly elected Prime Minister was an equally committed Atlanticist, resolute in her conviction that the maintenance of Britain's long-term security – the primary objective of UK foreign policy – lay in strengthening Britain's ties with the United States. Thatcher might not actually have had a 'mission' to restore the special relationship, but she certainly acted as if she had. From June 1979 onwards, the cultivation of Washington became a top priority.

In December 1979, the Thatcher Cabinet's efforts in this regard bore their first fruit when NATO foreign ministers resolved their internal differences over the deployment of cruise and Pershing II missiles in Western Europe. In January 1980, Britain announced its intention to allow 160 American-owned cruise missiles to be deployed in the United Kingdom.[25] This was an important symbolic affirmation of London's trust in Washington at a time when public opinion in Western Europe generally was becoming increasingly concerned about both the size and the character of American nuclear forces based in the European theatre. In July, agreement was reached over the purchase of the Trident I (C4) missile from the United States.[26] The new missile would replace the increasingly outdated Polaris system and provide for the continuance of the British independent deterrent well into the twenty-first century on terms equally favourable to those secured by Macmillan at Nassau. In January 1981, the task of promoting closer Anglo-American relations was rendered even easier when Ronald Reagan succeeded Jimmy Carter as President of the United States. Henceforward, Thatcher's natural Atlanticist inclinations would be firmly underpinned by a shared Anglo-American 'new right' ideology.[27] For both Reagan and Thatcher, the earthly salvation of all mankind, both at home and abroad, lay in the restoration of the market and the destruction of collectivism. Throughout the 1980s, this common ideological commitment to the rejuvenation of capitalism would be enough to ensure a remarkable degree of Anglo-American collaboration, even in situations where the immediate interests of London and Washington might appear – however temporarily – to diverge.

Thatcher and Reagan started as they meant to go on. In February 1981, Thatcher made a highly-publicised and extremely successful visit to the United States. Apart from further advancing the closeness of her personal relationship with the President, the visit produced a vigorous public statement of Britain's approval of the Reagan plan for the creation of a 'rapid deployment force' (RDF), a highly mobile military force which could be sent as and when necessary to trouble spots anywhere in the world (but most probably in the Middle East), in order to safeguard the strategic interests of the West. Although Britain's contribution (because of financial constraints) would be extremely limited, by expressing London's *preparedness* to contribute to RDF, Thatcher was providing precisely what Wilson had failed to give President Johnson in 1965; symbolic support and involvement in out-of-(NATO) area operations. This was very much what the US government needed in order to prosecute its continuing global campaign against Soviet-inspired subversion, while at the same time proclaiming to world opinion that it was not acting *unilaterally* to defend purely American interests.

Thatcher's reward for backing RDF arrived swiftly. In October 1981 the Reagan administration announced that Trident II (D5) would become fully operational well ahead of its original target date and that Britain was welcome to purchase it as a replacement for Polaris instead of Trident I. After six months of assessment, in March 1982, a contract for the British purchase of Trident II was duly signed, again, on terms extremely favourable to Britain.[28]

But even greater American largesse was close at hand. At the end of March 1982, the Argentinians invaded and occupied the Falkland

Islands. Thatcher's response was both decisive and determined. The Royal Navy declared an 'exclusion zone' around the islands and a task force was urgently despatched with orders to retake the islands. In terms of *realpolitik*, the United States was in a rather delicate position. First, if it followed Reagan's political instincts and sided with Britain, it risked damaging its good relations not only with Argentina, but also with the rest of non-Communist Latin America, where US companies had substantial investments. Second, the dispute itself had come to a head at a time when Britain was making common cause *against* the United States by siding with a number of EC countries that were resisting American efforts to dissuade them from building a gas pipeline to the Soviet Union. In addition, the United States was under no legal obligation to assist a NATO ally in this sort of out-of-area operation. Throughout April, therefore, the US government attempted to act as a mediator between Buenos Aires and London, though with both General Galtieri and Thatcher immovable, US efforts were entirely unsuccessful. By May, however, in the absence of a diplomatic settlement, Reagan's policy came out decisively in favour of Britain. Public statements of support were backed by the provision of refuelling facilities at Ascension Island and by the supply of satellite intelligence to the British War Cabinet. This latter factor in particular was extremely important in securing an early British victory in the actual military campaign.[29] Crucially, however, what the Falklands episode had demonstrated was that, in a serious crisis, Britain had been able to count on American support. Perhaps this was not quite a resurrection of the old wartime special relationship, but in the changed circumstances of the 1980s, in a world dominated by superpower *realpolitik*, it was a passable imitation.

Thatcher was able to repay her South Atlantic debt to the Americans relatively quickly, in the somewhat unusual forum of the Middle East. During the course of 1982, the Israelis had become increasingly embroiled in the internal politics of the Lebanon. They had successfully flushed the PLO out of Beirut but their efforts to effect a subsequent withdrawal were being thwarted by the increase in Syrian influence throughout Lebanon that seemed likely to follow an Israeli evacuation. In an attempt to facilitate an Israeli withdrawal – and at the same time perhaps win a few friends in the Middle East – the American government offered to cover the Israeli retreat by installing a peace-keeping force in and around Beirut. The force would interpose itself between the various rival Lebanese militias in an attempt not only to minimise the violence between them but also to avoid giving the Syrians a pretext for further intervention. As with Vietnam in 1965 and the Rapid

Deployment Force in 1981, it was important for propaganda purposes that the proposed peace-keeping force should be multinational, rather than an exclusively American one. And, as with the plans for an RDF, Thatcher was a ready accomplice in support of Washington's designs: in September 1983 a sizeable British contingent joined the American-dominated multinational force, remaining until the bulk of the force was evacuated in March 1984. Once again, Thatcher had demonstrated Britain's new-found support for the United States in out-of-area operations: an important symbol of Britain's determination to back American efforts to defend Western interests throughout the world.

The only major source of Anglo-American discord during Thatcher's first two periods of office was the Grenada affair of 1983. A former British colony and member of the Commonwealth, Grenada had been ruled until 1979 by a conservative, pro-Western government under Eric Gairey. In March 1979, however, the Gairey regime had been ousted in a *coup* by Maurice Bishop's New Jewel Movement (NJM), a Marxist–Leninist organisation which had close ties with the Castro regime in Cuba. In the belief that some kind of Caribbean domino effect might be in the making – with Cuba, Nicaragua and Grenada now all professing Socialist governments – the US government determined that if at all possible the NJM must be removed. Internal feuding within the movement, which provoked the assassination of Bishop by a rival faction under Bernard Coard, provided the Americans with the excuse they had been looking for. In October 1983, on the pretext of protecting the safety of American citizens stranded in Grenada, US forces invaded the island, removed the remaining NJM leaders from power and installed a pro-Western provisional government which subsequently held elections and delivered Grenada from the Soviet–Cuban embrace that the NJM government had favoured. The American action – judging by the welcome the invading US troops received – was popular with most Grenadians. It was also approved by the majority of other Caribbean governments: the State Department had even managed to persuade several of them to contribute troops to the invading force so that (as in Lebanon) the force could be invested with the epithet 'multinational'.

In terms of its effects (eliminating an unpleasant bunch of Marxists) the Grenadian invasion was warmly welcomed in London. What rankled, however, was the precipitate manner in which Washington had acted. Grenada, after all, was part of the Commonwealth, and accordingly Her Majesty's Government could reasonably expect to have at least been informed of American plans and intentions prior to the invasion. Yet only hours before the US action, Foreign Secretary

Howe had confidently told the Commons that in his view an American intervention was unlikely.[30] Notwithstanding the Thatcher government's resultant political and diplomatic embarrassment (Denis Healey described Thatcher as 'Mr Reagan's poodle'), Anglo-American relations were not seriously affected. What really mattered was that in at least one part of the Caribbean the creeping tide of Soviet-style socialism had been resisted and rolled back. If this meant that Washington had been obliged to keep an interested ally in the dark, then so be it. A satisfactory outcome, which the Americans had certainly achieved, was far more important than a few red faces either in Cabinet or in the Foreign Office. In these circumstances London did not make an issue of the affair but instead allowed it quietly to fade into the background, leaving the healthy state of relations between London and Washington virtually unimpaired.

This happy position continued throughout 1984 and 1985. On the great strategic issue of the day – the American Strategic Defense Initiative (SDI) – Britain firmly supported the United States in its decision to press ahead with research into the new 'defensive' technologies as rapidly as possible. Indeed, in October 1985, Defence Secretary Michael Heseltine was even able to sign with his American counterpart an agreement under which British companies would be eligible to undertake (what it was hoped would be extremely lucrative) SDI contract work for the US Department of Defense. Britain also found itself in agreement with the Reagan administration on the great international *moral* issue of the mid-1980s – what to do about South Africa now that it was experiencing increasing civil disorder as a result of an upsurge in black political consciousness. In a situation where the rest of the Commonwealth, as well as the vast majority of other countries, were strongly in favour of economic sanctions against Pretoria, Britain and the United States rejected such punitive measures out of hand. London and Washington justified this position on the grounds that economic sanctions would do nothing to bring about internal reform in South Africa (indeed they might succeed in driving the Afrikaners even further into their laager) and would merely damage the material position of the very people, the South African blacks, that they were designed to assist. Critics, in contrast, argued that white South Africa had already retreated into its laager as far as it was possible to go and that the majority of blacks were quite happy to see their material position damaged in the medium term if it meant an end to apartheid. In reality, of course, no one actually knew what the precise effects of imposing economic sanctions would be, and no one knew whether or not the majority of black South Africans genuinely welcomed their imposition. In any event, during the summer of 1986, the combination of British and American resistance effectively defeated a series of international moves to impose sanctions against South Africa. If such resistance perpetuated an outrageously unjust and inhumane system of government, then this was unfortunate but unavoidable. Reagan and Thatcher were in no doubt that South Africa was far too valuable a strategic resource to risk its loss to the Soviets in the bloody aftermath of a bloody revolution. A simple *realpolitik* principle was at work which the West could ignore only at its great peril: better the racist – but stanchly capitalist – tyranny you know than the anarchic, unstable and possibly pro-Moscow democracy you do not. Ron and Margaret understood one another: a common Anglo-American position on South Africa was necessary to secure the long-term strategic interests of the West.

At the same time as London and Washington were pursuing similar diplomatic policies towards South Africa, they were also involved in rather more intimate collaboration over Libya. Colonel Qadafi had been a thorn in the Americans' side for over a decade. His open espousal of revolutionary causes had been a source of constant irritation to Washington and his increasing willingness to provide both military hardware and training facilities to anti-Western terrorist groups a source of genuine alarm. The final straw came in March 1986 when American intelligence services purportedly intercepted a series of communications between Tripoli and the Libyan People's Bureau in West Berlin which – at least to President Reagan's satisfaction – provided incontrovertible evidence of Libyan government complicity in the deaths of numerous American servicemen in the bombing of a Berlin night club.[31] The US administration, already involved in a naval confrontation with the Libyans in the Gulf of Sirte, swiftly decided to take punitive action against Libya and sought the British government's permission to use American F-111 fighter aircraft stationed in Britain in order to effect a 'surgical strike' against Qadafi's capital.[32] With this permission readily given, on the night of 14–15 April American planes bombed selected targets in Tripoli and Benghazi.

Western reaction to the attack was perhaps more antipathetic than Thatcher had anticipated. The Labour Party, of course, fumed; but then that was entirely expected. More seriously, opinion polls showed that almost two-thirds of the British electorate – partly concerned that innocent civilians had been killed and partly fearful of Libyan reprisals to come – disapproved of the British government's tacit involvement in the American raid.[33] Meanwhile, Britain's EC partners were angry that on the day before the raid took place Sir Geoffrey Howe had failed to inform a meeting of European Foreign Ministers that Britain had already acceded to the American request to use British-based aircraft in the attack. Thatcher simply rode out the criticisms. She informed the Commons that it would have been 'inconceivable' for the British government to have refused the American request for assistance when all else had failed to subdue the Libyan 'mad dog'.[34] She emphasised the debt that Britain owed to the United States as a result of services rendered during the Falklands war. And she even suggested that from the humanitarian point of view the use of British-based F-111s had restricted Libyan civilian casualties: long-range bombers flying from bases in the United States would have been far less able to effect the sort of limited surgical strike that the Americans had attempted to undertake.[35]

The crucial point about the Libyan affair, however, was that yet again Thatcher had displayed her Atlanticist commitment. Assisting Washington was more important then keeping Paris or Bonn informed of policies which, should they backfire, might bring a new and virulent round of reprisal terrorism to the major cities of Western Europe. Moreover, as time passed and Qadafi's threatened terrorist response failed to materialise, Thatcher's supporters could reasonably claim that her pro-American stance had achieved its express objective: it had helped to chasten the Libyan regime into at least a temporary abandonment of 'state-sponsored terrorism'. Even the initially suspicious British electorate seemed to agree: by November 1986, the Libyan bombings had almost completely disappeared as a political issue.

During the course of 1987, Thatcher was presented with a new opportunity to strengthen Anglo-American collaboration in out-of-area operations: in the crisis in the Gulf. Iran and Iraq had been at war, with long interludes of military stalemate, since September 1980. The Western powers in general had an obvious interest in ensuring that the war did not seriously affect the export of oil from the Gulf. In addition, Britain also had specific responsibilities with regard to the defence of several of the Gulf sheikdoms.[36] From December 1980 onwards, Britain's contribution to the continued free movement of Gulf shipping was the provision of the 'Armilla patrol', an escort service to British shipping sailing between Bahrain and the Straits of Hormuz at the mouth of the Gulf. Until mid-1985, the patrol was broadly successful in deterring attacks on British merchant ships. Throughout 1986 and 1987, however, the Iraqis, unable to bring the Iranians to the negotiating table in order to end the war, increased their efforts to internationalise the conflict by stepping up the frequency of their attacks on Western shipping suspected of carrying Iranian oil. These attacks in turn increased the risks of Iranian reprisals and thereby threatened the security of *all* the shipping in the Gulf.

The Kuwaitis, given their geographical closeness to Iraq, were particularly alarmed by these developments: if the war at sea were to escalate, Kuwait's ability to export its oil would be seriously imperilled, with disastrous consequences for its domestic economy. In July 1987, in a neat diplomatic manoeuvre designed to obtain American protection of Kuwaiti shipping, the Kuwaiti government made informal approaches to Moscow aimed at soliciting *Soviet* protection for Kuwaiti oil tankers. The Americans were obliged to react quickly: while Iraqi attacks on Iranian shipping (though potentially dangerous) had been tolerable, a dramatic increase in Soviet military and diplomatic influence in the Gulf, which would surely follow if the Soviets were indeed allowed to act as Kuwait's protector, was wholly unacceptable. The result was that in late July the Reagan administration offered to 'reflag' Kuwaiti tankers under US colours and to provide naval protection if necessary to these newly-flagged 'American' ships. The Iranians in turn interpreted the American reflagging exercise as a cynical attempt to increase Washington's influence in the Gulf, possibly as a prelude to an American intervention, on the side of Iraq, in the Gulf war itself. As a result, Iranian revolutionary guards began to lay mines in and around the main shipping channels of the northern Gulf. It was particularly unfortunate for the Americans (indeed, to non-specialist observers it was almost unbelievable) that, in spite of their new commitment to the preservation of Gulf security, the US Navy did not possess the minesweeping capability necessary to protect either neutral merchant shipping or American warships.

Horribly embarrassed, in August 1987, the Americans requested assistance from their NATO allies. For the first time under Thatcher, the British government openly demurred. Aware of the political, as well as the naval, minefield that the United States was entering, and unconvinced that the Americans had really thought through the problems of military strategy which they might encounter in seeking to police the Gulf, London refused to be drawn. The American request for minesweeping assistance was politely rejected. In the last week of August, however, the Iranians stepped up the burgeoning conflict still further by mining the approaches to the Straits of Hormuz. This constituted a much more direct violation of the principle of free passage – as well as a more direct assault on *British* interests – and as a result Thatcher relented. Six minesweepers were duly despatched from the United Kingdom to assist the Armilla patrol in its regular escort operations. Indirectly, of course, the minesweepers would also be in a position to lend assistance to American warships in the Gulf. Once again, the Thatcher government had demonstrated its preparedness to make common cause with the Americans in the defence of the interests of the West as a whole.

The affair in the Gulf in the late summer of 1987 gave Britain the opportunity to show that the 'Reagan's poodle' characterisation of the Thatcher Cabinet's foreign policy was not entirely fair. The fact that Thatcher had starkly refused an American request for assistance – judging intervention at that stage to be contrary to British interests – suggested that, on the previous occasions when Britain had followed a policy which met with American approval, it had perhaps done so principally because the Cabinet's analysis of the situation – guided by Thatcher – had been similar to that of the US government. In the 1987 Gulf crisis, the British government's analysis had clearly been at variance with that of the Americans and the Cabinet had accordingly been reluctant to provide backing for the American position even when explicitly requested to do so. It had only been when the *situation* had dramatically altered, with the mining of the Straits, that the Cabinet's own analysis had changed. And it was on the basis of this new analysis that London subsequently decided to provide (something approaching) the sort of material support that Washington had originally requested.

By the late 1980s, then, it was clear that Thatcher was not an automatic supporter of American foreign policy in all of its out-of-area operations. Crucially, what she shared with the key decision makers in Washington was a *convergence of view* of the nature of international politics and of the character and seriousness of the global threats to Western interests. It was this more than anything else which produced the numerous examples of Anglo-American policy collaboration throughout the 1980s. Thatcher might not have restored *the* special relationship – in the changed circumstances of the postwar world this was an impossibility anyway – but she had without doubt established *a* special relationship with Ronald Reagan's America. In spite of Gorbachev's *glasnost*, the world was still a dangerous place in which only resolute strategies of *realpolitik* would prevail against the ubiquitous Soviet threat. Reagan's America was still the 'number one' defender of the capitalist values and interests of the West. Even if Britain no longer possessed the capability to be 'America's *universal* number two', it could at least provide assistance with all the resources at its command in certain limited contexts. What was good for American foreign policy was good for the capitalist West. And what was good for the capitalist West was good for Britain. This was the essential logic underlying

Thatcher's Atlantic circle foreign policy. Small wonder that she enjoyed a special relationship with Reagan.

Continuity and change in Anglo-American relations: some explanatory factors

It is clear, then, that the 'special relationship' underwent a number of important changes in the years after Suez. What is also clear, however, is that, even though the relationship certainly became less 'special' after 1963, relations remained sufficiently strong throughout the 1960s and 1970s to provide Thatcher with the firm diplomatic base which she needed in order to reinvigorate London's links with Washington in the period after 1979. What were the principal factors responsible for Britain's continued good relations with the United States? Why, within that framework of generally good relations, did the intimacy of Anglo-American co-operation vary over time? While it is not possible to answer these questions definitively, there are none the less several factors which were of such obvious and overriding importance that they merit review here.

Sources of continuity

Four main factors underpinned the basic stability of Anglo-American relations in the years after 1956. The first, though by no means the most significant, was *the continuing natural affinity which derived from a common language and a broadly similar culture.*[37] However, while similarities in language and culture were obviously relevant to the general feelings of mutual affect that were evident on both sides of the Atlantic,[38] they were clearly neither a necessary nor a sufficient condition for close *governmental* relations. Indeed, although sentiment derived from cultural affinities was frequently employed in public in order to justify or legitimise policy choices that had already been made, the available evidence suggests that most decisions affecting mutual bilateral relations were based primarily on tough, self-interested calculation.[39]

It is in this context that a second, and certainly more important, factor underlying the continuity in Anglo-American relations immediately assumes relevance: *the convergence of the two countries' economic interests.* One aspect of this convergence was *trade.* British exports to the United States remained at substantial levels throughout the postwar period, apparently unaffected by the fundamental shift in exports away from the Empire and towards Western Europe which occurred after 1955.[40] Bilateral trade alone, however, was never sufficiently important to produce a special relationship between London and Washington: while, on average, some 10 per cent of British exports were destined for the United States in the years 1945–85, only 5 per cent of American exports during the same period relied on markets in Britain.[41] The convergence of economic interest that really mattered was the *mutual benefit which Britain and the United States derived from the preservation of the existing capitalist system of world trade*. As relatively open economies with wide-ranging and diverse patterns of trade, Britain and the United States had a mutual interest, first, in preventing the 'loss' of any capitalist economies (together with their markets and raw material resources) to the rival 'socialist' camp; and second, in ensuring that the spectre of protectionism – which had surfaced so disastrously in the 1930s – was pushed further into the background by the progressive liberalisation of world trade. Even in the face of Britain's continuing relative economic decline, which was increasingly apparent to everyone after the mid-1950s, London and Washington retained both of these mutual interests which they continued to attempt to maximise jointly, albeit increasingly in cooperation with other OECD countries, and especially with the so called 'Group of 7'.[42]

Rather like 'cultural affinities', however, a mere convergence of general economic interests was not significant to produce the sort of intimate relations enjoyed by London and Washington for much of the postwar period. Certainly from 1968 onwards, when Britain was obliged to abandon the Overseas Sterling Area, Britain was no more important to the United States as an economic partner than any of the other Group of 7 countries. A third, and crucial, source of stability in postwar Anglo-American relations was, in classic *realpolitik* fashion, a *convergence of security interests*. For both countries it was of paramount importace that if at all possible the Soviet Union should be prevented not only from making any incursion into Western Europe but also from extending its influence in the third world. Any gain made by the Soviets would imply a commensurate loss for the West. In order to prevent the piecemeal dismantling of the Western sphere of influence in the third world it was necessary to maintain non-communist governments in as many countries as possible; to ensure that areas rich in raw material recources remainded under capitalist control; and to retain control of all the strategic sites necessary to keep open the world's major shipping lanes in times of both war and peace.

It was of course entirely natural for the United States, as the capitalist world's dominant power, to take a leading role in these efforts to protect the strategic interests of the West. American private enterprise was clearly deriving substantial benefit from the current international *status quo* and Washington accordingly had a strong interest in maintaining it. After 1956, however, it was less obvious why Britain should have attempted to play such a strong subsidiary role in support of the United States. For one thing, Suez itself had cruelly exposed the limitations of British power in the third world. For another, by the late 1950s formerly 'safe' British markets overseas were increasingly being eroded by American and West European (and later, Japanese) competition. In essence, Britain could not apparently do very much to protect the global interests of Western capitalism; and yet, even if the collective efforts of the Western Powers succeeded in fending off Soviet expansionism, the United Kingdom itself stood to gain very little in material terms. The British government was confronted with two alternative analyses of this situation. On the one hand, from the point of view of national self-interest, Britain's best course of action might be to devote the resources that were being spent on 'protecting western strategic interests' to the improvement of the country's domestic manufacturing base, thereby improving the efficiency of British industry and perhaps restoring Britain's competitive position in overseas markets. London could then follow the example of other OECD governments and attempt to 'free ride' on American largesse, leaving the United States to protect western strategic interests on its own. The alternative analysis, on the other hand, recognised that the United States was perhaps genuinely incapable of performing such an enormous task alone; that, in an age of decolonisation, with both Chinese and Soviet communism in the ascendant, Washington required the assistance of at least one other major Western power. In these circumstances, it was Britain's historical misfortune to be in possession of the remnants of an Empire which provided its government with a significant amount of political leverage in several strategically vital parts of the world: this uniquely qualified Britain to act as Washington's 'universal and indispensable number two'. For much of the period after 1956, it was this second analysis which dominated Britain's dealings with the United States. The main reason that it dominated, moreover, was that in spite of its veneer of altruism it was an analysis firmly grounded in *realpolitik*. What London shared with Washington was a realist world-view – a common commitment to Realism. In the face of the threat of communist encroachment, British and American policy makers alike were convinced that the world was an extremely dangerous place in which narrow calculations about the relative benefits likely to accrue to individual capitalist countries were clearly outweighed by the overriding need to maintain the security of the West as a whole. It was this shared *perception* of common security interests – as much as any *objective* interest convergence – that lay at the heart of the close relations between London and Washington throughout the postwar period.

A fourth major factor underlying Britain's consistently close relations with the United States, at least after 1958, was 'nuclear sharing'. The McMahon Act of 1946 had ended the vitally important atomic collaboration of the war years and obliged Britain to develop its own independent nuclear programme. The repeal of McMahon in 1958 and the subsequent signing of the Anglo-American treaty,[43] however, had effectively restored much of the old nuclear relationship. Not only could technical secrets once again be exchanged, but the path was now cleared for Britain to receive American nuclear hardware in the future – as the American decisions to supply first Skybolt and then Polaris were soon to demonstrate.

Of course, on both sides of the Atlantic an essential precondition for nuclear-sharing had been a high level of mutual intergovernmental trust. Significantly, it seems that the very act of nuclear sharing itself served to increase that sense of trust still further.[44] Even as London and Washington gradually drifted apart politically in the late 1960s and 1970s, relations between them still displayed an intimacy in nuclear matters that neither country ever achieved with a third party. And in the context of more contentious policy areas, such as out-of-area operations, this intimacy undoubtedly helped to promote smoother bilateral relations than might otherwise have been expected. The crucial feature of Anglo-American nuclear sharing after 1958, however, was that it cemented the informal understanding between Britain and the United States regarding their respective roles in the international system. The United States would effectively help Britain to maintain its Great Power status by supplying it with an up-to-date independent nuclear deterrent, while London for its part would provide 'independent' support for the Americans in their efforts to keep the world safe for capitalism and liberal democracy. It was a convenient arrangement for both parties and it certainly helped to underpin the generally good relations which London and Washington enjoyed throughout the post-Suez period.

Sources of change

While there were several factors encouraging stability in Anglo-

American relations after 1956, there were also a number of forces at work that were conducive to change. As noted earlier, in the immediate wake of Suez the need to prevent the growing Soviet influence in Egypt from spreading to other parts of the Middle East led to such a rapid restoration of relations that within a year London and Washington were engaged in joint military action to protect pro-Western regimes in Jordan and the Lebanon. Once Britain's 'second wave' decolonisation programme got under way after 1956, an even more potent source of Anglo-American cordiality came into operation: strong American approval of the revised 'world role' which the British government seemed poised to adopt. Successive US administrations had consistently voiced their suspicions of Britain's postwar imperial designs. The fact that London was now vigorously decolonising – which clearly demonstrated Britain's attachment to democratic ideals – was inevitably viewed with considerable favour in Washington. What pleased the Americans even more was that, notwithstanding the shedding of its colonial possessions, Britain still seemed to be committed to maintaining a military presence in enough strategic locations worldwide to enable Britain, should the need arise, to make a useful contribution to anti-communist trouble-shooting operations anywhere in the world. This was exactly the sort of burden sharing that the Americans wanted. With Washington clearly the senior partner, the United States and Britain could face the threat of communist encroachment together, as joint protectors of the strategic interests of the West.

From 1964 onwards, however, this vision of renewed Atlantic collaboration gradually began to fade as a series of developments – largely outside the British government's control – started to weaken the close diplomatic ties between London and Washington. The first of these was a consequence of the United Kingdom's long-term relative economic decline. Throughout the postwar period Britain had achieved significantly lower growth rates than its major industrial competitors and by the mid-1960s the cumulative effects of this poor performance were becoming all too apparent. Successive governments were being plagued by endemic balance of payments crises and by persistent pressure to cut government expenditure. Against this background of relative economic decline, the cost of maintaining a widely-dispersed overseas military presence was rising inexorably.[45] The logic of the situation was inescapable. The British economy was increasingly incapable of supporting the sort of political and military world role to which its government aspired, and cuts would have to be made. The immediate consequence of the Wilson government's resultant decision to cut defence spending by withdrawing from east of Suez was that

Britain simply became less *useful* to the United States in its efforts to resist communist expansionism in the third world. How could the Royal Navy help to protect democracy in Thailand, for example, if it had already evacuated Singapore? At the same time, moreover, Britain was being overtaken by West Germany as the main European contributor to NATO's conventional forces.[46] Both outside and inside the NATO context, therefore, Britain's significance as a militiary partner for the United States was in serious decline. In the harsh world of *realpolitik* such a development was bound to produce a cooling in Atlantic relations, especially at a time when Britain was looking to strengthen its ties with the European Community.

A second major source of the decay in Anglo-American relations after 1963 concerned the political and economic changes that were occurring inside the United States itself. Not least among these was the gradual shift in the geographical locus of American economic activity – away from the 'smoke-stack' industrial states of the eastern seaboard and towards the hi-tech sunrise states of the south and west. Beginning in the mid-1960s, this apparently autonomous shift in economic activity towards the west coast was reinforced by the dramatic growth over the next two decades of the Far Eastern economies of Japan, Taiwan, South Korea, Hong Kong and Singapore.[47] This expansion in turn created an awareness in Washington that US *economic* interests in this new 'Pacific Basin' region were just as important, if not more important, than those in Western Europe. Moreover this awareness was reinforced by the largely coincidental decline of the old east coast foreign policy establishment.[48] This process was accelerated in the late 1970s and 1980s by the retirement of a generation of politicians, administrators and military personnel who had established close personal and institutional links with Britain and Western Europe either during or immediately after the Second World War. Their successors were far less committed to the idea of the United States as a member of an *Atlantic* security community and concomitantly far more open to the idea of developing an alternative one in the Pacific. This gradual change in consciousness, combined with the change in material interests which the shift towards the Pacific Basin implied, inevitably resulted in the United States adopting a more critical approach to its dealings with Western Europe. This in turn caused Washington to attach rather less importance to its links with London, and, not surprisingly, the Anglo-American relationship suffered accordingly.

A third factor was the United States' increasing concern with *superpower* relations. Until the mid-1960s, Washington had tended to conduct its negotiations with the Soviet Union mainly on a multilateral

– rather than a bilateral – basis. The British Embassy in Moscow in particular had enjoyed intimate relations with its American counterpart and London had almost invariably been consulted when the United States administration was considering a major departure in its Soviet policy.[49] The negotiations preceding the Partial Test Ban Treaty in 1963 – in which Harold Macmillan had played a crucial role – were a typical case in point. From 1964 onwards, however, the United States was far more inclined to restrict formal negotiations over such a vital area as arms control to the Soviet Union alone. How far this was the result of American as opposed to Soviet preferences is uncertain, but the outcome was the same. There was no place for Britain in either the anti-ballistic missile (ABM) treaty negotiations in 1971/2 or in the negotiations that led up to the Strategic Arms Limitation Treaties (SALT) of 1972 and 1979. On the contrary, the high table was reserved exclusively for the superpowers. As a mere Great Power in decline, Britain could not reasonably expect to be represented. Indeed, even Margaret Thatcher's resuscitation of Anglo-American collaboration in the 1980s could not win Britain a place at the Reykyavik Summit in 1986. As a result, London had no hand in the negotiations that laid the foundation for the subsequent US–Soviet agreement to eliminate medium-range nuclear missiles in Europe, which was eventually signed in December 1987.

Yet Margaret Thatcher did re-establish a more intimate relationship with the United States than that enjoyed by any Prime Minister since Harold Macmillan. This intimacy was partly a result of Thatcher's instinctive Atlanticism, but it was also partly a consequence of the close correspondence between the Reagan and Thatcher views both of the seriousness of Soviet-inspired threats to Western interests and of the concomitant need to resist them with determination. Moreover, in 1979–80, when Thatcher and Reagan were assuming office, the world as viewed through the lens of Realism was beginning to look a distinctly more dangerous place for the Western democracies. During the mid-1970s, Vietnam, Laos, Cambodia, Ethiopia, Angola and Mozambique had all been 'lost' to the communist sphere of influence. In 1979, Nicaragua had been lost to the Cubans and Afghanistan to the Soviets. Iran was in the throes of an Islamic revolution. While it was perhaps not possible to do anything to restore these particular losses in the short term, Anglo-American collaboration might none the less serve to prevent *further* encroachment by the 'evil Empire'.[50] For the Americans, therefore, the possibility of renewed co-operation with London offered the prospect of 'independent' support for essential 'out-of-area' operations. For London, renewed co-operation with Washington represented an opportunity to effect a partial recovery of Britain's world role; to reverse the decline which had set in almost immediately after 1945 and which had accelerated with the withdrawal from east of Suez. It was an opportunity not to be missed, a chance to 'put the "Great" back into Britain', which Thatcher seized with both hands. Of course, how far the Thatcher government's foreign policy actually enhanced Britain's *general* international standing remains a matter for debate. And whether or not Britain's limited involvement in out-of-area operations in the 1980s objectively did anything to restore Britain's former 'world role' similarly remains open to question. There can be little doubt, however, that the 'Iron Maiden' significantly improved Britain's standing in *American* eyes. Under Thatcher, the would-be special relationship was not quite the one-sided affair that it had frequently appeared to be for the previous 30 years.

Summary and conclusions

One problem that confronts any analysis of Anglo-American relations in the postwar period is that the 'special relationship' itself is susceptible to such a wide range of interpretations. It has variously been claimed that the relationship was always much more 'special' for London than it was for Washington;[51] that, as an 'agreeable British myth to help cushion the shock of national decline', it never really existed at all;[52] that, on the contrary, it *did* exist until the mid-1960s, but faded as British and American interests diverged;[53] that in matters of military intelligence it survived throughout the postwar period;[54] that with regard to the crucial question of nuclear-weapons sharing it came fully to fruition only after 1958;[65] and that, having faded with the death of Kennedy and the resignation of Macmillan, it was revived on a tide of Thatcherism in the 1980s.[56] While all of these interpretations – and doubtless several others – can plausibly be derived from the history of postwar Anglo-American relations, it would certainly be beyond the scope of this study to attempt to decide between them. What is clear, however, is that in general relations between London and Washington were remarkably good throughout the postwar period, though whether this closeness constituted something which was at any stage *uniquely* 'special' remains a matter for speculation.

It has been suggested above that the continuing cordiality of Anglo-American relations was the result of four main factors: the broadly similar cultures; a shared economic interest in preserving the capitalist system of world trade; a common security interest in resisting communist expansionism; and the mutual intergovernmental trust which derived from the experience of nuclear sharing. However these factors did not operate uniformly throughout the postwar period. Indeed, their variable operation – together with other more temporally-specific factors – meant that in the years after Suez relations between London and Washington developed in three distinct phases: repair (1956–63); decay (1964–79); and revival (1980–8).

The Suez affair exercised a double-edged effect on Anglo-American relations. The short-term effect, since it was primarily US pressure which had forced the abrupt Anglo-French withdrawal, was clearly deleterious. In the medium term, however, the fact that Suez subsequently served to enhance Soviet influence in Egypt caused London and Washington to recognise the importance of their mutual security interest in preventing Moscow's malign influence from spreading further. Combined with the added danger in Europe that seemed to be implied by the Soviet intervention in Hungary, this renewed awareness of common security interests enabled the British and American governments to effect a rapid repair to their mutual relations. The new closeness was symbolised by the nuclear sharing agreement of 1958 and subsequently reinforced by the excellent personal relations enjoyed by Prime Minister Macmillan and President Kennedy.[57]

Within two years of the signing of the 1962 Nassau agreement, however, the 'special relationship' entered a long phase of decay. The new Labour government was less convinced of the enormity or the ubiquity of the Soviet threat outside Europe and accordingly was less prepared to provide automatic support for American efforts to defend what Washington still regarded as the global strategic interests of the West as a whole. The simultaneous attempts by the Wilson government to bring out-of-area operations more into line with the nation's straitened economic circumstances – moves which were not reversed by either the Heath or Callaghan governments – seriously reduced the United Kingdom's utility as a global military partner. This declining utility, together with the increasingly European focus of Britain's foreign policy, seemed to presage an inexorable divergence in British and American interests which would inevitably mean a further weakening of what remained of the 'special relationship'.

The revival phase in Anglo-American relations after 1979 was predicated entirely on the election of leaders in the two countries who shared very similar ideological convictions. Under Thatcher, Britain was no better placed in economic terms to perform an active support role for American global policing than it had been in the days of Wilson, Heath and Callaghan. Thatcher, however, firmly shared Reagan's fears about the seriousness of the Soviet global threat and his conviction that it must be pre-empted where possible and confronted where necessary. This meant that, even though the British government was now unable to provide the level of military support that it had in the 1950s, it could still bestow the appearance of 'multilateral' legitimacy on American-sponsored out-of-area operations. This was clearly valuable to Washington in its attempts to justify its own behaviour to world opinion. Yet it also provided Thatcher with the opportunity to demonstrate her credentials as Churchill's heir. Just as at home Thatcherite radicalism sought to reduce the role of the state and recreate an enterprise culture, so in foreign affairs it hoped to reverse 15 years of declining global involvement and falling international status. Britain would instead pursue an active, campaigning foreign policy which, in co-operation with the Americans and any other interested parties, would restore the West's primacy in the global balance of power and ensure that wherever possible its opponents were forced on to the defensive. It was a genuinely grand design, though only history would be in a position to judge its success.

7

The International Economic Dimension

In some respects it might appear unnecessary to delineate a separate area of a nation's foreign policy and designate it as 'economic'. After all, not only are self-evidently 'political' strategies frequently shaped by economic objectives and constraints, but decisions about economic policy are equally often guided by political criteria. In spite of the undoubted connections between 'the economic' and 'the political', there is still a distinctively economic area of British foreign policy which – if only because of its rather technical nature – merits separate investigation. As will be seen, in terms of foreign economic policy the postwar era can be conveniently partitioned into two distinct phases: from 1945 to 1968, when the 'reserve' role of sterling was finally abandoned; and from 1968 to the present day. During the first phase, successive governments sought to restore Britain's prewar international economic position by continuing to play a *dominant* and would-be guiding role in the international financial system. During the second phase, a less ambitious and rather more *reactive* strategy was adopted, a strategy that was in reality far better suited to Britain's straitened economic circumstances.

This chapter is concerned with two main questions: (1) what were the major external economic policies that Britain actually pursued in the years after 1945; and (2) why were they followed? Before the relevant policy developments can be described, however, a preliminary distinction is necessary. There are in fact three separate (though, inevitably, interrelated) aspects of foreign economic policy.

1. *Trade policy* is concerned primarily with the question as to who Britain's major trading partners should be and the extent to which those partners enjoy free access to British markets.

2. *Overseas investment policy* is concerned with the extent to which British companies are allowed or encouraged to export capital in order to build up overseas assets which will act as a source of future invisible exports in the form of repatriated profits.
3. *Currency policy* is concerned both with the extent to which the government stimulates the use of sterling as an 'international currency' and with the Treasury's efforts to influence the external value of the pound, that is, its price against other currencies.

Most of the discussion in this chapter focuses on aspect (3) and to a lesser extent on aspect (2). However, this is not to suggest that trade policy was unimportant in the postwar years. On the contrary, the promotion of Britain's export trade with the outside world was an important priority for governments of all political persuasions throughout the postwar era. The cursory treatment accorded to trade matters here largely reflects the sheer *continuity* of the trade policy which, within the limits imposed by Britain's membership of different international organisations, successive governments pursued for over four decades. This continuity stemmed mainly from the fact that all postwar governments maintained faith with the 'theory of comparative advantage': with the claim that trade stimulates economic growth by enabling different nation-states to specialise in producing those goods and services for which their natural factor endowments best qualify them.[1] As a result, successive governments consistently accepted that Britain, as a nation which traded a high proportion of its GDP,[2] should strive to follow the principles of the General Agreement on Tariffs and Trade (GATT) by removing mutual restrictions on trade wherever possible and by avoiding the illusory temptations of protectionism. In practice, therefore, Britain's postwar trade policy was to trade with as many foreign partners as possible (no matter what the political complexion of their governments) and to grant each partner access to British markets on conditions broadly similar to those enjoyed by British firms seeking market access abroad. These principles of reciprocity informed not only Britain's bilateral trading relations with a wide range of countries, but also its multilateral dealings with the Commonwealth in the 1950s, with EFTA in the 1960s and with the European Community after 1973.

The overall continuity of Britain's postwar trade policy, then, was considerable. While there were obviously some shifts in policy as Britain's involvement with different countries and with different international organisations varied over time, such changes were not of sufficient importance to warrant detailed discussion here. By far the most significant aspects of Britain's postwar foreign economic policy were the developments in its 'currency policy', developments which in turn affected the pattern of Britain's overseas investment. It is these changes which are now examined.

The attempt to preserve a dominant world financial role, 1945–68

The main theme of this section is that there were significant parallels between the 'overextended' *political* strategy that Britain pursued between 1945 and 1956 (discussed in Chapter 2) and the similarly overextended *economic* strategy that was pursued between 1945 and 1968. Just as the political strategy followed by successive British governments was not commensurate with Britain's depleted postwar resource base, so in the economic sphere London persistently attempted to project an economic role in the world which the domestic economy was not strong enough to support. As will be seen, the political strategy and the economic strategy had a common origin. They both derived from the postwar belief, widely held inside Cabinet and Whitehall, that Britain was still a Great Power and that its government should accordingly pursue foreign policies appropriate to that status. In the political sphere this meant a strategy designed to preserve British influence in all three of Churchill's 'circles'. In the economic sphere it meant a strategy designed to restore sterling to at least a semblance of the 'top currency' *reserve role* that it had enjoyed in the heyday of the Empire.[3]

This section is divided into two main parts. The first describes the major changes in Britain's currency policy that were made between 1945 and 1968. It tells the story of the progressive decline of sterling and (in the face of stubborn resistance from successive governments) the loss of its role as a reserve currency – a loss which was both a consequence and a symbol of Britain's declining status as a world power. The second part examines two alternative explanations (one Marxist, one non-Marxist) as to why successive governments sought for so long to maintain sterling's reserve role long after it had plainly outlived its usefulness.

The decline of sterling, 1945–68

Although it is possible to trace the decline of sterling as a major currency to at least 1914, the most useful place to begin for the purpose of the present exposition is September 1931, when Britain formally abandoned the Gold Standard. Under the Gold Standard (since 1925) the value of sterling had been tied to gold, and the values of most other currencies had been tied to sterling, the then 'top currency'. The main consequence of the abandonment was that the international financial system fragmented, splitting into a number of distinct 'currency blocs' based principally upon sterling, the dollar, the mark and the franc. Crucially, from the British point of view, the dominions of the Empire, together with several of the smaller European countries, continued to tie their currencies to the pound, forming an informal 'sterling bloc'. The independence and internal cohesion of this bloc was subsequently reinforced by Britain's abandonment of free trade in March 1932. Indeed the coalition government's introduction of a general external tariff (from which imports from the Empire were to be excluded) accelerated the development of a *sterling currency area* in which the participant members traded freely with one another but hardly at all with the outside world.

The American-sponsored Bretton Woods Agreement of 1944 sought to ensure that the anarchic international economic conditions of the 1930s, in which trade between member states of different currency blocs was difficult, would not be repeated in the postwar era. Put simply, Bretton Woods provided the basis for a new liberal international economic order. The newly established International Monetary Fund would help member states to finance short-term balance of payments deficits, thus promoting international trade. The World Bank would provide long-term funding for economic development projects. And the soon to be created GATT would facilitate the progressive multilateral reduction of tariff barriers. The cornerstone of the new regime, however, was a system of fixed parity exchange rates in which the value of the dollar was pegged to gold (at $35 per ounce) and all other national currencies were tied to the value of the dollar. (The pound, for example, was set at $4.03.) The fixed parity system was intended to provide a much needed stabilising mechanism for international trade: business certainty about the cost of imports and the value of exports would replace the high levels of uncertainty which had been associated with the fluctuating exchange rate anarchy of the 1930s.

From Britain's point of view, the crucial aspect of the Bretton Woods system was that its efficient operation required each participating state to hold *reserves* either of gold or of some 'hard' 'reserve' currency – reserves which each state could subsequently use if necessary to maintain its own currency's agreed par value. (For example, if a participating state experienced a balance of payments deficit – if the total value of its exports was less than the value of its imports – there would by definition be a lower demand for its currency. In these circumstances, the state's central bank would intervene in the currency markets, offloading some of its reserves in order to buy its own currency. This in turn would increase the demand for the currency and thereby restore its par value.) In deference to the United States' paramount position in the postwar economy, the dollar was designated as the major reserve currency. In recognition of Britain's continuing *de facto* economic dominance in the old 'sterling bloc' area and its still powerful (if relatively diminished) position in the world economy in general, sterling was also accorded the status of a reserve currency. Thus, although the post-Bretton Woods international order would undoubtedly be dominated by the United States, there would still be a special role for Britain: London would act as Washington's junior economic partner, giving strong diplomatic backing for American efforts aimed at expanding world trade and if necessary providing support for the dollar in times of crisis.

But if the foundations of the new world economic order – and Britain's place within it – were firmly in place by the end of the war, the war itself had affected Britain's international financial position in two important senses. On the credit side, the pre-war 'sterling bloc' had been transformed into the Overseas Sterling Area (OSA). As Strange observes, not only was the OSA 'almost a monetary union' in which the pound was employed as the major reserve currency, but the reserves of the OSA countries were held in a common pool in London under the control of the British government.[4] On the debit side, however, Britain emerged from the war with assets of £610m in gold and foreign currency reserves but with liabilities in excess of £3500m. These liabilities were almost entirely debts owed to Commonwealth governments as a result of their material assistance during the war, debts which became known as the 'sterling balances'.

The incoming Attlee government was thus faced with some very hard choices. On the one hand, the size of Britain's debts, its small asset base and its projected balance of payments deficit of £1000m for 1945–7 all pointed to the conclusion that the United Kingdom could not possibly afford the luxury of maintaining sterling's position as a reserve currency. The Bank of England simply did not have access to sufficient foreign currency reserves to maintain international confidence in the pound – confidence which was crucial if sterling was to continue to play a role as a major international currency. On the other hand, however, in the mid-1940s it was still believed that Britain should preserve sterling's reserve role. There were four main benefits that were assumed to follow from the maintenance of this role. The first was a simple matter of status. Britain was the capitalist world's second most important power, and if it wished to be acknowledged as such internationally it must continue to play a major role in the international financial system. Second, sterling's reserve role was thought to be a necessary condition for the continued extensive use of the pound as an international transactions currency,[5] a usage which was crucial to the invisible export-earning capacity of the City of London. Third, the fact that OSA governments held their reserves in London also meant that they were 'managed' in London and this in turn yielded valuable commission fees to financial institutions in the City. Fourth, it was widely recognised that Britain would be able to use the OSA to protect the overseas markets of British manufacturers. This possibility resulted from the fact that, through the Exchange Equalisation Account, the Treasury was able to determine the total number of pounds that could be exchanged for any other currency. This meant it could effectively ration the supply of *foreign* currency within the OSA and made it easier for businesses *inside* the OSA to purchase goods and raw materials from *other* OSA countries. This in turn provided relatively 'safe' markets for British manufacturers of both capital and consumer goods: deprived of foreign currency, importers in the dominions and colonies were obliged to buy from Britain (or from elsewhere in the OSA) or do without.

Thus the dilemma for the Attlee government was sharply focused. It wished to maintain sterling's reserve role status (and its corollary, the OSA) because of the considerable benefits that such status was assumed to bestow. Yet in 1945 Britain did not possess the financial wherewithal necessary to run a reserve currency. In the event, it was the Truman administration that came to Attlee's rescue. The 'American Loan' agreement of June 1946 provided Britain with a $3750 million loan sufficient to preserve sterling's status as a reserve currency and hence to preserve the OSA itself. It also made it possible for the British government to press ahead with its domestic expansion of the Welfare State and to maintain its global military capability. There were obvious benefits for both sides. The United Kingdom gained a welcome respite from what it was hoped would prove its temporary state of financial embarrassment and for the time being at least kept control of its protected markets in the OSA. The United States gained the promise of continued British military backing for its global struggle against communism. Washington also sought private assurances that in the near future sterling would be made freely convertible against the dollar, a development which would undoubtedly weaken Britain's hold over OSA markets and thereby increase the prospects for American export penetration. However, when the Attlee government duly abided by its tacit commitment (in July 1947), a disastrous run on the pound led to a rapid suspension of convertibility only one month later. Not wishing to witness a sterling crisis doing untold damage to the economy of its principal Cold War ally, the Truman administration accepted the swift ending of convertibility with relative equanimity. As a result – and more by luck than by judgement – the British government managed to preserve sterling's reserve role (courtesy of the American loan) *and* the integrity of the OSA and the 'safe' markets contained within it. Even when Dalton decided to devalue sterling in September 1949 (from $4.03 to $2.80) Washington continued to acquiesce, accepting that Britain's painful economic recovery could only be maintained if its exporters were allowed to benefit from the cheaper (and therefore more competitive) export prices that devaluation entailed.

If the 1940s had been characterised by the creation of a 'defensive' currency area safe for British exports, however, the 1950s witnessed a series of policy changes aimed at strengthening the international use of sterling as a transactions currency for worldwide financial operations.[6] Three institutional changes in particular contributed significantly to the revival of the City of London as a financial and commercial centre and thereby indirectly stimulated the growth of sterling's transactions role. In 1951, the City was reopened as an international market for foreign exchange dealing and for commodity trading. In 1954, various exchange controls were removed, thus allowing non-residents of the United Kingdom to deal more freely in sterling. And in 1958, the pound was made fully convertible. These changes certainly helped to maintain the international use of sterling as a reserve currency. More importantly still, they also allowed the City continuously to expand the range and sophistication of the services that it could offer the world financial and commercial community; as a result, there was a steady growth in Britain's 'invisible' export trade, without which the United Kingdom would have been in continuous balance of payments deficit since the early 1950s.

Yet in addition to the enormous benefits that this more liberal approach to Britain's currency policy bestowed in terms of the expansion of the City, there were also significant costs. Full convertibility in particular had two clearly damaging consequences. First, it reduced the 'safeness' of OSA markets for British exporters. With the pound freely convertible, OSA importers could now purchase goods or raw materials from *outside* the sterling area, using either dollars or some other convenient currency. Second, full convertibility rendered sterling increasingly vulnerable to speculative short-term capital movements.

Foreign speculators could now buy sterling more easily, but they could just as easily *sell* it. And, given the peculiar psychology of market behaviour, this in turn increased the tendency for speculators simultaneously to sell sterling for no other reason than their collective expectation (which subsequently became a self-fulfilling prophecy) that the value of sterling was about to fall. The main consequence of this tendency during the late 1950s and 1960s was a long-running series of 'runs on the pound'. And in response to each of these crises the Bank of England was obliged – under the Bretton Woods fixed parity arrangement – to intervene in the currency markets in order to support sterling; each intervention thus constituted a drain on Britain's gold and foreign currency reserves.

The situation came to a head in October 1967 after a series of abortive attempts at crisis management by the Treasury. In the face of continuous foreign and domestic speculation against sterling, and a disastrous fall in Britain's reserves, the Wilson government announced a devaluation of the pound; a reduction in its fixed parity from $2.80 to $2.40. The devaluation had the desired effect of staunching the short-term speculative outflow. Yet it also had the effect of devaluing the OSA governments' 'Sterling balances' – the long-term interest-yielding debts owed by the Treasury – by the same 14 per cent. As a result, the consequences of devaluation were dramatic. Fearful that yet more devaluations would follow, overseas sterling holders, especially OSA governments, began to move their long-term funds out of sterling: they quite simply stopped using the pound as their main reserve currency. This development effectively signalled the *de facto* demise both of the OSA and of sterling as a major reserve currency – without any specific policy decision to that end being taken by the British government. London nevertheless recognised a *fait accompli* when it saw one, and immediately began with the OSA governments a series of negotiations which culminated in the Basle Agreements of September 1987.[7] These agreements resolved a number of technicalities over the legal status of the remaining sterling balances and effectively terminated the Overseas Sterling Area.

Although the ending of sterling's reserve role was lamented in some quarters as being yet another indication of Britain's 'descent from power', many observers took the view that the termination of the reserve role had come not a moment too soon.[8] Between 1945 and 1968 the continued existence of the OSA and of the reserve role had had three profoundly disturbing consequences for Britain's domestic economy. First, the lack of constraints on the export of capital to OSA countries had encouraged a massive outflow of private long-term capital from Britain as investors strove to take advantage of the higher profits that, in the 1950s and 1960s, were available in Australia, South Africa and the Middle East. According to Andrew Shonfield this 'leakage of capital' led directly to lower investment levels in Britain and indirectly contributed to Britain's relatively poor industrial performance throughout the immediate postwar period.[9] Second, the system of discriminatory exchange controls which made it difficult for OSA countries to trade outside the Sterling Area, and which accordingly preserved 'safe' overseas markets for British exports, was a decidedly double-edged weapon. By insulating British industry from the energising effects of foreign competition, it ensured that even the most lethargic and inefficient of producers could sell their goods in the 'soft' OSA markets. By thus encouraging British inefficiency, therefore, the OSA – rather like the Empire before it – both masked and contributed to Britain's long-term industrial decline.[10]

A third consequence of the maintenance of sterling's reserve role was that the interest rate policies necessary for its smooth operation exacerbated the damaging stop–go fluctuations of the British domestic economy. The core of the problem in this context was psychological. In order to sustain the pound's reserve status, successive governments had to maintain international confidence in sterling – the confidence both of foreign governments and of private investors. Unfortunately, whenever the British balance of payments ran into deficit, 'confidence' in (as well as 'real', trade-related demand for) the pound almost invariably declined, thereby draining Britain's foreign exchange reserves as the Bank of England intervened in the market to maintain sterling's parity with the dollar. The Bank of England's typical response (after consultation with the Treasury) as each crisis loomed was to raise interest rates in London in order to attract short-term funds back into sterling. While this had the desirable consequence of relieving the pressure on the country's reserves, it also discouraged investment and inhibited economic growth at home by raising the domestic cost of borrowing. According to Brett, the alternate phases of growth and stagnation which characterised the British economy between the early 1950s and the late 1960s owed much to the currency policies of successive governments and their determination to preserve sterling's reserve status.[11] As Table 7.1 shows, during this period there were a series of expansionary phases in which the balance of payments shifted from a position of surplus to one of deficit. The resultant increase in interest rates, designed primarily to maintain international confidence in sterling, would then usher in a period of stagnation during which the balance of payments position would recover as a result of reduced

Table 7.1 The 'Stop–go' cycle of the UK economy during the 1950s and 1960s

	Annual growth in UK industrial production (%)	UK balance of payments, current account (£m)
1953–5 expansion	5.6	+ 145 to − 155
1955–8 stagnation	0.4	− 155 to + 336
1958–60 expansion	6.2	+ 336 to − 275
1960–2 stagnation	1.1	− 275 to + 101
1962–4 expansion	5.6	+ 101 to − 393
1964–6 stagnation	1.5	− 393 to − 61

SOURCE: E. A. Brett, *The World Economy since the War* (London: Macmillan, 1985) p. 155.

demand for imports. Interest rates could then be relaxed, thus stimulating more investment activity and economic growth. However the next balance of payments crisis – and the next run on the pound – would soon make itself felt.

Now, of course, it is easy to assert that many of the difficulties experienced by the British economy during the 1950s and 1960s were exacerbated – if not actually caused – by the attempts of successive governments to maintain sterling's international role. Unfortunately it is far more difficult to demonstrate that the pursuit of the reserve role actually had an effect on anything at all. This said, the broad consensus of informed opinion seems to suggest that the attempts to preserve the reserve role did indeed have a continuously damaging effect on Britain's domestic industrial development. Yet such a conclusion immediately begs an important question: why on earth did successive governments attempt to sustain sterling's reserve role – and its corollary, the OSA – when the consequences for the home economy appear to have been so consistently debilitating? It is this question that is now considered.

Explaining the reserve role strategy: Marxist and non-Marxist interpretations

The Marxist view.   For Marxist scholars, the puzzle concerning the protracted efforts to preserve sterling's reserve role can best be resolved by posing a further question: given that Britain's foreign economic strategy after 1945 produced so little benefit for the British economy as a whole, who did benefit from it? In the opinion of many Marxists the main beneficiaries were in fact that fraction of the capitalist class known as *'financial capital'*: the bankers, insurers, currency dealers and commodity traders whose activities were concentrated in the City of London. In essence, Marxists argue, the reserve role was maintained because it was in the interests of financial capital that it be maintained and because financial capitalists were sufficiently dominant within the British policy-making process to ensure that their own interests prevailed.[12]

How, then, did this come about? In the Marxist view, one of the key sources of the dominance of financial capital was the peculiar historical evolution of the British state apparatus. In most advanced capitalist countries, one of the primary functions of the state is to encourage the process of capital accumulation; this, after all, is the central economic activity of the capitalist mode of production. As a result the capitalist state typically contrives to maximise the interests of 'industrial capital', the fraction of the capitalist class that comprises the owners and controllers of the means of production and distribution. In Britain, however, financial capitalists managed to retain their hold on the levers of political power for longer than was typically the case elsewhere. In so doing, moreover, they ensured that in Britain at least it was the interests of financial rather than industrial capital that dominated foreign economic policy making well into the twentieth century. This continued dominance of financial capital stemmed partly from the generalised informal influence that City interests were able to exert over the decision-making apparatus of the British state and partly from the high level of decision-making autonomy retained (in spite of its formal nationalisation in 1945) by the Bank of England. In the Marxist view, from the late nineteenth century onwards, the City and the Bank of England were able to use the Bank's institutional links with the Treasury in order to exercise 'structural power' – to pressure successive governments into pursuing foreign economic policies that were conducive to the interests of financial capital.[13]

Contemporary Marxist scholars identify two major policy consequences of the dominance of financial capital in Britain's foreign economic policy making. One strand of Marxist opinion stresses the significance of the City's conviction during the 1950s and 1960s that the preservation of the OSA was essential for the maintenance of sterling's international transactions role. It was believed that without the transactions role the City's income from transactions fees would be seriously reduced. And, as a result, financial capital consistently exercised its 'structural power' over the political system by tacitly posing the threat of a disastrous 'flight of capital' from Britain if the reserve role were to be abandoned.[14] A second strand of Marxist opinion argues that, from the late nineteenth century onwards, the continued dominance of financial capital ensured that a central objective of Britain's foreign economic policy was the facilitation of capital exports. For Lenin, of course, this was what the Empire after 1870 had in any case been all about: the main purpose of the territorial acquisitions in Africa and the Far East in the late nineteenth century had been to resolve the crisis of capital over-accumulation at home by rendering the areas thus acquired safe for British capital exports. For contemporary Marxists, the OSA continued to perform a similar function in the postwar years: it remained an extremely congenial device for facilitating the export of capital to OSA countries where financial capitalists, together with large multinational industrial firms, could gain a higher return on their portfolio and direct investments.[15] And as long as the rate of profit remained higher in OSA countries than in Britain, financial capital had a clear incentive to ensure that the OSA itself was preserved. This, essentially, was why, in the face of the evident costs to the British economy as a whole, it did in fact survive for so long. According to the Marxist account, it was not until the late 1960s, when Britain's pattern of trade and investment had shifted 'naturally' towards Western Europe, that financial capital lost interest in the Sterling Area. The OSA, quite simply, was no longer required as a destination for British capital exports to anything like the extent that it had been in the past. The promise of profits from investment inside Europe clearly began to outweigh anything that the OSA had to offer. For the Marxists it was this autonomous change in the material interests of financial capital – away from the Empire and towards Europe – that led to the abandonment of the OSA and of sterling's reserve role. In short, financial capital was not only the chief beneficiary of the maintenance of the OSA, it was also the chief architect of its demise when the OSA was no longer needed.

The non-Marxist view.   The Marxists, then, emphasise the interests and the dominance of financial capital in their explanation of the survival of the OSA. The dominant non-Marxist view, associated most clearly with the writings of Susan Strange, is rather different. According to Strange, the OSA was perpetuated well beyond its useful life largely because the key decision makers in the British foreign policy elite adhered to a faulty analysis of Britain's postwar economic position.[16]

Strange argues that the postwar strategy of attempting to re-establish and maintain sterling's role as a major reserve currency was the result of two assumptions, both of which were incorrect. The first was the conviction that Britain shared an identity of material interest with the world economy: that what was good for the world economy was good for Britain. For Strange, this belief had made perfectly good sense before 1914. When British manufacturers were (among) the most efficient in the world, it was certainly in Britain's interest for the government to underwrite an international financial system that was designed to liberalise and expand world trade. After 1945, however, with the dollar clearly enthroned as the top currency, the coincidence between British interests and those of the world economy were no longer so clear-cut. Britain desperately needed to modernise and rationalise its industrial base. Yet it was unable to follow the defensive protectionist policies that might have effected such a modernisation as long as it remained committed to a strategy of trade and currency liberalisation designed to benefit the world economy as a whole. The essential problem in this context was that the British government was suffering from what Strange calls 'top currency syndrome', a damaging hangover from the days when sterling *had* been the top world currency and when Britain's economic interests and those of the world economy *had* coincided.

A second false assumption that led to the strategy of attempting to restore and maintain sterling's 'master currency' status derived from the continuing belief that the material benefits of running a reserve currency significantly outweighed the increasingly evident costs. These benefits and costs were reviewed above and they need not be described here. Following Strange, however, it is worth re-emphasising the importance of the belief, held by successive governments, that sterling's reserve status was a necessary precondition for the successful operation and expansion of the City as a financial and commercial centre (which was itself considered essential to the British economy's overall health). It was only as the 'top currency syndrome' faded – a decline which was obviously accelerated both by decolonisation and the realisation that it would soon be necessary to withdraw from east of Suez – that it was recognised that for the City to thrive it was just not necessary to maintain sterling's reserve role; the two, quite simply, were uncon-nected.

Strange's central point, then, is that the British government's foreign economic policy between 1945 and the late 1960s was predicated on a faulty analysis of Britain's postwar economic position and capabilities. It was believed that Britain was still a great economic power and accordingly that the benefits of operating a reserve currency would outweigh the costs. However the British economic recovery after the war was very slow in coming. And it was continually set back by balance of payments deficits which constantly weakened international confidence in sterling. In these circumstances the costs of running a reserve currency substantially outweighed the benefits. Unfortunately the 'top currency syndrome', born of earlier experiences in the heyday of the Empire, imposed on the key decision makers an intellectual strait-jacket which took time to break down. As a result it was only acknowledged that the abandonment of the reserve role would be to Britain's distinct economic advantage when the damage had already been done.

But which of these explanations – the Marxist or the non-Marxist – is correct? Unfortunately this is not a question that can be answered easily, if at all. The analyses make rather different assumptions about the nature of political and economic power in advanced capitalist societies, about where it is located and how it is exercised.[17] As a result it is not possible to adduce any specific piece of 'critical evidence' that might enable the disinterested observer to decide between the alternative analyses that are provided: both accounts are consistent with most of the 'known facts'; and each is capable of explaining, within its own terms of reference, why it took so long for Britain to abandon the OSA and sterling's reserve role. Choosing between the explanations is really a matter of choosing between two different intellectual traditions, a choice which the reader has probably already made on the basis of a wide range of other considerations.

The shift to a more reactive strategy, 1968–88

It was suggested in the previous section that the British government's efforts to play a major role in the international economic system between 1945 and 1968 were broadly unsuccessful. The benefits that were supposed to accrue from running a reserve currency failed to materialise because of the chronic weakness of the domestic economy, a weakness that was manifested in a series of balance of payments crises which progressively weakened sterling. This 'overextended' strategy of the early postwar years was brought to an abrupt end however with the termination of the OSA in 1968. It was replaced by a more flexible, reactive strategy that was much more suited to Britain's status as a 'major power of the second rank'.[18] Unfortunately, in terms of promoting the general health of the British economy and protecting its share of overseas markets, the foreign economic policies pursued after 1968 were not much more successful than those that had preceded it. As will be seen, some of the problems of the 1970s and 1980s, such as the implications of Britain's EC membership for its balance of trade deficit, were partly self-inflicted. But the main factor underlying the lack of success of Britain's foreign economic policy after 1968 was the dramatic changes that were taking place in the global economy: changes that were well outside London's ability to control and to which successive governments were obliged to react on a more or less *ad hoc* basis. This section begins by reviewing the main policy developments that occurred during the two subphases (1968–79 and 1979–88) of the post-OSA era. It then seeks to identify the major factors that constrained British foreign economic policy after 1968 and which contributed to the continuing difficulties that it encountered.

Policy developments, 1968–79

After 1968 Britain began to pursue a rather more 'self-sufficient' international economic strategy.[19] Without the burden of trying to maintain sterling's reserve role, the British economy should have been less vulnerable to the sort of speculative short-term capital movements which had continually provoked balance of payments crises and the need for stop–go since the early 1950s. The reason it should have been less vulnerable was simple: fewer people were holding sterling and therefore fewer could move out of it to cause a 'run on the pound'.

Unfortunately two related changes in the world economy contrived to undermine the new strategy. The first of these was the downturn in the world economy which began in the late 1960s and the effects of which were beginning to be felt worldwide by the early 1970s. The downturn made it even more difficult for Britain's already hard-pressed exporters to maintain – let alone expand – their overseas market share, and this in turn exacerbated the country's continuing balance of payments problems. By far the most important development in the world economy after 1968, however, was the collapse in 1971 of the Bretton Woods system of fixed exchange rates. During the 1960s the American government had massively increased the supply of dollars by running a continuous budget deficit. (This deficit enabled successive administrations to finance both the Kennedy–Johnson social welfare reforms and the escalating war in Vietnam without a significant increase in taxation.) However, contrary to its implied obligations under the Bretton Woods agreement, the US Treasury did *not* acquire additional gold stocks to back this increase in dollars. The result was that an informal market for gold developed in which gold was traded for more than its 'official' (Bretton Woods) price of $35 per ounce.

As Strange observes, the United States could have progressively (and unilaterally) raised the price of gold from the late 1960s onwards, in line with the increase in the supply of dollars.[20] For a variety of reasons (which need not concern us here), however, it chose not to do so. Instead, in August 1971, the Nixon administration simply abandoned the gold–dollar link altogether, in effect 'floating' the dollar and allowing market forces to determine its price against gold.[21] This flotation of the dollar broke the back of the Bretton Woods fixed parity exchange rate system, ushering in an era of generally floating exchange rates in which market forces, rather than Central Bank agreements, would determine the price of each currency against all the others.[22]

As far as Britain was concerned, it was somewhat ironic that, having battled for so long, and at such great cost, to maintain sterling at $2.80, less than three years after the battle had been lost the entire fixed exchange rate system should have collapsed. In common with the other major industrial trading nations, however, Britain was not yet ready for a floating free-for-all. In December 1971, the Smithsonian Agreement led to a temporary realignment of exchange rates among the major currencies. Unfortunately lack of American commitment to the new parities caused the agreement to collapse within six months.[23] By way of a substitute, in April 1972, the EEC countries together with Britain established the 'snake-in-the-tunnel', the forerunner of the European Monetary System (EMS). Under this arrangement each member state agreed that its Central Bank would intervene in the foreign exchange markets in order to maintain its currency's parity value, and/or pursue appropriate interest rates policies whenever the currency's market value went beyond certain defined bounds (the 'tunnel').[24] However each currency would be allowed to fluctuate – to 'snake about' – within these bounds without eliciting intervention. This, it was hoped, would bring a measure of stability to the foreign exchange markets, while at the same time permitting an acceptable degree of market flexibility. By June 1972, however, the Heath government had decided that participation in the snake was too much of a constraint on domestic economic policy making – particularly in terms of the adjustments in interest rate policy that it promised to require – and as a result Britain withdrew from the snake arrangement altogether. In spite of the United Kingdom's membership of the EC after January 1973, Britain did not participate fully in the monetary arrangements of the Community. (The main implications of Community membership for Britain's foreign economic policy in general are discussed on pp. 218–19 below.)

From June 1972 until 1976 successive British governments opted for a strategy of unilaterally managed floating. In principle sterling was allowed to find its own market value against other currencies, though in practice the Bank of England consistently intervened in the markets to prevent the pound from falling too far. The objective of these interventions was to prevent a falling pound from giving a further boost to domestic inflation (a lower pound would mean essential imports would be more expensive, thus fuelling inflation). The main consequence of the interventions, however, was a continuing decline in Britain's gold and foreign currency reserves, even though in theory a floating exchange rate should have relieved the pressure on the reserves to a considerable extent.

By March 1976, in spite of heavy Bank of England interventions, the combined effects of speculative pressure and persistent trade deficits had caused the pound to fall below $2 for the first time. An important psychological barrier – for the international speculators – had been broken and sterling continued its downward spiral. The crisis continued throughout 1976 and by October sterling had fallen to $1.56, notwithstanding the announcement by a consortium of Central Banks that they would provide the Bank of England with a stand-by credit of $5.5 billion. At this point the Labour government entered into negotiations with the IMF for a $3.5 billion *loan*. The granting of the loan certainly helped sterling to recover – to $1.71 by December – but the domestic costs were substantial. The conditions of the loan stipulated that the British economy should be subject to a hefty dose of deflation. Interest rates were gradually increased and as a result unemployment, which was already growing, further accelerated. These costs were unavoidable however. The loan had been necessary to prevent sterling from sinking even lower, which would undoubtedly have caused inflation to rise even higher. Fortunately the loan did enable the Callaghan government to maintain its earlier strategy of 'managed floating', providing it with access to sufficient reserves to keep sterling on a relatively even keel for the remainder of its period in office.

Policy developments, 1979–88

Margaret Thatcher's government achieved office in May 1979, committed to an ideology of economic liberalism which prescribed that market forces must be given free rein. The effects of this new, free market ideology were immediately felt in the field of foreign economic policy. Almost as soon as it came to power the new government abolished the few controls that still remained on foreign exchange dealings. Thatcher also initiated a series of discussions which led in October 1986 to the 'Big Bang' in the City of London, deregulating financial dealings and increasing both the competitiveness of the City and its attractiveness to foreign investors.

In relation to sterling, from May 1979 until early 1981 the Thatcher government adopted a genuinely floating exchange rate policy, with the Bank of England engaging in only minimal intervention in the foreign exchange markets. Unusually, during most of this two-year period, the pound floated upward rather than downward. This was partly because, with North Sea oil coming on stream, the pound was increasingly attractive to foreign speculators as a 'petrocurrency'. Yet it also resulted from the high interest rate policies that were pursued between 1979 and 1981. Here the Thatcher government encountered the contradiction that frequently besets interest rate policy. High interest rates have two major effects: internally, they restrict the expansion of the money supply and help to counter inflation; externally, they attract short-term capital movements from abroad and therefore (*ceteris paribus*) cause the exchange rate to rise. The high interest rate policies of the early Thatcher years certainly achieved their desired *internal* objective of reducing inflation. However they also had the undesirable *external* consequence of massively increasing the international value of sterling. This in turn effected a radical reduction in Britain's export competitiveness with devasting consequences for Britain's manufacturing base: it was only in 1987 that the official index of industrial production, which had fallen by over 20 per cent between 1979 and 1981, regained its May 1979 level.

From the beginning of 1981 onwards, therefore, the government began to recognise that it must act decisively to ameliorate the damaging consequences that an overvalued pound was having for Britain's manufacturing export performance. As a result, the management of the exchange rate once again became one of the government's clear policy objectives. Partly through Bank of England interventions and partly through a less doctrinaire interest rate policy, the exchange rate was gradually brought down from its peak of $2.40 in January 1981 to $1.54 in June 1983. Similar interventions and interest rate adjustments (though in the opposite direction) were employed in February 1985 when the exchange rate fell too low (to $1.08), thus threatening to give inflation an unwelcome boost in the run-up to the 1987 General Election. Interventionist policies were also pursued in 1985–6, following the 'Plaza Agreement' of September 1985, in which the 'Group of 7' top industrial nations agreed that joint measures should be taken to reduce the overvaluation of the dollar. Crucially, what all of these interventions demonstrated was that in spite of the flirtation with a freely floating exchange rate between 1979 and 1981, the Thatcher government in fact ended up pursuing a strategy of 'managed floating' similar to that which had been pursued by its predecessors between mid-1972 (when the Smithsonian Agreement collapsed) and May 1979.

By the late 1980s the Thatcher government's strategy of managed floating was achieving what appeared to be an optimal exchange rate level for sterling. The currency was fairly stable; it was sufficiently low against other currencies to prevent Britain's exporters suffering unduly; yet it was not so low as to threaten higher inflation through increased import costs. At the time of writing it appears to be the case that the fall in both the dollar and world-share values which began in October 1987 did not seriously damage the long-term position of sterling. However, in the months after October 1987, the Bank of England did participate in the extensive collaborative efforts of the major Central Banks, with the aim of preventing the dollar from 'sinking through the floor'. This participation, fully approved by the Treasury, indicated yet again that the days when the Thatcher government had been committed to the free operation of market forces on the foreign exchanges were long gone. In the context of currency policy at least, free market principles had proved to be a luxury that even the Thatcher government could not afford: it had accordingly been obliged to abandon them and revert to interventionism when external circumstances demanded it.

What can be said by way of summary of the developments in Britain's foreign economic policy between 1968 and 1988? The main conclusion, unsurprising though it may be, is that, as in the period before 1968, policy continued to be heavily constrained by external factors. The shift to a strategy of 'managed floating' after 1971 was due entirely to the collapse of the Bretton Woods system of fixed parities, a collapse which was itself the sole responsibility of the US Treasury. In the years after 1971, although sterling was no longer employed as a major reserve currency, it was still widely used as a transactions currency. This was particularly the case after 1973 when London became the temporary repository for billions of the petrodollars that flooded the international money markets in the wake of the first OPEC 'oil shock'. Given Britain's continuing balance of payments problems during the 1970s (which arose from the British consumer's preference for foreign imported manufactures and the lack of competitiveness of British exports), sterling remained vulnerable to short-term speculative pressures which continued to act as a drain on Britain's foreign exchange reserves and provoked the 1976 sterling crisis. Thatcher's ideology-driven determination to allow these 'speculative pressures' free rein – to allow the pound to find its own market value – foundered because of the effects which the policy had on the domestic economy. The combination of high interest rates and free market forces drove sterling so high that British exporters could not compete in foreign markets. The decline of Britain's manufacturing base forced a reduction in interest rates and a return to 'managed floating' in early 1981, a strategy that was continued through to the late 1980s.

Some explanatory factors: the major constraints after 1968

Three major factors served to constrain British foreign economic policy making in the years after the end of the Sterling Area: the increasing internationalisation of markets and of production; Britain's membership of the European Community; and the general crisis in the world economy.

The internationalisation of markets and of production.   Currency and commodity markets have always been to some degree international, with currencies and commodities being bought and sold by private individuals across national borders. After 1945 the extent of this internationalisation gradually increased. After 1980 it accelerated considerably. More currencies and more commodities were traded in more countries, and at significantly greater volumes, than ever before. After 1970, moreover, this internationalisation of currency and commodity markets was complemented by the increasing internationalisation of markets in government-issued stocks and in the shares of private-sector companies. The deregulation ideology of the Thatcher and Reagan governments, the ingenuity and inventiveness of the financial dealers in devising new methods of speculation, and the revolution in communications technology: all of these factors contributed to the internationalisation of markets throughout the world. By the late 1980s, currencies, commodities, stocks and shares were being traded round the clock world-wide, with near-instantaneous information links connecting all the major financial centres: a truly global market had been created, if not with the complete approval of the major capitalist governments, then at least with their acquiescence.

An analogous process was taking place simultaneously in patterns of manufacturing production. Multinational corporations (MNCs) were busily expanding and diversifying their activities across national frontiers. An MNC based in one country could readily circumvent tariff barriers by entering into a partnership with an existing corporation inside another 'host' country, or even by creating an entirely new subsidiary inside that host country. By this sort of institutional ploy, and by providing employment for the indigenous 'host' population, MNCs found that they could sidestep accusations that the domestic market was being swamped by foreign imports. The MNC also proved to be an extremely useful vehicle for transferring technology, capital and profits across national boundaries; and the complexity of the internal accounting procedures that were frequently employed made it extraordinarily difficult for national governments even to monitor such transfers, let alone control them.

Thus the fundamental consequence of the internationalisation of markets and of production was that it seriously impaired the decision-making autonomy of national governments, the British government included, in two senses. It meant, first, that individual governments found it increasingly difficult to intervene effectively in any given currency, commodity or stock market: there were simply too many other participants in each market to enable any one government to determine a particular market outcome. Acting on its own, even the US Federal Reserve would probably have been unable to support the dollar in the wake of the Wall Street 'crash' of October 1987: it required the assistance of other Central Banks in order to complete the task effectively. There is no telling what the Bank of England would have done if it had been obliged to cope alone with the effects of British budget and trade deficits of a magnitude comparable with those regularly encountered by the United States.

A second sense in which 'internationalisation' impaired the autonomy of governments was that it made it more difficult for them to constrain the behaviour of others. In the late 1980s, it was extremely hard to envisage, for example, how any British government – whatever its political complexion – could effectively reintroduce any sort of exchange controls on sterling. A large part of the problem was simple practicality: there was so much dealing in sterling going on overseas that it was completely outside the Bank of England's capability either to monitor or police it. Another aspect of the problem was that, even if the British government had attempted unilaterally to reimpose some sort of regulation on the financial markets, the costs would have been enormous: in all probability, foreign investors would have moved their funds out of London in droves, the City would have experienced a disastrous loss of confidence and sterling would have suffered a 'melt-down'. Such calamitous outcomes could not be seriously entertained: in the late 1980s, it looked as though Britain would be confronted and constrained by the power of the international markets for the foreseeable future.

Britain's membership of the European Community.   In principle, British membership of the EC could have exerted a powerful constraining influence on Britain's currency policy and on its trade policy. In fact, *currency policy* remained largely unaffected. This was mainly because, after its brief three-month involvement with the 'snake' in 1972, Britain consistently refused to become a full member of the European Monetary System which came into force in March 1979. Under this 'supersnake' arrangement, each member state was committed to intervening in the foreign exchange markets and to pursuing interest rate policies which would maintain the value of its currency within a 2.5 per cent band either side of its collectively agreed parity. Successive British governments, quite simply, were never prepared to commit themselves to this kind of arrangement. Although greater exchange rate stability would undoubtedly have been of considerable benefit to British exporters and importers, successive governments were not prepared to countenance the accompanying loss of national decision-making autonomy that EMS membership would have implied. As noted earlier, interest rate policy in particular has significant consequences for the domestic economy. The Thatcher government especially was not prepared to be unnecessarily constrained in its domestic policy options for the sake either of exchange rate stability or of yet another gesture aimed at 'restoring the supranational momentum of the EC'.

The effects of EC membership on Britain's *trade and trade policy*, however, were rather more substantial. Although *all* intra-community barriers against the free movement of capital, labour and goods were not scheduled to be removed until 1992, from 1973 onwards London was bound by the terms of accession to allow virtually free access to manufactured imports from EC countries. Notwithstanding the fact that British exporters also enjoyed freer access to markets in Europe, Britain's trade deficit with the EC certainly grew significantly after 1973. As Table 7.2 shows, in 1972 the United Kingdom had a visible trade deficit with the EC countries of £580m, which constituted just under 42 per cent of its total visible deficit. By 1986 the EC deficit had grown to £9503m, almost 73 per cent of the total deficit. Even taking account of the growing EC share of Britain's total trade (see the index figures at the bottom of Table 7.2), the visible deficits with the EC certainly worsened (from an index figure of − .35 to − .51) between 1972 and 1986. As Table 7.2 also indicates, the main source of the increasing deficit was Britain's bilateral trade with West Germany: this

Table 7.2 **UK visible trade deficit with the EEC 1972–86 (£m)**

	1972	1980	1986
Total deficit (all countries)	− 1302	− 6 288	− 13 058
West Germany			
imports from	841	5 778	14 139
exports to	589	4 218	8 542
Balance	− 252	− 1 500	− 5 598
Bilateral deficit as % of total deficit	18.1	24.8	42.8
EEC*			
imports from	3521	20 888	44 506
exports to	2941	17 479	35 003
Balance	− 580	− 3409	− 9 503
EEC deficit as % of total deficit	41.7	54.2	72.8
(a) EEC deficit as % of total deficit	41.7	54.2	72.8
(b) Trade with EEC as % of total trade	30.9	43.8	48.3
Relative contribution to deficit index ((b) − (a))/(b)	− 0.35	− 0.23	− 0.51

*All EEC figures refer to the Six plus Denmark and the Irish Republic.
SOURCE: *Annual Abstract of Statistics* (HMSO, various years).

constituted some 18.1 per cent of the total deficit in 1972 but had grown to a massive 42.8 per cent by 1986. As long as Britain remained inside the European Community, however, there was little or nothing that London could do – by way of changing its trade policy – either to remedy the imbalance with the Community in general or to reduce it with West Germany in particular: EC membership was a constraint that simply had to be accepted with equanimity.

The general crisis in the world economy. The most important constraint on British foreign economic policy after 1968, however, was almost certainly the continuing difficulties that were experienced by the entire world economy from the early 1970s onwards. In practical terms, the downturn – which was recognised world-wide in the wake of the 1973 'oil shock' – made it very difficult for British manufacturers to increase their share of overseas markets. This in turn perpetuated Britain's long-running balance of payments problems and thereby continued to exert downard pressure on the value of sterling throughout the 1970s.

However the nature of the crisis itself was characterised very differently by different observers. In government circles during the mid-1970s there was a tendency to attribute the crisis almost entirely to the machinations of OPEC: by quadrupling the price of oil in October 1973, the oil-exporting nations had massively increased world-wide inflation and pushed the world economy into recession. The optimistic implication of this interpretation, however, was that, as the United Kingdom was expected to be a net oil-exporter by 1980, Britain might well be able to turn the new situation to its advantage. Accordingly the main object of foreign economic policy in the 1970s was to hold the fort – to prevent anything too disastrous from happening either to sterling or to the balance of payments – until North Sea oil came fully on stream. Armed with its newly-won oil revenues, the British economy could face the future with confidence.

Yet, as the 1970s progressed, and the global recession showed few signs of abating, rather more sophisticated analyses of the nature of the world's economic problems began to emerge. Milton Friedman and his monetarist acolytes argued that the core of the problem derived from a long history of too much government interference in market mechanisms and too much trade restraint. For Friedman, a return to free market economics, avoiding protectionism, reducing state economic activity and deregulating markets, would restore the world economy to equilibrium, thereby creating optimal conditions for sustained recovery and growth.[25] Marxist analysts, in contrast, tended to follow Mandel's claims in the late 1960s that the capitalist world economy had begun to suffer from a serious crisis of capital over-accumulation. Entrepreneurs' increasing inability to find profitable outlets for their previously accumulated capital had led to a fall in the overall rate of profit and this in turn had thrown the entire capital system into a state of disorganisation and crisis that would probably last until the early 1990s.[26]

The 'hegemonic stability' theorists offered yet another analysis.[27] Their basic assumption was that any liberal system of international trade and finance can only function effectively when it is sponsored and controlled by a dominant hegemonic power. Between about 1840 and 1914 the role of 'international hegemon' was performed by Britain; between 1945 and 1970, by the United States. In both cases, however, the very effort of performing the hegemonic role sapped the economic strength of the hegemonic power: capital exports, intended to strengthen the economic system, constituted a 'leakage of capital' which depleted the hegemon's industrial base; and the out-of-area military commitments necessary to support and maintain foreign governments sympathetic to the liberal international regime were extremely expensive. According to the hegemonic stability thesis, by the late 1960s the United States was beginning to lose its hegemonic status. The collapse of the Bretton Woods system was the first major sign of America's relative economic weakness. The rising economic strength of Germany and Japan was another. And the defeat in Vietnam showed that American military power was also on the wane. With the strength of its hegemon in serious decline, the world economic system was incapable of functioning effectively. In the 1970s and 1980s, with no single power in control, both international trade and the system of international finance slowly drifted into a state of confusion that was beyond the power of any one state to control.

Whatever the relative merits of these competing characterisations of the world economic crisis, it was the Friedmanite model which guided Britain's external economic policy after 1976. For the Callaghan government (as noted earlier), the espousal of a strict monetarist domestic economic strategy and a managed floating exchange rate policy were the price that had to be paid for the IMF loan. For the Thatcher government after May 1979, however, tight money at home and a free-floating pound abroad were welcome ideological totems; indispensable elements in the new Tory strategy of exposing the British economy to the invigorating winds of international competition. For Thatcher, the long-running economic crisis of the 1970s had been the result of governments tampering with market mechanisms. Her government would follow Friedman's prescriptions: it would roll back the state, restore the market as the primary mechanism of distribution and deregulate wherever possible.

By the late 1980s, there were two broad sets of views as to how successful the Thatcher government's strategy of liberalisation had actually been. Government supporters emphasised the regeneration of British industry that the new competitive environment had made possible: the British economy had outridden the crises of the 1980s, and was set to surmount those of the 1990s, precisely because it had followed the principles of deregulation and market discipline. The government's critics were far less sanguine however. In line with Susan Strange's exposition of *Casino Capitalism*, they inclined to the view that the deregulation of the financial sector under Reagan in the United States and under Thatcher in Britain had seriously exacerbated the *instability* of markets world-wide. In the late 1980s the prices of currencies, of commodities, of credit and of stocks and shares were fluctuating ever more violently as speculative funds were transferred in and out of different markets at an increasing velocity. In the view of the pessimists, the stock market crash and 'dollar slide' of October 1987 were merely the first indications that the international financial casino – thanks to deregulation – was now out of control. Only time would tell whether it was the government or its critics that had been correct.

Summary and conclusions

Britain's external economic policy in the postwar period can be divided into two distinct phases. During the first phase, between 1945 and 1968, the main focus of Britain's foreign economic relations was its currency policy. Successive governments sought both to preserve the integrity of the Overseas Sterling Area and to maintain sterling's attendant role as a reserve currency. The preservation of the OSA in turn provided implicit guidelines for the British government's overseas investment and trade policies. The continued existence of the OSA made it relatively easy for British investors to export capital to OSA countries where it could frequently earn a higher rate of return than was readily available in the United Kingdom. And London's ability to control the sterling reserves of OSA countries enabled it to 'ration' currency in such a way as to preserve 'protected' markets for British exports in the dominions and colonies.

Until the late 1960s, therefore, Britain's economic links with most of the old Empire 'circle' remained quite strong, supported quite explicitly by the external financial policy of successive governments. Two factors served to change this situation. The first, documented in Chapter 5, was the autonomous shift in Britain's trade, away from the Empire and towards Europe, which began in the late 1950s. The second was the growing realisation in the mid-1960s that the postwar strategy of continuing to operate a reserve currency had been fundamentally misconceived; that it had in all probability acted as a drain on the strength of the British economy for over twenty years. The devaluation crisis of October 1967 presented the Wilson government with an opportunity to abandon sterling's reserve role which it was in no position – and had no desire – to oppose. The reserve role, and the Sterling Area with it, were duly ended under the terms of the Basle Agreements in 1968. Depending upon which account was believed, it had taken so long to abandon the reserve role either because of the vagaries of 'top currency syndrome' (which induced the key decision makers into making a faulty analysis of the costs and benefits of maintaining the OSA) or because of the predominant position within the British state apparatus of financial capitalists and their allies (who continued to derive enormous pecuniary advantage from the maintenance of the OSA until the mid-1960s).

Yet whatever the 'real' reason for the maintenance of the OSA, its termination certainly brought the 'overextension' of Britain's external economic policy to an end. During the second phase of the postwar period (1968–88) the British approach was less ambitious and more flexible. Currency policy, especially after the introduction of a floating exchange rate in 1972, retained its central importance, though after 1973 (when Britain joined the EC) trade policy and overseas investment policy became less dependent on what was happening to sterling and more dependent on the collective rules of the European Community.

But was the more flexible post-1968 strategy any more successful than its predecessor in its ultimate objective of strengthening Britain's international economic position? For much of the 1970s the answer would appear to be 'no'. Foreign economic policy during that period mainly consisted in the government adopting (virtually unavoidable) remedial measures in response to the latest crisis either in the world economy (the collapse of Bretton Woods in 1971; the 'oil shocks' of 1973 and 1979) or at home (the persistent balance of payments problems up to 1976). Thatcher's experiment with a freely floating exchange rate in 1979–80 – informed by firm ideological commitment rather than the pragmatism of the Heath/Wilson/Callaghan years – made the position even worse. An overvalued pound, buoyed up by North Sea oil revenues, wrought havoc with Britain's manufacturing export trade. The position was certainly eased by the return to managed floating from 1981 onwards. But by the late 1980s it was difficult to judge whether the Thatcherite economic programme, with its commitment to the restoration of market forces in both domestic and external contexts, had effected a genuine transformation in Britain's international economic position; or whether the apparent improvement in Britain's growth rate and balance of payments was the all too temporary consequence of the exploitation of North Sea oil.

What was certain about the post-1968 period, however, was that Britain's foreign economic policy was more heavily constrained by external factors beyond its control than ever before. To have attempted to insulate the British economy from the internationalisation of markets that was occurring in the 1970s and 1980s would have been both ineffectual and – in terms of the adverse foreign reaction it would have provoked – counterproductive. To have attempted to reduce the visible trade deficit with the European Community would have been impractical and equally counterproductive in terms of the likely reaction of

Britain's European partners. And there was certainly very little that Britain could do to pull the world economy out of the deep recession in which it had languished since the early 1970s. To be sure, the government could on occasion support multilateral efforts at crisis management, as it did in 1985 as one of the signatories to the Plaza Agreement progressively to devalue the dollar. But multilateral co-operation of this sort barely scratched the surface of the core problems of the global economy: the US budget deficit; the trade deficits of Japan's major trading partners; the unpaid – and unpayable – third-world debts and the out-of-control 'casino' of the financial markets. Since 1945, and especially since 1968, Britain's international economic position had been in secular decline and its foreign economic policy had accordingly been subject to increasing external constraints. In the late 1980s, it looked as though the next forty years would yield more of the same: further decline and ever more powerful constraints.

8

Defence Policy

Defence policy is that aspect of external policy concerned with maximising the nation-state's security interests. It consists in the construction of alliances and the development of military strategy designed to deter and/or counter potential foreign aggression. To the extent that foreign policy generally is also concerned in part with security calculations, a number of defence-related themes have already been discussed in previous chapters. This chapter seeks to draw these different themes together by summarising the major changes that characterised British defence policy in the postwar years and by outlining the main causal factors which provoked them. As will be seen, by far the most significant development of the period was the shift away from the defence of the 'Empire circle' that was associated with the 1968 decision to withdraw from east of Suez. This shift enabled successive governments to concentrate their defence efforts in the combined European and Atlantic 'circles', areas where Britain's primary economic interests were increasingly located. The first part of the chapter reviews London's increasingly laboured efforts in the 1940s and 1950s to continue to project a global military role; the contraction of that role in the 1960s and 1970s in the face of economic pressures; and the efforts at partial restoration which occurred during the 1980s. Since most of the developments have already been described in earlier chapters, the review provided is brief. The second – and most important – part of the chapter examines the origins and development of NATO, the 'Cold War' alliance of the 1950s which became the central focus of British defence policy from the late 1960s onwards.

Defence policy in the Empire circle, 1945–88

For two decades after 1945, the British government continued to take the sort of 'wide view' of British security that had characterised the outlook of successive governments since the early eighteenth century: that the security of the homeland was intimately bound up with the security of Britain's overseas possessions. There was nothing mystical about this belief. It derived, quite simply, from the Realist world-view of the key decision makers; from the conviction that, if London did not control the strategic bases and resource-rich territories of the Empire, then a potentially unfriendly power might – an eventuality that would seriously prejudice Britain's ability to prevail in any future war. In the immediate postwar years, this *realpolitik*-induced need to protect the security of the Empire was boosted by the emerging threat to Western interests posed by Soviet-style communism. What it meant in practice, as noted in previous chapters, was that London, in spite of its desire to reduce its overseas commitments if at all possible, found itself deploying military forces in almost every major theatre across the globe. As the February 1946 report on the defence estimates indicated, British forces in 1945–6 were not only concerned with administering the surrender and occupation of Germany, Austria, Italy and Japan: they were also providing assistance to the Greek government in its struggle to suppress a communist insurgency; attempting to keep law and order in Palestine; helping to maintain internal security and stability throughout the Empire; and safeguarding the global network of bases upon which Britain would rely in the event of any future global conflict.[1]

In the immediate postwar years, these responsibilities collectively imposed a considerable burden on Britain's defence budget. Given the competing resource demands at home, that budget was necessarily limited. Yet with its enormous commitments abroad, Attlee's government was still obliged to maintain defence forces far in excess of those necessary for the immediate protection of the United Kingdom itself. In this situation, Britain's postwar 'Empire circle' defence policy was driven by two conflicting objectives. On the one hand, the desire to see pro-British – or at least pro-Western – regimes proliferate throughout the third world encouraged support for almost any friendly government threatened by communist encroachment. On the other hand, the wish to reduce the worrying overextension of Britain's armed forces also encouraged Britain to seek to cut back its overseas responsibilities wherever withdrawal seemed unlikely to provoke serious local instability. The cynic would undoubtedly conclude that the simultaneous pursuit of these two contradictory objectives was bound to produce an inconsistent and directionless series of *ad hoc* policy decisions. The more generous observer, however, would recognise the British government's inability to abandon either objective in the threatening conditions of the Cold War and would probably conclude that, all things considered, successive governments made a series of intelligent compromises which successfully held communism at bay for over 30 years without bankrupting the Treasury.

The pressure to *increase* British involvement in the periphery made itself felt almost as soon as the war was over. In 1945–6 the War Office assumed control of the former Italian colonies of Somaliland, Libya and Eritrea in order to prepare them for independence in the early 1950s.[2] In 1948, British forces began extensive anti-insurgency operations in Malaya which were to last until 1958. In 1950, British forces joined the UN contingent which was fighting in Korea, a move that contributed to the near doubling of defence expenditure which subsequently occurred under the guise of the 1951–4 rearmament programme. In 1953, British troops became heavily involved in the struggle against the Mau-Mau nationalist movement in Kenya. And in the same year, Churchill's government bound itself by treaty to come to the aid of Libya in the event of its being attacked. Yet, even as these new deployments were being made, existing commitments also had to be met. In 1954, at perhaps the peak of Britain's postwar involvement in the Empire circle, sizeable British forces were stationed in the Mediterranean (in Gibraltar, Malta, Libya and Cyprus); in West Africa (in the Gambia, Sierra Leone, Ghana and Nigeria); in the Middle East (in the Canal Zone, at the Gulf of Aquabha and in Muscat); in East and Central–Southern Africa (in Kenya, Somalia, Sudan, Rhodesia, Nyasaland and Tanganyika); and in the Far East (in Korea, Japan, Hong Kong, Malaya and Singapore).[3] As if these commitments were not enough, in September 1954 Britain extended its obligations still further by guaranteeing the security of the Philippines, Thailand, Malaya and Singapore under the terms of the (SEATO) Manila Pact.[4] And the process was taken even further in February 1955 with the signing of the Central Treaty Organisation (CENTO) Baghdad Pact which committed Britain to the defence of Pakistan, Iran, Iraq and Turkey.[5] Finally, under the terms of the Simonstown Agreement of June 1955, the British government agreed to participate with Pretoria in joint naval operations to protect the shipping lanes around the Cape and in the Indian Ocean.[6]

Yet, although these alliances against the ubiquitous communist menace clearly *extended* Britain's *formal* responsibilities, in another sense they also reflected the government's contrary objective of *reducing* its global military commitments. Even before 1955, a communist attack on any of the countries that were to become either CENTO or SEATO signatories would almost certainly have resulted in Britain coming to the aid of the non-communist victim. By drawing the United States into SEATO, London ensured that, in the event of some future conflagration in the Far East, it would not find itself assisting a friendly regime without the support of the world's leading capitalist power: a burden shared with the United States, in this sense, was very much a burden halved.

Of course, the efforts to *reduce* Britain's overseas commitments had begun much earlier than the mid-1950s. Even while the Attlee government was increasing its activities in Malaya in the late 1940s, it was simultaneously withdrawing from India and from Palestine. After the Korean War the process of withdrawal accelerated. Under the terms of the Canal Zone Agreement of October 1954, Britain undertook to remove its forces from Suez within two years. In 1956, the 'second wave' phase of decolonisation began with the granting of independence to Sudan. Within ten years, in the face of escalating indigenous demands for change, Britain had removed the imperial yoke from all of its major colonies. And although Britain's withdrawal from each colony was generally accompanied by the promise of future support, if necessary, to the newly-independent government, the decolonisation process itself inevitably involved considerable reductions in the deployment of British forces overseas.

The crucial turning-point in 'Empire circle' defence policy, however, was the decision – announced in January 1968 – that all British military forces would be withdrawn from east of Suez by the end of 1971. Although the Royal Navy had been gradually slimmed down during the 1950s – the surface fleet had been reduced from 282 in 1952 to 110 in 1965[7] – in 1968 there were still over 57 000 troops and 14 000 naval personnel permanently deployed east of Suez,[8] their purpose not only to deter communist aggression in the Far East but also to '[safeguard] the trade and commerce of the free world'.[9] To maintain forces of this size, specifically designated for out-of-area operations, was, however, becoming a luxury that the hard-pressed Exchequer could no longer really afford. The 1966 Defence Review had announced the government's intention to cut defence spending from 7 per cent to 6 per cent of Britain's GNP by 1969–70. The Review had also intimated that the 'overstretch' of the country's defence forces would have to be eliminated in the near future: the situation in which London had been obliged to despatch emergency forces to eight trouble-spots around the globe in 1963, to sixteen in 1964, and to seventeen in 1965, could not be tolerated for much longer.[10] In these circumstances it was virtually inevitable that the government would soon seek to reduce the scope of Britain's defence efforts in order to concentrate on the one theatre – Western Europe and the North Atlantic – that was clearly of the most immediate relevance to the security of the United Kingdom itself.

Once the decision to withdraw from east of Suez had been taken, events moved rapidly. In December 1967, British forces withdrew from Aden, which accordingly achieved independence as the People's Republic of South Yemen. In October 1971, notwithstanding the election of a Conservative government in June 1970, British HQ Far Eastern Command was closed and the vast bulk of the British forces previously stationed in Singapore and Malaysia were withdrawn. (At a Five Power Defence Conference in London in April 1972, it was confirmed that the United Kingdom would cease to declare forces to SEATO and that Australia and New Zealand would effectively take over Britain's former role in the defence of Malaysia and Singapore.) However, Britain continued to garrison Hong Kong and retained five surface ships permanently on station in the Far East. In December 1971, HQ British Forces in the Gulf was withdrawn, leaving only a small garrison in Oman to assist the Sultan in counter-insurgency operations.[11] Moreover, while all of these changes were taking place east of Suez, Britain was also reducing its commitments in the Mediterranean, though not necessarily as a matter of choice. In 1970, the new Libyan government unilaterally terminated the 1953 Anglo-Libyan Defence Agreement and requested the prompt withdrawal of British forces and the closing of Britain's remaining bases. In 1972, the Maltese government made a similar request. In both cases, London quietly acceded to the demands of the host government: the cost savings were extremely welcome and confrontation would in all probability have been counter-productive in any case. By 1974, Britain's world role had been almost completely abandoned. Garrisons were still stationed in the remaining dependencies of Belize, Gibraltar, Hong Kong and the Falkland Islands. And a small force was still assisting the Sultan of Oman.[12] But plans to withdraw from Mauritius and Brunei (where the rump of the Brigade of Gurkhas was still deployed) were well advanced and negotiations had already been started with the South Africans with a view to terminating the 1955 Simonstown Agreement and abandoning the British base there. Indeed the March 1975 Defence White Paper could justifiably refer, without pretence or affectation, to Britain's '*former* aspirations to a world-wide role'.[13] By the mid-1970s, the British government's defence policy – as with its foreign policy in general – had clearly shifted away from the Empire circle and towards Europe.

Why had it been necessary to end Britain's world military role? Although the main reasons have already been considered in earlier chapters, it is nevertheless worth reviewing them briefly here. One of the major factors was undoubtedly the fact that decolonisation, irresistible in the face of rising indigenous nationalism and the increasingly European focus of Britain's trade, had robbed the bases at Aden, at Singapore, at Simonstown and on the Gulf of their principal strategic *raison d'être*. Once Britain *had* decolonised, the British government was no longer under quite the same obligation to guarantee the territorial integrity of its former possessions. This in turn meant that it did not need to maintain the same sort of permanent out-of-area capability which had been necessary to ensure the security of the Empire. However the main reason underlying the decision to withdraw from east of Suez, as noted in Chapter 4, was *cost*. Britain could not afford to make an effective contribution to the defence of Western Europe *and* to maintain a powerful military presence in the Gulf and in the Far East: if both tasks could not be accomplished properly because of scarce resources, it was far better to cut commitments and ensure that at least one was. With the Empire gone, Britain's interests were clearly moving towards Europe: it was thus inevitable that successive governments would choose to concentrate their defence efforts in the European theatre. An additional element in the decision calculus was that, even if Britain itself could no longer effectively participate in the protection of Western interests east of Suez, it had friends who could be relied upon to step into the breach: Australia and New Zealand willingly linked themselves to the security of Malaysia and Singapore; the United States (courtesy of the Wilson government's 'gift' of Diego Garcia)[14] took over responsibility for the Indian Ocean; and Iran (under its strongly pro-Western Shah) and the United States together looked set to mediate any local difficulty which might arise in the Gulf.

Yet there was one other security-based factor that was also relevant in the decision to withdraw from east of Suez. It was increasingly recognised in the 1960s that, if war were to break out between East and West, then it would probably 'go nuclear' very quickly. In these circumstances, the strategic value of a global network of bases would be highly questionable: what would be the point of controlling bases and sea-lanes if the home territory and population had already been eliminated? Although this possibility had been recognised since the late 1940s, it was not until the mid-1960s that the strategic planners became convinced of its importance. Once this shift in perceptions *had* occurred, however, it became clear that a British withdrawal from east of Suez was not as strategically 'risky' as it might have appeared 20 years earlier. Even if the worst happened and the Soviets, or their agents, gained control of the strategic bases vacated by Britain, Moscow would in all probability be unable to use its new-found assets to any great effect. Although the Soviets would almost certainly attempt to increase their influence in the territories from which British forces had been withdrawn (as they did in Aden, with some success, between 1969 and 1986), the potential strategic costs of such developments would no longer be so great as to prejudice the security either of Britain or of its NATO allies. By the late 1960s, in short, it could reasonably be argued that Britain could withdraw from its global role without appearing wildly irresponsible in the eyes of its allies and without leaving an enormous *realpolitik* vacuum that the Soviets would automatically fill to the serious detriment of the West.

With the withdrawal from east of Suez completed in 1972, the focus of British defence policy shifted firmly towards Europe. The bulk of Britain's trade was with Europe. And the United Kingdom had slipped so far down the GDP 'league table' that it was clearly no longer anything more than 'just another European power'. In these circumstances the British government neither needed nor could afford to take the sort of 'world-view' of British security interests which had characterised its defence policy for over two centuries. Although the threat of communist encroachment in the third world obviously still existed, the United States would simply have to continue the struggle alone: Britain no longer possessed the economic strength to assist in the task.

This rather more passive posture did not survive into the 1980s, however. Even if Britain now lacked a global military capability, the Conservative government which assumed office in May 1979 took a much 'wider' view of British security interests than its more 'Europeanist' predecessors. Reasoning along classic Realist lines, the Thatcher Cabinet insisted from the outset that the key feature of the contemporary international system was the global struggle between capitalism and communism. In Thatcher's view – and, even before the Falklands crisis, hers was the decisive voice in Cabinet – developments in every third-world theatre had a bearing on the global balance of power. This in turn meant that any incursion either into 'neutral' territory or into the capitalist sphere of influence constituted an erosion, however small, of the long-run security interests in the West. It was therefore in Britain's material interests for the government to resist attempts to extend socialist hegemony, wherever they might surface. And should anyone doubt the veracity of these claims, the Soviet invasion of Afghanistan in December 1979 provided a clear illustration of the threat that Soviet adventurism posed in the third world.

This 'wider view' of the Thatcher government did not mean, however, that British defence policy lost its primarily European focus. Thatcher, after all, was almost obsessively concerned with the need to make economies in all areas of government spending.[15] And having just renewed the Callaghan government's 1977 commitment to increase the Defence Budget by 3 per cent per year in real terms in order to strengthen NATO's defences, the Cabinet could hardly afford to embark on a massively expensive rearmament programme designed to restore Britain's out-of-area capabilities to pre-1968 levels. What the Thatcher government was prepared to do, however, was to lend unequivocal moral and political support to US efforts to protect the presumed world-wide interests of the Western capitalist powers, and to provide military assistance wherever it could. It was also prepared to take action on its own account if it considered that the rules of acceptable international behaviour were being seriously transgressed. While this shift in posture did not amount to Britain playing anything resembling 'an active world role' in the 1980s, it was certainly associated with a more active role than that pursued in the 1970s. Four episodes serve to illustrate this more active role. (1) In late 1980, in response to the threat posed to Western shipping by the outbreak of the Iran–Iraq war, the Royal Navy resumed its Armilla patrol in the Gulf of Oman.[16] As the Gulf war continued throughout the 1980s, the patrol increasingly took on the appearance of a permanent British commitment to the region. (2) Between April and July of 1981, British forces regained possession of the Falkland Islands: the fact that Argentina refused to bring a formal end to hostilities, however, meant that Britain seemed committed to garrisoning the islands for an indefinite period. (3) In 1982, a 100-man British contingent participated in the American-sponsored multinational peace-keeping force that was despatched to Lebanon in order to cover the Israeli retreat from Beirut. However this commitment was rather more temporary than those in the Gulf and the Falklands: British troops were withdrawn from Lebanon in January 1984. Finally (4) in September 1987, a contingent of six Royal Navy minesweepers was sent to the Persian Gulf in order to assist the US Navy, which was attempting to protect American-flagged oil tankers from Iranian attack. Notwithstanding UN attempts to bring the Gulf war to a satisfactory conclusion, in the late 1980s this commitment looked set to continue for several years to come.

Thus Britain's postwar Empire circle defence policy developed in three distinct phases. Between 1945 and the mid-1960s, London continued to adhere to the traditional belief that British security required not only geostrategic stability in western Europe but also the preservation of the Empire's global network of bases. The bases were considered essential both to the defence of the Empire itself and to the protection of the Western sphere of influence in the third world generally. By the mid-1960s, however, the burden of 'carrying two rifles instead of one' had proved too great. In order to prevent an unacceptable escalation in defence costs, successive governments between the mid-1960s and the late 1970s opted to concentrate the United Kingdom's defence efforts in the European theatre, where Britain's principal material interests were increasingly located. Notwithstanding the need to make limited deployments overseas,[17] therefore, Britain effectively withdrew from its 'world role', increasingly defining itself as a European power with primarily European interests. During the 1980s the pendulum swung back slightly. The Thatcher government took the same sort of wider, *realpolitik* world-view that had characterised British defence policy in the 1940s and 1950s. The need to confront any challenge to the interests of Western capitalism on a world-wide basis was central to Thatcher's understanding of international relations. To be sure, the simple facts of Britain's long-term relative economic decline ensured that there was no real prospect of London ever acquiring the permanent out-of-area capability necessary for it to resume its former world role. Nevertheless, the Thatcher government certainly strove to take a global view of developments in the old 'Empire circle' and, wherever possible, to act in concert with the United States in order to thwart communist (or even Islamic) efforts to weaken Western influence in the third world.

Defence policy in the European and Atlantic circles: NATO

Although the NATO alliance formed the basis of Britain's strategy for home defence from 1949 onwards, it was only in the mid-1960s that the forces which the government committed to NATO began to exceed those deployed in pursuit of Britain's 'world role'. While the shift in commitment had been signalled in the late 1950s – the 1957 Defence Review, for example, had identified 'deterring aggression in Europe' as the first aim of British defence policy[18] – the crucial policy change was announced in the Commons in January 1968. Henceforward the British government would concentrate its defence efforts in Europe and the North Atlantic. Although the specific form that this new 'concentration' took was undoubtedly the product of a complex set of negotiations in which the different service bureaucracies sought to preserve their own sectional interests, the shift in strategy itself resulted primarily from considerations of *cost*: from the perceived need to reduce defence spending to a level comparable to that incurred by Britain's major industrial competitors. That it was the 'world role' rather than the NATO role which was to be sacrificed reflected the government's recognition that it was in Europe, rather than in the Empire, that Britain's primary interests were now located.

This section focuses on four aspects of the NATO alliance. First, it examines the origins and development of the alliance and reviews the tensions that characterised it from its inception in 1949. Second, it assesses the political underpinnings of NATO and examines the varying perceptions of 'the Soviet threat' which were invariably invoked in order to justify its continuance. Third, it summarises the military principles which guided NATO strategy in the postwar era and reviews the role played by the British independent nuclear deterrent in the development of that strategy. Finally, it describes the main difficulties which Britain's NATO policy is likely to encounter in the future, focusing particularly on the problems of cost escalation and internal dissension over arms control negotiations.

Origins and development of NATO

As noted in Chapter 2, one of the important international developments of the late 1940s was the increasing potential threat posed to Western interests by Stalin's 'consolidation' of Eastern Europe. The pro-Moscow coup in Czechoslovakia and the Berlin crisis of 1948, together with the continuing electoral popularity of the French and Italian Communist Parties, caused considerable alarm in London and Washington. It was the Attlee government's view that, unless firm measures were taken to avoid it, Soviet 'consolidation' might easily mutate into an 'expansionism' which could envelop the whole of Western Europe. And London's preferred solution, founded on the belief that the Europeans were too weak to defend themselves, was an 'Atlantic alliance' in which the United States was firmly locked into the defence of Western Europe. Indeed what the British government wanted to ensure above all else was that, if war did break out in Europe, the Americans would be involved from the outset; that the Kremlin would be denied the possibility of achieving what Hitler had hoped for – 'a quick local success in Europe'.[19]

The Americans, unfortunately, were rather more equivocal. As also noted in Chapter 2, although the influential National Security Council (NSC) was broadly in favour of committing US ground forces to Western Europe's defence, the State Department, and, in particular, George Kennan, the Chief of its Policy Planning Staff, feared that American involvement would in the long run prove counter-productive. Articulating a widely held view in the United States, Kennan argued that the spectre of the Soviet threat – notwithstanding the recent events in Czechoslovakia and Berlin – had been considerably exaggerated. In Kennan's view it was extremely unlikely that the Soviet Union would attack Western Europe because, even in 1948, it was already strategically overextended. It was simply fanciful to suppose that the Soviets would attempt to extend their sphere of hegemony when they hardly possessed the military capability to retain control of their current imperial domain. If Kennan's views could have been dismissed as those of a misguided and ineffectual liberal, the Truman administration would have speedily rejected the State Department's position. Kennan, however, had been the chief architect of the postwar global strategy of 'containment' – of preventing the spread of communism in the third world – and had accordingly established his credentials as a respected practitioner of *realpolitik*. His was a powerful voice which had to be heard, and his fears that the creation of an Atlantic alliance would provoke the remilitarisation of a permanently divided Europe were widely shared.

Kennan's opponents in the NSC – as well as British Foreign Secretary Bevin – countered his claims by arguing that, with or without American participation, Europe was going to be remilitarised anyway. The fact that the Soviets might objectively be overextended at present did nothing to reduce West European fears about their long-term intentions and future capabilities. Western Europe itself, therefore, would be obliged to prepare for the worst in any case. The choice for Washington was whether it wanted to involve itself: whether or not it wished to commit itself to the defence of a region with which, in an age of ideological conflicts, it shared a common ideology and in which it had rapidly growing economic interests. Moreover, if the United States left the defence of Western Europe to the Europeans themselves, which in the late 1940s meant a disproportionately burdensome role for the British, then London would almost certainly have to run down its out-of-area capabilities and this in turn would render it less able to assist American efforts to resist communist expansion in the third world.

Bevin's efforts to convince Washington that its support was essential to Western Europe's security, and that the remilitarisation of Europe was already under way, first took shape with the signing of the Brussels Pact in March 1948, a politico-military alliance between Britain, the Benelux countries and France. The Attlee government's problem, however, was to convince Washington that, while the Pact demonstrated Western Europe's determination to contribute substantially to its own defence (which even the NSC considered to be a prerequisite for

American involvement), it did not also imply that European efforts alone would be sufficient to deter Soviet expansionism. By provoking the Berlin crisis, which began in May 1948, the Soviets unwittingly came to Britain's rescue. Stalin's blockade of the city not only confirmed the seriousness of the Soviet threat to geostrategic stability in west-central Europe, but also (as a result of the joint USAF–RAF airlift, mounted to defeat the blockade) helped to rekindle the spirit of Anglo-American military collaboration which had existed between 1941 and 1945. Subsequent events moved rapidly. In July 1948, the British government gave permission for the USAF to deploy a large contingent of (nuclear-capable) B-29s at air bases in Britain.[20] The concept of Britain as 'Airstrip 1' was born, with a clear message to the Soviets: even though the Americans were not formally committed to protecting Western Europe, any Soviet aggression in that region now risked provoking an American strategic response. In April 1949, the North Atlantic Treaty was signed, giving formal expression to the American commitment to Europe. In January 1950, NATO itself was officially constituted. Covering the United States, Canada and most of Western Europe, the new organisation was a mutual assistance pact with a permanent military command structure.[21] Decisions on military strategy were to be collectively determined and each member state would designate part of its military forces for permanent NATO-assigned duties.

Throughout the 1950s and 1960s – as the Cold War deepened and then receded – NATO constituted the basis of Western Europe's defence. The Americans not only provided an 'extended nuclear deterrent' as protective cover, but also contributed over 300 000 military personnel, most of them permanently stationed in West Germany. Britain, for its part, committed some 77 000 troops to the British Army of the Rhine and the Berlin Brigade (reduced to 64 000 in 1957 and to 55 000 in 1958);[22] a large contingent of aircraft and aircrew to RAF Germany; a significant porportion of the fleet to patrolling the channel and the eastern Atlantic; over 100 000 troops to the defence of British sovereign territory; and, from the mid-1950s onwards (and in varying forms), the British independent nuclear deterrent. NATO itself was bolstered by the admission of Greece and Turkey in 1952 and (following the abortive Franco–German attempt to form a European Defence Community in 1953–4) by the inclusion of the newly rehabilitated Federal German Republic in 1955. At the same time, the Federal Republic, together with Italy, joined the Brussels Pact Signatories to form the Western European Union.[23]

In 1966, NATO was rocked by the French decision to withdraw from its military wing. (Paris retained its contacts with the *political* institutions of the alliance.) De Gaulle had been increasingly concerned about American dominance of the alliance and, having failed to entice Britain into a closer Anglo-French military relationship, decided that France would be less of a target for Soviet aggression if all American bases and forces – as well as NATO's Paris HQ – were removed from French soil. As far as London was concerned, the potential danger of the French withdrawal was that it might lend weight to those voices in Washington that were already pressing for a reduction in American involvement in European security matters: if the Europeans were not prepared to organise their own defence properly, then why should the United States continue to underwrite it? Three developments helped to suppress this incipient American neo-isolationism. The first was the British decision to withdraw from east of Suez and to concentrate its still substantial military forces in the European theatre. Although this shift of emphasis did not entirely replace the forces which had been lost to NATO as a reult of the French withdrawal, it did mean that no additional American deployments were required in order to meet the shortfall. The second development originated – ironically – in Moscow. The Soviet intervention in Czechoslovakia in May 1968, just like Stalin's blockade of Berlin 20 years earlier, served both to dispel West European suspicions that 'the Soviet threat' might be receding and to reinforce the belief that the threat must continue to be actively deterred through a strong and united NATO. The third development was the creation of NATO's 'Eurogroup' in January 1969. Intended partly as a vehicle for improving Anglo-German defence collaboration, the Eurogroup was warmly welcomed by the Nixon Administration on the grounds that a strengthening of NATO's 'European Pillar' would relieve the military pressure on the United States, an important consideration when American forces were heavily committed to an extended campaign in Vietnam.[24]

The political climate within NATO changed yet again in the early 1970s as the United States and the Soviet Union entered a period of 'détente' in which the traditional need for confrontation between East and West was de-emphasised. This relaxation of tension did not mean, of course, that the Soviet threat had diminished or that the NATO countries could contemplate dropping their military guard. None the less, in addition to producing the Anti-Ballistic Missile Treaty of 1972 and the Strategic Arms Limitation Treaty of 1974, the détente process did facilitate NATO–Warsaw Pact negotiations on conventional arms reductions (the long running Mutual Balanced Force reduction talks in Vienna) and, through the Helsinki Final Act of August 1975, Europe-wide participation in a series of conferences on security and co-operation in Europe.

The spirit of détente did not last for long, however. As the 1970s progressed, it was increasingly felt within NATO circles that the Soviets had merely used the détente process as a cover for a massive expansion of their own military capability, which was now in danger of outstripping that of the West.[25] Accordingly, at a meeting of NATO Defence Ministers in May 1977, it was agreed that NATO countries would redress this capability imbalance by increasing their defence expenditure by 3 per cent per annum, in real terms, for the period 1979–84.[26] It is quite possible that these targets would have been conveniently forgotten had East–West relations not suffered a further series of setbacks during the course of 1979. In June, the Sandinista victory in Nicaragua precipitated American fears that 'another Cuba' was imminent; in mid-December the NATO decision to deploy cruise and Pershing II missiles in Europe (in response to the earlier Soviet deployment of SS-20s in eastern Europe) provoked Soviet threats of retaliatory deployments; and in late December, the Russian invasion of Afghanistan reinforced Western convictions that the Soviet Union was still an expansionist power which continued to pose a threat to the interests of the Atlantic alliance both inside and outside the European theatre. As a result of all of these developments, East–West relations entered a new era of 'Cold War' (1979–83). In the Thatcher government's view, NATO needed seriously to consider the possibility of extending its operations to out-of-area activities in the third world.[27] Notwithstanding the multinational force that was despatched to Lebanon in 1983, this idea failed to gain allied support. However the practitioners of *realpolitik* now in power in London and Washington did press ahead with the putative '3 per cent solution' and, though not fully backed by other NATO member-states, succeeded in giving the East–West arms spiral yet another upward twist.

Critics on the left argued, predictably perhaps, that this renewed arms race was necessary not because of any 'real' increase in the Soviet threat but because higher arms spending was in the material interests of the ubiquitous 'military–industrial complex'. The government, in contrast, pointed to the softening of the Soviet position in the mid- and late 1980s, claiming that its origins lay in the tough uncompromising stance which NATO had taken between 1979 and 1983: the increased defence spending of the NATO countries had forced the Kremlin, with its vastly inferior economic capacity, to compromise on the question of its own military deployments; the conciliatory Soviet posture of the Gorbachev years – which had produced the Intermediate Nuclear

Force (INF) agreement in December 1987 – was merely the West's reward for its earlier fortitude. Which of these opposing interpretations was correct was, of course, extraordinarily difficult to establish. In any event, in the late 1980s, it was clear that, even if the Soviets did still threaten West European security, Gorbachev was far more willing than any of his predecessors to engage in a constructive dialogue with the West aimed at achieving genuine arms reductions both in the European theatre and world-wide. After 40 years of near-continuous confrontation, this was progress indeed. Yet, as far as London was concerned, it did not mean that NATO could lower its defences significantly. Gorbachev's strategy of *glasnost* and *perestroika* at home and co-operative diplomacy abroad might, for whatever reason, disappear just as quickly as they had emerged. A strong and determined NATO would still be necessary to maintain West European – and especially British – security for the foreseeable future.

The political underpinnings of NATO: perceptions of the Soviet threat

From the foregoing discussion it is clear that from its inception the continued existence of NATO was predicated on the presence of 'the Soviet threat'. Yet, paradoxically, it was never possible to assess with certainty whether the threat was real or not. Since the Kremlin – obviously – did not (and does not) publish its geostrategic plans, it was always necessary to infer its intentions from its actions, its military capabilities and the public posturings of its leaders. NATO, in this sense, was always Western Europe's, and Britain's, *realpolitik* safety net. Simple prudence dictated that the Western powers should combine in order to deter Stalin from further expansionism; that if they wanted peace, they should prepare for war.[28] The suspicion that the Korean War might be a communist feint designed to put NATO off its guard in Europe merely added to the fears that Stalin's ruthless campaign of 'consolidation' in Eastern Europe had already engendered.

Yet, even at the height of the Cold War in the late 1940s and early 1950s, London was not entirely convinced that Britain was 'really' threatened by the Soviets. To be sure, the post-1945 '10-year rule' (which advised service chiefs to assume for planning purposes that Britain would not be engaged in a major war for ten years) had been abandoned by mid-1948.[29] Moreover, by December 1950, as noted in Chapter 2, the Chiefs of Staff Committee was advising Cabinet that war was 'probable in 1952; possible in 1951'.[30] In spite of such warnings, however, governmental doubts about the magnitude of the Soviet threat remained. A significant minority of Attlee's Cabinet at the time of the rearmament decision in December 1950, for example, were not convinced that Britain's security was seriously threatened by the Soviets.[31] And in the Eden Cabinet of 1954–6, even the Prime Minister himself, on at least one occasion, voiced the opinion that it was no longer necessary to take the Soviet threat altogether seriously.[32]

During the détente era of the 1970s, the doubts about the 'threat' that had for so long received wide (if not majority) currency in defence policy circles started to be reflected in public opinion. It was increasingly suggested that in the late 1940s Stalin had perhaps only been concerned to defend socialism from attack and to create a strategic buffer in east-central Europe which would insulate Soviet territory from yet another invasion. Perhaps, it was suggested, the Russians would not have invaded Western Europe even if NATO had not been there to 'deter' them. In the late 1970s and 1980s a voluble minority throughout Europe, and particularly in Britain, increasingly asked: is there *really* a Soviet threat to the security of Western Europe?

There were clearly two broad sets of answers to this question. Those who subscribed to the thesis that there was now no longer such a threat (even if there had been one in 1948–9) possessed a powerful array of arguments. First, some suggested, the 'Soviet threat' had from the outset been a propaganda ploy of Western capitalist elites who created the threat partly because they wished to discredit socialism in general and partly because they sought to divert mass attention away from injustice and inequality at home. Second, it was suggested that Soviet adventurism in the 1940s had stemmed from a situation in which the lines of partition in Europe were relatively fluid. By the late 1970s, however, the lines of partition had solidified; this enormously increased the likely costs of any new Soviet adventurism and accordingly reduced its probability. In the British context, a third set of arguments concerned internal institutional factors. It was alleged that, even before the broad bipartisan consensus on foreign policy broke down in the late 1970s, it was always in the Conservative party's political interests to bolster the idea of the Soviet threat in the public imagination. This increased the salience of defence as an electoral issue which in turn worked to the electoral advantage of the Conservatives because they were traditionally seen by the electorate as being 'strong on defence'. It was also alleged that inter-service rivalry might have served to exaggerate the sense of an external threat. The series of Defence Reviews, which from 1946 onwards sought to cut unnecessary defence expenditure,[33] encouraged each service to identify aspects of the Soviet threat which could only be countered if its share of the defence budget was maintained. This in turn tended to magnify the apparent size of the overall threat as each service sought to protect its own projected programmes and deployments, producing a considerable disparity between collective perceptions of the threat and its objective magnitude.

The final reason why the size of the threat needed to be exaggerated, according to the thesis that 'there is no longer a Soviet threat', derived from the British government's fears of an American withdrawal from the NATO alliance. If the threat receded sufficiently, Washington might well be tempted to save some foreign exchange and entrust the defence of Western Europe to the Europeans themselves. In these circumstances London would certainly lose what residual ability it still possessed to influence American strategic planning. More seriously, the Europeans would be extremely vulnerable in the event of any future resurgence of Soviet adventurism: the task of bringing the Americans back into the alliance might well prove as difficult as that of securing their wartime participation in 1917 and 1941; and in the likely conditions of the Third World War a repetition of this sort of prevarication would probably be fatal. In classic *realpolitik* fashion, therefore, inflating the threat was simply a device for maintaining alliance unity in order to protect against future unforeseen contingencies.

Needless to say, most – if not all – of these arguments were rejected out of hand by NATO's protagonists. In their view, the Soviet threat in the 1980s was just as real as it had been in the 1940s; it had merely assumed a more benign form. Soviet ideology still favoured and still anticipated the world-wide spread of communism. Just as détente had crumbled in the late 1970s, there was no telling when Moscow might revert to a more virulent anti-capitalist posture. Obviously there was no direct evidence of Soviet aggressive intent in Europe: forty years of NATO deterrence had put paid to that. Yet there was abundant indirect evidence of Moscow's commitment to a ruthless and acquisitve form of *realpolitick*. The suppression of dissent in Hungary in 1956, in Czechoslovakia in 1968 and (indirectly) in Poland in 1980 clearly demonstrated the Kremlin's determination to preserve its hegemony in Eastern Europe. Moscow's support for Vietnam in its invasion of Kampuchea in 1978; its use of its Cuban proxy in Angola in 1974–5 and in Ethiopia in 1977–8; its financing of Cuban support for the Sandinistas in Nicaragua in 1978–9; its invasion of Afghanistan in December 1979: all of these developments revealed an aggressive superpower intent on the gradual incorporation into its own sphere of influence of as many lesser powers as possible. Only 'eternal vigilance', or at least the preservation of NATO in more or less its present form, would prevent Soviet expansionism from spreading from the third world (where it was already widespread) to Europe. Indeed, if the Soviets were *not* intent on expanding their sphere of influence, it was asked, why had they massively expanded the Soviet Navy in the period since 1965 and simultaneously poured resources into the strategic bases that they had acquired: into Aden (in South Yemen) after 1968; into Mogadishu and Berbera (in Somalia) after 1971; into Asmara (in Ethiopia) after 1977; and into Cam Rann Bay (in Vietnam) after 1975? Why, on the European central front, did Moscow insist on preserving a 2.7:1 Warsaw Pact superiority in tanks, a 2.5:1 superiority in field guns, and a 2.3:1 superiority in tactical aircraft – as well as a 2:1 superiority in surface ships and submarines in the Eastern Atlantic – if it had no agressive intentions towards Western Europe?[34]

In the Thatcher's government's view, Moscow's actions in the third world demonstrated its *intent* and its deployments in the European theatre demonstrated its *capability*. Notwithstanding Gorbachev's apparent willingness to compromise, these were the 'facts' that mattered most. The Soviet threat remained real and pervasive. The necessity of opposing it accordingly remained undiminished.

As in so many other areas of Britain's external policy, it was not possible to determine which of these rival interpretations was 'correct'. Although protagonists on each side could cite some empirical evidence in support of their position, neither had access to the evidential source that mattered: the calculations and objectives of the strategic planners and decision makers inside the Kremlin. In the absence of decisive evidence, NATO's critics were prepared to conclude that the Soviets posed no threat in Western Europe because they were already overextended and would gain nothing materially even from a successful military campaign. Its protagonists were rather more cautious. In their view, it was easy to construct a *plausible* argument which concluded that 'the Soviet threat' was largely an illusion in an uncertain world. However the costs of being wrong about the Soviet threat were so enormous that NATO's leadership was obliged to play safe; to build its defences as if there were a Soviet threat even though that assumption might be incorrect.

NATO's military strategy and the British independent deterrent

As an essentially defensive alliance, NATO military strategy was always based on a two-dimensional concept of deterrence. First, the British and American forces (supplemented after 1955 by troops from the FRG) stationed in West Germany were from the outset intended to provide a conventional weapons 'shield', a 'denial deterrent' which would halt, or at least delay, any conventional attack by Soviet bloc forces. Initially, NATO's conventional forces were committed only to defending the territory west of the Rhine; the admission of FRG to the alliance in 1955, however, resulted in the 'forward strategy' of setting NATO's defensive line at the Federal Republic's eastern border.[35] The second aspect of NATO's deterrent posture was the nuclear 'sword', a 'punishment deterrent' which would inflict unacceptable damage on the Soviet Union if the denial deterrent failed or if the Soviets used nuclear weapons against the West.

What complicated NATO's calculation from 1949 onwards, however, was the recognition that the conventional 'denial deterrent' was not very effective. Soviet bloc forces possessed an enormous conventional superiority in east-central Europe and it was generally accepted that NATO's conventional shield would at best *delay* a Soviet conventional advance, perhaps only for a matter of hours. To have built up NATO's *conventional* forces to match those of the Soviet bloc would have been prohibitively expensive: NATO always made it clear, therefore, that it was quite prepared to use *nuclear* weapons in order to prevent a quick Soviet conventional victory. NATO's problem in this context was that the threat to use nuclear weapons if its conventional deterrent failed was not entirely credible. Notwithstanding the presence of over 300 000 American troops in Europe, would Washington really engage in 'massive (nuclear) retaliation' (and therefore invite Soviet counter-reprisals) just because of a conventional invasion of, say, West Germany? In the mid-1960s, the possibility that the Soviets no longer regarded the massive retaliation threat as credible induced NATO to shift to a strategy of 'flexible response'. The new strategy, announced in December 1967, was based on two principles. First, NATO would keep its response options open and would not reveal in advance how it would respond to a conventional attack on any of its members. Second, NATO committed itself to developing and maintaining a credible capability across as wide a range of weapon-systems as possible. This meant that, if it so desired, NATO could provide a *graduated* response to any Soviet attack which was commensurate with the form and intensity of that attack. This in turn was intended to increase the chances that any overt conflict could be restricted to the lowest possible rungs of the 'escalation' ladder. By the late 1980s, assuming that there really was a serious Soviet threat, flexible response had enjoyed over two decades of unbroken success, bolstered by new conventional strategies (such as 'deep strike' attacks on Soviet bloc 'follow-on forces')[36] which were intended to prevent any conventional exchange from crossing the nuclear threshold.

Yet there was an additional element in NATO's deterrent strategy that could also claim some credit (albeit contentiously) for preserving the peace in Europe: the British 'independent' nuclear deterrent. When NATO had been created, only the United States and the Soviet Union had possessed any kind of nuclear capability. In 1951, however, the new Conservative government determined that Britain should develop its own independent deterrent force.[37] Following a series of atomic tests in 1952–3, the RAF was supplied with nuclear bombs capable of being delivered by its ageing fleet of Canberra aircraft in 1954.[38] In March 1955, Defence Secretary Macmillan announced that Britain's new V-bomber force was now nuclear-armed.[39]

Throughout the 1950s there was considerable rivalry between the RAF and the Royal Navy as to which service was best equipped to deliver nuclear warheads to enemy territory.[40] The Navy's case centred on the doubts that were increasingly being voiced about NATO's post-1956 threats of 'massive retaliation' which, it was argued, invited the Soviets to engage in a pre-emptive 'first strike' against the West's nuclear arsenals. Nuclear bombs stored at airfields in Western Europe were prime targets for such a first strike. What was needed was a 'second strike capability' which could plausibly threaten to hit back at Soviet targets even if Warsaw Pact forces launched a successful *blitzkrieg* – nuclear or otherwise – against Britain itself.[41] With developments in ballistic missile technology gradually weakening the RAF's case for a manned-aircraft delivery system, the Navy's case began to prevail. The decision to purchase Polaris – a submarine-launched ballistic missile system – from the Americans in December 1962 decided the matter. From the time that Polaris became operational in 1968, Britain's independent deterrent was based on a small submarine fleet which was permanently designated for NATO responsibilities but which could be withdrawn specifically for British use in an emergency. The secret 'Chevaline' upgrade of the Polaris warhead authorised by the Heath, Wilson and Callaghan governments during the 1970s continued the commitment.[42] And the Thatcher government's decision to purchase, first, Trident I (C4) and then Trident II (D5) – again from the Americans – in 1980–2 meant that Britain could expect to maintain a credible independent deterrent capability well into the twenty-first century.[43]

But why had it been necessary for Britain to possess an independent deterrent in the first place? Why could not London have relied on the Americans to protect Britain, as well as the rest of Western Europe, with their extended nuclear deterrent? Four factors seem to have been particularly significant, although, as is frequently the case, it is difficult to determine their relative importance. One factor, in the early 1950s at least, was the need for Britain to retain its prominent position in what was already an American-dominated alliance. As a government Global Strategy Paper argued in 1952, the United Kingdom could only expect to influence the development of American nuclear strategy if it possessed its own independent nuclear capability.[44] A second, and related, factor was the question of prestige. If Britain wished to retain its Great Power status and to continue to exercise influence in the international corridors of power, it had to have a share in the awesome destructive potential of the latest military technology. A fashionable pun of the mid-1950s was that nuclear weapons were 'great levellers' – both of buildings and of the power differentials between nation-states.[45] Nuclear weapons seemed to provide middle-range powers like Britain and France with the opportunity to achieve strategic equality with the two recently-emerged superpowers. The attraction of thereby retaining a leading position in world diplomacy proved too much for both Labour and Conservative governments: the development of an independent nuclear capability accordingly became an important defence policy priority.

A third factor underlying the British decision to press ahead with its own independent deterrent was the implicit message that such a programme sent to the Kremlin. In the mid-1950s, it was entirely possible that Moscow simply found American threats of 'massive retaliation' non-credible; that the Soviets did not believe that Washington would unleash what would inevitably be a mutually-fatal nuclear exchange merely because of a Soviet conventional incursion into western Europe. In these circumstances, Britain's possession of an independent nuclear capability not only provided another decision-centre that Moscow was now obliged to consider in its calculations about the credibility of NATO threats of 'nuclear punishment'; it also provided a Western punishment deterrent that was far more likely to be *used* if Moscow were to call Washington's bluff and to attempt to take advantage of its conventional superiority in Europe. A prime function of the independent deterrent in this sense was to make NATO's nuclear sword more *credible*.

The fourth main factor was that the independent deterrent provided an insurance policy against the possibility of future American withdrawal from NATO. Although in the late 1980s such a withdrawal still looked a distant possibility, it was none the less reassuring to NATO's European wing to know that, even if Washington were to decide at some future date that it no longer had any interest in defending Western Europe, the Eurogroup would still possess its own nuclear deterrent capability. Either alone, or in combination with the French *force de frappe*, the British deterrent would still provide a formidable counter-threat to any future Soviet challenge.

Future problems for British defence policy

Britain's defence planners confronted two major problems as they approached the 1990s: (1) the growing internal tensions within NATO itself; and (2) the seemingly endless escalation in equipment costs which are imposed by advances in weapons technology. The first of these problems was certainly not new. Since the early 1950s NATO had frequently been characterised as 'an alliance in crisis', with disagreements both over burden sharing and over Washington's preponderant role in the determination of military strategy, disagreements which were largely responsible for the French withdrawal from NATO's military wing in 1966. In the late 1980s these difficulties looked set to intensify, for at least three reasons. In the first place, European public opinion over previous decades had become increasingly concerned that the deployment of American nuclear forces on their soil turned European countries into even more obvious targets for Soviet missiles. In Britain, particularly, these fears were compounded by doubts about the efficacy of the so-called 'dual-key' arrangement which was supposed to guarantee equal British participation in any decision to *use* British-based American nuclear weapons. To be sure, the government had stated unequivocally that, since the secret Attlee–Truman accords of 1951, the United States had fully accepted that such usages would require the express agreement of the British Prime Minister.[46] Nevertheless it was increasingly suspected that Washington's NATO-designated, European-theatre nuclear weapons were intended primarily to serve the security interests of the United States rather than those of Western Europe; that the British government would in reality have virtually no operational control over United Kingdom-based American capabilities. The United States, it was often suggested, had fought two world wars in Europe; perhaps it had the same strategy in mind for the Third World War.

The wider articulation of views such as these was not well-received in Washington. In the American view, the Europeans, with the possible exception of the British, had never made a proportionate contribution to the costs of their own defence: in spite of Western Europe's increasing prosperity its security continued to be subsidised by the

American taxpayer. Worse still, the Europeans were now complaining about the way in which Washington sought to organise Europe's defence. Such sentiments could only serve to reinforce the growing chorus of voices in the United States which was arguing that America's principal material interests were shifting away from the Atlantic and towards the Pacific Basin; that unless the Europeans were prepared to allow the United States to protect them properly, there was little point in trying to do the job at all; and that it might be better to reduce the Federal Budget deficit and let the 'ungrateful' Europeans make their own security arrangements. At the time of writing, Washington's public commitment to European defence remains as firm as ever. There is no denying, however, that the Kennanism of the late 1940s is experiencing something of a revival. It is by no means unlikely that the next decade or two will witness a significant reduction in Washington's military deployments in Europe. NATO's Eurogroup strategists will have to produce realistic contingency plans accordingly.

The danger of a reduced American commitment to NATO was exacerbated by a second potential source of NATO disunity: the threat of a Labour government in Britain committed to a radical, 'unilateralist' defence policy. The Labour Party had dabbled with the idea of unilateral nuclear disarmament in the late 1950s but had adopted a pro-nuclear posture by the time of its election in 1964, a position which it maintained until 1979. The general radicalisation which affected Labour doctrine in the early 1980s, however, brought about a distinct change in its defence policy, a change which marked a clear break with the broadly bipartisan defence consensus of the previous 30 years. Labour's official stance in the late 1980s was that the next Labour government would rapidly decommission all British nuclear weapons, insist on the speedy withdrawal of all American nuclear bases and forces from British soil and assume a non-nuclear role within NATO. Although this position was moderated in Labour's 'Multilateralist' Policy Review in the Spring of 1989, the fact that such dramatic actions had been seriously entertained by a major political party caused some consternation in Washington. Here was yet more evidence of Western Europe's lack of commitment to its own defence. Indeed any such developments in Britain would not be welcomed in the United States and would certainly invoke a serious reappraisal of Washington's NATO commitments. Labour's implicit riposte to suggestions that its new defence policy might lead the United States to withdraw both its extended nuclear deterrent and its conventional and nuclear forces from Western Europe was to argue that NATO could then be transformed into a European, *conventional* alliance, well suited to fending off any conventional Soviet attack. The problem with this conclusion, of course, was that a purely conventional NATO would be highly vulnerable to any threat of 'nuclear blackmail' which a nuclear-armed potential aggressor might, at some later date, choose to pose. In the absence of compelling empirical evidence, however, it was only possible to speculate about such matters. Labour argued that the Soviet threat had long ago receded; its critics asserted that the threat was still all too real. Neither side could demonstrate that its case was actually correct. To be sure, the British electorate on balance remained unconvinced of Labour's claims. None the less the possibility that Labour might be elected – for reasons other than its defence policy – remained a continuing irritant inside NATO, a constant reminder that Washington's commitment to the alliance might well decline alarmingly if the British domestic political map were to shift to the left.

A third reason why internal tensions within NATO appeared likely to increase in the late 1980s was the increasing rapprochement between the United States and the Soviets over arms reductions. The Intermediate Nuclear Force (INF) agreement of December 1987 and the Reagan–Gorbachev summit on strategic arms reductions in June 1988 caused some disquiet in the capitals of Western Europe. Were these accords part of a deliberate Soviet ploy to unravel the Atlantic alliance? How credible would NATO's nuclear deterrent posture be if it was stripped of its intermediate range (Cruise and Pershing II) missiles and if its strategic missile capability was significantly reduced? Did Washington's increased willingness to do a bilateral deal with the Soviets presage a decline in American concern for the security interests of the West Europeans? Uncertain about the answers to any of these questions, European governments prepared for the worst. As soon as the INF deal was announced, the Thatcher government reiterated its determination to exclude the British independent deterrent from any superpower agreement on strategic arms. It also entered into discussions with other Eurogroup members with a view to establishing a common position on the need to strengthen NATO's conventional and tactical nuclear capabilities, in order to compensate for the restrictions on US intermediate-range nuclear weapons imposed by the INF agreement. Thatcher even saw fit to publicise her continuing doubts about the Soviet Union's long-term intentions towards the West, doubts which remained in spite of her good personal relations with Gorbachev. These developments most certainly did not constitute anything approaching an open breach between Europe and the United States. None the less they did indicate a distancing, a preparation for unwanted – but probably unavoidable – disagreements ahead.

The second major problem confronting British defence policy in the 1980s was cost escalation. Successive governments had, of course, traditionally experienced difficulties in keeping defence expenditure down. The 'three circle' strategy of the postwar years had imposed an ever-increasing burden on the defence budget. The increasing restlessness of the Empire during the 1950s had coincided with the historic decision to maintain a permanent peace-time military presence in continental Europe. And London's insistence on developing an independent deterrent had made matters even worse. Yet it had certainly been necessary to confront the problem of 'overstretch', and given Britain's continuing relative economic decline and the relatively high proportion of GNP which the United Kingdom was already spending on defence, the only plausible solution had been to reduce Britain's overseas responsibilities.[47] The decision to withdraw from east of Suez was thus taken principally in order to cut costs. It was part of the Wilson government's strategy not only of moving Britain more solidly into the European circle but also of reducing defence expenditure from 7 per cent of GNP in 1965 to 6 per cent by 1970. Indeed, by 1972 only 5.5 per cent of GNP was devoted to defence.[48] Even after the withdrawal, however, the concern for economies continued. By 1979, defence spending had been further cut to 4.7 per cent of GDP, bringing it within sight of the French figure of 4.0 per cent and the German figure of 3.9 per cent.[49]

With the Conservative election victory in 1979, this 15-year downward trend went into reverse. There was no doubt that Thatcher's government was as committed as any of its predecessors to eliminating waste. However it was also determined to ensure that NATO forces were equipped with the up-to-date weaponry necessary to deter the newly-resurgent Soviet threat that was (in its view) evident both from the Soviet invasion of Afghanistan and from the Warsaw Pact's recent deployment of eighty SS-20 missiles in Eastern Europe.[50] The problem, inevitably, was that, in an era of rapidly evolving technology, new weaponry was *increasingly* expensive. This exerted upward pressure on defence costs in three different ways. The incoming Conservative Cabinet was confronted, first, with the unanticipated extra cost (estimated at £1000m)[51] of developing the Chevaline warhead for Polaris, a commitment secretly entered into by the previous Labour government. Second, following an unenviable tradition which stretched back to Blue Streak in the 1950s and TSR-2 in the 1960s, the Thatcher government inherited a number of projects which encountered such enormous technical difficulties that some were shelved before completion. The most notable – and the most costly – of these was undoubtedly the

Nimrod air-borne warning system that was abandoned in 1987. However, as late as March 1988, a confidential Ministry of Defence (MoD) report noted that technical failures and over-optimistic expectations about the feasibility of new technical developments in weapon systems were still costing taxpayers some £3–4000m annually. Indeed, the report concluded: 'The cost escalation figures imply that about 40% of the MoD equipment budget represents expenditure which has not been foreseen when projects started, and about 22% was not foreseen when projects entered full development.'[52]

A third source of upward pressure on defence costs was the need for British (and NATO) weapon systems to match both recent and anticipated developments in Warsaw Pact weapons technology in order to prevent a technological 'weapons gap' from emerging. As generals throughout history have discovered to their cost, there is nothing so ineffective as an out-of-date weapons-system. This problem was particularly noticeable in the nuclear weapons field, where a credible deterrent has to incorporate the latest design features. In the government's view it was thus necessary to replace Polaris with Trident because the number of missiles which Polaris could expect to deliver to Soviet territory was insufficient given the advances which the Soviets had made in anti-ballistic missile technology (notwithstanding the 1972 ABM Treaty) in the period since Polaris had been deployed. Trident, because it could deliver many more warheads, could restore the declining credibility of the British independent deterrent. Similar problems were also encountered in the conventional weapons sphere. In order to match the performance of their Warsaw Pact counterparts, British tanks and artillery not only needed to be increasingly mobile but also needed to be fitted with the latest targeting technology; the RAF's fighter squadrons required the most up-to-date radar and stealth technologies, in addition to being highly manoeuvrable at speed; and the Royal Navy's frigates and destroyers had to possess the latest sonar and anti-guided missile technologies. Overarching all of these requirements, moreover, was the need to devise and deploy communications systems that were immune to deliberate Warsaw Pact efforts either to jam or to distort NATO's battlefield transmissions.

As noted above, all of these developments were expensive. Each time a new generation of weapons was procured, the improved design features necessarily engendered an additional cost burden over and above the simple replacement cost. In this situation it was inevitable that, even if the number of ships, tanks, guns, bombs and aircraft was held constant, Britain's overall defence costs would continue to rise inexorably in real terms. And, unless GDP rose faster than the 'add-on'

Table 8.1 The Royal Navy's shrinking fleet 1948–88*

	1948	1957	1958	1963	1967	1968	1969	1970	1971	1972	1973	1976
Aircraft carriers, battleships and destroyers	137	97	77	53	34	33	30	25	22	20	16	17
Frigates	161	138	84	68	71	60	68	66	65	65	62	60
Submarines	57	60	57	53	48	44	41	35	36	35	34	32

	1977	1978	1979	1980	1981	1982	1983	1984	1985	1986	1987	1988
Aircraft carriers, battleships and destroyers	18	21	20	19	19	20	18	20	21	20	19	18
Frigates	56	66	55	54	46	44	46	43	41	40	40	39
Submarines	31	31	31	32	32	32	31	32	33	34	32	32

*Figures include vessels active and in reserve.
SOURCE: Annual Defence White Papers, 1948–88.

cost of new defence technology, then the defence budget (*ceteris paritus*) was destined to swallow an ever larger percentage of GDP. Yet, if Britain was to continue to discharge its NATO responsibilities in Central Europe and the eastern Atlantic, none of these 'add-on' costs could be easily avoided.

All too aware of these problems, the Thatcher government strove to make economies. One apparent answer was the decision, anounced in 1981, to cut the size of the surface fleet. As Table 8.1 indicates, the size of the Royal Navy had been reduced progressively throughout the postwar period. In general the cuts had been instituted gradually, though there had also been brief periods of acceleration in the late 1950s and mid-1960s. However, John Nott's plans for a new round of accelerated cuts were firmly thwarted by the pivotal role played by the Royal Navy in the 1982 Falklands War. In the wake of the campaign, it was all too evident that an undiminished naval capability of at least the size still in existence in 1982 would be necessary for essential out-of-area operations for the indefinite future. The Thatcher government's major response to the need for defence economies, however, was to initiate an investigation – the so-called Rayner Review – into MoD contract procedures, a process which later resulted in the closure of the Royal Dockyards at Chatham and a series of attempts to increase competition among defence contractors. The government's problem was to balance the need for a thriving domestic arms industry – which contributed employment, profit and export revenues to the British economy[53] – with the need to ensure that the MoD procured the best possible weapon-systems at the lowest possible cost. In the late 1980s, in spite of the Thatcher government's considerable endeavours, the correct balance had yet to be struck. In far too many contexts, the most sophisticated and most reliable systems could only be obtained from foreign suppliers; the government's political need to 'buy British' (in order to appease the pressures of employment and private profit at home) thus continued to inhibit genuine competition over MoD contracts and in consequence continued to contribute to Britain's escalating defence costs.[54]

Summary and conclusions

Defence is the one area of external relations in which policy is almost invariably guided by considerations of *realpolitik*. What matters is not good intentions and the mutual benefits of economic intercourse, but the balance of military capabilities and the convergence or divergence of security interests. Britain's postwar defence policy was consistently overshadowed by the spectre of the Soviet threat both to Europe and the third world. Whether or not this threat was 'real', it was entirely understandable that Britain's postwar defence planners should have based their decision calculus upon it. There were two main reasons for this. First, the Soviets vociferously expounded an *ideology* which characterised the contemporary international system in terms of a zero-sum conflict between capitalism and socialism. It was a conflict, moreover, in which the Soviets would play a central role and which was destined to result in the victory of socialism. This was dangerous stuff indeed if the Soviets really believed it. Yet in addition to this implicitly expansionist ideology, the Soviets also possessed an enormous *military capability*. Moreover, not content with the massive conventional superiority which they had enjoyed in the European theatre since 1945, in the early 1960s the Soviets embarked on a rapid expansion of both their surface and submarine fleets. As far as the British government was concerned this combination of Messianic ideology and preponderant capability meant only one thing: aggressive Soviet intent. Thus was the Soviet threat created and sustained.

Against this background of the ever-present Soviet threat, Britain's postwar defence policy sought to provide the military underpinning for the 'three-circle' strategy which it had already decided would guide its foreign policy in general. Given that the British government wished to preserve its influence in each of the three circles, it would only be possible to meet the Soviet challenge if its limited military capabilities were distributed judiciously. In the event, through NATO, London was able to combine its security interests in the European and Atlantic circles by drawing the United States into the defence of Western Europe. The *quid pro quo* of greater US involvement, however, was that in order to *keep* the Americans in Europe, Britain was obliged to enter into an open-ended military commitment on the continent of Europe, a development unknown in peace-time since the Hundred Years War. Yet in the Empire circle, too, Britain remained heavily committed. So long as large parts of the Empire remained – even after the loss of India in 1947 – they had to be protected. This in turn required the maintenance of a significant out-of-area capability which would permit the rapid deployment of troops, air squadrons and naval forces to almost any part of the world.

By the mid-1960s, the United Kingdom's heavy NATO commitments, its continuing efforts to project a world role for the sake of British interests in the Empire, and the costs associated with the independent deterrent had all combined to overstretch Britain's military forces. However, rather than spend more on defence as a whole, the Wilson government sought selective cuts in both commitments and capabilities. The decision to withdraw from east of Suez announced in 1968 aimed these cuts at the Empire circle. With the Empire itself all but gone, there was little military purpose in attempting to pursue a world policing role which, because of a lack of resources, was bound to be ineffectual. To be sure, a residual capability sufficient for minor emergencies (such as the Falklands crisis) was retained, but from the early 1970s onwards, British defence efforts were concentrated almost exclusively in Europe, where Britain's primary economic interests had been increasingly located since the late 1950s.

During the 1970s, debates over British defence policy lost some of their edge. The withdrawal from east of Suez was now a *fait accompli*. Superpower détente had lowered the profile of East–West security issues generally. And the deepening crisis of the domestic economy had further diverted public attention away from matters of defence. Indeed, whenever the question of 'the Soviet threat' was raised, it was tempting to conclude that the Soviets could not possibly want to seize control of a country where industrial relations were unmanageable and where the economy staggered from one crisis to another. The election of Margaret Thatcher in 1979 changed the situation quite markedly, however. The issue of the Soviet threat was revived. The Soviets had used détente as a blind for extending their sphere of influence in the third world. They could still not be trusted in Europe: any doubters should ask the 'proud people of Afghanistan'.[55]

But was the Soviet threat any greater in the early 1980s than it had been in the mid-1970s? Or was NATO 'deterring' a threat which no longer existed? Was all the calculation about 'flexible response' and 'follow-on force attack' an irrelevance that was no longer necessary? And if the Soviet threat had indeed receded, was it because internal changes in the Soviet Union had rendered its foreign policy benign, or was it precisely because the long-term effectiveness of the NATO deterrent had neutralised Soviet ambitions? Unfortunately none of these questions could be definitively answered.

NATO's critics on the left argued that the threat was negligible for at least three reasons. First, the peoples of Eastern Europe had enjoyed forty years of rising living standards which their governments would not wish to prejudice by initiating what would inevitably be a highly destructive war, even if the nuclear threshold was not crossed. Second, when the Warsaw Pact's military capabilities were compared with those of the West in general (including Japan) it was evident that the West was in a far superior military position.[56] And third, Gorbachev's reforming zeal at home had only been possible because of a profound material and ideological shift within Soviet society itself: a new Soviet ideology was emerging which recognised the importance of market mechanisms and which was well suited to achieving a genuine 'peaceful coexistence' between East and West. Taken together, these three factors meant that Britain's cost escalation problem and its fear of a gradual decoupling of the United States from Western Europe could both be easily resolved. Britain's defence policy should move with the tide of history. The United Kingdom should abandon its 'unusable' and costly independent deterrent and encourage the Americans to leave the Atlantic alliance. The American presence had only been necessary because Europe had not been strong enough to meet the Soviet threat alone. Now that the threat had dissipated, the Americans were no longer needed: let them concentrate their defence efforts elsewhere.

For Thatcher and her government, however, none of these arguments was compelling. Of course the Soviets did not relish the prospect of a highly destructive European war. Of course the West, with its superior system of economic organisation, could out-produce the Soviet bloc in terms of military capabilities. Of course Soviet ideology was far less stridently aggressive than it had been thirty years earlier. The crucial question, however, was whether the Soviets could be *trusted* when they claimed they had no designs on the West. And in Thatcher's Hobbesian view, they could not. As long as the Soviets continued to expound even a sanitised version of communist ideology and continued to support communist regimes and insurgents throughout the world, there could be no real trust between East and West. And in the absence of trust, as viewed in true *realpolitik* fashion, there would always be a potential threat which would always need to be deterred.

For Thatcher, therefore, keeping the Americans in Europe was of paramount importance. Without them, the European conventional deterrent would be ineffecutal, unless there was a massive (and politically unacceptable) increase in European defence spending. By the same token, an American withdrawal would leave NATO's Eurogroup dependent upon the British (and possibly the French) nuclear deterrent. The danger here was that NATO without the Americans would mean less opportunity for Anglo-American defence collaboration. This in turn would weaken relations between London and Washington and make it less likely that at some future date Britain would be able to purchase an off-the-peg independent deterrent from the United States as it had done with both Polaris and Trident. Without the promise of American assistance, Britain would be obliged – if it wished to maintain its independent deterrent – to relaunch its own nuclear weapons programme, which would add significantly to its already serious cost escalation problems. For an instinctive Atlanticist like Margaret Thatcher none of this was to be welcomed. The best way of dealing with the lingering Soviet threat was for the West to be united. Britain's security for the foreseeable future would continue to be based upon the NATO alliance, where the European and Atlantic circles were firmly bonded together.

9

The Relevance of Foreign Policy 'Theory'

In the introduction to this book it was indicated that the present study would seek to explain the major developments in Britain's postwar foreign policy at two different levels. On the one hand, it would examine the calculations that underpinned the foreign policy decisions of successive governments, paying particular attention to the 'Realist' world-views of the policy makers themselves. On the other, it would simultaneously attempt to identify the most significant underlying 'structural' factors that seem to have influenced Britain's changing international position, again making particular use of the Realist model. Given this intrusion of Realism at both the 'decision making' and 'structural' levels of investigation, it was acknowledged from the outset that the analysis provided in this book adopted a broadly state-centric, 'Realist' approach. It is clear from the foregoing chapters, however, that some of the other 'theoretical perspectives' outlined in the Introduction have also found their way into this dicussion. In these circumstances, the purposes of this chapter are to review the main theoretical perspectives that could have been used in order to analyse Britain's postwar foreign policy and to assess the relevance of each of these perspectives to the particular analysis conducted here. Not surprisingly, a substantial part of the discussion is devoted to an exposition of Realism, the approach that has featured most significantly in previous chapters. The chapter itself is divided into two parts. The first provides a formal statement of the Realist model and outlines its main uses and limitations in the context of the present study. The second briefly describes (in rather more detail than was possible in the Introduction) the 'Rational Actor', 'Bureaucratic Politics', 'Marxist' and 'World Society' perspectives and examines the way in which each has provided additional insights into Britain's postwar foreign-policy behaviour.

Realist world-views and the Realist model

One of the distinguishing features of the Realist approach to foreign policy analysis is that Realism is both an 'academic' theory about the nature and workings of international politics and a way of characterising the 'world-views' of the policy makers themselves. What has been referred to as 'Structural-Realism' consists of a set of propositions (specified below) that purport to describe and explain the foreign policy behaviour of nation-states. By extension, a 'Realist world-view' is an adherence on the part of the policy maker to the basic tenets of Structural-Realism, even though he (or she) may only dimly understand the full model itself, relying instead on a simplified version of it. Short definitions are easy to provide, however. What, precisely, does Structural-Realism entail?

Modern Realist or 'power politics' thinking has a long pedigree. Derived from the writings of Thucydides, Machiavelli and Hobbes, among others, it has been reinforced by the researches of generations of diplomatic historians who have sought to analyse the motives and calculations underlying foreign policy strategy.[1] The foundation of Realism is the claim that the international state system is essentially anarchic: that there is no overarching authority that can adjudicate in important or serious disputes between nation-states and that, as a result, the nation-state must ultimately rely upon its own efforts and resources to sustain it in a dangerous and threatening world.

The recognition of the anarchic nature of the international system has led to the use by Realists of the 'Hobbesian analogy'. This device suggests that there is a strong analogy between the situation that confronts the nation-state (or bloc) in the international system and the situation that confronts the individual in Hobbes' State of Nature, where life is 'poor, solitary, nasty, brutish and short'. In both situations, the individual actor is in a continuing state of fear and uncertainty, unsure as to whether, and which, other actor(s) might launch an unprovoked and unanticipated attack. Thus, just as Hobbesian man is motivated by his desire for safety, for the satisfaction of his 'appetites' and for the enhancement of his reputation, so the nation-state is driven primarily by its need to promote its security, its material–economic well-being and its international reputation. Similarly, just as Hobbesian man can best reduce his overwhelming sense of fear by developing whatever power capability is available to him, so the nation-state (or bloc) can best protect its security and material interests by pursuing a strategy of either maximising its own power capabilities or seeking to avoid the development of any power preponderance elsewhere.[2]

There are, of course, a number of serious objections that can be raised against the use of the Hobbesian analogy in this way.[3] It has often been observed that states are unlike individuals in so many important ways that the attempt to draw an analogy between them is worthless. Unlike individuals, states vary enormously in the power capabilities at their disposal (compare, for example, the United States and Bangladesh). Unlike an individual whose interests are broadly unitary, states are usually composed of a variety of competing factions and groupings with an equally variegated set of contradictory interests and goals. And, unlike an individual whose allotted life-span is relatively short, most states endure for long periods of time. Similarly, it is often argued that, whereas Hobbes's model of the State of Nature refers to the 'war of all against all', in the international system stable and long-lasting alliances and informal understandings are frequently in evidence. All these differences, it is alleged, mean that the sorts of motivation and calculation that prevail in Hobbes's anarchical and dangerous State of Nature cannot be systematically transferred to an analysis of the international system, even though that system might appear to be just as anarchic and dangerous as its Hobbesian counterpart.

The Realists' response to these criticisms is to acknowledge freely that Hobbes's theoretical model of anarchy obviously cannot be applied mechanically to contemporary nation-state behaviour: of course there are significant imbalances of power across the state system; of course states frequently pursue contradictory goals; of course the life of the state is not 'short' (though, with the advent of nuclear weapons, the accuracy of this assertion is not as self-evident as it once was); and of course long-term alliances enable the boundaries of Hobbesian fear to be redrawn so as to exclude longstanding 'friends'. In the Realist view, however, these concessions do not in any sense diminish the value of the fundamental insight into international conflict that the Hobbesian analogy provides. It is simply not necessary, the Realist argues, to adopt the entire paraphernalia of the Hobbesian model to recognise the general applicability of the core of that model to the adversarial relationships between nation-states. Of course the condition of Hobbesian fear is clearly not particularly valuable for describing the postwar relationships between, say, Belgium and the Netherlands. However, it is axiomatic to the Realist position that the international system is divided into a complex network of overlapping and to some degree interlocking 'security complexes', any of which may at any time erupt into violent conflict.[4] It is in the context of these security complexes that the concept of Hobbesian fear is relevant as a means of characterising the relations between, for example, the United States and USSR; between NATO and the Warsaw Pact; between Israel and the Arab states of the Middle East; between China and Taiwan; between India and Pakistan; between China and Vietnam; between North and South Korea; and between South Africa and its northern neighbours. In each of these relationships, the intense mutual mistrust felt by the two sides produces mutual postures of confrontation, which in turn encourage further mutual antagonism – a vicious circle from which there is no easy release. As noted earlier, the fact that the boundaries of Hobbesian fear can be redrawn so as to exclude fellow members of one's own 'bloc' does not mean that those boundaries can be removed altogether. In the Realists' view, only the creation of an international Leviathan could achieve such a feat, and since this is neither practicable nor desirable (who would control it?) nation-states simply have to devise foreign policy strategies that enable them to cope with the problem of Hobbesian fear as best they can.

Six Realist propositions[5]

Indeed, with the concept of Hobbesian fear very much in mind, Realism offers a series of propositions which apply to all potentially conflictual situations in international politics. The first of these, in direct contrast to the Marxist position examined below, is that *the character of international relations is shaped primarily by political factors: the fundamental driving force behind the foreign policies of all states is the search for national and/or bloc security.* This is not to say that motives of economic gain and personal or national glory do not also operate, neither is it to deny that the form that the search for security takes will vary enormously over time and from country to country. It is merely to suggest that, in conditions of Hobbesian fear, the security motive is invariably the dominant one in the determination of foreign policy strategies.

A second proposition that Realism makes is that in any given security complex *the need to prevent 'the other side' from becoming too powerful acts as a powerful stimulus to pre-emptive expansionism.* Such expansionism tends to take two forms. On the one hand, it can involve a direct pre-emptive strike against an opponent's military capabilities. On the other, it can involve an attempt to wrest control of part of an opponent's territory or 'sphere of influence'. The principle at work in both cases is simple: 'Do unto others before they do unto you'. Consider two relatively powerful states, A and B, which are located in the same security complex. If *A* fears that *B* may achieve a position of military superiority in the future – which may damage *A*'s interests – *A* will be strongly tempted to deprive *B* of part of something important now in order to prevent *B* from achieving superiority in the future. *B*, in turn, fearful that *A* may be about to engage in some sort of pre-emptive strike, will be tempted to launch its own. In such a situation of Hobbesian fear, both *A* and *B* are predisposed to engage in expansionism of some kind.

What is even more disturbing about this condition of Hobbesian fear, however, is that even self-avowed neutrals are endangered by it. *A* is well aware that *B* might attempt to strengthen its resource base (and therefore its power capabilities) by extending its sphere of influence into the territory of a neutral state, *C*. Thus *A* has a strong incentive to try to incorporate *C* into *its* sphere of influence before *B* does. According to Realists, *A*'s principal motive in seeking to dominate *C* may well be unrelated to any desire to exploit *C* economically. Rather, *A*'s primary motive in expansion and domination is a self-protective, defensive one, deriving from the anarchic nature of the international system. If *A* does not dominate *C*, then eventually *B* (or *D* or *E* . . .) will, and *A*'s relative power position (plus, therefore, its security) will be accordingly diminished. In the Realist view, as long as there is more than one state in *A*'s position (and invariably there is), expansionism and domination – that is, imperialism – will be an inevitable feature of international politics.

A third basic proposition concerns the role of co-operation in international affairs. According to the Realist model, *patterns of international friendship and antagonism are determined by the convergence or divergence of material and/or security interests.* Where material interests converge (for example, where there is abundant mutually beneficial trade) or where security interests converge (for example, where there is a 'common enemy' or a 'common threat'), then states will enjoy good relations. Conversely, where material or security interests diverge, inter-state relations will be at best tense and at worst overtly conflictual. The crucial corollary to this claim is that *both the extent and the consequences of co-operation in international politics are subordinated to the calculus of realpolitik.* Co-operation between nation-states is only possible to the extent that it is underpinned by a prior convergence of material–security interests. However such co-operation has no real autonomy. It will only endure so long as the convergence of material–security interests itself endures; if national interests – for whatever reason – subsequently diverge, then no amount of prior co-operation will improve the prospects for good mutual relations in the future. All of this means that, given that the material and security interests of states tend to shift over time, so patterns of interest convergence and divergence also undergo continuous transformation and change. Indeed, in the Realist view, convergences of interest between nation-states are rarely stable in the long term, and foreign policy makers must accordingly make contingency plans for the protection of the nation's material and security interests which recognise that current friends, partners and allies may not remain so in the future. In the harsh world of international politics, it is the nation's 'vital interests' that matter, not emotional attachments to friends or former allies who may well have outlived their usefulness.

Realism's fourth proposition is concerned with the question of peace and war. From the discussion above, it is obvious that, in those situations where nations' material and security interests converge, peace is likely to ensue between or among them. The Realist does not argue, however, that interest divergence necessarily leads to war. On the contrary, if conditions are right, interest divergence can also be consistent with the maintenance of international peace. The crucial condition for the Realist in this context is the 'balance of power' or, more correctly, the prevailing 'balance of power capabilities'. *In any given security complex, if power capabilities are relatively evenly distributed between (or among) the potential protagonists, then a balance of power can be said to exist between (or among) them. Such a balance, in turn, produces a position of mutual deterrence in which each party calculates that it would incur more overall cost than overall benefit if it were to engage in aggression.* In these circumstances, for the Realist, peace is the consequence of a military 'stand-off' which is itself the consequence of a balance of power. Should the balance for whatever reason be broken then the result is likely to be a military confrontation between or among the states (or blocs) involved in the particular security complex, with the attendant danger of outside intervention from states located in other security complexes. In any event, the outcome of any conflict (like all outcomes in international politics) will be determined by the existing balance of *realpolitik* resources. In the world of the Realist, national (or bloc) ascendancy derives fundamentally from superior military and/or economic capability combined with political will. The strongest, the best organised and the most determined prevail.

A fifth Realist assertion states that the *role of legal and moral considerations in international politics is an ineffectual one.* For the Realist, the frequent claims of statesmen that they are acting according to the precepts of international law or some other 'higher morality' are largely if not entirely fraudulent. Rather, law and morality are used principally as *ex post* justifications for decisions already arrived at on the basis of hard-headed *realpolitik* calculations. According to the Realist account, this is indubitably true with regard to those issues that concern the nation's vital interests (that is, those areas that directly affect either national security, the fundamental character of the domestic political order or the fundamental health of the economy). Whenever conflicts involving vital interests arise, states not only refuse to refer unresolved disputes to any international legal process: they regard themselves as being unconstrained by prior legal commitments and obligations. Legal rectitude is invariably subordinated to Realist calculations aimed at protecting the national interest.

There is, however, one set of circumstances in which the Realist does allow a minor role for international law. With regard to issues that do not concern vital interests, decision makers can afford to be magnanimous. Accordingly in 'areas that do not really matter' nation–states can contentedly sign bilateral treaties and multilateral conventions that constrain their behaviour; they can likewise refer unresolved disputes to judicial tribunals with the full intention of accepting the tribunals' rulings even if they turn out to be unfavourable. For the Realist, however, such actions do not in any sense represent a commitment to the higher principle of the legal regulation of nation–state behaviour. Rather, both treaty making and the acceptance of judicial rulings are cynically derived from a self-interested belief in the value of reciprocity ('I am prepared to do *x* and/or not to do *y* if you will do the same'); and for the Realist reciprocity is based on nothing more than a cost-benefit 'What is in it for us?' *realpolitik* calculation aimed at advancing the nation–state's material and/or security interests.

The sixth and final proposition at the heart of the Realist approach concerns the role of economic motivations and forces in the determination of foreign policy behaviour. According to the Realist, as noted earlier, *the sense of Hobbesian fear that pervades inter-bloc and inter-state relations invariably relegates economic factors to a subsidiary role in comparison with the deep-seated political imperatives of maximising security.* This is not to imply that economic forces cannot play an important role in certain situations. For example, in the relations between the rich countries of North America and Western Europe and the poorer countries of Africa and Latin America, economic factors are of obvious importance. American and European corporations wish to operate in the poorer countries in order to make profits that can be repatriated to the metropolitan homeland: Western governments, thankful of anything that will strengthen their balance of payments position, thus pursue policies that facilitate both the extraction of this economic surplus from the poor 'periphery' and its transfer back to the prosperous 'centre'.

For the Realist, however, even this kind of process, which at least superficially seems to be almost entirely economics-driven, is based on the political foundation of the need to enhance (in this case, Western) bloc security. In essence, what the Realist argues in this context is that the formally non-aligned states of the third-world periphery cannot simply be left as genuine neutrals in the global Cold War security complex. In line with the arguments about 'pre-emptive expansionism' advanced earlier, the West will probably need in practice to exercise some form of informal political dominion or hegemony over the third world because, if it does not, the Soviet bloc will. Thus the 'defection' of even one Western periphery country (such as Nicaragua in 1979) is likely to constitute not only a small but measurable depletion of the Western bloc's informal resources but also a corresponding gain for the Soviet bloc.

In the Realist's view, therefore, it is the West's desire to prevent the Soviet bloc – 'the other side' – from moving towards a position of power preponderance that acts as the fundamental driving force behind Western attempts to dominate the periphery. In these circumstances, so the argument runs, nation–states or blocs of nation–states simply employ whatever political and/or economic mechanisms are available to them in order to sustain their domination and thereby avoid the development of power preponderance elsewhere. Capitalist countries will obviously employ capitalist methods of domination, just as social- ist countries will employ socialist methods of domination – for precisely the same purpose. Crucially, however, for the Realist, it is not the capitalism of capitalist countries that causes them to behave in this dominating way (no more than it is the socialism of powerful socialist countries that causes them to attempt to dominate their less powerful peripheries). Rather, Western governments pursue, for example, for- eign policies conducive to the operation of transnational corporations, simply because the building of economic links between centre and periphery reinforces the centre's ability to exercise informal *political* dominion over the periphery – a dominion that is essential if the rival claims and pressures of the other side are to be resisted. In short, for the Realist, economics is simply the tool of politics. The purpose of the capitalist domination of the periphery is not to make the world safe *for* investment; it is to make the world safe *by* investment.

This, then, is the Structural-Realist model. It regards international politics as being fundamentally conflictual in character. It considers that the achievement and maintenance of national security is the paramount foreign policy goal. And it argues that national interests can only be maximised by the pursuit of cautious, self-regarding foreign policy strategies that are alert to the threat posed by potential aggressors abroad. The unspoken assumption in this latter context, moreover, is that, in an age of ideological divisions, the threat to the security interests of the West derives from the countries of the communist world; and concommitantly, that the threat to communist security lies in the capitalist West.

The uses of the Realist model

As I have repeatedly observed, throughout the present study the Structural Realist model has been employed both as a means of describing the world-view of Britain's key foreign policy makers and as a vehicle for identifying the underlying structural factors that influenced the course of Britain's postwar foreign policy. What, precisely, has each of these usages entailed?

As a means of describing policy makers' world-views, the formal Structural Realist model described above certainly requires some modification. Indeed, of the many policy makers who are committed to a Realist world-view, few would articulate their Realist convictions in quite such a formalised way as that presented in the preceding pages. None the less the Realism that has dominated British foreign policy thinking since the late 1930s has undoubtedly been based on a number of simplified propositions, all of them directly traceable to the Structural Realist model outlined above. The more important of these simplified propositions – the practical principles of *realpolitik* – are summarised in Table 9.1.

The crucial sense in which these propositions are relevant to the analysis of Britain's postwar foreign policy is the way in which they informed the policy makers' priorities. As the rational actor model contends, successive British governments during the postwar period certainly made reasoned calculations about the probable costs and benefits of alternative foreign policy actions and about the likelihood that a given course of action would maximise British interests. The important point is that these calculations rested on Realist foundations: the policy makers' Realist beliefs resulted in their insistence, on the one hand, that the paramount foreign policy goal would be the maintenance of national security and, on the other, that this primary objective could only be achieved if Britain possessed a strong defensive capability. Even before the Second World War was over, the British Cabinet had been convinced that the Soviet Union was pursuing an aggressive *realpolitik* strategy designed to erode the international

Table 9.1 Simplified *realpolitik* principles illustrative of the Realist policy maker's world-views

Principle	Examples of application of the principle in twentieth-century British foreign policy
(a) In wartime	
1. My enemy's enemy is my friend. If enemy **A** starts to fight enemy **B**, befriend whichever of the two represents the more distant threat in order jointly to eliminate the more immediate threat. However, prepare for renewed conflict with your new-found ally once the common threat has been eliminated.	Churchill's approaches to Stalin after the German invasion of the Soviet Union in June 1941. Even before the end of the war, Churchill was preparing to meet what he regarded as the inevitable postwar Soviet challenge to Europe's geostrategic stability.
(b) In peacetime	
2. If war seems imminent but you are militarily unprepared for it, play for time by using whatever diversionary tactics can be improvised.	Chamberlain's acquiescence to Hitler's demands to annex the Sudetenland in 1938 can be interpreted as following this proposition. However, the historical record (see Chapter 1) seems to contradict this interpretation.
3. Potential aggressors will remain unmoved by generous attempts to understand past injustices; by reasoned arguments about mutual interests in avoiding war; or by patient efforts aimed at securing an equitable compromise. Potential aggressors can only be deterred by firm and unambiguous threats, backed, if necessary, by credible military force.	(i) The creation of NATO in 1949 constituted a clear deterrent threat intended to thwart what were presumed to be Soviet designs on Western Europe (ii) The Anglo-French intervention at Suez was in part intended to deter Egypt from taking any further aggressive action against Western interests in that country.

4. Avoid situations where a potential aggressor possesses a preponderant military capability. Counter any significant military imbalance either by forming an alliance with a powerful state which shares your own security fears or by increasing your own military capability.

(i) The 1951–4 rearmament programme, initiated by Labour but continued by the Conservatives, aimed to reduce the alarming conventional imbalance between Soviet and NATO forces in the European theatre.

(ii) NATO's 3 per cent per annum increase in real defence spending 1979–84, to which Britain adhered, was intended to reinforce the credibility of NATO's anti-Warsaw Pact deterrent posture.

5. Since international politics, like nature, abhors a vacuum, retain control of overseas possessions for as long as possible. However, once effective control has either been lost or is about to be lost, a rapid withdrawal combined with the installation of a friendly government is preferable to a protracted withdrawal, because the latter is likely to strengthen the hand of indigenous forces antagonistic to your interests.

(i) The 'first-wave' decolonisations in India and Palestine in 1947–8.

(ii) The 'second-wave' decolonisations in Malaya, Africa and the Caribbean after 1956.

6. If you are forced to withdraw from potentially useful strategic locations because of commitments elsewhere, ensure that the territory thus vacated becomes part of the sphere of influence of your firmest and most trustworthy ally.

(i) The Attlee government's announcement in 1947 that it would no longer underwrite the anti-Communist regimes in Greece and Turkey, on the understanding that under the newly-proclaimed Truman Doctrine the Americans would take over these responsibilities.

(ii) The Labour government's granting of base facilities to the Americans at Diego Garcia after 1975 was intended to assist the US Navy in its efforts to police the Indian Ocean, following the Royal Navy's withdrawal in the early 1970s.

position of the Western democracies. Moreover, from the mid-1940s through to the late 1980s, the Soviets did little to disabuse Britain's policy makers of this conviction. In the European theatre, the Soviets maintained a position of massive military superiority. In the third world they provided backing for almost any regime or insurgent movement that challenged Western interests. And underscoring all of Moscow's actions was its commitment to an apparently aggressive ideology that both urged and predicted the universal spread of communism. As far as successive British governments were concerned, the Soviet Union's enormous military capability, its growing influence in the third world and its expansionist ideology combined to constitute a profound Realist threat to Western interests that demanded a determined Realist response. Although London could afford to be distinctly un-Hobbesian in its approach to its current friends, adopting a broadly co-operative posture towards them in matters of mutual economic benefit, the first priority of Britain's postwar foreign policy was always to ensure that the Soviets would never be tempted to take direct military action against Britain or its allies.

The Realist world-views of Britain's postwar foreign policy makers thus meant that they viewed developments in world politics, and especially those pertaining to the actions and pronouncements of the Soviet Union, through the 'lens' of Structural Realism. What the analysis presented in preceding chapters sought to demonstrate was that this realist world-view profoundly affected the development of Britain's postwar foreign policy. In the European and Atlantic 'circles' it played a crucial role in the creation of NATO in 1949. In the Empire circle – in a series of moves designed to inhibit communist encroachment in the Far East – it led Britain into Korea in 1950 and subsequently into SEATO in 1954 and CENTO in 1955. And as late as the 1980s it was also partly responsible for the firmly anti-Soviet posture adopted by the Thatcher government during the so-called 'Second Cold War'.

Yet, in addition to providing valuable insights at the decision-making level of analysis, the Structural Realist model has also been used in the present study to identify the major 'structural' factors that affected Britain's postwar foreign policy. The main contribution of Structural Realism in this regard derives from its assertion that the external behaviour of any nation–state depends fundamentally on the pattern of its economic and security interests: when these interests change, adjustments in foreign policy are likely to follow. Given the difficulty of objectively assessing the extent to which the *security* interests of different states either diverge or converge, the analysis presented in this book has not made substantial use of Structural Realist arguments about the role of changing security interests in the determination of Britain's foreign policy. Such a restriction has not been necessary, however, with regard to Britain's changing *economic* interests. In this context the pattern of Britain's external trade can be regarded as a plausible indicator of where Britain's major overseas economic interests lie: an increase in trade with a given country over time can be considered to indicate a growing convergence of economic interests; a decline, to indicate a growing divergence. Using these notions, the Structural Realist model provides a fairly compelling partial explanation for the major strategic shift in Britain's postwar foreign policy strategy, away from the Empire-cum-Commonwealth and towards Western Europe, that occurred in the 1960s. The argument upon which this conclusion is based can be summarised as follows. In the 1940s and 1950s Britain's intimate military and political ties with the Empire circle were underpinned by its extensive trading relationship with Empire and Commonwealth countries. (In 1955, for example, over half of British exports went to Empire circle destinations.) During the late 1950s and the 1960s, however, the focus of Britain's export trade experienced a marked and autonomous shift toward western Europe: between 1955 and 1965 Western Europe's share of Britain's export trade rose from a third to a half; the Empire circle share fell from a half to a third over the same period. In different historical circumstances the effects of these changes might have been limited. However, at a time when, for other reasons, the 'three circle' strategy was being seriously reviewed, the fact that Britain's economic interests were rapidly shifting towards Europe provided the British government with a powerful stimulus to concentrate more of its foreign policy and defence efforts in the European circle. In Structural Realist terms, in short, both the downgrading of the Empire and the higher priority accorded to Europe that occurred in the 1960s were the result, at least in part, of earlier and continuing shifts in Britain's material economic interests.

The limitations of the Structural Realist model

Despite the extensive use that has been made of the Realist model in foreign policy analysis generally, the model itself is by no means immune from criticism. Indeed, as a characterisation of the worldviews of Britain's postwar foreign policy makers, Realism can be subjected to two main criticisms. First, it could be argued, Realism's initial description of world politics as an essentially conflictual system populated by interest-maximising, self-regarding nation–states is wrong. For one thing, there is far less conflict and far more co-operation about than the Realist model anticipates.[6] For another, the Realist's emphasis on the pattern of diverging and converging state interests significantly underemphasises the extent to which certain sub-national economic and political groupings in different countries (for example, 'financial capital') can share common interests that transcend national boundaries. Although this 'alternative characterisation' argument is a powerful one, it does not in fact constitute an attack on the way that Realism has been used in the present work to study British foreign policy decision making. Rather, it represents an implicit criticism of the policy makers themselves, suggesting that their 'Realist world-views' have not accorded with 'reality'; that their analysis of world events – and therefore, presumably, their policies – have in some sense been faulty. All of this may well be true but it misses the point. If policy makers believe that international politics is a *realpolitik* game, whether or not it 'really' is, they will frame their policies on the basis of that belief. In order to understand why a particular foreign policy decision was taken, the analyst needs to know how the policy makers perceived the situation that confronted them, rather than the 'objective' features of the situation itself. Indeed any analysis that stressed the former at the expense of the latter would risk seriously misunderstanding the motives and calculations underlying particular decisions. The claim that the policy makers' world-views did not reflect 'the way things really were' – though it may be correct – is thus irrelevent to the sort of decision-making analysis presented here.

A second way of criticising the use that the foregoing analysis has made of Realism is to suggest that Britain's postwar foreign policy makers may not actually have held Realist world views at all. This criticism alludes in part to a more general accusation that is frequently levelled at the Realist model: that it is so amorphous and flexible that supporting evidence for *realpolitik* calculation can be found in almost every decision-making situation. Indeed, the argument continues, the present analysis has consistently found evidence of such calculation in foreign policy decision making simply because it has consistently looked for it: if the analysis had searched for evidence of something else, it might have found that instead. One response to this criticism is to argue (1) that the mere fact that an analyst finds something, for example *realpolitik* calculation, almost every time he looks for it cannot be taken as evidence that the phenomenon in question does *not* exist; and (2) that accordingly it is incumbent upon the critic to demonstrate that the policy makers' world-views were based on something other than Realism.

Such a response, however, does not demonstrate definitively that Realism did indeed constitute the world-views of Britain's postwar foreign policy makers. Moreover it has to be admitted that the analysis presented here has not provided such a demonstration. It is certainly the case that Britain's postwar foreign policy makers behaved *as if* they adhered to a Realist world-view. Unfortunately the present study has not been able to show in detail that the key members either of particular Cabinets or of particular policy committees were indisputably committed to a Realist world-view. To be sure, the key decision makers' public pronouncements, their published memoirs and the official public record (in so far as it is currently available) are all consistent with their holding such a world-view. But such indirect evidence does not – indeed could not – demonstrate that Realist thinking guided their unspoken thoughts and calculations and therefore, by implication, their policy decisions. We simply do not know what goes on inside policy makers' heads, even though we can make informed inferences on the basis of their spoken and written comments. In practical terms, what all of this means is that, at worst, the present study has provided a series of *metaphorical* explanations for the foreign policy decisions of successive postwar British governments: it has 'explained' those decisions 'as if' they were based on the Realist calculations of the policy makers. (In the difficult world of social science 'explanation', this is not quite as unimpressive an achievement as it sounds.)[7] At best, it has provided a set of falsifiable *causal* explanations (that posit causal connections between the policy makers' Realist world-views and their policy decisions) that are in principle testable but which still await definitive confirmation because the necessary empirical evidence has yet to be assembled.[8]

Thus the main criticisms of the use of Realism as a description of policy makers' world-views can be answered reasonably satisfactorily – even if certain qualifications have to be made. How far can the same conclusion be sustained with regard to the use of Realism as a means of identifying the structural influences on British foreign policy?

Apart from the general criticism that can be levelled against any theoretical perspective – that its characterisation of the global economy and polity is incorrect in the first place – the most important criticism that is made of Realism as structural theory is that it is non-falsifiable. It is alleged that, because of the flexible way in which the theory is formulated, no empirical evidence could ever be adduced that could not somehow be interpreted as being consistent with it: to the extent that

Realism offers a 'true' analysis of international politics, it is an analysis that is true by definition – not one that has been rigorously tested against the available empirical evidence. In short, Realism is accused of providing nothing more than a series of tautologies masquerading as explanations.

In the present author's view this particular criticism of Realism as structural theory is unjustified. It is certainly the case that many Realist propositions are *not* falsifiable. However a similar limitation also applies to almost all theories in the social and physical sciences.[9] Indeed, the analytic core of most theories is couched in an abstract language that is rarely susceptible to empirical testing. What matters is that the theory generates at least some propositions that are capable of being tested. The way that Realism has been employed as a structural theory in the present analysis belies the accusation that Realism offers little more than sophisticated tautology. The substantive argument advanced earlier – that the changing pattern of Britain's economic interests in the 1950s and 1960s provided the main impetus behind the British government's strategic shift towards the European 'circle' during the 1960s and 1970s – certainly involved a non-tautological hypothesis that was in principle capable of being falsified. The statistical evidence that was reported regarding the changes that occurred in Britain's overseas trade after 1955 provided empirical corroboration for the hypothesis that changing national interests were at the root of the changes in Britain's foreign policy strategy. In short, the foregoing analysis did treat Realism as a falsifiable structural theory: it simply established that one of Realism's key falsifiable predictions was supported by the available empirical evidence.

Realism, then, though it has certain limitations, has undoubtedly provided valuable explanatory insights into Britain's postwar foreign policy at both the decision-making and structural levels of analysis. What of the other theoretical perspectives that were reviewed earlier?

The contribution of other theoretical approaches

As noted above, although Realism has been the dominant theoretical perspective employed in the present study, the discussion has also been informed by several other approaches: at the decision-making level, by the 'Rational Actor' and 'Bureaucratic Politics' approaches; and, at the structural level, by the 'Marxist' and 'World System' perspectives.

The Rational Actor and Bureaucratic Politics approaches

The 'Rational Actor' approach seeks to understand foreign policy behaviour as the goal-directed consequence of rational calculation by decision makers; calculation that aims in some sense to maximise the national interests of the nation-state which the decision makers represent.[10] Not surprisingly, according to this model it is the policy makers' decision calculus that is the stuff of foreign policy analysis. What were the major aims of a particular foreign policy decision? Why was this option chosen from among the available alternatives? What calculations were made about the intentions and capabilities of military rivals or enemies? What assumptions were made about the likely behaviour of other nation-states? And so on. While these questions offer only a glimpse into the kind of elements that might enter into a full analysis of foreign policy based on the Rational Actor model, they do indicate where the analyst should look both for 'explanatory factors' and for evidence: at the decision makers themselves, at their sources of information, at their purposes, intentions and beliefs, as revealed both in personal memoirs and in official minutes, memoranda and briefing papers.

The 'Bureaucratic Politics' approach to foreign policy analysis makes two central assumptions: first, that nation-states are not necessarily unitary actors; and, second, that policy may be the result more of a political compromise among competing bureaucratic and political elites than of a rational attempt by decision makers to maximise the attainment of a defined and agreed set of goals.[11] Thus the Bureaucratic Politics model is concerned to establish, for example, how far different intra-party factions and within-Cabinet groups seek to effect foreign policy decisions commensurate with their preferred goals; how the different administrative departments and different factions within them vary in importance; what strategies are pursued by particular factions and groupings in order to ensure that *their* conception of 'departmental' or 'national' interest prevails. The Bureaucratic Politics model, in short, focuses on a much wider set of actors and influences than the Rational Actor model would seem to allow – though, significantly, the evidential base required for the application of both models is broadly the same.

While the foregoing discussion treats the Rational Actor and Bureaucratic Politics approaches as being separate models (in the theoretical literature the distinction between them is almost axiomatic), in fact the distinction can be pressed too far. As Freedman has noted, most contemporary narrative analysts of British foreign policy actually use a mixture of both models.[12] On the one hand, following the Rational Actor approach, they are concerned to identify the main policy objectives that decision makers set themselves and to show why those decision makers believed that the policy options eventually selected would achieve their objectives more effectively than the available alternatives. On the other hand, following the Bureaucratic Politics approach, they are also concerned to examine the inter- and intra-departmental manoeuvring that preceded the taking of a given decision, as different factions jockeyed to ensure that the policy which was finally selected accorded as closely as possible with their own preconceptions. Contemporary writings thus frequently incorporate both perspectives into the same analysis. Despite being conceptually distinct, the two models are in fact mutually compatible and can be jointly applied to the same empirical materials without serious difficulty or contradiction.

In the preceding discussion of Realism it was hinted that, in its analysis of postwar foreign policy decision making, the present study made indirect use of the Rational Actor model: although the policy priorities and calculations of Britain's policy makers were bounded by their Realist world-views, they in general followed a rational calculus in arriving at their policy decisions. There was one major context, however, in which rational calculation did manage to break free of its Realist bonds: in the matter of the retreat from Empire between 1956 and 1971.

Put simply, the retreat from Empire was an entirely rational response to the changed situation in which Britain found itself in the 1950s and 1960s. The world role and the intimate connection with the Empire circle had been established at a time when Britain was one of the world's richest states and when the Royal Navy really did rule the waves. The postwar world was very different, and there was virtually nothing that successive governments could do to change it. The two superpowers – and especially the awful Soviets – could not be magically demoted to mere 'Great Power' status. The rising tide of indigenous nationalism in the colonies could not be reversed by Parliamentary fiat. And the problems of the ailing British economy seemed to defy all efforts to remedy them. In this new situation, old solutions promised scant return. To have attempted to repress indigenous nationalism throughout the whole of British Africa and the Caribbean – along the lines so successfully pursued in Malaya and Kenya – would have been far beyond the physical capabilities of Britain's armed forces. And there was no prospect whatsoever of securing the assistance of some powerful ally whose collaboration in the task of imperial repression might make a military solution viable. In these circumstances, rapid decolonisation was the rational, indeed the only, solution: a reduction in commitments to a level commensurate with Britain's reduced relative capabilities. This way, the War Office would not be consigned to fighting a never-ending and probably ever-widening series of colonial emergencies; the defence budget might not consume an ever-greater proportion of national income; Britain would undoubtedly lose an Empire, but it might emerge from the process fitter, leaner and better equipped to adapt to the rapidly changing circumstances of the modern world.

In the retreat from Empire, then, reason prevailed over Realism. According to orthodox Realist thinking, the principal risk of imperial withdrawal was that it would result in a rapid increase in communist influence in the territories thus vacated. This was a prospect which should be studiously avoided if Moscow was to be prevented from further weakening the global strategic position of the West. A strict adherence to *Realpolitik* reasoning, therefore, implied that Britain should make ever-greater sacrifices at home in order to sustain the increasing, but unavoidable, military burden of protecting the Empire. In London's view, however, the costs of such a strategy were increasingly unacceptable. The extra sense of national security that Britain might have gained from the continued possession of the Empire was more than outweighed by the monetary and political costs that would doubtless be incurred if Britain was obliged to fight a series of deeply unpopular colonial wars. As a result, successive governments began to subscribe to the view that the preservation of the Empire was no longer quite so crucial to the maintenance of Britain's national security. The government's unswerving loyalty to Realism could be relaxed and reason – at least for the time being – could hold sway. Even in these circumstances, however, Realism was not entirely forgotten: as noted earlier, in its continuing efforts to preserve British influence as widely as possible, London consistently sought to follow Realist principles by installing post-colonial regimes that were well-disposed to the interests of the West. If reason had supplanted Realism over the momentous decision to decolonise, imperial withdrawal itself would still be implemented with *realpolitik* firmly in mind.

Although the present study has not accorded much explicit emphasis to the Bureaucratic Politics model, this should not be taken to imply that the interplay of bureaucratic and interest group pressures were unimportant in the determination of Britain's postwar foreign policy. On the contrary, there were at least three occasions when such pressures achieved some prominence in the policy process. The Attlee government's decision to embark on a massive rearmament pro-gramme in December 1950, for example, was influenced to a consider-able – and unusual – degree by the advice proffered by the Joint Chiefs of Staff regarding the seriousness and the imminence of the Soviet threat to British security. In a similar vein, in the run-up to the Suez fiasco in October 1956, the deliberations of the pivotal 'Egypt Commit-tee' paid rather too much attention both to the sensationalist xenopho-bia of the popular, right-wing press and to the propagandist outpour-ings of the influential 'Suez group' of Tory MPs. Finally, throughout the debate on the acquisition of Britain's 'independent nuclear deter-rent', there was tremendous factional rivalry among the three service ministries as to what sort of delivery system the deterrent should use; a competition that was duly won by the Royal Navy in December 1962 when Macmillan and Kennedy struck their deal over Polaris.

Yet, although bureaucratic pressures of various sorts were undoubtedly important as background factors in the formation of Britain's foreign policy throughout the postwar period, it seems unlikely that they were of critical importance in determining any of these decisions. Attlee's rearmament decision in 1950 was more a straightforward *realpolitik* response to an extremely dangerous external situation than the result of a nimble piece of bureaucratic footwork on the part of the Joint Chiefs. The Egypt Committee's decision to attempt to remove Nasser by force was influenced more by Eden's long-standing determination to avoid repeating the errors of 'appeasement' than it was by the bureaucratic machinations of the popular press and the Suez group. And the Navy's 'victory' in the inter-service competi-tion over the manner of delivery of the 'independent deterrent' in the end owed nothing to Admiralty politicking in Whitehall and everything to the American decision at Nassau to supply Britain with a cheap and ready-made submarine-launched ballistic missile system which, by definition, could only be operated by the Royal Navy.

There were, none the less, two senses in which bureaucratic pressures clearly seem to have exerted a *generalised* effect on Britain's postwar foreign policy. The first was in relation to the size of the defence budget. Notwithstanding a long-running series of cost-cutting 'defence reviews' (in 1947–8, 1957, 1965, 1966, 1975 and 1981), and notwithstanding the ending of the world role, the proportion of national GDP devoted to defence remained remarkably stable (around 5–7 per cent) throughout the postwar period.[13] The stability of this figure was testimony to the tenacity of both the service chiefs and the defence industry lobby in persuading a succession of governments that Britain's security relied upon the continuation of a strong – and up-to-date – military capability. The second sense in which bureaucratic pressures seem to have been of generalised importance (in the making of foreign economic policy) is discussed below in the section on Marxist approaches.

One final point needs to be made about the Bureaucratic Politics model. A thorough-going Bureaucratic Politics analysis of British foreign policy would undoubtedly require access to the official minutes (and related correspondence) associated with the major foreign policy decisions taken by successive governments. Under the 30-year rule, the relevant documents are at present available only up to the late 1950s. Although the present study could perhaps have made greater use of the Bureaucratic Politics model in its analysis of the 1945–58 period, such an approach would not have been possible for the years after 1958. Rather than present an unbalanced analysis, therefore, this study has consistently emphasised Cabinet calculations rather than bureaucratic pressures in the determination of policy. However it may well be that, when the history of the last 30 years comes to be written, with the benefit of both hindsight and the official record, the Bureaucratic Politics model will feature rather more significantly than it has here. We shall see.

Marxist approaches

Two factors complicate any attempt to incorporate Marxist ideas into the sort of non-Marxist analysis of British foreign policy that has been provided here. First, given that there are often quite considerable disagreements among Marxist scholars themselves, there is no single 'Marxist position' upon which all Marxists would be likely to agree. Second, without providing what would in effect be a full-blooded Marxist analysis of Britain's postwar foreign policy, it is extremely difficult to do justice to the subtleties and complexities of argument that are developed by different Marxist theorists. This said, even though Marxist analyses of Britain's postwar foreign policy are not sufficiently important to warrant an exclusively Marxist approach being taken here, they are too important to ignore altogether.

Bearing all of these qualifications in mind, there are two main fields of Marxist scholarship that have proved relevant to the foregoing discussion. The first of these concerns contemporary Marxist analyses of imperialism. These analyses derive principally from Lenin's historical account of the way the European Powers originally came to acquire and expand their colonial possessions in the late nineteenth century.[14] According to Lenin, the territories colonised after 1870 were acquired primarily for economic reasons: to secure supplies of the raw materials that were increasingly required for industrial production, to provide new market opportunities and – most particularly – to facilitate the export of capital abroad in order to resolve the crisis of capital over-accumulation at home. This export of capital had two profound consequences: it incorporated into the capitalist system parts of the world that had hitherto been free from capitalist patterns of production, exchange and domination; and it enabled the rich 'metropolitan' powers to extract a substantial economic surplus from the colonial territories in the form of 'repatriated profits'.

Most contemporary Marxists argue that in spite of decolonisation the rich metropolitan countries have continued to dominate and exploit the third world. Indeed modern Marxist writers have variously identified three principal economic mechanisms through which the underdevelopment of the countries of the 'periphery' is maintained. The first is the repatriation to the metropolitan countries of profit (derived from the production activities of multinational corporations) and interest (derived from bank loans, usually to third-world governments). For Marxists, this repatriation of funds is frequently underpinned by a 'class alliance' between the international banks and corporations on the one hand and the indigenous bourgeois elites of the dependent countries on the other. The former act as a guarantor of the domestic position of the local elites while the local elites ensure the continuing free flow of profit and interest payments abroad. Crucially, for Marxist analysts, the repatriation of funds constitutes an important leakage of capital which could otherwise be used for productive investment and development in the peripheral country.[15]

A second mechanism that helps to maintain the dependence of the periphery is the position that the peripheral economies are obliged to occupy in the international division of labour.[16] The crucial point in this context is that production patterns in the dependent countries are geared not to the needs of their own populations but to the requirements of the international capitalist system. In the Marxist view, the global capitalist system typically requires third-world countries to provide only certain kinds of input into the international economy. At worst, a peripheral country will be required to provide a single cash crop or a single raw material for sale on the world market, a position that leaves it extremely vulnerable to the seemingly autonomous fluctuations that occur in world prices for primary commodities. Yet in these circumstances most peripheral countries find that virtually all private externally funded investment (investment that obviously yields a profit to the investor) is devoted to increasing the production of that single cash crop or raw material. External investment funds are rarely directed towards creating the sort of diversified pattern of industrial or agricultural production that might serve to further the dependent country's own interests. Thus, in the Marxist view, the dependence of the periphery is maintained: the operation of the international capitalist system simply starves it of the kind of capital investment that might enable it to exploit its own manpower and natural resources for its own benefit.

The final mechanism reinforcing the subordinate position of the periphery and operating to the enormous benefit of the metropolitan economies of the North is unequal exchange.[17] While the precise terms of the debate about 'unequal exchange' are highly technical, the fundamentals of the principle are simple. The dominant world-market position of the developed capitalist economies, with their large market shares, their highly diversified production patterns and their wide range of trading partners, enables them to ensure favourable terms of trade for themselves in their dealings with the periphery's less developed economies. For Marxists, an elementary principle is at work: in any market system of bargaining and distribution (perfect competition excepted), the already powerful do best. In the capitalist world economic system, this effectively means that the rich and powerful countries of the North extract an economic surplus from the periphery of the South in two ways. Not only does the North benefit from repatriated profits and interest payments on investments in capital projects that themselves reinforce the South's vulnerable trade dependence: the North also benefits disproportionately in its straightforward trade dealings with the South. This is power indeed.

How, if at all, do these ideas contribute to our understanding of Britain's postwar foreign policy? As we saw in Chapter 4, the notions of profit repatriation, dependent investment patterns and unequal exchange cannot easily be used to demonstrate empirically that postcolonial Britain continues to act as a 'neo-imperialist' power. Nevertheless, for many Marxists, the mere fact that Britain, as a rich, northern power, occupies a dominant position in the global economy gives its financiers and industrialists a vested interest in the preservation of the international economic *status quo*. In the Marxist view, the strength of this vested interest has constituted an important and continuing structural constraint on British foreign economic policy making throughout the post-colonial era, encouraging governments to resist international efforts to reform the global economy in favour of the impoverished economies of the third world. The reluctance of successive governments to be more generous in donating aid to the third world;[18] their rejection of the proposals for restructuring the world economy along the lines suggested variously by UNCTAD, the Brandt Commission and others;[19] and their unwillingness to make substantial provision for writing off third-world debts: all of these postures reflected the structural constraint upon British foreign policy making that was imposed by the material benefits deriving from Britain's position within the international economy.

The idea of structural constraints on policy making is also relevant to a second field of Marxist scholarship that has been alluded to in the present analysis: the implications of the ascendancy in Britain of 'financial capital'. In Marxist analyses it is generally taken as axiomatic that in capitalist societies the interests of capital will predominate over the interests of labour. What is less certain, however, is which particular fraction of the capitalist class will dominate the state apparatus during any given historical period. Most contemporary Marxists argue that, owing to a particular configuration of historical circumstances, the British state since about 1870 has in fact been dominated by the interests of financial, as opposed to industrial, capital.[20] This in turn has meant that since the late nineteenth century the entire strategy underlying Britain's foreign economic policy has been guided by a desire to protect and promote the profits of financial capital. In matters of trade relations, overseas investment and the external value of sterling, British foreign policy has been dominated by the interests of financial capital. And, as a result, the banks, the finance houses and the foreign exchange dealers have prospered – often at the expense of the interests of manufacturing industry.

For Marxist analysts, this dominance of financial capital within the British policy making process has been created and sustained by the development of an 'institutional nexus' which links together the ideology, the personnel and the material interests of the City, the Bank of England and the Treasury.[21] Although the precise workings of this nexus are too complicated to review here, its fundamental consequence has been to set the parameters of debate about foreign economic policy, allowing certain policy options to be considered, but ensuring that others are excluded. In particular, the threat of a 'flight of capital' – of both domestic and foreign finance capitalists moving investment funds overseas if some 'unacceptable' policy were to be implemented – has acted as an important structural constraint on the decision-making autonomy of successive British governments. In the days of the Gold Standard, for example, when British finance capital benefitted enormously from sterling's status as the 'Master Currency' of the international economic system,[22] the idea that Britain should abandon the Gold Standard (in order to boost the export competitiveness of its manufacturing sector) was regarded as a dangerous heresy that could not be seriously entertained. Similarly, during the time of the Overseas Sterling Area in the 1950s and 1960s the view that the OSA was damaging Britain's industrial performance was countered by pointing to the disastrous 'capital flight' that was bound to ensue if sterling's reserve role were to be terminated. In the 1980s, even within the Opposition Labour Party, debates on foreign economic policy were overshadowed by this continuing threat of capital flight. Suggestions that Labour, if elected, should reimpose exchange controls, and perhaps even attempt to introduce controls on the export of capital, invariably met with the response that such actions would inevitably result in a crisis of confidence and massive withdrawals of capital from Britain. Given that such an outcome was certainly not be be countenanced, even Labour avoided advocating the introduction of controls on international financial transactions. Thus, in the Marxist view, was finance capital able to set the political agenda. Thus was it able to exercise 'structural power' over the foreign policy making process.

Marxist theories, then, are relevant to the analysis of British foreign policy primarily in terms of the structural constraints that they identify in the economic sphere. In analysing the actual policy decisions of postwar British governments most Marxist analysts would probably acknowledge the value of the sort of Rational Actor/*realpolitik* calculation approach that has been employed throughout the present study. They would also be likely to argue, however, that such a decision-making approach merely concerns itself with the 'surface features' of foreign policy and that its underlying determinants could only be uncovered through a more sophisticated (and Marxist) structural analysis.

Such criticisms, of course, are both easy to make and difficult to defend. What appears to be a surface feature to one analyst may seem utterly profound to another: such is the power of the analyst's initial 'theoretical position'. While the importance of structural constraints in foreign policy making cannot be denied, I remain convinced not only that the foremost task of foreign policy analysis is to understand the decisions of the policy makers themselves but also that this undertaking can only be satisfactorily completed if a serious attempt is made to reconstruct the policy calculations underlying those decisions. The key problem of the Marxist approach is that what it deems to be a structural constraint may also be capable of being analysed in state-centric decision-making terms as something that policy makers did consider but which (for good and clearly articulated reasons) weighed so heavily against a particular policy alternative that that alternative was immediately rejected. The threat of a flight of capital, for example, certainly constrains a government's decision-making autonomy. However, where the Marxist endows that threat with the status of a structural constraint, the Realist views it merely as an entry on the debit side of a rational calculation about the likely costs and benefits of a particular policy option. For the Realist, the fact that the rejection of a particular option appears to be 'in the interests of financial capital' is an incidental artefact of the policy decision: it does not mean that the option was rejected (or not even considered) because of the 'structural power' of financial capital.[23]

All of this in a sense leaves us where we began: with the observation that the analyst's initial theoretical position strongly influences both his characterisation of 'that which is to be explained' and the explanations that he offers for it. Indeed all that can be said definitively in the matter of the structural constraints identified by Marxists is that the Marxists and the Realists differ in the explanations that they provide. The question as to which analysis is 'better' remains a matter for debate.

Idealism and the World Society perspective

It was noted earlier that the Realist model provides both a description of the world-views of policy makers and an academic theory about the nature and workings of international politics. Although Idealism has so far been identified primarily as an alternative way of characterising policy makers' world-views, it, too, offers – albeit in a relatively rudimentary form – a formal theoretical analysis of foreign policy behaviour.

The immediate problem with the Idealist approach as a vehicle for analysing foreign policy is that it is self-avowedly concerned just as much with making *pre*scriptions about the way states ought to behave as it is with making *de*scriptions of the actual character of international politics.[24] Advocates of the Idealist approach tend to assert that scholars should emphasise the co-operative aspects of nation-state behaviour: the failure to do so, it is alleged, merely contributes to the hardening of attitudes on the part of policy makers. Academic analysis based on the Realist model, it is argued, underpins (and even justifies) Realism in the minds of the politicians. The task of the scholar, on this analysis, is to develop ideas that encourage policy makers to recognise the virtues and benefits of co-operation.

Regardless of the merits (or otherwise) of this missionary aspect of Idealism, however, the approach does contain, in addition, a relatively plausible analytic core. The basic theoretical premise of Idealism is extraordinarily simple. If Structural Realism is correct in its assertion that the primary source of international conflict lies in the anarchic structure of the state system itself, then the obvious way out of that condition of anarchy is to pursue the Hobbesian logic and create an international Leviathan. Just as in the Hobbesian State of Nature men resolve their sense of Hobbesian fear by ceding sovereignty to an all-powerful state capable of imposing domestic order by force of arms, so nation-states can reproduce the process at the international level by ceding their sovereignty to a supranational authority which, backed by coercive force, would impose order at the international level.

Realism, of course, replies that such a solution is impractical: not only do nation-states' fundamental interests inevitably diverge and conflict with one another, but, in any case, why should states that are powerful *now* entrust the protection of their vital interests for the foreseeable future to some supranational authority that they cannot control? The Idealist, in contrast, argues that such divergences of national interest stem solely from the existing condition of international anarchy and are far more apparent than real. If the problem of anarchy could be resolved, then there would be a universal recognition of the fact that there is in reality a global harmony of interests. Indeed, the interests of all states would be maximised if an ordered international system could be devised which was capable of increasing the possibilities for mutually beneficial economic exchange and of preventing war.

As discussed in Chapter 1, Idealist principles received relatively wide currency in the years after 1918. The apparent failures of the 'Idealist experiment' of the 1920s and 1930s, however, seriously damaged the Idealist cause. Indeed the fact that the strategy of co-operative diplomacy advocated by the Idealists became castigated as 'appeasement' had two profound consequences in the postwar years: it convinced the British foreign policy elite that a Realist approach to international affairs offered the only viable response to the machinations of an acquisitive potential aggressor; and it ensured that all postwar governments would be almost pathologically averse to any policy option which had even the faintest whiff of appeasement about it. The failure of interwar Idealism, in short, was a critical source of the Realist world-view which so consistently informed British foreign policy throughout the postwar period.

Yet notwithstanding the triumph of Realism during the war years, traces of Idealist thinking can still be discerned in the strategy of 'partial co-operation' that successive governments pursued towards the Soviet Union after 1957. Although Britain (along with its NATO allies) consistently maintained a strong defensive posture towards the Warsaw Pact, it simultaneously followed neo-idealist principles by *co-operating* with Soviet bloc countries in relatively non-contentious policy areas. Such partial co-operation, it was hoped, would serve indirectly to reduce both East–West tensions and the sense of Hobbesian fear that had characterised East–West relations since the late 1940s. The partial co-operation strategy manifested itself in a series of summit meetings between British and Soviet leaders which began in 1957, and in a long-running series of cultural/scientific (and, latterly, trade) agreements betwęen Britain and a number of Warsaw Pact countries. Even such a seasoned *realpolitik* campaigner as Margaret Thacher, in the late 1980s as committed as ever to the need for NATO to confront the continuing Soviet military threat, recognised the parallel importance of 'jaw-jawing' with the potential enemy and of seeking to identify areas of policy where mutually beneficial co-operation might be encouraged. This double-pronged strategy was not in any sense woolly-minded Idealism. On the contrary, it was a prudent combination of 'safety-first' Realism and 'co-operative diplomacy' Idealism. During the Gorbachev years, at least, the strategy even looked as though it might yield positive results.

While traditional Idealism maintains a state-centric focus, the most important modern variant of Idealist thinking – the 'World Society' perspective – de-emphasises the role of the nation-state, preferring instead to concentrate on the behaviour of transnational actors and transnational processes.[25] In the view of World Society theorists, the growing interdependence of the advanced market economies is gradually usurping the role of the nation-state, providing an opportunity for the breakdown of that condition of Hobbesian fear that, in the Realist view, is so fundamental to the genesis of international conflict. Crucially, the World Society model – like the Marxist approach – offers a structural rather than a decision-making approach to foreign policy behaviour. It pays particular attention to the rapid processes of internationalisation that are now affecting both markets and production and communication patterns world-wide. The central contention of the World Society perspective is that these developments have collectively served to reduce the decision-making autonomy of the nation-state, to constrain its policy choices to a serious degree, and to increase the global role of transnational actors at the nation-state's direct expense. What is clear from the discussion in the preceding chapters is that in terms of *non*-economic policy, the British government continued to possess a relatively high degree of decision-making autonomy throughout the postwar years. Successive British governments were certainly subjected to enormous external constraints. But this had always been the case, since long before 'interdependence' became so evident in the 1960s. Even in the late 1980s, it was still the British government that decided who Britain's enemies were and how the threat that they posed to British interests could best be countered. It was still the government that decided which friendly powers shared a convergence of security interests with Britain and which could be regarded as economic and military allies. And it was still the government that decided which international organisations Britain should belong to, with which it should co-operate, and which it should ignore or confront.

But if the British government still enjoyed considerable decision-making autonomy in the political and security spheres, it was less evident by the late 1980s that this luxury extended to economic matters. Here increasing interdependence and internationalisation were beginning to constrain the government's freedom of action to a degree never encountered before. Such was the power and volatility of the financial markets that the Treasury was unable effectively to monitor – let alone control – foreign dealing in sterling. A sizeable body of opinion in Cabinet – which reportedly included the Prime Minister herself – was convinced that a long-term policy for managing the external value of the pound was impractical. The ingenious accounting procedures of the ever more powerful multinational corporations made it increasingly difficult for any government to control transnational capital flows. And Britain's membership of the European Community by definition reduced London's ability to conduct an independent trade policy capable of discriminating in favour of British producers and consumers. Given the likelihood of yet more market and production internationalisation in the future, at the time of writing it seems likely that in the economic sphere at least the World System approach will assume increasing relevance in the study of British foreign policy.

Summary and conclusions

Foreign policy research, indeed, social research of any sort, is rarely conducted in a theoretical vacuum. What this chapter has endeavoured to show is the extent to which the narrative account of Britain's postwar foreign policy provided in the previous chapters was guided by different theoretical considerations. This is not to say that any of the 'theories' described in this chapter have been systematically tested against Britain's postwar foreign policy experiences. Rather, the different theories have been used to inform description and explanation, to provide guidelines and signposts as to which observations are important and which are not.

What is clear from the foregoing discussion is that each of the theoretical approaches identified earlier has made some sort of contribution to the analysis present here. Indeed, although each perspective has been presented as a discrete position, the ideas summarised under the different headings are in many ways quite compatible with one another. At the decision-making level – as was indicated at the outset – the main emphais has been placed on the Realist and Rational Actor models. The Rational Actor model has been relevant because in arriving at their decisions Britain's postwar foreign policy makers have in general engaged in a process of rational calculation, weighing the likely costs and benefits of different policy options and selecting the option that appeared most likely to maximise what they perceived to be British interests. The relevance of the Realist model has derived from the way in which the policy makers' Realist world-views informed both their policy priorities and their interpretations of the actions of potentially hostile states. Their Realist world-views ensured that the top policy priority was always the maintenance of national security and that potentially hostile states were invariably seen as following an aggressive *realpolitik* strategy that required a resolute British response. As we saw in previous chapters, when there was good reason to suppose that the threat from hostile states was real, this 'resolute' combination of Realism and Reason resulted in policies that were entirely 'realistic' in the everyday sense of the word. This was certainly the case, for example, when the Attlee government responded to Stalin's actions in Eastern Europe in the late 1940s by joining with other Western powers to create the NATO alliance. However when the policy makers' subjective perceptions of an external threat to British interests were significantly greater than the threat's objective magnitude, as occurred during the Suez crisis, the resolute approach was equally capable of producing policies which with hindsight appeared neither rational nor realistic. The question that remains unanswerable at the time of writing is how far the 'resolute Realism' of the present Thatcher government is capable of producing realistic policies – again, in the everyday sense – in an age of *perestroika* and *glasnost*.

At the structural level, the Structural Realist, Marxist and World Society approaches all proved useful for identifying the general constraining conditions that have shaped the foreign policy choices of successive postwar British governments. Structural Realism was of particular value in specifying the origins of the major strategic shift which occurred in British foreign policy during the 1950s and 1960s. The downgrading of the empire circle and its replacement by Britain's increasing involvement with Europe was in large measure the result of the changing pattern of Britain's overseas economic interests. The Marxist and World Society approaches were both of value in the economic sphere, pointing to the constraints on governmental decision-making autonomy that are imposed by the structure of the world economy and by the increasing internationalisation of markets and production.

The power of Structural Realism as an explanatory tool may well diminish in the future, however. It is frequently argued that the game of international politics has in recent years become less concerned with competing for the control of territory and populations and more with competing for market shares and repatriated profit. If this is indeed the case, then Britain's future foreign policy is likely to focus more on economic affairs and the role of transnational actors and less on matters of high politics and national security. In these circumstances, the state-centric Realist model will perhaps lose some of its theoretical relevance. By the same token, the Marxist and World Society approaches may prove rather more useful for explanatory purposes than they have done in the past.

10

Conclusions

Given that each of the preceding chapters ended with a 'summary and conclusions' section, this chapter does not provide a summary statement of the major developments in Britain's postwar external policy. It does, however, seek to review the main substantive and theoretical arguments that have been advanced in previous chapters. The first section re-examines the problem of 'overextension', the notion that, notwithstanding imperial withdrawl, Britain's foreign policy strategy – and especially its defence policy – remained fundamentally overextended throughout most of the postwar period. The second section examines the changing nature of the role that Britain has played in international affairs in the postwar era and offers some speculations as to how that role might develop in the future.

The problem of overextension

The overriding constraint which profoundly affected all of Britain's postwar foreign policy was the relative decline of its economic base. This economic decline in turn engendered a progressive diminution in the ability of successive governments to project a world military role. It meant, in effect, that the 'three circle' strategy of seeking to preserve British power and influence in the Empire, in North America and in Europe could not be sustained. Yet even though Britain was soon obliged to withdraw from both India (in 1947) and Palestine (in 1948) because of the strength of local demands for independence, the process of imperial retreat was not at that stage allowed to develop further. Britain still had extensive economic ties with the Empire and it was still capable of undertaking 'out-of-area' military operations on a world-wide scale. After the 'loss' of India and Palestine, therefore, successive Labour and Conservative governments embarked on a final phase of imperial retrenchment in which they sought simultaneously to maintain

Britain's global network of military bases, to preserve British industry's 'safe' imperial markets, and to prevent the general spread of communism to indigenous populations in the third world. With these objectives broadly in mind, successful holding operations were duly conducted in Malaya (1948–58) and in Kenya (1954–8). The direct and indirect costs of the retrenchment strategy were considerable however. First, Britain was obliged to spend a much higher proportion of GDP on defence than any of its major European competitors. Unlike its European allies, Britain had to 'carry two rifles': one for its NATO commitments and the other for its continuing global role. Second, the preservation of the Empire's financial system – the Overseas Sterling Area – continually impaired the operation of Britain's domestic economy by provoking a series of sterling crises which reinforced the endemic, and debilitating, 'stop–go' cycle of the 1950s and 1960s. Quite simply, the military and economic burdens of the 'three circle' strategy were too great for a power in serious economic decline to sustain.

In the years immediately after Suez the pressures for a radical change in the 'three circle' strategy grew rapidly. At the structural level, two developments were decisive. The first, during the 1950s, was the growth of indigenous nationalist sentiment in the colonies themselves. Whatever its origins, this new political consciousness threatened to make the remainder of the Empire as unmanageable as India and Palestine had become in the late 1940s. Such indigenous pressures could only be short-circuited, moreover, by making real concessions to nationalist demands for autonomy. The second structural development was the autonomous shift in the pattern of Britain's overseas trade, away from the Empire and towards Europe, which became evident from the late 1950s onwards. This shift marked a change in Britain's economic interests which reduced the material need for a continuing close political connection between London and its former dependencies. Concomitantly, of course, the *increasing* economic importance of (Western) Europe provided the material basis for the British government's subsequent attempts to join the EEC.

Added to these two structural factors was an important change in decision-making psychology. The trauma of Suez, in which 'the lessons of the 1930s' had been seriously misapplied, made it possible for British governments subsequently to distinguish between the need to avoid appeasing unprincipled men of violence and the competing need to recognise legitimate nationalist demands for self-determination. After Suez, giving way to indigenous pressures for independence tended to be seen far less in terms of appeasement and far more in terms of the ceding of sovereignty to peoples who were now 'ready' for self-rule. As far as London was concerned, the 'second wave' decolonisations after 1957 and the military withdrawal from east of Suez after 1968 were merely rational responses to the exigencies of a changing situation. The overextension of Britain's foreign and defence policies could only be resolved by significantly reducing its overseas commitments, by bringing its obligations into line with its relatively reduced capabilities. And if Britain's role and influence in the Empire circle were thus in rapid decline, the obvious substitute was to strengthen the United Kingdom's ties with Western Europe. Thus, from the early 1970s onwards, Europe became the primary focus of Britain's external policy.

Yet, even after decolonisation and the withdrawal from east of Suez, the problem of overextension lingered on. Part of the problem was that Britain still had certain residual colonial responsibilities, notably in Gibraltar, Belize, the Falkland Islands and Hong Kong, which required it to maintain a credible out-of-area military capability for use in emergencies. Perhaps more profound, however, was the problem of 'imperial overhang', the tendency of the foreign policy elite to continue to view the world from the old imperial perspective, to persist with old habits of thinking, long after the Empire itself had disappeared. It is extraordinarily difficult to demonstrate that this particular affliction did indeed influence the formulation of British foreign policy in the period after 1965. Nevertheless, in the same way that 'top currency syndrome' misled the framers of foreign economic policy into preserving sterling's reserve role long after its usefulness had been exhausted, it seems likely that an analogous 'post-imperial Great Power syndrome' did continue to affect British foreign policy long after the formal retreat from the world role had been accomplished in 1971–2.

The critical – and essentially indirect – supporting evidence for this proposition lies in the persistent tendency of successive governments to maintain a set of military capabilities which reflected Britain's international position before decolonisation, rather than after it. In the late 1980s, in spite of decolonisation and the withdrawal from east of Suez, Britain still spent around 5 per cent of national GDP on defence (compared with figures of 4.1 per cent in France and 3.3 per cent in West Germany) and still maintained a viable independent out-of-area capability. In spite of a GDP per capita some 60 per cent less than that of West Germany and 30 per cent less than that of France, Britain still contributed massively to NATO's land-based and airborne permanent forces in central Europe and still provided the bulk of NATO's maritime capability in the eastern Atlantic. And crucially, in spite of the continuing American nuclear guarantee and the apparently diminished Soviet threat to British security, the United Kingdom retained its independent nuclear deterrent, its insurance policy against an American withdrawal from NATO and its supposed passport to continuing Great Power status. That a country which by the early 1980s had slipped to twenty-first position in the world economic league could still exhibit undiminished 'Great Power' aspirations was testimony to the hold which 'Great Power syndrome' continued to exercise over the British government's collective imagination. Indeed during the 1980s the Thatcher government even sought to reinvigorate Britain's moribund world role by co-operating with the United States in a series of 'out of area' operations ranging from the joint intervention in Lebanon in 1982 to the policing of the Persian Gulf in 1987–8. Moreover it was argued that, by maintaining a credible nuclear deterrent, whatever the opportunity cost, and by collaborating with Washington in its global efforts to defend the West's general interests, Britain could expect both to maintain its Great Power ranking and to ensure that its voice was still heard in the international corridors of power. Curiously, neither the precise benefits of Great Power ranking nor those of maintaining an audible – but almost invariably ineffectual – voice in international diplomacy were ever clearly articulated. This was 'Great Power syndrome' operating at its most vexacious: Britain had always been a Great Power and must therefore continue to be one regardless both of the changed world in which it now found itself and of the stark facts of its long-term economic decline. In the late 1980s, given that the Thatcher economic revolution at home had not yet propelled the United Kingdom *up* the international GDP per capita league table, Britain looked set to continue with its overextended defence strategy into the indefinite future.

Postscript: Britain's international role

Between 1945 and the late 1950s the United Kingdom's role in world affairs was both extensive and clear-cut. Britain was the proud possessor of a contracting but still enormous Empire; a major naval power responsible, in tandem with the United States, for the world-wide protection of the West's sea-routes; the junior sponsor of the capitalist world's international monetary system; the leading European member of the NATO alliance; and an active permanent member of the prestigious UN Security Council. Britain was not a superpower but it was still a 'Great Power of the first rank' with immense world-wide power and influence.

During the 1960s almost everything changed. The decolonisations of

1957–65 robbed Her Majesty's Government of its Empire. The defence cuts of 1966 and the decision to withdraw from east of Suez in 1968 anticipated the rapid termination of Britain's world-wide naval role. The demise of the Overseas Sterling Area (in 1968) and the subsequent collapse of Bretton Woods (in 1971) ended Britain's co-sponsorship of the international currency system. West Germany overtook Britain as the European mainstay of NATO's continental defence. And the Security Council – long regarded as ineffectual – ceased to be important as a forum for the world's leading statesmen. By 1968, even the government admitted publicly that Britain was merely a 'Great Power of the second rank'. With its 'world role' vanishing, London had turned to Europe, making two unsuccessful attempts to join the EEC in 1961/2 and 1967/8: Europe, unfortunately, had spurned its advances. In the late 1960s, Britain was no better off than it had been in 1962 when Dean Acheson had uttered his famous epithet that Britain had 'lost an Empire [but] not yet found a role'. Indeed, with its Empire and its world role gone, what on earth was the United Kingdom going to do?

In the early 1970s, Europe became more accommodating and Britain more enthusiastically 'European'. Not only did the United Kingdom become a full member of the EC in 1973 – thus enormously strengthening its economic and political ties with Europe – but it also concentrated its defence efforts in the European theatre, becoming at the same time a leading participant in NATO's 'Eurogroup'. Britain looked set to pursue a primarily European role in the international system. It would focus its diplomacy on Europe and join with other EC member-states in developing a common European position on the major international issues of the day. In spite of this strategic shift towards Europe, however, it became clear as the 1970s progressed that the British government's enthusiasm for a primarily European role in international affairs was far from unbridled. Indeed it became increasingly apparent to the Europeans that Britain had sought Community membership not because of any deep-seated commitment to European ideals but because of the presumed economic benefits which membership would bestow. When these benefits failed to materialise, disillusion had set in. The British were certainly not committed Europeans and their government frequently hampered EC efforts to develop a distinctively European position in world affairs.

In the 1980s, the situation, if anything, deteriorated further. The Thatcher government's continual wrangling over both the Common Agricultural Policy and the size of Britain's budget contribution, together with its refusal to join the EMS 'exchange-rate' mechanism, contrived to exasperate Britain's European partners. In their view, even

London's concession on '1992' – the planned removal of all intra-community trade barriers by 1992 – had resulted from an ideological commitment to free market forces rather than from a principled commitment to European economic integration. How could Britain play an appropriate role in Europe, and how could Europe fashion a role for itself in the world, if London continually questioned Community rules and sought to participate only in those aspects of Community activity that could be turned to national advantage?

To make matters worse, Thatcher's 'wider view' of Britain's interests seemed to entail a partial restoration of Britain's global military role. In the 1980s, not content with forcibly retaining its foothold in the South Atlantic, London renewed its interest in general 'out-of-area' operations. Regardless of the consequences for Britain's relations with Europe, and for Europe's relations with the world, London offered consistent military and political backing to Washington's efforts to counter either socialist- or Islamic-inspired challenges to the material interests of the West. Of course, Britain's out-of-area military capabilities could never again hope to match those that had been discarded in the 1960s. None the less the pretensions to a renewed global role were real; and they undoubtedly made the pursuit of the European role much more difficult to sustain.

As Britain approached the 1990s, its foreign policy makers were confronted with a choice between three alternative role models, each of which corresponded to a different point on the political spectrum. The political *left* broadly favoured a position of 'concerned independence',[1] in which Britain, though recognising its geographical position as a European power, would seek to disengage itself from Europe both militarily and economically by withdrawing from NATO and the EC. Using what remained of its political influence throughout the world, it would seek to act as an international mediator, a diplomatic bridge between North and South and between East and West, preaching a doctrine of non-exploitation and peace-with-justice for all. The political *centre* (which, at the time of writing, seemed increasingly to include the Labour leadership) regarded such a scenario as impractical. In its view, Britain's primary economic and political interests lay in Western Europe and as such the British government's best long-term strategy was to act as a genuine partner in Europe: to co-operate in the development of a common European foreign policy which would ensure a prominent position on the world stage for Western Europe as a whole. For the political *right*, what mattered most in international affairs was the maximisation of the economic and security interests of the entire developed capitalist world. In its view, the interests of all the rich capitalist powers were now so inextricably linked that they would prosper or fall together. Britain's preferred international role was accordingly as Washington's 'junior partner', assisting American efforts to defend the West's long-term economic and security interests throughout the world. In the economic sphere this would be achieved by fostering a reliance on market discipline in as many forums as possible. In the military sphere the task would be accomplished by out-competing the Soviet bloc in the arms race and by coercing it into arms reductions wherever possible.

During the Thatcher years, the international role that Britain adopted corresponded most closely to that advocated by the political right. Although significant concessions were made to the 'Europeanist' lobby – in the economic field, at least – the Anglo-American connection was accorded considerable emphasis. At 'Group of 7' summits in the 1980s, British representatives were just as likely to side with the Americans as with the Europeans on issues ranging from global economic strategy to international terrorism. Similarly, in discussions of military strategy inside NATO, British negotiators were far more likely to find themselves making common cause with their American counterparts than with their colleagues in Europe. Yet this was not simply a matter of London following where Washington chose to lead: of Thatcher being 'Reagan's poodle'. What mattered was the common realist 'world-view' shared by the White House and Downing Street; a world in which the tide of socialism had to be rolled back by a concerted and united effort on the part of the Western Powers. It was this common world-view that lay at the heart of the renewed Anglo-American collaboration of the 1980s, though whether the British government's perceptions in this regard were consistent with Britain's post-imperial position as a power with primarily European interests was a matter of some contention. The survival of the 'common view' would undoubtedly depend on the balance of political forces inside Britain itself: a victory for either the left or the centre seemed likely to produce a decisive change in the sort of international role that Britain would seek to play. The apparent solidity of Thatcher's domestic position in the late 1980s, however, suggested that in the foreseeable future any such change was unlikely. Britain's foreign policy strategy would continue to straddle the European and Atlantic circles through to the end of the century.

Appendix: Treaties and Agreements entered into by the UK Government, January–December 1967

	Country/ institution	Form of agreement	Topic
January	United States	2 Exchanges of notes	Space tracking
	Yugoslavia	Exchange of notes	Import of books and films
	Laos	Exchange of notes	Finance
	Netherlands	Exchange of notes	Air transport
	Paraguay	Exchange of notes	Trade
February	Israel	Exchange of notes	Visas
	Italy	Exchange of notes	Air travel
	France	Exchange of notes	Administrative agreement
	United States	Exchange of notes	Education
	Argentina	Exchange of notes	Visas
	Lesotho	Agreement	Public Officers/independence
	Soviet Union	Agreement	Scientific/cultural
	Ghana	Agreement	Debts
March	GATT	Agreement	Entry of Korea to GATT
	Austria	Exchange of notes	War cemeteries
	Romania	Agreement	Scientific co-operation
	Paraguay	Exchange of notes	Trade
	International Olive Oil Convention		
April	Ethiopia	Exchange of notes	War graves
	Irish Republic	Exchange of letters	Air services
	Egypt (UAR)	Exchange of notes	Finance
	European Convention on Adoption		

	Country/ institution	Form of agreement	Topic
May	Jordan	Exchange of notes	Finance
	France	Exchange of notes	Film co-productions
	Federal . German Republic	Agreement	Offset arrangements for BAOR
	India	Exchange of letters	Air transport
	Luxembourg	Convention	Taxation
	GATT	Protocol	Cotton textiles
	International Wheat Agreement		
June	Italy	Exchange of notes	Social insurance
	United States	Exchange of notes	N. S. Savanah
	South Africa	Protocol	Taxation
	Guyana	Exchange of letters	Armed services assistance
	Cameroon	Exchange of notes	Loan
	Dominican Republic	Exchange of notes	Visas
	El Salvador	Agreement	Technical co-operation
	Sweden	Exchange of notes	Radio licensing
	Yugoslavia	Agreement	Exchange of money orders
	GATT	Protocol	Accession of Argentina, Iceland, Poland and Irish Republic
July	Turkey	Exchange of notes	Finance
	Malta	Agreement	Air services
	Kenya	Exchange of letters	Status of UK forces in Kenya
	Kenya	Exchange of letters	Training of Kenyan army
	Malaysia	Agreement	Taxation
	United States	Exchange of notes	Bahamas testing grounds
	Irish Republic	Exchange of letters	Air services
	FAO	Exchange of letters	Locusts
	International Agreement on Tariffs for Scheduled Air Services		
August	Indonesia	Agreement	Commercial debts
	Malaysia	Agreement	Air services
	Singapore	Agreement	Air services
	Hungary	Agreement	Scientific co-operation

	Country/ institution	Form of agreement	Topic
	Jordan	Exchange of notes	Loan
	Japan	Exchange of notes	Air services
	Soviet Union	Agreement	Establishment of telephone 'hotline'
September	Paraguay	Exchange of notes	Trade and payments
	Sweden	Exchange of notes	Peaceful use of nuclear power
	Japan	Agreement	Safety standards
	Italy	Agreement	Film co-productions
	European Agreement on the International Carriage of Dangerous Goods		
October	Denmark	Exchange of notes	Taxation
	Sweden	Agreement	Scientific information exchange
	Netherlands	Convention	Taxation
November	Muscat	Treaty	Cession of Kuria Muria Islands
	South Africa	Exchange of notes	Consular privileges
	France	Exchange of notes	Radio licences
	Argentina	Exchange of notes	Military service
	GATT	Process verbal	Accession of Tunisia and UAR
	European Space Research Organisation	Agreement	Use of Falkland telemetry station
December	Indonesia	Exchange of notes	Loan
	Malaysia	Exchange of letters	Training assistance for Malaysian army
	Australia	Agreement	Taxation
	Botswana	Exchange of letters	Amendment to Public Officers agreement
	Peru	Exchange of notes	Loan
	Norway	Exchange of notes	Peaceful use of nuclear power
	Brazil	Exchange of notes	Taxation

Notes and References

Introduction

1. Under the '30-year rule' British official documents are not released for general viewing until 30 years after the events with which they are concerned. This rule applies to diplomatic correspondence, internal Departmental memoranda, Cabinet minutes and the minutes of Cabinet committees.
2. For a sophisticated discussion of the relevant issues, see Anthony Giddens, *Central Problems in Social Theory: Action, Structure and Contradiction in Social Analysis* (London: Macmillan, 1979).
3. The definitive study of foreign policy making in Britain is William Wallace, *The Foreign Policy Process in Britain* (London: Royal Institute of International Affairs, 1976). For an excellent 'update', see Michael Clarke, 'The Policy-Making Process', in Michael Smith, Steve Smith and Brian White (eds), *British Foreign Policy: Tradition, Change and Transformation* (London: Unwin Hyman, 1988) pp. 71–96. The two most authoritative texts covering the substance of Britain's postwar foreign policy are F. S. Northedge, *Descent From Power: British Foreign Policy 1945–1973* (London: George Allen & Unwin, 1974) and Joseph Frankel, *British Foreign Policy 1945–1973* (London: Oxford University Press, 1975).

Chapter 1

1. For a brief review see John P. Mackintosh, 'Britain in Europe: historical perspective and contemporary reality', *International Affairs*, vol. 45, no. 2 (1969) pp. 246–58.
2. Sir Eyre Crowe, 'Memorandum on the Present State of British Relations with France and Germany' (1 Jan. 1907) cited in Graham Spry, 'Canada, the Emergency Force and the Commonwealth', *International Affairs*, vol. 33, no. 3 (1957) p. 290.
3. Mackintosh, 'Britain in Europe', p. 248.
4. For a detailed analysis of the British government's military objectives during this period, see V. H. Rothwell, *British War Aims and Peace Diplomacy 1914–1958* (Oxford: Clarendon Press, 1971).
5. David Thomson, 'General De Gaulle and the Anglo Saxons', *International Affairs*, vol. 41, no. 1 (1965) p. 11. After 1918 the need to maintain a strong France became a basic axiom of Britain's European policy.

6. Mackintosh, 'Britain in Europe', p. 247.
7. W. L. Wright, 'Truths about Turkey', *Foreign Affairs*, vol. 26 (1948) pp. 349–59.
8. H. Kuyacek, 'Anglo-Turkish economic relations', *South Asian Review*, vol. 37 (1941) pp. 91–100.
9. Peter J. Beck, 'A tedious and perilous controversy: Britain and the Settlement of the Mosul dispute, 1918–1926', *Middle East Studies*, vol. 17, no. 2 (1981) pp. 256–76; Robert W. Olson and Nurham Ince, 'Turkish Foreign Policy from 1923–1960: Kemalism and its legacy, a review and critique', *Oriento Moderno*, vol. 57 (1977) pp. 227–41.
10. Porter notes that during the nineteenth century Latin America was very much part of the United Kingdom's 'informal' Empire. There was a greater degree of British capital penetration in Argentina, for example, than in many of Britain's actual colonies. See Bernard Porter, *The Lion's Share: A Short History of British Imperialism*, 2nd edn (London: Longmans, 1984) ch. 1.
11. Mackintosh, 'Britain in Europe', p. 249. For a detailed analysis see Bradford Perkins, *The Great Rapprochement: England and the US 1895–1914* (London: Victor Gollancz, 1969).
12. Nicholas Mansberg, 'Britain, the Commonwealth and the Western Union', *International Affairs*, vol. 24, no. 4 (1948) pp. 491–504.
13. In fact, France and Russia already possessed sufficient capability to outweigh the Royal Navy in the late 1880s. See Porter, *The Lion's Share*, pp. 123–5.
14. Keith Wilson, 'British Power in the European Balance 1906–14' in David Dilks (ed.), *Retreat from Power: studies in Britain's Foreign Policy of the Twentieth Century, Volume I, 1906–1939* (London: Macmillan, 1981) p. 26.
15. Quincy Wright provides an admirable summary. See Quincy Wright, *A Study of War*, vol. II (Chicago: Chicago University Press, 1942) especially pp. 727–8.
16. D. Dilks, 'Introduction' in Dilks (ed.) *Retreat from Power* pp. 19–20.
17. See Porter, *The Lion's Share*, pp. 239–51.
18. On the dismemberment of the Ottoman Empire after 1918, see R. R. Kasliwal, 'The Foreign Policy of Turkey Since 1919', *Indian Journal of Political Science*, vol. 7 (1946) pp. 38–97.
19. On the new Soviet government's approach to the postwar settlement, see J. M. Thompson, *Russia, Bolshevism and the Versailles Peace* (Princeton NJ: Princeton University Press, 1966).
20. M. Kajima, *The Emergence of Japan as a World Power 1895–1925* (Rutland, Vermont: Tuttle, 1978).
21. For a discussion of these treaties, see H. M. Swanwick, *Collective Insecurity* (London: Jonathan Cape, 1937) pp. 53–9.
22. H. A. L. Fisher, *A History of Europe, Volume II: From the Early Eighteenth Century to 1935* (London: Fontana, 1975) p. 1275. Cited in Porter, *The Lion's Share*, p. 249.
23. C. E. Callwell, *Field Marshall Sir Henry Wilson* (London: Cassell, 1927) pp. 240–1. Cited in *The Lion's Share*, p. 252.

24. In 1922 Britain's armed forces personnel numbered 200 000. It was not until 1937 – in Duff Cooper's 1937 Army Estimates – that serious reform was considered. Hore-Belisha introduced further changes in 1938. See Liddell Hart, *The Defence of Britain* (London: Faber & Faber, 1939) especially pp. 251–309.

25. On the background to this progaganda, see Philip Taylor, 'Publicity and Diplomacy: the impact of the First World War upon Foreign Office attitudes towards the Press', in Dilks (ed.), *Retreat from Power*, pp. 42–63.

26. Cited in Porter, *The Lion's Share*, p. 255.

27. See Hersch Lauterpacht, *The Function of Law in the International Community* (London: Oxford University Press, 1933).

28. The three major League institutions were the Council, the Assembly and the Permanent Court of International Justice, which were intended to constitute, respectively, an embryonic supranational executive, legislature and judiciary. For a definitive review of the operations of the League, see F. P. Walters, *A History of the League of Nations* (London: Oxford University Press, 1960).

29. Ibid., chapters 3–6.

30. Dilks, *Retreat from Power*, p. 11.

31. Swanwick, *Collective Insecurity*, pp. 36 ff.

32. The discussion of Anglo-Turkish relations provided here is derived from David Sanders, *Lawmaking and Co-operation in International Politics: the Idealist Case Re-examined* (London: Macmillan, 1986) ch. 5.

33. For details, see Walters, *League of Nations*, pp. 465–99 and 623–91.

34. Vansittart, a confirmed 'Realist' of long standing, was Permanent Under-secretary at the Foreign Office between 1930 and 1938. He was reportedly ousted at Eden's instigation and replaced by Sir Alexander Cadogan who remained in office until 1946: John Colville, *The Fringes of Power: Downing Street Diaries 1939–1955* (London: Hodder & Stoughton, 1985) p. 162.

35. For a detailed analysis of British policy during the Abyssinian crisis, see Norton Medlicott, 'The Hoare–Laval Pact Reconsidered', in Dilks (ed.), *Retreat from Power*, pp. 118–38.

36. C. J. Bartlett, *The Global Conflict: the international rivalry of the great powers, 1880–1970* (London: Longmans, 1984) pp. 182–3.

37. Ruth B. Henig (ed.), *The League of Nations* (Edinburgh: Oliver & Boyd, 1973) p. 117.

38. Bartlett, *The Global Conflict*, p. 175.

39. Ibid., p. 176.

40. Norton Medlicott, 'Britain and Germany: the search for agreement 1930–37' in Dilks (ed.), *Retreat from Power*, pp. 78–101.

41. Bartlett, *The Global Conflict*, p. 176.

42. Ibid., p. 177.

43. Medlicott, 'Britain and Germany', p. 92.

44. Ibid., pp. 94–5. In June 1936 Eden proudly informed the Commons that the government's aim with regard to the German question was a general 'European settlement and appeasement'. The latter term – as late as 1936

– was still not tainted with the pejorative connotations it was later to acquire. See Bartlett, *The Global Conflict*, p. 185.

45. Chamberlain's commitment to appeasement eventually got too much even for Eden, who resigned in February 1938 over Chamberlain's efforts to conciliate Mussolini over the latter's African policy: Eden was by then convinced of the need to resist aggression – or the threat of it – with force. See Bartlett, *The Global Conflict*, pp. 207–8.

46. William Wallace, *The Foreign Policy Process in Britain* (London: Royal Institute of International Affairs, 1976) p. 75. For a critique of Henderson's diplomacy, see Sir Charles Webster, 'Munich Reconsidered: A Survey of British Policy', *International Affairs*, vol. 37, no. 2 (1961) pp. 137–53.

47. Bartlett, *The Global Conflict*, p. 197.

48. Sir Keith Feiling, *The Life of Neville Chamberlain* (London: Macmillan, 1947) p. 401, cited in *The Global Conflict*, p. 202.

49. Foremost among the scholars' contributions was E. H. Carr's *The Twenty Years' Crisis 1919–1939* (London: Macmillan, 1946).

50. DP(P) 32, CAB 16/183A; 'Appreciation by the Chiefs of Staff of the Situation in the Event of War with Germany' (4 Oct. 1938). Cited in Michael Howard, 'British Military Preparations for the Second World War', in Dilks (ed.), *Retreat from Power*, p. 114.

51. Webster, 'Munich Reconsidered', p. 151.

52. Kenneth Younger, 'Public Opinion and British Foreign Policy', *International Affairs*, vol. 40, no. 1 (1964) p. 24.

53. As Vansittart put it: the government's task was 'how to induce the unwilling to accept the unavoidable'. Cited in Joseph Frankel, 'Conventional and theorising diplomats: a critique', *International Affairs*, vol. 57, no. 3 (1981) p. 544.

54. The need for an Anglo-German alliance had, after all, been a major theme of Hitler's *Mein Kampf*. See Medlicott, 'Britain and Germany', pp. 78–82.

55. Webster, 'Munich Reconsidered', p. 149.

56. The definitive work is E. L. Woodward, *British Foreign Policy in the Second World War (5 vols)* (London: HMSO, 1970–6). See also Christopher Thorne, *Allies of a Kind: the United States, Britain and the War Against Japan, 1941–42* (London: Hamish Hamilton, 1978); A. P. Adamthwaite, *The Making of the Second World War* (London: George Allen & Unwin, 1977); Elisabeth Barker, *Churchill and Eden at War* (London: Macmillan, 1978); David Dilks (ed.), *The Diaries of Sir Alexander Cadogan 1938–45* (London: Cassell, 1971); Michael Howard, *The Mediterranean Strategy in the Second World War* (London: Weidenfeld & Nicolson, 1968).

57. For a detailed analysis of Soviet actions during this period, see J. E. McSherry, *Stalin, Hitler and Europe, 1933–41 (Vol. 2)* (New York: World Publishing Co., 1970).

58. William Hardy McNeill, *Survey of International Affairs 1939–1946: America, Britain and Russia, their Co-operation and Conflict 1941–1946* (London: Oxford University Press for the Royal Institute of International Affairs, 1953) p. 49.

59. See Colville, *Fringes of Power*, pp. 158–66.
60. Churchill's first telegram as Prime Minister (15 May 1940) was to Roosevelt, urgently requesting 50 destroyers for Britain's war effort. Cited in John Baylis, *Anglo-American Defence Relations, 1939–1984*, 2nd edn (London: Macmillan, 1984) p. 3.
61. Ibid., p. 3.
62. Colville, *Fringes of Power*, pp. 331, 347.
63. McNeill, *Survey*, p. 139.
64. This 'public declaration of solidarity' was signed 12 July 1941. See McNeill, ibid., p. 52. Subsequently, on 26 May 1942, an Anglo-Soviet Mutual Assistance Treaty was also signed. See Max Beloff, 'Some aspects of Anglo-Soviet Relations', *International Affairs*, vol. 21, no. 2 (1945) pp. 168–79.
65. McNeill, *Survey*, p. 52.
66. William Roger Louis, 'American anti-colonialism and the dissolution of the British Empire', *International Affairs*, vol. 61, no. 3 (1985) p. 400.
67. McNeill, *Survey*, pp. 129, 111, 148.
68. Baylis, *Anglo-American Defence*, p. 8.
69. McNeill, *Survey*, p. 95.
70. Ibid., pp. 139–41.
71. Ibid., pp. 402–3.
72. Ibid., p. 456.
73. This was the so-called 'Declaration on liberated Europe'. See Bartlett, *The Global Conflict*, p. 249.
74. McNeill, *Survey*, p. 532.
75. Ibid., pp. 533–4.
76. Ibid., p. 139.
77. Ibid., p. 668.
78. Sir Henry Tizzard's 'Scientific and Technical Information Mission' first went to Washington in August 1940. See Baylis, *Anglo-American Defence*, p. 5. Baylis also notes that British participation in nuclear research on the Manhattan project was euphemistically recorded officially as involvement in 'Tube alloys' research.
79. Colville, *Fringes of Power*, p. 331.
80. This 'mixing up' had been anticipated by Churchill in the Commons on 20 Aug. 1940. See Baylis, *Anglo-American Defence*, p. 4.
81. Ibid., p. 15.
82. The worst disaster was probably the ill-fated Arnhem expedition of September 1944.
83. These principles had originally been enshrined in the Atlantic Charter signed by Churchill and Roosevelt in August 1941.
84. The definitive work on the subject is William Roger Louis, *Imperialism at Bay: the United States and the Decolonisation of the British Empire, 1941–1945* (London: Oxford University Press, 1977).
85. McNeill, *Survey*, p. 453.
86. Ibid., p. 524.
87. The campaign itself had been initiated by Cordell Hull, Roosevelt's Secretary of State, as early as 1933. See Dean Acheson, *Present at the*

Creation: My Years in the State Department (New York: Norton, 1987). ch. 2.

88. Ibid., pp. 667–76.
89. These issues are discussed in more detail in Chapter 8.
90. This, of course, was precisely what the Treaty stipulated. For a discussion of the limitations of the General Treaty, see Swanwick, *Collective Security, passim.*

Chapter 2

1. The problems of the British economy in the immediate postwar years are discussed in more detail in Chapter 7.
2. *CMND 6707, Statistical Materials Presented During the Washington Negotiations* (HMSO, 1945) pp. 5–8.
3. McNeill, *Survey of International Affairs 1939–46*, p. 676.
4. Bernard Porter, *The Lion's Share*, pp. 260–1.
5. For a review of the debate, see Andrew Gamble, *Britain in Decline: Economic Policy, Political Strategy and the British State* (London: Macmillan, 1985); David Coates and John Hillard (eds), *The Economic Decline of Modern Britain: The Debate Between Left and Right* (Brighton: Wheatsheaf, 1986).
6. *Monthly Digest of Statistics No. 49* (HMSO, January, 1950) p. 89. The annual deficits reported here are the published monthly averages multiplied by 12.
7. *CMND 6743, Statement Relating to Defence* (HMSO, February, 1946).
8. *CMND 7327, Statement Relating to Defence* (HMSO, February, 1948).
9. Ibid., p. 62.
10. A good example of the 'turning-point' thesis can be found in Christopher Mayhew, 'British Foreign Policy Since 1945', *International Affairs*, vol. 26, no. 4 (1950) pp. 477–86.
11. Several of the subsequent departures both from the tacit agreements made at Yalta and from the more explicit declarations made at Potsdam are catalogued in Anne Whyte, 'Quadripartite Rule in Berlin', *International Affairs*, vol. 23, no. 1 (1947) pp. 30–41.
12. Arnold Toynbee, 'A Turning Point in the Cold War?', *International Affairs*, vol. 26, no. 4 (1950) p. 459.
13. Repayments of the loan were not to begin until December 1951. They would then be paid in 50 annual installments at 2 per cent interest with no interest payable if Britain's trade balance fell below the 1936–8 level. McNeill, *Survey*, p. 683.
14. Ibid., pp. 652–3.
15. Cited in ibid., p. 731.
16. Cited in Bartlett, *The Global Conflict*, p. 263.
17. Geoffrey Warner, 'The Truman Doctrine and the Marshall Plan', *International Affairs*, vol. 50, no. 1 (1974) p. 83.
18. Mayhew, 'British Foreign Policy', p. 480.
19. 'Containment', of course, was identified most closely with George Kennan, a senior policy adviser within the US State Department.

20. Reynolds attributes this remark to Paul Hoffman, one of the Marshall Aid administrators. See David Reynolds, 'A special relationship'? America, Britain and the international order since the Second World War', *International Affairs*, vol. 62, nol. 1 (1986) p. 8.

21. The calculations underlying British decisions over the Brussels Treaty are discussed in John Baylis, 'Britain, the Brussels Pact and the continental commitment', *International Affairs*, vol. 60, no. 4 (1984) pp. 615–30.

22. Bartlett, *The Global Conflict*, p. 275.

23. A. H. Head, 'European Defence', *International Affairs*, vol. 27, no. 1 (1951) pp. 1–9. See also M. L. Dockrill, 'The Foreign Office, Anglo-American relations and the Korean War, June 1950–June 1951', *International Affairs*, vol. 62, no. 3 (1986) pp. 459–78; Peter Truscott, 'The Korean War in British Foreign and Domestic Policy, 1950–52' (PhD dissertation, Exeter College, Oxford, 1984) p. 24.

24. Bartlett, *The Global Conflict*, pp. 280–1.

25. The rearmament package was intended to cost some £4700m over the period 1951–4 (Truscott, 'The Korean War', pp. 108–10). This included a quadrupling of expenditure on military hardware by 1953–4 (*CMND 8146, Defence Programme Statement Made By the Prime Minister in the House of Commons, January 29th 1951* (HMSO, 1951)).

26. The Federal German Republic achieved independence in September 1949.

27. The signatories were France, the Federal German Republic, Italy, Belgium, Luxembourg and the Netherlands.

28. The phrase 'third world' was not itself widely used until the 1960s.

29. The Elbe was assumed to constitute the West German border and the Rhine, the French border.

30. Anglo-American policy towards the oil states during the 1930s and 1940s is discussed in Sir Arthur Hearn, 'Oil and the Middle East', *International Affairs*, vol. 24, no. 1 (1948) pp. 63–75.

31. Bartlett, *The Global Conflict*. p. 272.

32. Ibid.

33. The express reason for the Soviets' action was the Americans' refusal to allow the People's Republic of China a seat at the UN.

34. Kenneth Younger, 'Public Opinion and British Foreign Policy', *International Affairs*, vol. 40, no. 1 (1964) p. 26.

35. CAB 128/18 CM (50) 79, (11 Nov. 1950) cited in Truscott, 'The Korean War', p. 18.

36. Bartlett, *The Global Conflict*, p. 298.

37. Note from Dean Acheson to Ernest Bevin (10 July 1950) cited in Truscott, 'The Korean War', p. 3.

38. Ibid., p. 4.

39. Bartlett, *The Global Conflict*, p. 299.

40. This was certainly what Truman – according to his memoirs – told Attlee at their meeting in Washington in December 1950. See Truscott, 'The Korean War', p. 38.

41. Kenneth Younger, then Minister of State at the Foreign Office, observed: 'We were simply resigned to the fact that MacArthur had gone mad and was totally out of control'. See ibid., pp. 58–59.

42. Ibid., p. 68.
43. Ibid., p. 14.
44. Ibid., pp. 14–16.
45. N. Henderson, 'Britain's Decline: its Causes and Consequences', *The Economist* (2 July 1979) p. 34.

Chapter 3

1. Porter, *The Lion's Share*, p. 240.
2. John Darwin, 'Imperialism in decline? Tendencies in British Imperial Policy between the Wars', *Historical Journal*, vol. 23, no. 3 (1980) pp. 657–79.
3. Anthony Howard, *RAB: The Life of R. A. Butler* (London: Jonathan Cape, 1987) pp. 57–8.
4. Y. Krishan, 'Mountbatten and the Partition of India', *History*, vol. 68, no. 1 (1983) pp. 22–37.
5. Ibid., p. 22.
6. I. A. Talbot, 'Mountbatten and the Partition of India: A Rejoinder' *History*, vol. 69, no. 1 (1984) pp. 29–35.
7. In 1922 there were some 48 000 Jews in Palestine. By 1948 the figure had increased to 640 000. See Sir Alan Cunningham, 'Palestine: the last days of the Mandate', *International Affairs*, vol. 24, no. 4 (1948) pp. 481–90.
8. Ritchie Ovendale, 'The Palestine Policy of the British Labour Government 1945–1946', *International Affairs*, vol. 55, no. 3 (1979) pp. 409–31.
9. Quoted in Michael Howard, *'The Continental Commitment: the Dilemma of British Defence Policy in the Era of Two World Wars* (Harmondsworth: Penguin, 1974) p. 14.
10. T. H. Silcock, 'Policy for Malaya, 1952', *International Affairs*, vol. 28, no. 4 (1952) pp. 445–51.
11. *CMND 9688, Memorandum of the Secretary of State for War Relating to the Army Estimates 1956–57* (HMSO, February 1958).
12. C. W. Greenidge, 'The present outlook in the British West Indies', *International Affairs*, vol. 25, no. 2 (1949) pp. 175–81.
13. Southern Rhodesia did not achieve legal independence – as Zimbabwe – until 1980.
14. Martin Wight, 'Brutus in Foreign Policy: the memoirs of Sir Anthony Eden', *International Affairs*, vol. 36, no. 3 (1960) p. 309.
15. This theme is developed in F. S. Northedge, 'Britain as a Second-rank Power', *International Affairs*, vol. 46, no. 1 (1970) pp. 37–47.
16. Doreen Warriner, 'Land Reform in Egypt and its repercussions', *International Affairs*, vol. 29, no. 1 (1953) pp. 1–10.
17. William Roger Louis, 'American anti-colonialism and the dissolution of the British Empire', *International Affairs*, vol. 61, no. 3 (1985) p. 413.
18. Ibid.

19. Geoffrey Warner, '"Collusion" and the Suez crisis of 1956', *International Affairs*, vol. 55, no. 2 (1979) pp. 226–39.
20. Reynolds, 'A Special Relationship', p. 10.
21. John Baylis, *Anglo-American Defence Relations 1939–1984*, 2nd edn (London: Macmillan, 1984) p. 73.
22. Anthony Howard, *RAB*, pp. 239–41.
23. Wight, 'Brutus', p. 306.
24. William Wallace, *The Foreign Policy Process in Britain* (London: Royal Institute of International Affairs, 1976) p. 75.
25. Sir Anthony Eden, *The Memoirs of the Right Hon. Sir Anthony Eden: Full Circle* (London: Cassell, 1960) p. 579.
26. David Sanders, *Lawmaking and Co-operation in International Politics: the idealist case re-examined* (London: Macmillan, 1986) ch. 5.

Chapter 4

1. William Wallace, *The Foreign Policy Process in Britain*, p. 82.
2. Wight, 'Brutus in Foreign Policy', p. 305; Elisabeth Monroe, 'British bases in the Middle East – assets or liabilities?,' *International Affairs*, vol. 42, no. 1 (1966) pp. 25–7.
3. Graham Spry, 'Canada, the UN Emergency Force and the Commonwealth', *International Affairs*, vol. 33, no. 3 (1957) pp. 289–300.
4. This reasoning had already been articulated in the early twentieth century. See, for example, Leopold Amery, *My Political Life (Volume 1): England Before the Storm, 1896–1914* (London: Hutchinson, 1953).
5. Indeed, in 1955 serious consideration had been given to consolidating the Commonwealth by increasing its membership from eight (United Kingdom, Canada, New Zealand, Australia, South Africa, India, Pakistan, Ceylon) to thirteen, through the creation of new dominions in the Caribbean, in West Africa, in the Rhodesias and Nyasaland, in East Africa and in Greater Malaya. See C. E. Carrington, 'A New Theory of the Commonwealth', *International Affairs*, vol. 31, no. 2 (1955) pp. 137–148.
6. Wight, 'Brutus in Foreign Policy'; *CMND 150, Memorandum of the Secretary of State for War Relating to the Army Estimates 1957–8* (HMSO, April 1957).
7. For a summary of the changed establishment position, see Earl of Home, 'Interdependence: the British role', *International Affairs*, vol. 37, no. 2 (1961) pp. 154–60.
8. For review, see R. I. Rotberg and Ali Mazrui (eds), *Protest and Power and Black Africa* (New York: Oxford University Press, 1970), especially sections 4–6.
9. The table is derived partly from Porter, *The Lion's Share*, pp. 335–6.

10. This view was by no means confined to the British popular press. In July 1960, for example, the US representative on the UN Security Council (Henry Cabot Lodge) observed that the Soviet Union was 'evidently seeking to bring the Cold War to the heart of Africa' (*Keesings Contemporary Archive, 1960*, p. 17648).

11. For a detailed description of the process of social mobilisation, see Karl Deutsch, 'Social Mobilisation and Political Development', *American Political Science Review*, vol. 55 (1961) pp. 494–512.

12. As Porter so succinctly puts it: 'colonialism was breeding its own antidote'. See Porter, *The Lion's Share*, pp. 322 ff.

13. Deutsch, 'Social Mobilisation', pp. 495–7.

14. For a review of the impact of social mobilisation on political developments throughout the third world generally, see Samuel P. Huntington, *Political Order in Changing Societies* (New Haven: Yale University Press, 1968).

15. In Mozambique and Angola the settler regimes were also in the fortunate position of receiving the full backing of the Salazar dictatorship in Lisbon: it was only when Salazar was ousted in an army coup in 1974 that independence was secured.

16. Iraq had also been a signatory to the pact, though it abrogated the agreement in 1958.

17. *CMND 2902, Statement on the Defence Estimates 1966 Part II; Defence Estimates 1966–67* (HMSO: Feb. 1966).

18. Wallace, *Foreign Policy Process*, pp. 138–9.

19. Ibid., pp. 119–120.

20. Ibid., p. 136.

21. Alistair Buchan, 'Britain and the Indian Ocean', *International Affairs*, vol. 42, no. 2 (1966) pp. 184–193.

22. *CMND 2901 Statement on the Defence Estimates 1966 Part I: The Defence Review* (HMSO: Feb. 1966).

23. *CMND 3540, Statement on the Defence Estimates 1968* (HMSO: Feb. 1968).

24. *CMND 3701, Supplementary Statement on Defence Policy 1968* (HMSO: July 1968).

25. In 1965 the United States devoted 7.6 per cent of GNP to defence expenditure. The UK figure was 5.9 per cent. The comparable figures for Britain's major competitors were as follows:

France	5.5	Netherlands	4.0	Denmark	2.9
Sweden	4.4	Italy	3.4	Austria	1.3
FRG	4.4	Belgium	3.0	Japan	0.9

Source: Charles Lewis Taylor and Michael C. Hudson, *World Handbook of Social and Political Indicators*, 2nd edn (New Haven: Yale University Press, 1972) pp. 34–6.

26. Wallace, *Foreign Policy Process*, p. 134.

27. Michael Howard, 'Britain's Strategic Problem East of Suez', *International Affairs*, vol. 42, no. 2 (1966) pp. 179–83; *CMND 2592: Statement on the Defence Estimates 1965* (HMSO: Feb. 1965).

28. See, for example, Roger Owen and Bob Sutcliffe (eds), *Theories of Imperialism* (London: Longmans, 1972). The phrase 'imperialism without colonies' is the subtitle of the contribution by Harry Magdoff.
29. The 20-year UK–Libya Treaty of Friendship and Alliance had been signed in July 1953.
30. The 1953 Treaty was terminated by an Exchange of Notes in January 1972.
31. The Foreign Office and the Colonial Office were merged in 1968 to form the Foreign and Commonwealth Office.
32. Ghana experienced *coups* in 1972, 1978, 1979 and 1982; Nigeria in 1975, 1983 and 1985.
33. Treaties were signed with Bahrain in August 1971, with Qatar in September and with the United Arab Emirates in December. Note that it was partly these commitments – as well as the need to protect western shipping – that led to the renewed British naval presence in the Gulf in the late 1980s, as the spill-over from the Iran–Iraq war threatened the security of western shipping in the region.
34. *CMND 4890, Exchange of Notes between ... the United Kingdom ... and ... Malaysia regarding Assistance for the Malaysia Armed Forces and the Arrangements for a United Kingdom Force in Malaysia* (1 Dec. 1971).
35. Ibid.
36. *CMND 3231, Exchange of Notes between the Government of the United Kingdom and the Government of the United States of America concerning the availability for defence purposes of the British Indian Ocean Territory* (30 Dec. 1966).
37. *CMND 6413 Exchange of Notes between ... the United Kingdom ... and ... the United States of America concerning a United States Navy Support facility on Diego Garcia, British Indian Ocean Territory* (25 Feb. 1976).
38. Training agreements were signed with Zambia, Cyprus and Botswana in 1968; with Nigeria in 1969; with Malawi in 1970; with Malaysia and Kenya in 1973; and with Zimbabwe in 1980.
39. *CMND 8288, The United Kingdom Defence Programme: The Way Forward* (HMSO: 1981).
40. There is no direct evidence to support the view that Thatcher's stance was a calculated move to increase her own domestic popularity. The effects of the Falklands War on the government's popularity are the subject of some contention. See, for example, David Sanders, Hugh Ward and David Marsh, 'Government Popularity and the Falklands War: a reassessment', *British Journal of Political Science*, vol. 17, no. 2 (1987) pp. 281–313.
41. In 1986, the annual cost of maintaining the garrison was estimated to be £250m. Tony McGrew, 'Security and Order: the Military Dimension', in Michael Smith, Steve Smith and Brian White (eds), *British Foreign Policy: Tradition, Change and Transformation* (London: Unwin Hyman, 1988) p. 107.
42. *CMND 9543, Joint Declaration of the Government of the United Kingdom ... and the Government of the People's Republic of China on the question of Hong Kong* (19 Dec. 1984).

43. The literature on this subject is voluminous. Probably the most authoritative work is still Ernest Mandel, *Late Capitalism* (London: New Left Books, 1975).
44. The two most significant UNCTAD meetings were UNCTAD IV (in Nairobi in 1976) and UNCTAD V (in Manila in 1979).
45. The most prominent of these agreements was the STABEX mechanism introduced in April 1975. For a good introduction to these schemes, see W. Brandt *et al.*, *North–South: A Programme for Survival* (The Brandt Report) (London: Pan Books, 1980),
46. The ACP were initially a group of some 46 African, Caribbean and Pacific (Far Eastern) countries which signed the Lomé Convention with the EEC states in 1974.
47. Jonathan Kimber, 'Dependence, Cooperation and the Lomé Convention: the cases of Mauritius, the Ivory Coast and Ghana' (PhD dissertation, University of Essex, 1983).
48. Andre Gunder Frank, *Crisis: In the Third World* (London: Heinemann, 1981). These matters are discussed further in Chapter 9.
49. Moreover the complex internal and external accounting procedures used by contemporary multinational corporations make systematic profit-tracing an almost impossible exercise anyway.
50. It can of course be argued that some third-world politicians corruptly welcome foreign multinational investment for their own private gain. However such an argument does not confront the crucial question as to the balance of cost and benefit that accrues from the activities of multinational corporations in third-world countries.
51. This is generally achieved by examining over time movement in the relative prices of raw materials as against manufactures. See, for example, Michael Beenstock, *The World Economy in Transition* (London: George Allen & Unwin, 1983) p. 101.
52. The phrase 'emptying out' is derived from Northedge. See F. S. Northedge, 'Britain as a Second-Rank Power', *International Affairs*, vol. 46, no. 1 (1970) p. 40.

Chapter 5

1. The Council of Europe was loosely based on an idea mooted by Churchill in September 1945. The original members were Britain, France, Belgium, the Netherlands, Luxembourg, Sweden, Norway, Denmark, Ireland and Italy. They were subsequently joined by Iceland, West Germany, Greece, Turkey and Austria.
2. See, for example, Altiero Spinelli, *The Eurocrats, Conflict and Crisis in the EEC* (trans. C. Grove Haines) (Baltimore: Johns Hopkins Press, 1966).
3. See J. S. Nye, *Peace in Parts: Integration and Conflict in Regional Organisation* (Boston: Little, Brown, 1971) especially chs 1–3; Ernst B. Haas, *The Uniting of Europe* (London: Oxford University Press, 1958).

4. The original 'six' of the subsequent EEC were: France, the Federal Republic of Germany, Italy, Belgium, the Netherlands and Luxembourg.
5. *CMND 13, Agreement concerning the Relations between the United Kingdom and the European Coal and Steel Community* (21 Dec. 1954). This in many respects unique agreement in fact gave the UK government and industry direct access to the High Authority and, therefore, to the decision-making structure of the ECSC itself.
6. This is not to say, however, that Whitehall was entirely unaware of the changes that were under way. The shift in the pattern of Britain's external trade was certainly anticipated by Sir Frank Lee, then Permanent Undersecretary at the Board of Trade.
7. An additional reason for Britain's lack of interest in the EEC at this stage was the belief – widely held in British foreign policy circles – that French opposition would prevent the plans for the proposed EEC from coming into fruition. It was only after Suez had 'bounced' the French into the EEC and Euratom ventures that the British realised that they would indeed have to face a *de facto* customs union among the Six.
8. *CMND 9842, Agreement between . . . the United Kingdom and . . . the Federal Republic of Germany for Co-operation in the Peaceful Uses of Atomic Energy* (31 July 1956).
9. *CMND 458, Agreement between . . . the United Kingdom and the Government of the Italian Republic for Co-operation in the Peaceful Uses of Atomic Energy* (23 Dec. 1957).
10. *CMND 1313,* [Three] *Exchanges of Notes between . . . the United Kingdom and . . . the Federal Republic of Germany concerning Local Defence Costs of UK forces stationed in the Federal Republic . . .* (7 June 1957).
11. *CMND 1080, Exchange of Notes between the Government of the United Kingdom and the Government of the Kingdom of the Netherlands concerning the Arrangements to Facilitate Travel between the United Kingdom and the Netherlands* (1 April 1960); *CMND 1157* (20 June 1960: as *CMND 1080* but refers to the Federal German Republic); *CMND 1357 Exchange of Notes between the . . . United Kingdom and . . . Luxembourg concerning the Acceptance of the British Visitors Passport for Travel between the UK and Luxembourg* (21 Feb. 1961); *CMND 1354* (21 Feb. 1961: title as *CMND 1357* but refers to Belgium); *CMND 1355* (21 Feb. 1961: title as *CMND 1357* but refers to the Netherlands).
12. David Coombes, *Politics and Bureaucracy in the European Community: A Portrait of the Commission of the EEC* (London: George Allen & Unwin, 1970) p. 75.
13. Peter Calvocoressi, *World Politics since 1945, Fourth Edition* (London: Longman, 1982) pp. 167–8.
14. *CMND 2108 Polaris. Sales Agreement between the Government of the United Kingdom . . . and the Government of the United States of America* (4 June 1963).
15. Wallace, *The Foreign Policy Process* pp. 85–6.
16. Alan Campbell, 'Anglo-French relations a decade ago: a new assessment (1)', *International Affairs*, vol. 58, no. 2 (1982) pp. 237–53.
17. *CMND 5179, Treaty concerning the Accession of . . . the United Kingdom*

... *to the European Economic Community and the European Atomic Energy Community including the Act concerning the conditions of Accession and the Adjustment to the Treaties* ... (1 Jan. 1973).

18. The Warsaw Treaty Organisation was created in 1955. Its members are USSR, Poland, the German Democratic Republic, Hungary, Czechoslovakia, Romania and Bulgaria.

19. Sanders, *Lawmaking and Cooperation*, pp. 21–7.

20. Colville, *The Fringes of Power*, p. 683.

21. *The Oxford Dictionary of Quotations* (Oxford University Press, 1985) attributes the phrase to Theodore Roosevelt (p. 408).

22. *CMND 1076, Five Year Trade Agreement between the Government of the United Kingdom and the Government of the Union of Soviet Socialist Republics* (24 May 1959); *CMND 917, Agreement between the* ... *United Kingdom and* ... *the Union of Soviet Socialist Republics on relations in the Scientific, Technological, Educational and Cultural fields, 1960–61* (1 Dec. 1959); *CMND 2557, Protocol for the prolongation of the Five Year Trade Agreement between* ... *the United Kingdom and* ... *the Union of Soviet Socialist Republics* (23 April 1964).

23. *CMND 4705, Long-Term Economic and Trade Agreement between the Government of the United Kingdom* ... *and the Government of the Polish People's Republic* (21 April 1971).

24. *CMND 5016, Long-Term Economic and Trade Agreement between the Government of the United Kingdom* ... *and the Government of the Hungarian People's Republic* (21 March 1972); *CMND 5074, Long-Term Economic and Trade Agreement between the Government of the United Kingdom* ... *and the Government of* ... *Czechoslovakia* (27 June 1982); *CMND 5106, Long-Term Economic and Trade Agreement between the Government of the United Kingdom* ... *and the Socialist Republic of Romania* (15 June 1972).

25. *CMND 5286, Long-Term Agreement on the Development of Economic, Industrial, Scientific and Technical Co-operation between the Government of the United Kingdom* ... *and the Government of the Polish People's Republic* (20 March 1973); *CMND 5552, Agreement between the Government of the United Kingdom* ... *and the Government of the German Democratic Republic on the Development of Economic, Industrial, Scientific and Technical Co-operation* (18 Dec. 1973).

26. The actual figures were: in favour, 48 per cent; opposed, 26 per cent; don't know, 26 per cent. See Younger, 'Public Opinion and British Foreign Policy' p. 31.

27. Calvocoressi, *World Politics*, p. 171. For a discussion of the Kennedy Round negotiations, see Coombes, *Politics and Bureaucracy*, pp. 166–216.

28. For a provocative – and entertaining – view of the decline, see Corelli Barnet, *The Audit of War: the Illusion and Reality of Britain as a Great Nation* (London: Macmillan, 1986).

29. This tendency is documented extensively in Peter Willetts, *The Non-Aligned Movement: The Origins of a Third World Alliance* (London: Frances Pinter, 1978).

30. See, for example, C. E. Carrington, 'Between the Commonwealth and Europe', *International Affairs*, vol. 38, no. 2 (1962) pp. 449–455.

31. The three exceptions were Finland, Norway and Denmark.

32. See, for example, Frank Longstreth, 'The City, Industry and the State', in Colin Crouch (ed.), *State and Economy in Contemporary Capitalism* (London: Croom Helm, 1979) pp. 157–90.

33. Jonathan Lynn and Anthony Jay, *Yes, Prime Minister: the Diaries of the Right Hon. James Hacker, Volume II* (London: BBC Books, 1987).

34. France (after 1966) and the Irish Republic were not full NATO members.

35. There were nine such decisions in 1974 and 10 in 1975. See, for example, *CMND 6258, Decisions of the Representatives of the Governments of the Member States of the European Coal and Steel Community meeting in Council, opening, allocating and providing for the allocation of Tariff Quotas and opening Tariff Preferences for certain Steel Products originating in Developing Countries* (2 Dec. 1974).

36. A 2:1 majority voted in favour of continued membership of the Community in June 1975 (67.2 per cent Yes; 32.8 per cent No).

37. See Helen Wallace, 'The British Presidency of the European Community's Council of Ministers: the opportunity to persuade', *International Affairs*, vol. 64, no. 4 (1986) pp. 583–99.

38. For details, see Jan-Erik Lane and Svante O. Ersson, *Politics and Society in Western Europe* (London: Sage, 1987).

39. Joseph Frankel, 'Conventional and theorising diplomats: a critique', *International Affairs*, vol. 57, no. 3 (1981) p. 547.

40. Wallace, 'The British Presidency of the European Community's Council of Ministers', p. 585.

41. See, for example, Leon Lindberg, *Political Dynamics of European Economic Integration* (London: Oxford University Press, 1963).

42. Lord Gladwyn, 'Western Europe's Collective Defence', *International Affairs*, vol. 51, no. 2 (1975) p. 168.

43. Douglas Hurd, 'Prospects for Europe: Political Co-operation', *International Affairs*, vol. 57, no. 3 (1981) p. 383. It is also worth noting that the Single European Act of 1986 extended EPC still further. The aim before 1986 was to provide a consultative framework that *could* be used if the political will was there: after 1986, consultation through EPC became a legal requirement.

44. James Eberle, John Roper, William Wallace and Phil Williams, 'European Security Cooperation and British interests', *International Affairs*, vol. 60, no. 4 (1984) p. 546.

45. Evan Luard, 'A European Foreign Policy?' *International Affairs*, vol. 62, no. 4 (1986) p. 576.

46. The Independent European Arms Procurement Group was created in 1975.

47. These took place largely within the framework of the Conference on Security and Co-operation in Europe which arose out of the Helsinki Final Act of 1975.

48. Hurd, 'Prospects for Europe', p. 386.

49. For details of these matters, see Geoffrey Edwards, 'Europe and the

Falkland Islands crisis 1982', *Journal of Common Market Studies*, vol. 22, no. 4 (1984) pp. 295–313.

50. Greece became a full EC member in January 1981; Spain and Portugal in January 1986.

51. Luard, 'A European Foreign Policy?', p. 580.

Chapter 6

1. A large part of the problem, in fact, was Washington's refusal to assist Britain's efforts to pacify the growing intercommunal conflict. See Bradford Perkins, 'Unequal Partners: The Truman Administration and Great Britain', in William Roger Louis and Hedley Bull (eds), *The Special Relationship: Anglo-American Relations Since 1945* (Oxford: Clarendon Press, 1986) pp. 43–65; Ritchie Ovendale, 'The Palestine Policy of the British Labour Government, 1947: the decision to withdraw', *International Affairs*, vol. 56, no. 1 (1956) pp. 73–93.

2. Susan Strange, *Sterling and British Policy* (London: Oxford University Press, 1971) p. 62.

3. Other commentators offer slightly differing periodisations from that presented here. Reynolds, 'A "special relationship"?', for example, views the entire 1945–63 period as a single phase of generally close relations which was followed by two periods of cooling (1963–73 and 1973+). Baylis, *Anglo-American Defence Relations*, in contrast, partitions the post-Suez period into four phases: the 'preferential relationship', 1957–62; the 'close relationship', 1963–9; the 'natural relationship', 1970–9; and the extraordinary alliance', 1980–7.

4. *CMND 537, Agreement between the Government of the United Kingdom . . . and the government of the United States . . . for co-operation on the uses of atomic energy for mutual defence purposes* (3 July 1958).

5. Baylis, *Anglo-American Defence*, p. 95.

6. For details, see ibid., pp. 96–7.

7. Ibid., pp. 97–101.

8. The precise details of the financial charges to be made by Washington were given in Article XI of *CMND 2108* (6 April 1963). As *The Times* Defence Correspondent observed on 27 Jan. 1983, this constituted '. . . a bargain that for most of its life has cost the Government less than 2% of its defence budget'. Cited in Alistair Horne, 'The Macmillan Years and Afterwards', in Louis and Bull (eds) *The Special Relationship*, p. 98.

9. See Graham Allison, *Essence of Decision: Explaining the Cuban Missile Crisis* (Boston, Mass.: Little, Brown, 1971).

10. See, for example, John Mander, *Great Britain or Little England* (London: Penguin, 1963) p. 21. Cited in Baylis, *Anglo-American Defence* p. 106.

11. Horne, 'Macmillan Years', pp. 92–3.

12. Ibid., p. 100. The Partial Test Ban Treaty itself was signed in August 1963.

13. Ibid., pp. 95–6.
14. Baylis, *Anglo-American Defence*, p. 147.
15. Cited in ibid., p. 154–5.
16. Cited in Ibid., p. 155.
17. *CMND 6413* (25 Jan. 1976).
18. Peter Unwin, 'British Foreign Policy Opportunities Part I – the Global context', *International Affairs*, vol. 57, no. 2 (1981), p. 226.
19. David Watt, 'Introduction: the Anglo-American relationship', in Louis and Bull (eds), *The Special Relationship*, p. 13.
20. Cited in Baylis, *Anglo-American Defence*, p. 151.
21. Reynolds, 'A "special relationship"?', p. 13.
22. See Chapter 8.
23. The result of Carter's efforts was the 1979 Israeli–Egyptian Peace treaty. See Henry Kissinger, *Years of Upheaval* (Boston, Mass: Little, Brown, 1982).
24. David Owen, *Personally Speaking to Kenneth Harris* (London: Weidenfeld & Nicolson, 1987).
25. Baylis, *Anglo-American Defence*, p. 182.
26. Ibid., pp. 182–3.
27. For review, see Roger Scruton, *The Meaning of Conservatism*, 2nd edn (London: Macmillan, 1984). For the new right's views of the left, see Roger Scruton, *Thinkers of the New Left* (Harlow: Longman, 1985).
28. Baylis, *Anglo-American Defence*, p. 184. See *CMND 8517*, *The British Strategic Nuclear Force* (HMSO: March 1982).
29. Admiral Sir James Eberle, 'The Military Relationship', pp. 157–8, and Ernest R. May and Gregory F. Treverton, 'Defence Relationships: American Perspectives', in Louis and Bull (eds) *The Special Relationship*, pp. 175–6.
30. Baylis, *Anglo-American Defence*, p. 192.
31. *The Times*, 16 April 1986.
32. The British government's permission was necessary under the terms of the 'Truman–Attlee Understandings' of 1951. See Baylis, *Anglo-American Defence*, p. 186.
33. Two polls conducted in by-election constituencies (Ryedale and Derbyshire West) immediately after the Libyan bombing indicated that 61 per cent of the sample disapproved of the British government's decision to allow US bombers to fly from British bases (*Guardian*, 30 April 1986).
34. 'Mad dog' was the deliberately provocative phrase used by President Reagan to describe Colonel Qadafi on 9 April. (See the *Observer*, 20 April 1986.)
35. *Guardian*, 21 April 1986, p. 17. Cynics noted that the 'surgical strike' had not been carried out particularly accurately. Most of the Libyan casualties were civilian. Colonel Qadafi himself – the presumed target of the attack – was unharmed.
36. See Chapter 4, pp. 114–15.
37. On both the similarities and differences of the British and American political cultures, see Gabriel Almond and Sidney Verba, *The Civic Culture* (Boston, Mass.: Little, Brown, 1965).

38. At the mass level, these feelings of affect have consistently been reflected in opinion poll responses. Eurobarometer polls, for example, have consistently shown the British to be more trusting of Americans than any other nationality. (See, for example, *Eurobarometer 17* (April, 1982; ICPSR Study No. 9023).) Polls conducted by the Chicago Council on Foreign Relations have similarly shown that Americans generally regard the British as being highly trustworthy. (See, for example, J. E. Rielly (ed.), *American Public Opinion and US Foreign Policy* (Chicago: Chicago Council on Foreign Relations, 1983).) Although there are no comparable data at the elite level, there is no reason to suppose that British or American elites are any less favourably disposed towards one another than their respective populations.

39. This is certainly the case for those periods where the official records have been opened. See, for example, Ritchie Ovendale, 'The Palestine Policy of the British Labour Government, 1945–46', *International Affairs*, vol. 55, no. 3 (1979) pp. 409–31; Ritchie Ovendale, 'Britain, the US and the Cold War in SE Asia 1949–50', *International Affairs* vol. 58, no. 3 (1982) pp. 447–64.

40. Indeed, if anything, the United States became even more important as a trade partner for the United Kingdom. British exports to the United States increased from 6.3 per cent of total United Kingdom exports in 1955 to 14.4 per cent of total exports in 1984. (See Table 5.4.)

41. United States exports to the United Kingdom constituted 4.5 per cent of all United States exports in 1952; 5.5 per cent in 1960; 5.5 per cent in 1970; 5.3 per cent in 1980; and 5.2 per cent in 1986. Source: *United Nations Yearbook of International Trade Statistics* (New York: United Nations, various years).

42. The G7 group is comprised of the United States, the United Kingdom, France, Italy, FRG, Japan and Canada.

43. *CMND 537*.

44. Andrew Pierre, *Nuclear Politics: The British Experience with an Independent Strategic Force, 1939–70* (London: Oxford University Press, 1972) p. 144.

45. This became particularly noticeable in the early 1960s, when decolonisation should perhaps have been reducing Britain's overseas defence burden. From 1955/6 through to 1959/60, the Defence Estimates were in the region of £1500m per annum (1955/6 = £1548m; 1959/60 = £1514m). From 1960 onwards, however, costs rapidly escalated, even allowing for inflation. In 1960/1 the Defence Budget was £1629m; in 1961/2 £1655m; in 1962/3 £1721m; in 1963/4, £1838m. By 1966–7, the total annual estimate had risen to £2250m. (Source: Annual Statement(s) on the Defence Estimates 1955–1966).

46. Reynolds 'A "Special Relationship"?' p. 13.

47. Michael Clarke, 'American reactions to shifts in European Policy: the changing context', in John Roper (ed.), *The Future of British Defence Policy* (Aldershot: Gower, 1985) pp. 83–4.

48. Sir Michael Howard, 'Afterword: the "Special Relationship"', in Louis and Bull (eds), *The Special Relationship*, p. 391.

49. On the extent of this consultation, see, for example, Harold Macmillan, *Riding the Storm, 1956–1959* (London: Macmillan, 1971).

50. The 'evil Empire' was, of course, one of President Reagan's favourite euphemisms for the Soviet Union.

51. Watt, 'Introduction: the Anglo-American relationship', p. 7.

52. Max Beloff, 'The Special Relationship: an Anglo-American myth', in Martin Gilbert (ed.), *A Century of Conflict 1850–1950: Essays for A. J. P. Taylor* (London: Hamish Hamilton, 1966) pp. 151–71.

53. Reynolds, 'A "special relationship"?', pp. 13–18.

54. Eberle, 'The Military Relationship', p. 154; May and Treverton, 'Defence Relationships' pp. 168–9.

55. Margaret Gowing, 'Britain, America and the Bomb', in Dilks (ed.), *Retreat from Power*, Vol. 2, p. 137.

56. This seems most closely to accord with Thatcher's own view. In December 1979 she referred to the Anglo-American relationship as 'the extraordinary alliance'. Cited in Baylis, *Anglo-American Defence*, p. 182.

57. Horne, 'Macmillan Years', pp. 90–2. Horne quotes Joe Hersch's comment that Macmillan was '. . . one of the few living British politicians who can manage to sound convincingly patriotic without sounding anti-American' (p. 91).

Chapter 7

1. See James E. Alt and K. Alec Chrystal, *Political Economics* (Brighton: Wheatsheaf Books, 1983) for a concise review of this theory.

2. In 1950, for example, Britain's overall trade volume (exports plus imports divided by two) constituted some 20.0 per cent of national GDP. Source: *Annual Abstract of Statistics, 1952*. In 1975, the equivalent figure was 20.9 per cent. The West German figure for 1975 was 19.5 per cent, the French figure 15.8 per cent and the United States figure 6.8 per cent. Source: *United Nations Statistical Pocket/Second Edition, World Statistics in Brief* (New York: United Nations, 1977).

3. The technical aspects of the discussion that follows are largely derived from Susan Strange's *Sterling and British Policy* (London: Oxford University Press, 1971). The reader familiar with this study will realise the considerable debt that the present chapter owes to Professor Strange's work. Strange makes a number of technical distinctions that are relevant to the ensuing discussion.

   (i) *Master Currency*: the dominant currency of a particular currency area. The pound was in effect a master currency in the British Empire currency area from the mid-nineteenth century onwards. The German mark acquired a similar status in central Europe in the 1930s; the franc in the French colonies from 1920 onwards. The pound was the master currency in the 'Overseas Sterling Area' from the early 1930s until the late

1960s; though according to Strange, it was losing its master currency status from 1931 onwards. The essential feature of a master currency is that the master currency state has sufficient political and military dominance over the subordinate states in the currency area that it can determine (1) the official exchange rate with other currencies; (2) the volume and types of trade permitted both among members and between members and states outside the currency area; (3) the money supply and the rate of credit expansion.

(ii) *Reserve Currency*: a master currency used by the governments of subordinate states as a *contingency asset*. The subordinate state holds reserves of the reserve currency that can be used if necessary in the event of some future balance of payments deficit. The pound sterling was a reserve currency for the OSA from 1945 until 1968. Since then its role as a reserve currency has been minimal. The main reserve currency since 1945 (and especially since 1968) has been the dollar.

(iii) *Vehicle or transactions currency*: a currency used commercially by private individuals or organisations in financial or trade transactions. For example, a Nigerian businessman might use dollars to buy Ghanaian goods. Until the 1970s, sterling was a popular transactions currency; today the dollar is the main transactions currency.

(iv) *Top Currency*: the dominant master currency which is also the main reserve currency and the main transactions currency. From 1815 to 1918 the pound occupied this role. After 1918 it was gradually shorn of its top currency status. Since 1945 the top currency has clearly been the dollar. It is generally considered that the top currency state has a vested interest in the health of the *world* economy and that its international economic and political strategy should aim to sustain and develop the strength of the world economy.

(v) *Official vs Market Convertibility*: market convertibility refers to the *unofficial* or market-determined price at which currencies change hands. (For example, how many roubles do you need to buy a dollar?) For all currency exchanges there is always a market rate, but the market rate is often higher than the official rate. States can impose an official rate by making certain (or all) forms of currency dealing *illegal*. The intention is to *ration* spending of the state's own currency (for example, roubles) abroad in order to keep imports down. Individuals can thus only change the domestic currency for foreign currency through official channels. 'Free' or 'full' convertibility means that all exchange controls are removed: anyone can exchange the domestic currency for foreign currency anywhere in 'the market'. 'Official' and 'market' exchange rates are in this context the same.

4. Strange, *Sterling*, pp. 56–7.
5. See note 3 above for a definition of this term.
6. Strange, *Sterling*, pp. 64–9.
7. *CMND 3834, Sterling. Exchange of Notes and Letters concerning the Guarantee by the ... United Kingdom and the Maintenance of the Minimum Sterling Proportion by certain Overseas Sterling Area Governments (the Sterling Area Agreements)* (25 Sept. 1968).

8. Strange, *Sterling*, *passim*.
9. See, for example, Andrew Shonfield, *British Economic Policy Since the War* (Harmondsworth: Penguin, 1958).
10. For a development of this theme, see Porter, *The Lion's Share*, *passim*.
11. E. A. Brett, *The World Economy Since the War* (London: Macmillan, 1985).
12. As in many areas of academic debate, there is, strictly, no *single* 'Marxist view' concerning the role of financial capital in the formation of British foreign economic policy. The characterisation provided here is a simplified (though, it is hoped, not a simplistic) amalgam of several works: Frank Longstreth, 'The City, Industry and the State', in Colin Crouch (ed.), *State and Economy in Contemporary Capitalism* (London: Croom Helm, 1979) pp. 157–90; Grahame Thompson, 'The relationship between the financial and industrial sector in the United Kingdom economy', *Economy and Society*, vol. 6, no. 3 (August 1977) pp. 235–83; and Geoffrey Ingham, *Capitalism Divided? The City and Industry in British Social Development* (London: Macmillan, 1984).
13. See for example, Bob Jessop, 'The transformation of the State in Post-War Britain' in R. Scase (ed.), *The State in Western Europe* (London: Croom Helm, 1980) pp. 23–93.
14. Ingham, *Capitalism Divided?*
15. Whether or not there was an explicit 'alliance' between financial capital and multinational industrial capital in this context remains a matter for debate. See, for example, the exchanges between Overbeek and Minns: Henk Overbeek, 'Financial Capital and the Crisis in Britain', *Capital and Class*, vol. 11 (1980) pp. 99–120; Richard Minns, 'A Comment on "Financial Capital and the Crisis in Britain"', *Capital and Class*, vol. 14 (1982) pp. 98–110.
16. Strange, *Sterling, passim*.
17. In Lukes's terms, while the Marxists take a three-dimensional, 'radical' view of power, Strange takes a one-dimensional, 'liberal' view. See Stephen Lukes, *Power: A Radical View* (London: Macmillan, 1975).
18. The government-sponsored Duncan Report used this phrase in 1969. See *CMND 4107, Report of the Review Committee on Overseas Representation 1968–9* (HMSO 1969).
19. Brett, *World Economy*, p. 157.
20. Susan Strange, *Casino Capitalism* (London: Basil Blackwell, 1986) p. 68.
21. This move – though costly to the world economy – was enormously beneficial to the United States. Although the dollar–gold link had been broken, most other countries continued to hold the bulk of their reserves in dollars, thus ensuring that the value of their currencies were still defined in dollar terms. This effectively gave the American government 'unlimited reserves of dollars' (Strange, p. 9): the dollar was the standard against which all other currencies were valued and yet the United States government was free to determine how many dollars it wished to print. The resultant dollar flood was largely responsible for the world-wide inflation crisis of the 1970s. The OPEC 'oil-shock', often blamed for the

downturn in the world economy after 1973, was merely a symptom of an inflation that had already begun, not a cause of it.

22. Floating exchange rates confer both costs and benefits on different national economies. The major cost is the *uncertainty* which floating rates engender for importers and exporters: an exporter may find that the price he receives for a particular commodity falls alarmingly if, for some exogenous reason, the value of his own currency rises. Similarly, an importer may find that the cost of a particular good rises alarmingly, purely as a consequence of an autonomous fall in the value of his own currency.

    The main benefit of floating exchange rates is that they reduce the need for reserves. Indeed freely floating rates obviate the need for reserves of any sort. With floating rates, if a country experiences a balance of payments deficit, its Central Bank does not need artificially to prop up the international value of its currency by drawing on its reserves of gold and foreign currency. It simply allows the value of the currency to fall. This makes exports cheaper (and therefore more are sold) and imports dearer (and therefore less are bought) and this brings the balance of payments back into equilibrium: floating exchange rates, in this sense, are self-equilibrating. The problem with this self-equilibration, however, is that most currency movements today are *not* trade-related. Instead, they reflect speculation about future movements in currency values. It is thus entirely possible (and quite common) for a currency to experience a serious decline even though its actual international trading position is extremely healthy. In these circumstances, remediable measures to redress the currency imbalance have to be taken, in spite of the undesirable consequences they might have for the (currently successful) domestic economic programme.

23. Strange, *Casino Capitalism*, p. 39.

24. Raising interest rates (in Britain, via the Bank of England's minimum lending rate) is another way of checking a declining currency. The rise in interest rates attracts short-term funds back into the currency, thereby raising its value. The problem is that raising interest rates also has domestic economic consequences (raising the cost of borrowing and therefore reducing both consumer demand and investment) which may damage the government's domestic economic strategy.

25. See, for example, Milton Friedman, *Prices of Money and Goods across Frontiers: the Pound and the Dollar over a Century* (London: Trade Policy Research Centre, 1980).

26. Ernest Mandel, *Late Capitalism* (London: New Left Books, 1975).

27. See, for example, C. Kindleberger, *The World in Depression 1929–1933* (London: Allen Lane, 1973); R. Gilpin, *US Power and the Multinational Corporation* (New York: Basic Books, 1975); Robert O. Keohane, *After Hegemony* (Cambridge, Mass.: Harvard University Press, 1984).

Chapter 8

1. *CMND 6743, Statement Relating to Defence* (Feb. 1946).
2. See D. C. Cumming, 'British Stewardship of the Italian Colonies', *International Affairs*, vol. 29, no. 1 (1953) pp. 11-21.
3. *CMND 9075, Statement on Defence, 1954* (HMSO, Feb. 1954); *CMND 9072, Memorandum of the Secretary of State for War relating to the Army Estimates 1954–55* (HMSO, Feb. 1954).
4. *CMND 265, South East Asia Collective Defence Treaty*, 8 Sept. 1954.
5. *CMND 9859, Pact of Mutual Co-operation between His Majesty the King of Iraq and the President of the Republic of Turkey* (Accessions: United Kingdom 5 April 1955; Pakistan 23 Sept. 1955; Iran 3 Nov. 1955).
6. *CMND 9520, Exchange of letters with the Government of the Union of South Africa on the transfer of the Simonstown Naval Base and arrangements for its future use* (30 June 1955).
7. *CMND 8476, Statement of the First Lord of the Admiralty explanatory of the Navy Estimates 1952–3* (HMSO, Feb. 1952); *CMND 2902, Statement on the Defence Estimates 1966 Part II The Defence Estimates 1966–7* (HMSO Feb. 1966). The detailed figures were as follows:

	1952		1965	
	active	*reserve*	*active*	*reserve*
carriers	5	—	4	1
battleships, cruisers, destroyers	43	88	20	15
frigates	36	110	56	14

8. *CMND 3540, Statement on the Defence Estimates 1968* (HMSO, Feb. 1968).
9. *CMND 1936, Statememt on Defence 1963* (including memoranda to accompany the Navy, Army and Air Estimates 1963–4) (HMSO, Feb. 1963) p. 15.
10. *CMND 2901, Statement on the Defence Estimates 1966, Part I, The Defence Review* (HMSO, Feb. 1966).
11. *CMND 4891, Statement on the Defence Estimate, 1972* (HMSO, March 1972).
12. *CMND 5976, Statement on the Defence Estimate, 1975* (HMSO, March 1975).
13. Ibid., p. 13.
14. See Chapter 5.
15. See, for example, Peter Riddell, *The Thatcher Government*, 2nd edn (Oxford: Basil Blackwell, 1985).
16. *CMND 8212–I, Statement on the Defence Estimate 1981* (HMSO, April 1981).
17. In the late 1980s these involved a continuing British presence (i) in Cyprus as part of UNICYP, the UN forces in Cyprus; (ii) in the dependencies of Belize, Hong Kong, Gibraltar and the Falkland Islands; (iii) in Oman and Brunei in support of the incumbent regimes.
18. *CMND 124, Defence: Outline of Future Policy* (HMSO, April 1957).

19. Sir John Slessor, 'The Place of the Bomber in British Policy', *International Affairs*, vol. 29, no. 3 (1953) p. 303.
20. Baylis, *Anglo-American Defence Relations*, p. 40.
21. The original members were: the United States, the United Kingdom, Canada, France, Belgium, the Netherlands, Luxembourg, Italy, Denmark, Norway, Iceland and Portugal.
22. *CMND 124; CMND 363, Report on Defence: Britain's contribution to Peace and Security* (HMSO, Feb. 1958).
23. The Western European Union (WEU) was intended to provide a forum in which the West European states could discuss their common political and security interests. However it rarely achieved the status of anything more than a sophisticated 'talking shop', in spite of efforts to revive its use, first, in 1967–8 (as an accompaniment to Britain's second attempt to join the EC) and subsequently, in the mid-1980s. At the time of writing it is too early to assess how successful this more recent venture has been. For review, see James Eberle, John Roper, William Wallace and Phil Williams, 'European Security Co-operation and British interests', *International Affairs*, vol. 60, no. 4 (1984) pp. 545–60.
24. *CMND 4290, Statement on the Defence Estimates 1970* (HMSO, Feb. 1970) p. 8.
25. Fred Halliday, *The Making of the Second Cold War* (London: Verso, 1983) pp. 75–80.
26. *CMND 7099, Statement on the Defence Estimates 1978* (HMSO, Feb. 1978) p. 10.
27. See, for example, *CMND 8212-I*, p. 5.
28. *Si vis pacem, para bellum. The Oxford Dictionary of Quotations* attributes this dictum to Vegetius (p. 556).
29. Alfred Goldberg, 'The Military Origins of the British Nuclear Deterrent', *International Affairs*, vol. 40, no. 4 (1964) pp. 601, 609.
30. Truscott, 'The Korean War' p. 14.
31. Ibid., p. 17.
32. Eden reports that he told the Cabinet in April 1956: 'I do not believe that the Russians have any plans at present for military aggression in the West'; Sir Anthony Eden, *The Memoirs of the Right Hon. Sir Anthony Eden: Full Circle* (London: Cassell, 1960) p. 363.
33. Defence Reviews were carried out in 1947 (reported in CMND 7327), 1953 (CMND 8768), 1956–7 (CMND 124), 1962 (CMND 1639), 1966 (CMND 2901), 1968 (CMND 3701), 1975 (CMND 5976) and 1981 (CMND 8288).
34. *CMND 6432, Statement on the Defence Estimates, 1976* (HMSO, March 1976).
35. John Garnett, 'BAOR and NATO', *International Affairs*, vol. 46, no. 4 (1970) pp. 673–4.
36. These alternative conventional strategies are briefly discussed in Ken Hunt, 'Comment on Williams and Booth', in John Roper (ed.), *The Future of British Defence Policy* (Aldershot: Gower, 1985) pp. 61–77.
37. Richard Gott, 'The evolution of the British Independent Deterrent', *International Affairs*, vol. 39, no. 2 (1963) pp. 238–9. For a comprehensive

review of Britain's nuclear strategy through to the mid-1970s, see A.J.R. Groom, *British Thinking about Nuclear Weapons* (London: Frances Pinter, 1974).

38. Goldberg, 'Military Origins', p. 610.
39. Gott, 'The evolution of the British Independent Deterrent', p. 243.
40. See N. J. Wheeler, 'British nuclear weapons and Anglo-American relations 1945–54', *International Affairs*, vol. 62, no. 1 (1986) pp. 83–4.
41. John Strachey, 'Is our deterrent vulnerable? A discussion of western defence in the 1960s', *International Affairs*, vol. 37, no. 1 (1961) pp. 1–8.
42. Baylis, *British Defence*, p. 182.
43. *CMND 8529–I*.
44. Baylis, *British Defence*, pp. 68–9.
45. See, for example, Julian Amory's speech in the Commons on 28 May 1956, cited in Gott, 'The evolution of the British Independent Deterrent', p. 242.
46. *CMND 8951–I, Statement on the Defence Estimates 1983 (Vol. 1)* (HMSO, Feb. 1983) p. 6.
47. 'Overstretch' had been a central theme of Denis Healey's 1966 Defence Review (*CMND 2901*), moving Healey to observe that 'Defence must be the servant of foreign policy, not its master' (p. 4). It was not until the 1977 White Paper, however, (*CMND 6735, Statement on the Defence Estimates, 1977*) (HMSO, Feb. 1977) that the Government published cross nationally comparable figures:

Defence expenditure on a percentage of GDP (1976)

Greece	6.5	France	3.9	Denmark	2.6
US	5.9	FRG	3.2	Italy	2.6
UK	5.1	Netherlands	3.3	Canada	2.0
Portugal	4.2	Belgium	3.1		
Turkey	3.9	Norway	3.0		

48. *CMND 4891, Statement on the Defence Estimates 1972* (HMSO, Feb. 1972).
49. *CMND 7474, Statement on the Defence Estimates 1979* (HMSO, Feb. 1979).
50. See, for example, *CMND 7826–I, Defence in the 1980s: Statement on the Defence Estimates 1980 vol. 1* (HMSO: April 1980) pp. 5–6.
51. *CMND 8212–I*, p. 15.
52. David Hencke, 'Secret MoD report urges radical reforms for weapons contracts', *Guardian*, 13 March 1988, p. 2.
53. British governments began to boast officially about the export performance of the domestic arms industry in the mid-1970s. The 1976 *Statement on the Defence Estimates (CMND 6432)*, for example, noted that overseas *defence* sales for 1976/7 were estimated to be £700m (p. 59). By 1983 (*CMND 8951–I*), the figure had increased to £2400m; by 1987 to £3500m (*CMND 344–I Statement on the Defence Estimates 1988 Vol. I*, p. 43).
54. The government was assisted, however, by the continuous growth of the economy as a whole from the mid-1980s onwards. Although defence costs continued to increase, they did not grow as fast as the economy. This meant that, in the late 1980s, defence expenditure as a percentage of GDP

actually fell to 4.7 per cent in 1986/7. See *CMND 9763–I, Statement on the Defence Estimates 1986* (HMSO, Feb. 1987).

55. Richard Nixon, *Real Peace* (Boston: Little Brown, 1984).
56. Halliday, *The Making of the Second Cold War*, pp. 56–77.

Chapter 9

1. Thucydides, *The History of the Peloponnesian War* (translated by R. Crawley) (London: Everyman's Library, 1952); Niccolo Machiavelli, *The Prince* (translated by G. Bull) (Hardmondsworth: Penguin, 1961); Thomas Hobbes, *Leviathan* (Harmondsworth: Pelican, 1968). For a recent summary statement of the Power Politics approach, see Martin Wight, *Power Politics*, 2nd edn (Harmondsworth: Penguin, 1986).
2. Kenneth Waltz, *Theory of International Politics* (Reading, Mass.: Addison–Wesley, 1979).
3. See, for example, Hedley Bull, 'Society and Anarchy in International Relations', in Herbert Butterfield and Martin Wight (eds), *Diplomatic Investigations: Essays on the theory of international politics* (London: George Allen & Unwin, 1966) pp. 35–50.
4. On the notion of 'security complex', see Barry Buzan, *People, States and Fear: the National Security Problem in International Relations* (Brighton: Wheatsheaf Books, 1983).
5. A 'definitive' list of 'Realist propositions' would be difficult to provide. The propositions summarised here are a revised and extended version of those developed in Trevor Taylor, 'Power Politics' in Trevor Taylor (ed.), *Approaches and Theory in International Relations* (London: Longman, 1978) pp. 122–40.
6. See, for example, Hedley Bull, *The Anarchical Society: A Study of Order in World Politics* (London: Macmillan, 1977).
7. See Norwood Russell Hanson, *Patterns of Discovery* (Cambridge: Cambridge University Press, 1958).
8. On the general relationship betwen theory and evidence, see A. F. Chalmers, *What is this thing called Science?*, 2nd edn (Milton Keynes: Open University Press, 1986); note, however, that Chalmers's references to philosophical 'Realism' do not refer to the 'Realism' discussed here.
9. See Imre Lakatos, 'Falsification and the Methodology of Scientific Research Programmes', in Imre Lakatos and Alan E. Musgrave (eds), *Criticism and the Growth of Knowledge* (Cambridge: Cambridge University Press, 1974) pp. 132–5.
10. The most impressive applications of the Rational Actor model have undoubtedly been undertaken in the field of Game Theory. For a wide-ranging application see Glenn H. Snyder and P. Diesing, *Conflict Among Nations: Bargaining, Decisionmaking and System Structure in International Crises* (Princeton NJ: Princeton University Press, 1977).
11. The best known study using the Bureaucratic Politics approach is probably Graham T. Allison, *The Essence of Decision* (Boston: Little, Brown, 1971).

12. Lawrence Freedman, 'Logic, Politics and Foreign Policy Processes: a critique of the Bureaucratic Politics model', *International Affairs*, vol. 52, no. 3 (1976) pp. 434–49.

13. The only exceptions to this general pattern were during the Korean War rearmament programme of the early 1950s (when defence expenditure rose as high as 11 per cent of GDP) and during the late 1980s (when a sustained rise in GDP enabled relative defence expenditure to fall to 4.5 per cent of GDP). See Peter Byrd, 'Defence Policy', in Peter Byrd (ed.), *British Foreign Policy Under Thatcher* (Oxford: Philip Allan, 1988) p. 171.

14. V. I. Lenin, *Imperialism, the Highest Stage of Capitalism*, 13th edn (Moscow: Progress Publishers, 1966).

15. This theme is developed in P. A. Baran and Paul M. Sweezy, *Monopoly Capital* (New York: Monthly Review Press, 1966).

16. This theme has been extensively developed in the writings of Gunder Frank. See, for example, Andre Gunder Frank, *Capitalism and Underdevelopment in Latin America* (Harmondsworth: Penguin, 1971); *Crisis: in the Third World* (London: Heinemann, 1981). On the development of capitalism as a global system, see Immanuel Wallerstein, *The Capitalist World Economy* (Cambridge: Cambridge University Press, 1979).

17. A. Emmanuel, *Unequal Exchange: a Study in the Imperialism of Trade* (London: New Left Books, 1972).

18. See, for example, C. R. Hensman, *Rich Against Poor: The Reality of Aid* (London: Allen, Lane, 1971); Teresa Hayter, *Aid as Imperialism* (Harmondsworth: Penguin, 1971).

19. See, for example, UNCTAD, 'Restructuring the international economic framework. Report by the Secretary-General of UNCTAD to the fifth session of the Conference' (Geneva: UNCTAD TD/221, 1979); W. Brandt *et al. North-South: A Programme for Survival*.

20. See, for example, Ingham, *Capitalism Divided*.

21. Frank Longstreth, 'The City, Industry and the State', in Colin Crouch (ed.), *State and Economy in Contemporary Capitalism* (London: Croom Helm, 1979) pp. 160–1; Bob Jessop, 'The Transformation of the State in Post-War Britain', in R. Scase (ed.), *The State in Western Europe* (London: Croom Helm, 1980) pp. 30–8.

22. See Strange, *Sterling and British Policy*, pp. 212.

23. For a sophisticated critique and re-interpretation of these issues, see Robert A. Stones, 'The Myth of Betrayal: Structure and Agency in the Labour Government's Policy on non-devaluation 1964–67', PhD dissertation, University of Essex, 1988.

24. Classical Idealism was a powerful influence upon international organisation during the interwar period. For review, see David Sanders, *Lawmaking and Co-operation in International Politics: The Idealist case re-examined* (London: Macmillan 1986).

25. See, for example, John W. Burton, *World Society* (Cambridge: Cambridge University Press, 1972); John W. Burton, *Global Conflict: The Domestic Sources of International Crisis* (Brighton: Wheatsheaf Books, 1984); Edward Azar (ed.), *The Theory and Practice of Conflict Resolution* (Brighton: Wheatsheaf Books, 1985).

Chapter 10

1. For a highly readable statement of this position, see John Burton *et al.*, *Britain Between East and West: A Concerned Independence* (Aldershot: Gower, 1984).

Bibliography

Acheson, Dean, *Present at the Creation: My Years in the State Department* (New York: Norton, 1987).

Adamthwaite, A. P., *The Making of the Second World War* (London: George Allen & Unwin, 1977).

Allison, Graham T., *Essence of Decision: Explaining the Cuban Missile Crisis* (Boston, Mass.: Little, Brown, 1971).

Almond, Gabriel and Sidney Verba, *The Civic Culture* (Boston, Mass.: Little, Brown, 1965).

Alt, James E. and K. Alec Chrystal, *Political Economics* (Brighton: Wheatsheaf Books, 1983).

Amery, Leopold, *My Political Life (Volume 1): England Before the Storm, 1896–1914* (London: Hutchinson, 1953).

Azar, Edward (ed.), *The Theory and Practice of Conflict Resolution* (Brighton: Wheatsheaf Books, 1985).

Baran, P. A. and Paul M. Sweezy, *Monopoly Capital* (New York: Monthly Review Press, 1966).

Barker, Elisabeth, *Churchill and Eden at War* (London: Macmillan, 1978).

Barnet, Corelli, *The Audit of War: the Illusion and Reality of Britain as a Great Nation* (London: Macmillan, 1986).

Bartlett, C. J., *The Global Conflict: the international rivalry of the great powers, 1880–1970* (London: Longmans, 1984).

Baylis, John, *Anglo-American Defence Relations, 1939–1984*, 2nd edn (London: Macmillan, 1984).

Baylis, John, 'Britain, the Brussels Pact and the continental commitment', *International Affairs*, vol. 60, no. 4 (1984) pp. 615–30.

Beck, Peter J, 'A tedious and perilous controversy: Britain and the Settlement of the Mosul dispute, 1918–1926', *Middle East Studies*, vol. 17, no. 2 (1981) pp. 256–76.

Beenstock, Michael, *The World Economy in Transition* (London: George Allen & Unwin, 1983).

Beloff, Max, 'Some aspects of Anglo-Soviet Relations', *International Affairs*, vol. 21, no. 2 (1945) pp. 168–79.

Beloff, Max, 'The Special Relationship: an Anglo-American myth', in Martin Gilbert (ed.), *A Century of Conflict 1850–1950: Essays for A. J. P. Taylor* (London: Hamish Hamilton, 1966) pp. 151–71.

Brandt, W., *et al.*, *North–South: A Programme for Survival* (The Brandt Report) (London: Pan Books, 1980).

Brett, E. A., *The World Economy Since the War* (London: Macmillan, 1985).

Buchan, Alistair, 'Britain and the Indian Ocean', *International Affairs*, vol. 42, no. 2 (1966) pp. 184–93.

Bull, Hedley, 'Society and Anarchy in International Relations', in Herbert Butterfield and Martin Wight (eds), *Diplomatic Investigations: Essays on the Theory of International Politics* (London: George Allen & Unwin, 1966) pp. 35–50.

Bull, Hedley, *The Anarchical Society: A Study of Order in World Politics* (London: Macmillan, 1977).

Burton, John W., *World Society* (Cambridge: Cambridge University Press, 1972).

Burton, John W., *Global Conflict: The Domestic Sources of International Crisis* (Brighton: Wheatsheaf Books, 1984).

Burton, John et al., *Britain Between East and West: A Concerned Independence* (Aldershot: Gower 1984).

Buzan, Barry, *People, States and Fear: the National Security Problem in International Relations* (Brighton: Wheatsheaf Books, 1983).

Byrd, Peter, 'Defence Policy', in Peter Byrd (ed.), *British Foreign Policy Under Thatcher* (Oxford: Philip Allan, 1988) pp. 157–79.

Calvocoressi, Peter, *World Politics since 1945, Fourth Edition* (London: Longman, 1982).

Campbell, Alan, 'Anglo-French relations a decade ago: a new assessment (1)', *International Affairs*, vol. 58, no. 2 (1982) pp. 237–53.

Carr, E. H., *The Twenty Years' Crisis 1919–1939* (London: Macmillan, 1946).

Carrington, C. E., 'A New Theory of the Commonwealth', *International Affairs*, vol. 31, no. 2 (1955) pp. 137–48.

Carrington, C. E., 'Between the Commonwealth and Europe', *International Afairs*, vol. 38, no. 2 (1962) pp. 449–55.

Chalmers, A. F., *What is this thing called Science?*, 2nd edn (Milton Keynes: Open University Press, 1986).

Clarke, Michael, 'American reactions to shifts in European Policy: the changing context', in John Roper (ed.), *The Future of British Defence Policy* (Aldershot: Gower, 1985) pp. 83–4.

Clarke, Michael, 'The Policy-Making Process', in Michael Smith, Steve Smith and Brian White (eds), *British Foreign Policy: Tradition, Change and Transformation* (London: Unwin Hyman, 1988) pp. 71–96.

Coates, David and John Hillard (eds), *The Economic Decline of Modern Britain: The Debate Between Left and Right* (Brighton: Wheatsheaf, 1986).

Colville, John, *The Fringes of Power: Downing Street Diaries 1939–1955* (London: Hodder & Stoughton, 1985).

Coombes, David, *Politics and Bureaucracy in the European Community: A Portrait of the Commission of the EEC* (London: George Allen & Unwin, 1970).

Cumming, D. C., 'British Stewardship of the Italian Colonies', *International Affairs*, vol. 29, no. 1 (1953) pp. 11–21.

Cunningham, Sir Alan, 'Palestine: the last days of the Mandate', *International Affairs*, vol. 24, no. 4 (1948) pp. 481–90.

Darwin, John, 'Imperialism in decline? Tendencies in British Imperial Policy between the Wars', *Historical Journal* vol. 23, no. 3 (1980) pp. 657–79.

Deutsch, Karl, 'Social Mobilisation and Political Development', *American Political Science Review*, vol. 55 (1961) pp. 494–512.

328   *Bibliography*

Dilks David (ed.), *The Diaries of Sir Alexander Cadogan 1938–45* (London: Cassell, 1971).
Dilks, David, (ed.), *Retreat From Power: Studies in Britain's Foreign Policy of the Twentieth Century (2 Volumes)* (London: Macmillan, 1981).
Dockrill, M. L., 'The Foreign Office, Anglo-American relations and the Korean War, June 1950–June 1951', *International Affairs*, vol. 62, no. 3 (1986) pp. 459–78.
Eberle, James, John Roper, William Wallace and Phil Williams, 'European Security Co-operation and British Interests', *International Affairs*, vol. 60, no. 4 (1984) pp. 545–60.
Eberle, Admiral Sir James, 'The Military Relationship', in William Roger Louis and Hedley Bull (eds), *The Special Relationship: Anglo-American Relations Since 1945* (Oxford: Clarendon Press, 1986) pp. 151–60.
Eden, Sir Anthony, *The Memoirs of the Right Hon. Sir Anthony Eden: Full Circle* (London: Cassell, 1960).
Edwards, Geoffrey, 'Europe and the Falkland Islands crisis 1982', *Journal of Common Market Studies*, vol. 22, no. 4 (1984) pp. 295–313.
Emmanuel, A., *Unequal Exchange: a Study in the Imperialism of Trade* (London: New Left Books, 1972).
Fisher, H. A. L., *A History of Europe, Volume II: From the Early Eighteenth Century to 1935* (London: Fontana, 1975).
Frank, Andre Gunder, *Capitalism and Underdevelopment in Latin America* (Harmondsworth: Penguin, 1971).
Frank, Andre Gunder, *Crisis: In the Third World* (London: Heinemann, 1981).
Frankel, Joseph, *British Foreign Policy 1945–1973* (London: Oxford University Press, 1975).
Frankel, Joseph, 'Conventional and theorising diplomats: a critique', *International Affairs*, vol. 57, no. 3 (1981) p. 544.
Freedman, Lawrence, 'Logic, Politics and Foreign Policy Processes: a critique of the Bureaucratic Politics model', *International Affairs* vol. 52, no. 3 (1976) pp. 434–49.
Friedman, Milton, *Prices of Money and Goods across Frontiers: the Pound and the Dollar over a Century* (London: Trade Policy Research Centre, 1980).
Gamble, Andrew, *Britain in Decline: Economic Policy, Political Strategy and the British State* (London: Macmillan, 1985).
Garnett, John, 'BAOR and NATO', *International Affairs*, vol. 46, no. 4 (1970) pp. 670–7.
Giddens, Anthony, *Central Problems in Social Theory: Action, Structure and Contradiction in Social Analysis* (London: Macmillan, 1979).
Gilpin, R., *US Power and the Multinational Corporation* (New York: Basic Books, 1975).
Gladwyn, Lord, 'Western Europe's Collective Defence', *International Affairs*, vol. 51, no. 2 (1975) pp. 166–74.
Goldberg, Alfred, 'The Military Origins of the British Nuclear Deterrent', *International Affairs*, vol. 40, no. 4 (1964) pp. 600–18.
Gott, Richard, 'The evolution of the British Independent Deterrent', *International Affairs*, vol. 39, no. 2 (1963) pp. 238–52.

Gowing, Margaret, 'Britain, America and the Bomb', in Dilks (ed.), *Retreat from Power*, vol. 2, 1981, pp. 120–37.

Greenidge, C. W., 'The present outlook in the British West Indies', *International Affairs*, vol. 25, no. 2 (1949) pp. 175–81.

Groom, A. J. R., *British Thinking about Nuclear Weapons* (London: Frances Pinter, 1974).

Haas, Ernst B., *The Uniting of Europe* (London: Oxford University Press, 1958).

Halliday, Fred, *The Making of the Second Cold War* (London: Verso, 1983) pp. 75–80.

Hanson, Norwood Russell, *Patterns of Discovery* (Cambridge: Cambridge University Press, 1958).

Hart, Liddell, *The Defence of Britain* (London: Faber & Faber, 1939).

Hayter, Teresa, *Aid as Imperialism* (Harmondsworth: Penguin, 1971).

Head, A. H., 'European Defence', *International Affairs*, vol. 27, no. 1 (1951) pp. 1–9.

Hearn, Sir Arthur, 'Oil and the Middle East', *International Affairs*, vol. 24, no. 1 (1948) pp. 63–75.

Henderson, N., 'Britain's Decline: its Causes and Consequences', *Economist* (2 July 1979).

Henig, Ruth B. (ed.), *The League of Nations* (Edinburgh: Oliver and Boyd, 1973).

Hensman, C. R., *Rich Against Poor: The Reality of Aid* (London: Allen Lane, 1971).

Hobbes, Thomas, *Leviathan* (Harmondsworth: Pelican, 1968).

Home, Earl of, 'Interdependence: the British role', *International Affairs* vol. 37, no. 2 (1961) pp. 154–60.

Horne, Alistair, 'The Macmillian Years and Afterwards', in Wm Roger Louis and Hedley Bull (eds) *The Special Relationship: Anglo-American Relations since 1945* (Oxford: Clarendon Press, 1986) pp. 87–102.

Howard, Anthony, *RAB: The Life of R. A. Butler* (London: Jonathan Cape, 1987).

Howard, Michael, 'Britain's Strategic Problem East of Suez', *International Affairs*, vol. 42, no. 2 (1966) pp. 179–83.

Howard, Michael, *The Mediterranean Strategy in the Second World War* (London: Weidenfeld & Nicolson, 1968).

Howard, Michael, *The Continental Commitment: the Dilemma of British Defence Policy in the Era of Two World Wars* (Harmondsworth: Penguin, 1974).

Howard, Michael, 'Afterword: the "Special Relationship"', in Wm. Roger Louis and Hedley Bull (eds), *The Special Relationship: Anglo-American Relations since 1945* (Oxford: Clarendon Press, 1986) pp. 387–92.

Howard, Michael, 'British Military Preparations for the Second World War' in Dilks (ed.), *Retreat from Power*, 1981, vol. 2, pp. 102–118.

Hunt, Ken, 'Comment on Williams and Booth', in John Roper (ed.), *The Future of British Defence Policy* (Aldershot: Gower, 1985) pp. 61–77.

Huntington, Samuel P., *Political Order in Changing Societies* (New Haven: Yale University Press, 1968).

Hurd, Douglas, 'Prospects for Europe: Political Co-operation', *International Affairs*, vol. 57, no. 3 (1981) pp. 383–93.

Ingham, Geoffrey, *Capitalism Divided? The City and Industry in British Social Development* (London: Macmillan, 1984).

Jessop, Bob, 'The transformation of the State in Post-War Britain', in R. Scase (ed.), *The State in Western Europe* (London: Croom Helm, 1980) pp. 23–93.

Kajima, M., *The Emergence of Japan as a World Power 1895–1925* (Rutland, Vermont: Tuttle, 1978).

Kasliwal, R. R., 'The Foreign Policy of Turkey Since 1919', *Indian Journal of Political Science*, vol. 7 (1946) pp. 38–97.

Kimber, Jonathan, 'Dependence, Cooperation and the Lomé Convention: the cases of Mauritius, the Ivory Coast and Ghana' (PhD dissertation, University of Essex, 1983).

Kindleberger, C., *The World in Depression 1929–1933* (London: Allen Lane, 1973).

Kissinger, Henry, *Years of Upheaval* (Boston, Mass.: Little, Brown, 1982).

Krishan, Y., 'Mountbatten and the Partition of India', *History*, vol. 68, no. 1 (1983) pp. 22–37.

Kuyacek, H., 'Anglo-Turkish economic relations', *South Asian Review*, vol. 37 (1941) pp. 91–100.

Lakatos, Imre, 'Falsification and the Methodology of Scientific Research Programmes', in Imre Lakatos and Alan E. Musgrave (eds), *Criticism and the Growth of Knowledge* (Cambridge: Cambridge University Press, 1974) pp. 132–5.

Lane, Jan-Erik and Svante O. Ersson, *Politics and Society in Western Europe* (London: Sage, 1987).

Lauterpacht, Hersch, *The Function of Law in the International Community* (London: Oxford University Press: 1933).

Lenin, V. I., *Imperialism, the Highest Stage of Capitalism*, 13th edn (Moscow: Progress Publishers, 1966).

Lindberg, Leon, *Political Dynamics of European Economic Integration* (London: Oxford University Press, 1963).

Longstreth, Frank, 'The City, Industry and the State', in Colin Crouch (ed.), *State and Economy in Contemporary Capitalism* (London: Croom Helm, 1979) pp. 157–90.

Louis, William Roger, *Imperialism at Bay: the United States and the Decolonisation of the British Empire, 1941–1945* (London: Oxford University Press, 1977).

Louis, William Roger, 'American anti-colonialism and the dissolution of the British Empire', *International Affairs*, vol. 61, no. 3 (1985) pp. 395–420.

Luard, Evan, 'A European Foreign Policy?', *International Affairs*, vol. 62, no. 4 (1986) pp. 575–82.

Lukes, Stephen, *Power: A Radical View* (London: Macmillan, 1975).

Lynn, Jonathan and Anthony Jay, *Yes, Prime Minister: the Diaries of the Right Hon. James Hacker, Volume II* (London: BBC Books, 1987).

Machiavelli, Niccolo, *The Prince* (translated by G. Bull) (Hardmondsworth: Penguin, 1961).

McGrew, Tony, 'Security and Order: the Military Dimension', in Michael

Smith, Steve Smith and Brian White (eds), *British Foreign Policy: Tradition, Change and Transformation* (London: Unwin Hyman, 1988) p. 107.

Mackintosh, John P., 'Britain in Europe: historical perspective and contemporary reality', *International Affairs*, vol. 45, no. 2 (1969) pp. 246–58.

Macmillan, Harold, *Riding the Storm, 1956–1959* (London: Macmillan, 1971).

McNeill, William Hardy, *Survey of International Affairs 1939–1946: America, Britain and Russia, their Co-operation and Conflict 1941–1946* (London: Oxford University Press, for the Royal Institute of International Affairs, 1953).

McSherry, J. E., *Stalin, Hitler and Europe, 1933–41 (Vol. 2)* (New York: World Publishing Co., 1970).

Mandel, Ernest, *Late Capitalism* (London: New Left Books, 1975).

Mansberg, Nicholas, 'Britain, the Commonwealth and the Western Union', *International Affairs*, vol. 24, no. 4 (1948) pp. 491–504.

May, Ernest R. and Gregory F. Treverton, 'Defence Relationships: American Perspectives', in Louis and Bull (eds), *The Special Relationship* pp. 161–84.

Mayhew, Christopher, 'British Foreign Policy Since 1945', *International Affairs*, vol. 26, no. 4 (1950) pp. 477–86.

Medlicott, Norton, 'The Hoare–Laval Pact Reconsidered', in David Dilks (ed.), *Retreat from Power: Studies in Britain's Foreign Policy of the Twentieth Century, Volume 1, 1906–1939* (London: Macmillan, 1981) pp. 118–38.

Medlicott, Norton, 'Britain and Germany: the Search for Agreement 1930–37', in Dilks (ed.), *Retreat from Power, Volume 1*, pp. 78–101.

Minns, Richard, 'A Comment on "Finance Capital and the Crisis in Britain"', *Capital and Class*, vol. 14 (1982) pp. 98–110.

Monroe, Elisabeth, 'British bases in the Middle East – assets or liabilities?', *International Affairs*, vol. 42, no. 1 (1966) pp. 24–34.

Nixon, Richard, *Real Peace* (Boston: Little, Brown, 1984).

Northedge, F. S., 'Britain as a Second-rank Power', *International Affairs*, vol. 46, no. 1 (1970) pp. 37–47.

Northedge, F. S., *Descent From Power: British Foreign Policy 1945–1973* (London: George Allen & Unwin, 1974).

Nye, J. S., *Peace in Parts: Integration and Conflict in Regional Organisation* (Boston: Little, Brown, 1971).

Olson, Mancur, *The Rise and Decline of Nations: Economic Growth, Stagflation and Social Rigidities* (Cambridge Mass.; Harvard University Press, 1982).

Olson, Robert W. and Nurham Ince, 'Turkish Foreign Policy from 1923–1960: Kemalism and its legacy, a review and critique', *Oriento Moderno*, vol. 57 (1977) pp. 227–41.

Ovendale, Ritchie, 'The Palestine Policy of the British Labour Government 1945–1946', *International Affairs*, vol. 55, no. 3 (1979) pp. 409–31.

Ovendale, Ritchie, 'The Palestine Policy of the British Labour Government, 1947: the decision to withdraw', *International Affairs*, vol. 56, no. 1 (1980) pp. 73–93.

Overbeek, Henk, 'Financial Capital and the Crisis in Britain', *Capital and Class*, vol. II (1980) pp. 99–120.

Owen, David, *Personally Speaking to Kenneth Harris* (London: Weidenfeld & Nicolson, 1987).

Owen, Roger and Bob Sutcliffe (eds), *Studies in the Theory of Imperialism* (London: Longmans, 1972).

Perkins, Bradford, 'Unequal Partners: The Truman Administration and Great Britain', in William Roger Louis and Hedley Bull (eds), *The Special Relationship: Anglo-American Relations Since 1945* (Oxford: Clarendon Press, 1986), pp. 43–65.

Perkins, Bradford, *The Great Rapprochement: England and the US, 1895–1914* (London: Victor Gollancz, 1969).

Pierre, Andrew, *Nuclear Politics: The British Experience with an Independent Strategic Force, 1939–70* (London: Oxford University Press, 1972) p. 144.

Porter, Bernard, *The Lion's Share: A Short History of British Imperialism*, 2nd edn (London: Longmans, 1984).

Reynolds, David, 'A "special relationship"? America, Britain and the international order since the Second World War', *International Affairs*, vol. 62, no. 1 (1986) pp. 1–20.

Riddell, Peter, *The Thatcher Government*, 2nd edn (Oxford: Basil Blackwell, 1985).

Rotberg, R. I. and Ali Mazrui (eds), *Protest and Power and Black Africa* (New York: Oxford University Press, 1970).

Rothwell, V. H., *British War Aims and Peace Diplomacy 1914–1958* (Oxford: Clarendon Press, 1971).

Sanders, David, *Lawmaking and Co-operation in International Politics: the Idealist Case Re-examined* (London: Macmillan, 1986).

Sanders, David, Hugh Ward and David Marsh, 'Government Popularity and the Falklands War: a reassessment', *British Journal of Political Science*, vol. 17, no. 2 (1987) pp. 281–313.

Scruton, Roger, *The Meaning of Conservatism*, 2nd edn (London: Macmillan, 1984).

Scruton, Roger, *Thinkers of the New Left* (Harlow: Longman, 1985).

Shonfield, Andrew, *British Economic Policy Since the War* (Harmondsworth: Penguin, 1958).

Silcock, T. H., 'Policy for Malaya, 1952', *International Affairs*, vol. 28, no. 4 (1952) pp. 445–51.

Slessor, Sir John, 'The Place of the Bomber in British Policy', *International Affairs*, vol. 29, no. 3 (1953) pp. 302–8.

Snyder, Glenn H. and P. Diesing, *Conflict Among Nations: Bargaining, Decisionmaking and System Structure in International Crises* (Princeton NJ: Princeton University Press, 1977).

Spinelli, Altiero, *The Eurocrats, Conflict and Crisis in the EEC* (trans. C. Grove Haines) (Baltimore: Johns Hopkins Press, 1966).

Spry, Graham, 'Canada, the Emergency Force and the Commonwealth', *International Affairs*, vol. 33, no. 3 (1957) pp. 289–300.

Stones, Robert A., 'The Myth of Betrayal: Structure and Agency in the Labour Government's Policy on non-devaluation 1964–67' (PhD Dissertation, University of Essex, 1988).

Strachey, John, 'Is our deterrent vulnerable? A discussion of western defence in the 1960s', *International Affairs*, vol. 37, no. 1 (1961) pp. 1–8.

Strange, Susan, *Sterling and British Policy* (London: Oxford University Press, 1971).

Strange, Susan, *Casino Capitalism* (London: Basil Blackwell, 1986).

Swanwick, H. M., *Collective Insecurity* (London: Jonathan Cape, 1937).

Talbot, I. A., 'Mountbatten and the Partition of India: A Rejoinder', *History*, vol. 69, no. 1 (1984) pp. 29–35.

Taylor, Charles Lewis and Michael C. Hudson, *World Handbook of Social and Political Indicators*, 2nd edn (New Haven: Yale University Press, 1972).

Taylor, Philip, 'Publicity and Diplomacy: the impact of the First World War upon Foreign Office attitudes towards the Press', in David Dilks (ed.), *Retreat from Power: Studies in Britain's Foreign Policy of the Twentieth Century, Volume 1, 1906–1939* (London: Macmillan, 1981) pp. 42–63.

Taylor, Trevor, 'Power Politics', in Trevor Taylor (ed.), *Approaches and Theory in International Relations* (London: Longman, 1978) pp. 122–40.

Thompson, Grahame, 'The relationship between the financial and industrial sector in the United Kingdom Economy', *Economy and Society*, vol. 6, no. 3 (August 1977) pp. 235–83.

Thompson, J. M., *Russia, Bolshevism and the Versailles Peace* (Princeton N. J.: Princeton University Press, 1966).

Thomson, David, 'General De Gaulle and the Anglo Saxons', *International Affairs*, vol. 41, no. 1 (1965) pp. 11–21.

Thorne, Christopher, *Allies of a Kind: the United States, Britain and the War Against Japan, 1941–42* (London: Hamish Hamilton, 1978).

Thucydides, *The History of the Peloponnesian War* (translated by R. Crawley) (London: Everyman's Library, 1952).

Toynbee, Arnold, 'A Turning Point in the Cold War?', *International Affairs*, vol. 26, no. 4 (1950) pp. 457–62.

Truscott, Peter, 'The Korean War in British Foreign and Domestic Policy, 1950–52' (PhD dissertation, Exeter College, Oxford, 1984).

United Nations Statistical Pocket Book/Second Edition, World Statistics in Brief (New York: United Nations, 1977).

Unwin, Peter, 'British Foreign Policy Opportunities Part I – the Global Context', *International Affairs*, vol. 57, no. 2 (1981) pp. 394–408.

Wallace, Helen, 'The British Presidency of the European Community's Council of Ministers: the opportunity to persuade', *International Affairs*, vol. 64, no. 4 (1986) pp. 583–99.

Wallace, William, *The Foreign Policy Process in Britain* (London: Royal Institute of International Affairs, 1976).

Wallerstein, Immanuel, *The Capitalist World Economy* (Cambridge: Cambridge University Press, 1979).

Walters, F. P., *A History of the League of Nations* (London: Oxford University Press, 1960).

Waltz, Kenneth, *Theory of International Politics* (Reading, Mass: Addison-Wesley, 1979).

Warner, Geoffrey, 'The Truman Doctrine and the Marshall Plan', *International Affairs*, vol. 50, no. 1 (1974) pp. 82–92.

Warner, Geoffrey, '"Collusion" and the Suez crisis of 1956', *International Affairs*, vol. 55, no. 2 (1979) pp. 226–39.

Warriner, Doreen, 'Land Reform in Egypt and its repercussions', *International Affairs*, vol. 29, no. 1 (1953) pp. 1–10.

Watt, David, 'Introduction: The Anglo-American Relationship' in Wm. Roger

Louis and Hedley Bull (eds), *The Special Relationship: Anglo-American Relations since 1945* (Oxford: Clarendon Press, 1986) pp. 1–14.

Webster, Sir Charles, 'Munich Reconsidered: A Survey of British Policy', *International Affairs*, vol. 37, no. 2 (1961) pp. 137–53.

Wheeler, N. J., 'British nuclear weapons and Anglo-American relations 1945–54', *International Affairs*, vol. 62, no. 1 (1986) pp. 71–84.

Whyte, Anne, 'Quadripartite Rule in Berlin', *International Affairs*, vol. 23, no. 1 (1947) pp. 30–41.

Wight, Martin, 'Brutus in Foreign Policy: the memoirs of Sir Anthony Eden', *International Affairs*, vol. 36, no. 3 (1960) pp. 299–309.

Willetts, Peter, *The Non-Aligned Movement: The Origins of a Third World Alliance* (London: Frances Pinter, 1978).

Wilson, Keith, 'British Power in the European Balance 1906–14', in David Dilks (ed.), *Retreat from Power Vol. 2.* (1981) pp. 21–41.

Woodward, E. L., *British Foreign Policy in the Second World War (5 vols)* (London: HMSO, 1970–6).

Wright, Quincy, *A Study of War*, vol. ii (Chicago: Chicago University Press, 1942).

Wright, W. L., 'Truths about Turkey', *Foreign Affairs*, vol. 26 (1948) pp. 349–59.

Younger, Kenneth, 'Public Opinion and British Foreign Policy', *International Affairs*, vol. 40, nol. 1 (1964) pp. 22–33.

HMSO (Command) publications

CMND 6707 Statistical Materials Presented During the Washington Negotiations (1945).

CMND 6743 Statement Relating to Defence (Feb. 1946).

CMND 7327 Statement Relating to Defence (Feb. 1948).

CMND 8146 Defence Programme Statement Made by the Prime Minister in the House of Commons, January 29th 1951.

CMND 8476 Statement of the First Lord of the Admiralty explanatory of the Navy Estimates 1952–3 (Feb. 1952).

CMND 9075 Statement on Defence, 1954 (Feb. 1954).

CMND 9072 Memorandum of the Secretary of State for War relating to the Army Estimates 1954–55 (Feb. 1954).

CMND 265 South East Asia Collective Defence Treaty, 8 Sept. 1954).

CMND 13 Agreement concerning the Relations between the United Kingdom and the European Coal and Steel Community (21 Dec. 1954).

CMND 9859 Pact of Mutual Co-operation between His Majesty the King of Iraq and the President of the Republic of Turkey (Accessions: UK 5 April 1955; Pakistan 23 Sept. 1955; Iran 3 Nov. 1955).

CMND 9520 Exchange of letters with the Government of the Union of South Africa on the transfer of the Simonstown Naval Base and arrangements for its future use (30 June 1955).

CMND 9842 Agreement between ... the United Kingdom and ... the Federal

Republic of Germany for Co-operation in the Peaceful Uses of Atomic Energy (31 July 1956).

CMND 150 Memorandum of the Secretary of State for War Relating to the Army Estimates 1957–8 (April 1957).

CMND 1313 [Three] *Exchanges of Notes between . . . the United Kingdom and . . . the Federal Republic of Germany concerning Local Defence Costs of UK forces stationed in the Federal Republic . . .* (7 June 1957).

CMND 124 Defence: Outline of Future Policy (April 1957).

CMND 458 Agreement between . . . the United Kingdom and the Government of the Italian Republic for Co-operation in the Peaceful Uses of Atomic Energy (28 Dec. 1957).

CMND 9688 Memorandum of the Secretary of State for War Relating to the Army Estimates 1956–57 (HMSO, Feb. 1958).

CMND 537 Agreement between the Government of the United Kingdom . . . and the government of the United States . . . for co-operation on the uses of atomic energy for mutual defence purposes (3 July 1958).

CMND 363 Report on Defence: Britain's contribution to Peace and Security (Feb. 1958).

CMND 1076 Five Year Trade Agreement between the Government of the United Kingdom and the Government of the Union of Soviet Socialist Republics (24 May 1959).

CMND 917 Agreement between the . . . United Kingdom and . . . the Union of Soviet Socialist Republics on relations in the Scientific, Technological, Educational and Cultural fields, 1960–61 (1 Dec. 1959).

CMND 1080 Exchange of Notes between the Government of the United Kingdom and the Government of the Kingdom of the Netherlands concerning the Arrangements to Facilitate Travel between the United Kingdom and the Netherlands (1 April 1960) *CMND 1157* (20 June 1960: as *CMND 1080* but refers to the Federal German Republic).

CMND 1357 Exchange of Notes between the . . . United Kingdom and . . . Luxembourg concerning the Acceptance of the British Visitors Passport for Travel between the UK and Luxembourg (21 Feb. 1961); *CMND 1354* (21 Feb. 1961: title as *CMND 1357* but refers to Belgium); *CMND 1355* (21 Feb. 1961: title as *CMND 1357* but refers to the Netherlands).

CMND 2108 Polaris. Sales Agreement between the Government of the United Kingdom . . . and the Government of the United States of America (4 June 1963).

CMND 1936 Statement on Defence 1963 (including memoranda to accompany the Navy, Army and Air Estimates 1963–64) (Feb. 1963).

CMND 2557 Protocol for the prolongation of the Five Year Trade Agreement between . . . the United Kingdom and . . . the Union of Soviet Socialist Republics (23 April 1964).

CMND 2592 Statement on the Defence Estimates 1965 (Feb. 1965).

CMND 2901 Statement on the Defence Estimates 1966 Part I: The Defence Review (Feb. 1966).

CMND 2902 Statement on the Defence Estimates 1966 Part II: Defence Estimates 1966–67 (Feb. 1966).

CMND 3540 Statement on the Defence Estimates 1968 (Feb. 1968)

CMND 3231 Exchange of Notes between the Government of the United Kingdom and the Government of the United States of America concerning the availability for defence purposes of the British Indian Ocean Territory (30 Dec. 1966).

CMND 3540 Statement on the Defence Estimates 1968 (Feb. 1968).

CMND 3701 Supplementary Statement on Defence Policy 1968 (July 1968).

CMND 3834 Sterling. Exchange of Notes and Letters concerning the Guarantee by the ... United Kingdom and the Maintenance of the Minimum Sterling Proportion by certain Overseas Sterling Area Governments (the Sterling Area Agreements) (25 Sept. 1968).

CMND 4107 Report of the Review Committee on Overseas Representation 1968–9 (1969).

CMND 4290 Statement on the Defence Estimates 1970 (Feb. 1970)

CMND 4705 Long-Term Economic and Trade Agreement between the Government of the United Kingdom ... and the Government of the Polish People's Republic (21 April 1971).

CMND 4890 Exchange of Notes between ... the United Kingdom ... and ... Malaysia regarding Assistance for the Malaysia Armed Forces and the Arrangements for a United Kingdom Force in Malaysia (1 Dec. 1971).

CMND 4891 Statement on the Defence Estimates 1972 (Feb. 1972).

CMND 5016 Long-Term Economic and Trade Agreement between the Government of the United Kingdom ... and the Government of the Hungarian People's Republic (21 March 1972).

CMND 5074 Long-Term Economic and Trade Agreement between the Government of the United Kingdom ... and the Government of ... Czechoslovakia (27 June 1972).

CMND 5106 Long-Term Economic and Trade Agreement between the Government of the United Kingdom ... and the Socialist Republic of Romania (15 June 1972).

CMND 5179 Treaty concerning the Accession of ... the United Kingdom ... to the European Economic Community and the European Atomic Energy Community including the Act concerning the conditions of Accession and the Adjustment to the Treaties ... (1 Jan. 1973).

CMND 5286 Long-Term Agreement on the Development of Economic, Industrial, Scientific and Technical Co-operation between the Government of the United Kingdom ... and the Government of the Polish People's Republic (20 March 1973); *CMND 5552 Agreement between the Government of the United Kingdom ... and the Government of the German Democratic Republic on the Development of Economic, Industrial, Scientific and Technical Co-operation* (18 Dec. 1973).

CMND 6258 Decisions of the Representatives of the Government of the Member States of the European Coal and Steel Community meeting in Council, opening, allocating and providing for the allocation of Tariff Quotas and opening Tariff Preferences for certain Steel Products originating in Developing Countries (2 Dec. 1974).

CMND 5976 Statement on the Defence Estimates 1975 (March 1975).

CMND 6413 Exchange of Notes between ... the United Kingdom ... and ... the United States of America concerning a United States Navy Support Facility on Diego Garcia, British Indian Ocean Territory (25 Feb. 1976).

CMND 6432 Statement on the Defence Estimates 1976 (March 1976).

CMND 6735 Statement on the Defence Estimates 1977 (Feb. 1977).

CMND 7099 Statement on the Defence Estimates 1978 (Feb. 1978).

CMND 7474 Statement on the Defence Estimates 1979 (Feb. 1979).

CMND 7826–I, Defence in the 1980s: Statement on the Defence Estimates 1980 Vol. 1 (April 1980).

CMND 8212–I, Statement on the Defence Estimates 1981 (April 1981).

CMND 8288 The United Kingdom Defence Programme: The Way Forward (1981).

CMND 8517 *The British Strategic Nuclear Force* (March 1982).

CMND 8951–I, Statement on the Defence Estimates 1983 (Vol. 1) (Feb. 1983).

CMND 9543 Joint Declaration of the Government of the United Kingdom . . . and the Government of the People's Republic of China on the question of Hong Kong (19 Dec. 1984).

CMND 9763–I, Statement on the Defence Estimates 1986 (Feb. 1987).

CMND 344–I, Statement on the Defence Estimates 1988, Vol. I (Feb. 1988).

Author Index

Subject Index